로제타 홀 일기

5

Diary of Rosetta S. Hall 1893.11.10–1902.11.10

셔우드 홀 육아일기

Journal of Sherwood Hall

표지 사진

1895년 5월경, 셔우드 홀이 한 살 반 때 외할아버지와 함께 찍은 사진.
셔우드는 아버지인 윌리엄 제임스 홀 선교사가 순직한 후
로제타 홀의 고향으로 돌아가 외할아버지 집에서 약 한 달 동안 지냈다.

로제타 홀 일기

5

Diary of Rosetta S. Hall
1893.11.10-1902.11.10

셔우드 홀 육아일기
Journal of Sherwood Hall

로제타 홀

김현수 · 문선희 옮김 | 양화진문화원 편

홍성사.

차례

일러두기

- 로제타 홀은 총 여섯 권의 일기를 남겼다. 네 권은 선교일기, 두 권은 육아일기이다. 《로제타 홀 일기 5》는 육아일기 첫 번째 권이다. (로제타 홀이 한국에 오기까지 그리고 한국에서 선교 사역을 감당해 나간 내용을 담은 선교일기는 《로제타 홀 일기 1-4》로 출간되었다.)
- 본서는 내용적으로 크게 세 부분으로 구분된다. 1893년 11월 10일 셔우드 홀의 탄생부터 아빠인 윌리엄 제임스 홀이 서거한 후 양화진에 묻히기까지, 1894년 12월 14일 박에스더 부부와 함께 미국으로 돌아가 지내던 시기, 1897년 11월 10일 셔우드 홀의 네 번째 생일에 다시 한국에 도착하여 이전의 선교 사역을 계속 이어나가는 내용이 셔우드 홀의 성장 과정과 함께 전개된다.
- 본서의 1부는 일기 원본 사진으로 구성하였고, 2부는 원본의 영문을 한글로 번역한 것이다.
- 2부에서 한글로 번역된 내용을 원본에서 찾아보기 쉽도록, 해당 한글 번역 부분에 원본 일기의 쪽수를 기입해 놓았다.
- 로제타 홀은 일기 중간 중간에 사진이나 문서, 편지들을 스크랩했다. 스크랩에 대한 설명글은 2부 본문에서 해당 내용이 나오는 부분에 실었으며 으로 표시해 놓았다.
- 로제타 홀은 일기 내용을 보완할 필요가 있을 때 그 날짜에 해당하는 일기 페이지의 여백에 주로 세로 글씨로 추가 기록했는데, 이에 대한 번역은 { } 안에 넣었으며 책 뒤의 주에서 설명했다.
- 옮긴이가 추가한 내용은 [ ] 안에 표기했다.
- 책에 나오는 주는 옮긴이가 달았으며, 성경구절 번역본은 개역개정판 성경을 사용했다.
- 본문에 나오는 연도와 날짜에는 원문과 다르게 색을 넣어 구별되도록 했다.
- 로제타 홀은 일기의 첫 부분에 날짜, 인용 성경구절, 인용 시를 쓰고 그날 있었던 일들을 기록했는데, 원문은 그 요소들의 행갈이가 일정하지 않아 우리말 번역문에서는 가독성을 고려해 일괄적으로 행을 띄워 정리했다.
- 본서에 나오는 사진은 남기용 사진작가가 찍었으며, 모든 사진의 저작권은 양화진문화원에 있다.

1부

영인본

Journal of Sherwood Hall

1893.11.10-1902.11.10

Journal of
Sherwood Hall, from birth
Nov. 10th 1893 until able to write himself
" " 1902, with a glimpse of
His "First 'Teen" — 1906 —

Journal of Sherwood Hall
Nov. 10, 1893 – 1902.

DR. WILLIAM JAMES HALL.
施病院
京大貞洞美國胡醫員

1
Sherwood Hall.
대개하느님이셰샹을사랑ᄒᆞ샤그
외아들예수크리스도ᄭᅳ를주어므
릇밋는쟈는망ᄒᆞᆷ을면ᄒᆞ고기리살

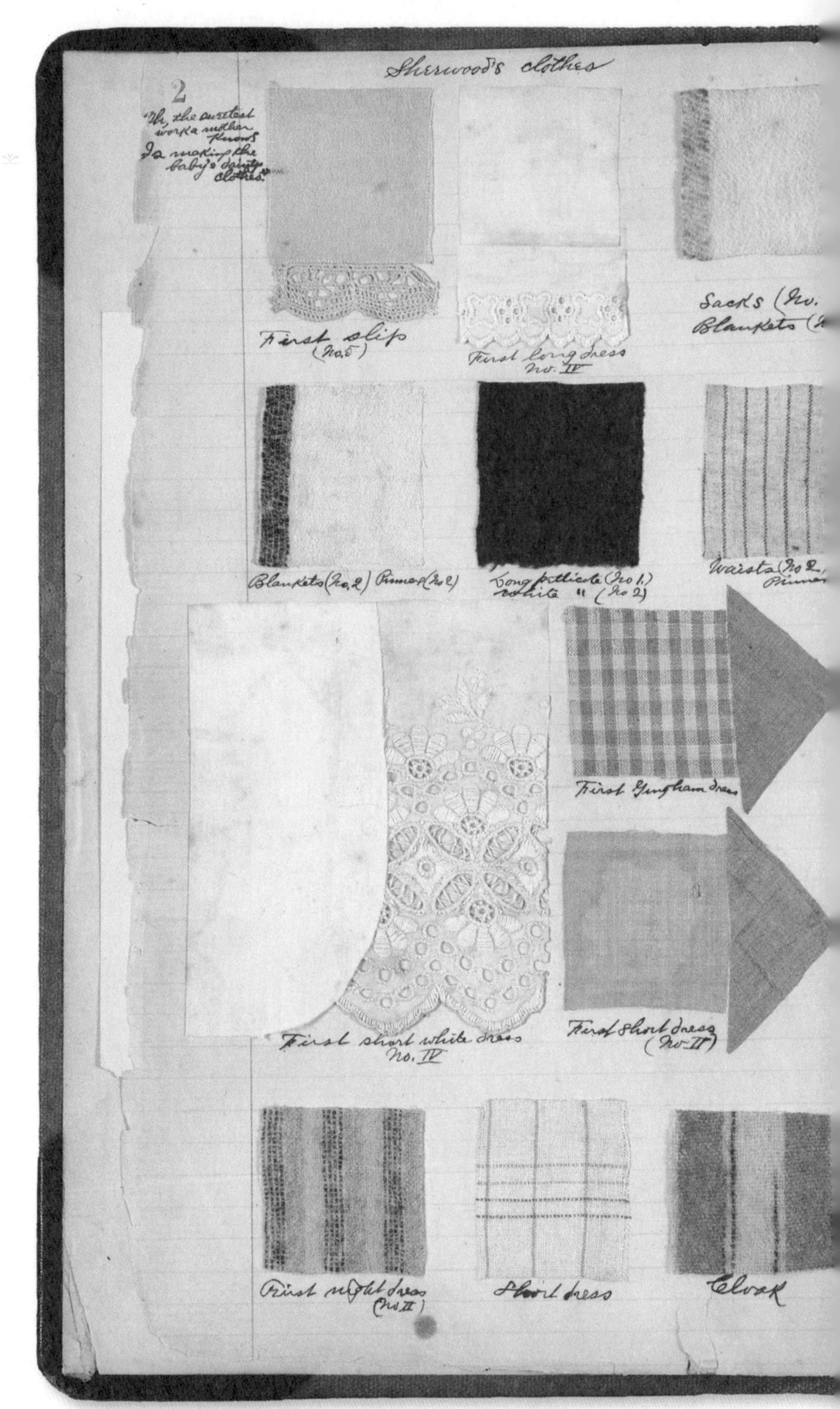
Sherwood's clothes
2
"Oh, the sweetest work a mother knows Is making the baby's dainty clothes."
First slip (No. 5)
First long dress No. IV
Blankets (No. 2) Pinner (No 2)
Long petticoat (No 1.) white " (No 2)
First short white dress No. IV
First Gingham dress
First short dress (No II)
First night dress (No II)
Short dress
Cloak

3
First aprons No II
1st Short white flannel petticoat No II
1st Short flannel petticoat No II
Winter apron (2)
Winter apron (1)
Sherwood's birthday anniversary dress.
Two dresses
Lawn Guimpes (4)

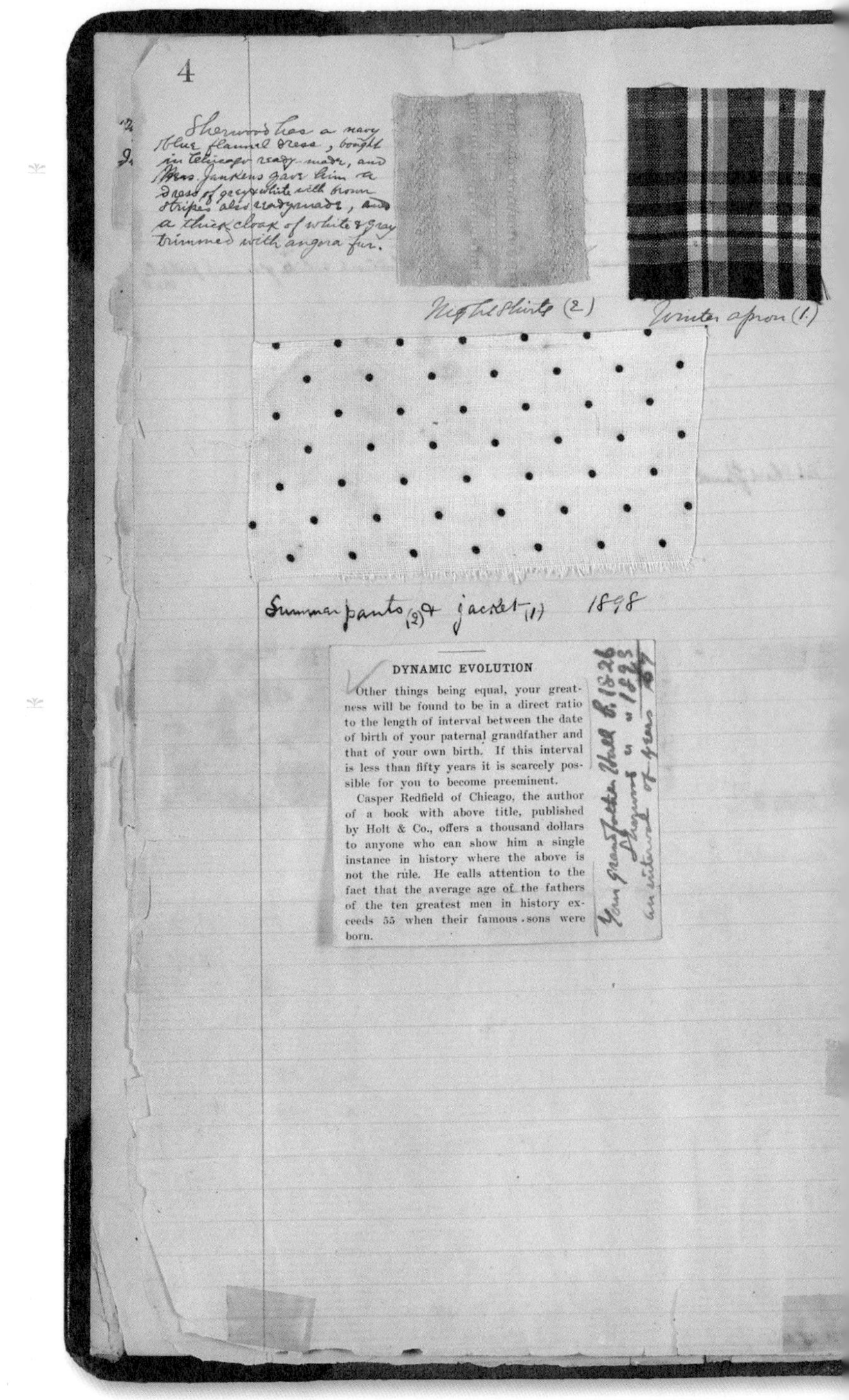
4

Sherwood has a navy blue flannel dress, bought in Chicago ready-made, and Mrs. Jankens gave him a dress of grey & white with brown stripes also readymade, and a thick cloak of white & grey trimmed with angora fur.

Night Shirts (2)

Winter apron (1.)

Summer pants (2) & jacket (1) 1898

DYNAMIC EVOLUTION

Other things being equal, your greatness will be found to be in a direct ratio to the length of interval between the date of birth of your paternal grandfather and that of your own birth. If this interval is less than fifty years it is scarcely possible for you to become preeminent.

Casper Redfield of Chicago, the author of a book with above title, published by Holt & Co., offers a thousand dollars to anyone who can show him a single instance in history where the above is not the rule. He calls attention to the fact that the average age of the fathers of the ten greatest men in history exceeds 55 when their famous sons were born.

Your grandfather Ruel b. 1826
Sherwood " " 1893
an interval of years 67

5
IN GOD WE TRUST

6
"The house where I was born"
Photo taken summer of 99

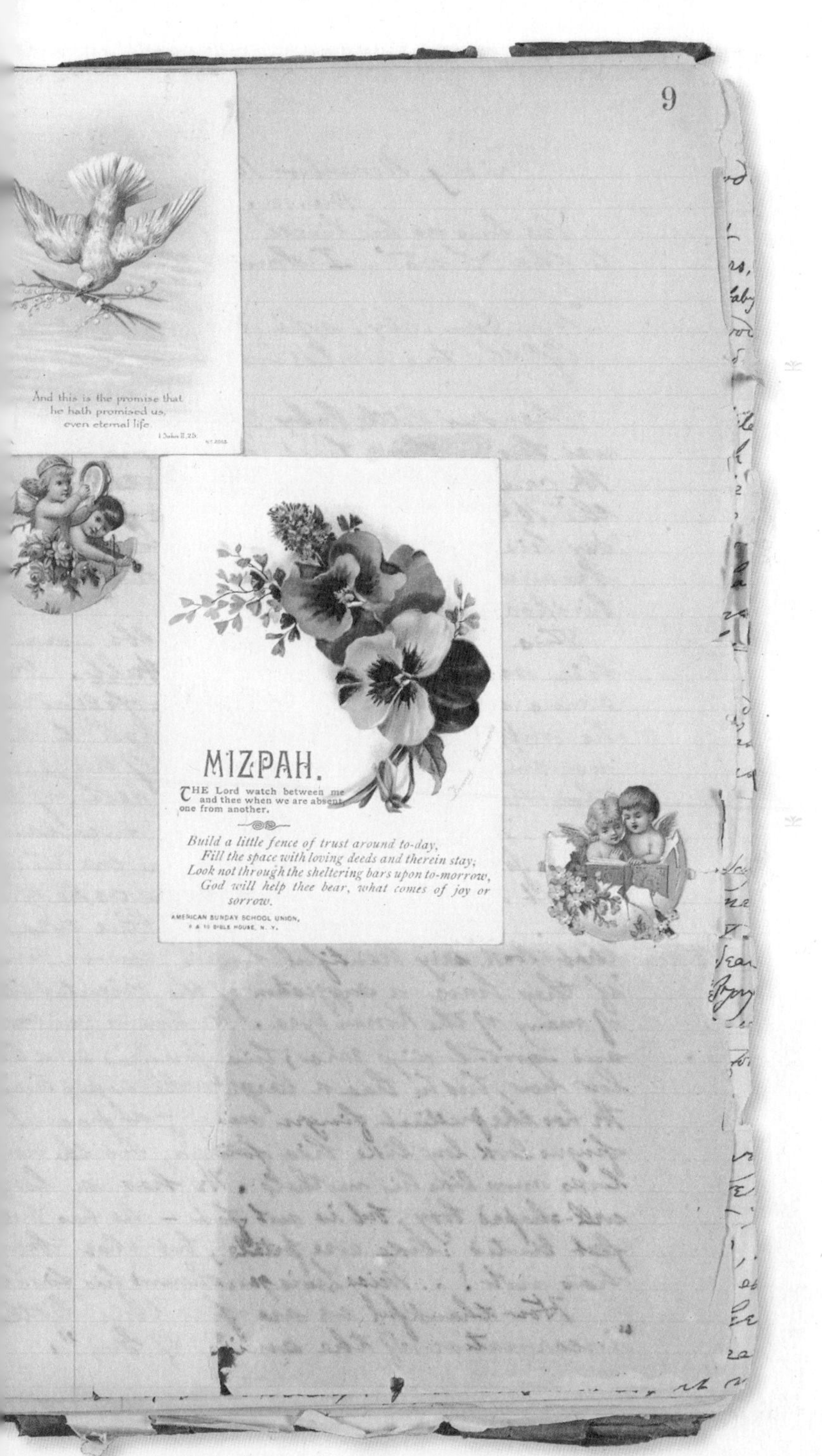
9
And this is the promise that
he hath promised us,
even eternal life.
I John II, 25.
MIZPAH.
THE Lord watch between me
and thee when we are absent
one from another.
Build a little fence of trust around to-day,
Fill the space with loving deeds and therein stay;
Look not through the sheltering bars upon to-morrow,
God will help thee bear, what comes of joy or
sorrow.
AMERICAN SUNDAY SCHOOL UNION,
8 & 10 BIBLE HOUSE, N. Y.

Friday, November 10th, 1893.
10 a.m.

'As long as he liveth he is grante[d]
to the Lord' I Sam. I, 28

"New-born baby, soft and pink
Of the two worlds on the brink."

The dear little baby boy is here. "Our ba[by]"
was his mother's first greeting to him.
He came at 10 o'clock on the 10th day [of]
the Korean 10th moon, which was just [the]
day his mother had hoped he would come
because it was his Grandfather Sherwo[od's]
birthday; — he is 89 to-day.

This baby is a big boy of 9 lbs. and
his name is Sherwood Hall. He
seems like a patient little fellow a[s]
he only cried once just enough to let
us know he had a good pair of lungs, an[d]
then he was very quiet the rest of th[e]
day. He is not pretty, his nose is
large for a baby and his features are all boy.
No doubt he will grow better looking as he grow[s]
older. Little Sherwood has true blue eyes
that look very beautiful to his mama even
if they have a suggestion of the oriental sla[nt]
of many of the Korean eyes. He has a good mou[th]
and good-looking ears; his forehead is a bit
low now, but he has a large well shaped head.
He has the prettiest finger nails; — at present h[is]
fingers look long like his father's, but the hand
looks more like his mother's. He has a long
well-shaped body, but is not fat — he has pretty
feet tinted like rose petals, but what baby
has not! Miss Lewis gave Sherwood his first ba[th].

How thankful we are for this little
"incarnation of the smile of God".

11

Sunday, Nov. 12th. Baby Sherwood smiled for the first to-day. He is a good baby, and his papa keeps him in a basket up on the shelf the most of the time. Mrs. Greathouse came in to see him, Aunt Esther washes baby

Sunday, Nov. 26th, The first time Sherwood was washed by his mama, His Dr. Cutler called.

Thursday Nov. 30th Thanksgiving day. Baby Sherwood had on one of his long white dresses, and a pretty wool sack trimmed with pink to-day. Heretofore, he has worn his little baby-blue wrappers. This is his papa's last day home for sometime. To-morrow he leaves for Pyong Yang. Sherwood has gained one pound, and is nearly over the jaundice which he has had since he was 4 days old. During this time he has been so constipated that he has required ... day. Otherwise he has ... and has given no ...

... 25th Christmas day ... forth of the dust, ne... of the ground. - Job V ... ich I can not see ... ould so stricken by ... the rest ... as well as for them, ... rest!"

... ood's papa went aw... ick, and was ve... month. He seemed ... - his mama dieted, ... and did everything ... milk right for her dear little baby, but though it had agreed with him nicely up to this time, it ...

Nurse Lewis who gave baby Sherwood his first bath.

12

seemed too rich for the extremely delicate state that his little baby stomach soon got into, and from the 1st of Dec. there were days and nights when in the whole 24 hours he could retain but 2 or 3 nursings and sometimes a little barley water. When six weeks old he weighed a little less than he did when he was born. The neighbors began to think this little boy was not very long for this world, and his papa came home about this time, and he feared the same and use to talk to Sherwood's mama sometimes to try to get her reconciled to thought of their little boy going back to God who gave him.

However, papa's presence proved a great help to mama, and therefore to baby too. There was some one to share the responsibility and to lighten the burdens, and it was not long before there was a marked improvement in little Sherwood.

To-day he was invited by the Allen boys to a Christmas tree, but he was not well enough to go. However, he was remembered with several toys. All the other babies were there.

Sherwood received a great many Christmas presents — a beautiful cloak and hood from Mrs. Moore, a pretty dress from Mrs. Reynolds, a nice blanket from Mrs. Noble, a pair of Korean stockings from Mrs. Kim, and another pair from Lucy Mo, and a jumping

Record Kept during the latter part of baby's sickness

Dec. 13th from 2 a.m. vomited all but one nursing until 2 a.m. the 14th.
Dec 14 Retained food till 1 p.m. [illegible] nothing more till 2 a.m.
Dec 15 Vomited 4 a.m. nursing
Retained Barley water at 10 a.m.
" Milk & water at 12 M.
Threw up all of 4 p.m.
Retained the most of 10 p.m. [illegible]
Dec. 16th Vomited all of 6 a.m.
Retained 10 a.m. & 12 M.
Vomited all of 4 p.m.
Retained some of 7 p.m.
During the last 3 days has taken 20 Bismuth & Pancreatine powders — the stools have been made darker & reduced in number to one a day, and this can not be had without an injection — it begins to appear when baby feels in need of a stool & can't have it, if he is nursed during that time he is sure to vomit —
9 p.m. retained barley water & went to sleep 12 M water
2 a.m. water & milk 6 a.m. water & milk
Slept all [illegible] at 9 p.m. & slept till 3.30 a.m.

Has had 10 [illegible] of powders [illegible] of Bismuth with Pepsin in his water to-day. Has also has pepsin
28th Commenced Horlicks for

-94 black wooly dog from Dr. Busteed. That was a very merry Christmas for such a little sick boy. He continues to need an enema night and morning.

Jan 10th Sherwood two months old, and weighs just ten pounds. He is doing quite nicely now on his mamas milk and Horlick's food alternately. His papa started for Pyong Yang again to-day. Expects not to return for eight or ten weeks.

Sherwood's Amah is so good to him and such a help to ~~Mama~~, but she has to work so hard during the day that she can't stay at night as she has her own little boy and husband too, ~~but~~ when papa was away she would often stay till 11 or 12 p.m. with the sick baby and be back at 5 or 6 a.m. She did all his washing and ironing, kept the fire and did the room work, but papa thought this time when he went away it would be better to have ~~another~~ to help, one who could stay nights, he was sorry that mama had not thought of this before when he was away – it would have been such a help to both her and baby, for when mama was tired out and couldn't rest well it would react upon baby. Also our dear little faithful Amah couldn't go with us to Pyong Yang in the Spring, and therefore it seemed wise to try and secure someone who could, and get her trained in to take the place of the other in time if possible.

Jan 29 "Sylvia" the widow of Mr. Ro's younger brother began work to-day. Think we shall like her. Poor woman she is all alone in the world, her parents are dead, her husband died recently and her only child a little girl was burned to death in our Girl's school. She often feels sad, and she says why should she want to earn money, she has no one to give it to

4

Number	Name	Ages	Nativity	Address
1.	Mrs. Maggie O'Neil		Ireland	56 Oak st

11-16-89 Symptoms. Temp. 100.4° P. 120 R. 3
lungs in bad condition. Patie
and expectorates a great

11-20-89 Temp. 100 P. 160 R. 56
11-23 " 100 " 138 " 48
11-30 "
Face, feet + hands much swolle
to patient, and talked to her
live long, and that she felt
prayer for her, and bade her
12-4-89 Patient died this p.m

2.	James Robinson	2 wks	N.Y. city	62 Oliver st.

before being able to urinate. The
to the hospital 11-22-89 – she
came d about 10 p.m.; from that
convulsion which was follow
in 4 hrs. Child screams, closes
come opisthotonos. Examinatio
11-23-89 a.m tracted Temp. 101.4° Pulse 150
Space of 20 sec between in one instan
11 a.m Enema of soap + water followed
stool by 3 p.m. Rx Sod. Brom
gr iii ev. 2 hrs alternating the
11-23-89 p.m 5 o'clock Temp. 100.6°. Better color
11-24 '89 P.m " " 99° P 130 R. 24
through the night. Looks quite
11-28-89 doing nicely except still some
from prea. ...'s, but it was adhe
12-7 + 14th Baby growing ...ly – troubles

...p powder for eruption about arms & thighs

Patient has always been well — drinks no

1-27-'89 Labor began at 3 a.m.

Membranes ruptured at 5.30 a.m.

Reached patient at 11 a.m. Not very strong pains but regular about ev. 15 min.

...lls, not tense. Larger on R. side. Foetal heart ...the back. Os scarcely penetrable by 2 fingers, but

Labor went on very slowly owing to absence of ...he position vertex, right-occipito-posterior

...8 p.m. Os size of $1. Pains ev. 4-5 min, only ...red. (and veratrum)

...p oedematous — had to hold it back during several 11 p.m. Head posteriorly down to floor of pelv...

...ad patient move changing position from back to L side ...hange from diagonal pos. to ant-posterior position ...ip and swept downward. Held it back till the ...ne more pain brought the rest — a fine large

...maternal pulse 88 Foetal 150 was correct basis for progn...

...aned up. Temp. 99. P. 68. R. 24

12-1-89 8 p.m. T. 100.8° P. 96. R. 24. Patient said

Gave Calomel gr ii Sod-bicarb gr v at 9 p.m. & ordered

...ormal — fundus a little below umbilicus

sleeplessness — ordered Pot. Brom gr x Morph. Sulph. gr 1/16 at

12-8-89. Patient doing well — Sup today. Baby splendid

...er body, and baby also somewhat affected. Inquired

headache & sleeplessness ... relieved, but rash has been

...ulph. ℥ii at 9 p.m. & repeat if bowels don't move before ... at brin...

18

However she borrowed $10 of Doctor for the burial of her husband, so she wants to earn enough to save that much, and by that time she will probably become interested in Sherwood and her work here, and feel again that "Life is worth living." She is a Christian, and so will make good help for Byong Yang.

Feb. 6th Korean New Year's day. Sherwood weighs 11 pounds now, he seems quite well except for constipation. He is very sunny-hearted the most of the time, laughing and cooing. He will lie in his basket for a long time playing with his pretty baby fingers which he seems to admire almost as much as his mama does. He also enjoys playing with a bone ring that is tied with a blue ribbon to the side of the basket, he knocks it with his hand to hear it rattle against the basket. He amuses himself with this for a half hour sometimes. He also likes to lie where he can see a bright Korean lantern suspended from the ceiling with a little wax baby hanging beneath, he will watch it a long time and laughs and talks to it in great style. His mama's Korean teacher is so good to him, and Sherwood likes him so much. The teachers wife has sent Sherwood two very pretty pair of Korean socks, one of silk and one of wool, both embroidered with silk.

March 10th Sherwood four months old, he weighs 12 lbs, is 24 inches long, and his head 16 inches in circumference. He has been quite sick for a few days the last of the month, but so far this month is quite well again. He still needs his enema and for over 3 weeks now has used a little "Yokon" at the suggestion of his grandma. It is easier for him than to be pinned up in his napkin, and he does look so cunning sitting there, his Amah holding up his long clothes and supporting his back, while he grunts and looks down at the little red socks on his feet which just touch the floor. He often has a pretty hard time, and the tears come to his eyes, but he is a brave little man, and is generally happy for a long time after. For more than two weeks now he has enjoyed looking at the face of a big rag doll, he pats it and talks baby talk to it sometimes gets quite hilarious over it. The rag doll is dressed in Korean boy's clothes, and his Amah calls it Sherwood's "elder brother". He also enjoys shaking a Korean rattle that my teacher gave him.

I wanted to take Sherwood "out" to-day as it is his birthday, but it rained. He was out for the first 3 days ago, and watched Mr. Noble sow grass seed.

h 12th Sherwood called on little Miss Max Scranton and cooed at her as sweet as you please.

rch 17th Sherwood's papa returned after an absence of nearly ten weeks. Sherwood is so glad to have some one that can sing to him again. He enjoys his papa pretty much, but he will pull his whiskers. Doctor hardly knows his son, he has changed so much for the better. Sherwood is quite well and happy now, and enjoys his baths so much.

pr. 10, 1894. A little child shall lead them, —
Isa XI, VI

"'Only a baby!' Ah! do you not know
That little feet walk where no others can go
That soft little fingers
Laid on the chords
Make music that lingers —
Sweeter than words?
That the touch of a baby has magic that brin

1) 20

Harmonies rich from discordant heartstrings,
That in his little voice all the melodies swee
Which are sung in the home, in unison mee

Sherwood is 5 mos old to-da
and such a dear little boy as he i
Mrs. Isabella Bird Bishop says he is a
"very intelligent looking baby", and
General Greathouse said he never saw
a baby laugh so much.

He weighs 13 1/2 lbs now, he
is not fat, but has been doing wel
upon his mama's milk pieced out w
strained oatmeal gruel and Highland Evapo
cream, until recently he began using the
Eagle brand of condensed milk, as the cr
got so acid. If he could only have so
of the nice milk and cream from his
Grandpa Sherwood's farm he would su
thrive.

Grandma Sherwood writes &
wants Sherwood's mama to kiss him
every day for her until she can see him
and kiss him for herself. "Old Fe
Joe" sent a U.S. dollar to Sherwo
Aunt Maggie writes it does not seem poss
to think of such a dear little baby being
born away out in that heathen land,
that they are all so surprised and pl
Uncle Frank says "The boy will sca
know his nationality – kiss him for
the darling little Sherwood – supp
he will be a missionary sure

Pampie Gray wants to know
his eyes slant, and if he will w
his hair in a pig-tail – and his
little cousin Maud Gray is so worried
fear he will not be a white baby
she will not want to own him.

Really our little Sherwood is a good boy, he has no bad habits — doesn't cry to be walked with, or to be rocked, he doesn't suck his thumb or anything else, he doesn't soil his napkins but uses the Korean "yokon" every morning like a little man. He nurses mama regularly after breakfast, dinner and supper, and once in the night, seldom wakes more than ~~twice~~ once in the night — somewhere between 12 & 2 a.m. he nurses a half hour and goes to sleep till 6 or 7 a.m. Between each nursing he has one feeding of oatmeal and condensed milk. He is having his short dresses made now, and is getting ready to go to Pyong Yang and be a little pioneer missionary.

As Sherwood is so soon to get in short dresses we had his first pictures taken in his long baby dress. The one taken alone looks fatter than Sherwood does, and has not his expression, so we had none finished up like it. The one on his mama's lap doesn't do him justice as his head is not in good position, and he moved his hands, but after all both papa & mama and his friends ~~thought it~~ resembled him the most as it contained more of the peculiar little expression he is apt to wear when not smiling.

"Oh the sweetest work a mother knows
Is making the baby's dainty clothes."

Thursday, May 10, 1894.

As thy days, so shall thy strength be
Deut. XXXIII

We are immortal till our work is done. - Whi[illegible]

This is Sherwood's six month's birth[day] and he is spending it in Pyong Yang. How he has grown - one would scarcel[y] recognize him for the same baby tha[t] left Söul three weeks ago. We spe[nt] two weeks in Chemulpo at Mrs. Jones's waiting for the Pyong Yang Steamer, a[nd] while there Youdanie carried him ou[t] for long walks each fair day, and he g[ot] a good start there. Then we had a typhoon after starting and had to anc[hor] for 33 hrs, so we were from Friday noon until Tuesday noon upon the salt wa[ter]. Everyone else was very sea-sick, but he thought all the rocking and rolling wa[s] for his amusement, and he profited [there]by, he was so good, and slept so well [and] ate so much. Sylvia was too sick a[ll] the time to do anything for him, and [one] day both his papa and his mama were [too] sick too, but the dear good-natured little ba[by] had already ~~made his~~ friends among t[he] Japanese and Korean seamen, and a ve[ry] kind Korean (the interpreter for the Japanese) too[k] good care of him till we reached quieter wat[er].

He is as rosy, plump and stro[ng] now as one could wish to see, a[nd] is a good looking baby in the eyes of oth[er] people as well as of his fond parents. [He] is 26½ in. long and the circumf. of his he[ad] is 17 in. There is no way of weighing he[re] but he must weigh at least 16 lbs. He is just begining to learn to kiss, a[nd] he is a real little lover. He is cutti[ng] his first two teeth, and he says, da da, and papa, and sometimes 'a ma.

Yesterday, he got his first fall, rolled off of a box over 2 ft high where he had been laid down to take a nap.

The ~~[illegible]~~ fully 1500 women and children came to see Sherwood, the first foreign baby ever in Pyong Yang and to-day though there has been much trouble to make them afraid to come here just now, there have been 150 or more here in groups of tens or so staying five or ten minutes, some longer, Sherwood proves the great attraction for all.

Early this morning came word that Chong Sikey doctors evangelist, and Han Mr. Moffetts evangelist had been cast into prison, other Christians were beaten, a little later Mr. O the teacher of Dr's boys school was taken right from our yard to prison. Sherwood and his mama were left [illegible] hours at a time, while his [illegible] [illegible]ted the poor men in prison, [illegible] the Governor, and was at [illegible]ph office sending messages to [illegible] Esther & Sylvia kept in Esther's [illegible] the most of the time, but [illegible]ng women and children kept [illegible] they scarcely noticed any thing [illegible] house, but everything about the [illegible] the greatest interest. They [illegible] him 기특 "lovely."

[illegible]wood got his bath as usual at [illegible] and was soundly sleeping when [illegible] suddenly awakened by a noise [illegible] like a mad bull pawing [illegible]. It was old Capt. Kim in [illegible]est rage come to demand a [illegible] had been left at the house

To Myself, at Six Months.

YOUNG rascal, with your bland surprise;
Your corrugated, lofty brow;
The look of marvel in your eyes,
As asking, "*What* is coming *now?*"
I know not if you're he or she—
Your clothes say naught. No doubt it's true
They called you "it." Please speak to me—
Whose wondrous prodigy are *you*?

They claim that you are I—are I!
I' faith, this portrait bears attest
(A fact that I will not deny)
The first edition is the best.
And was I "cunning," "cute," and "sweet"?
And did I bleat "goo-goo," "goo-wah"?
And kick my tootsies—now but feet?
And thrill with pride my fond ma-ma?

Deep-nestled in your wayward brain,
What thoughts were hid, so none might know?
Or were your bounds the counterpane,
A rubber ring, a new-found toe?
Did phantoms of another life
You just had left still dwell within?
Or were those movements, meaning-rife,
Aroused by some obtrusive pin?

Did you, impatient, long for day
When you would be as old as eight?
And in your odd, capricious way
The very name of "baby" hate?
Ah, babe, the pity is that here
You did not stay content, I see;
But onward led from year to year,
Behold the thing you grew to be!

Edwin L. Sabin.

this afternoon and he had sent t[illegible]
servants after once but doctor th[illegible]
best not to give it up at first, and
out and tried to quiet him, ~~[illegible]~~
Lanie happened to be out there,
not daring to lay his hands o[illegible]
doctor he pitched upon Jon Lanie took [illegible]
by the top-knot kicked and beat [illegible]
and ordered his men to carry him o[illegible]
prison, but doctor then quickly got the [illegible]
for him, and he let Jon Lanie off [illegible]
left, and after it was quiet ag[illegible]
Sherwood went to sleep.

May 14th One tooth cut through the skin, but can['t]
see it yet – Sherwood has loose bowels [illegible]
have not had to give him but one or two ene[illegible]
since we reached Pyeng Yang.

May 17th Sherwood not very well – he misses t[illegible]
long walks he had at Chemulpo, too t[illegible]
him out doors for the whole day at Ke[illegible]
grave. Ketjah was the founder of Kore[illegible]
civilization in 1122 B.C. can see Sh[illegible]
wood's first little pearl to-day. 21st May

May 22nd Sherwood some better. He says "Papa
"A-ma" surely now. His 2nd tooth is al[illegible]
in sight. He tore his first paper i[illegible]
with great interest to-day; but he m[illegible]
be taught not to tear paper; Hi[illegible]
mama treats from 8 to 19 patients daily
and after dispensary ~~this~~ papa, mam[illegible]
and Chang Sikay take little Sherw[illegible]
out for a long walk every day. Th[illegible]
is what is bringing the roses ba[illegible]
into his cheeks again. It hailed to-[illegible]

May 26th 2nd tooth all through. Began givin[illegible]
lime water in Sherwood's milk,
tooth was extracted at Seoul just 5 yrs later; and the perma[illegible]
incisors soon made their appearance.

Sunday, June 10, 1894.

When thou passest through the waters I will be with thee. Isa 43:2.

"Rocked in the cradle of the deep,
I lay me down to in peace to sleep.
Secure I rest upon the wave
For thou, Oh Lord, hast power to save.
I know thou wilt not slight my call,
For thou dost mark the sparrow's fall:
And calm and peaceful is my sleep
Rocked in the cradle of the deep."

Emma Willard, 1832

Sherwood is out on the Yellow sea to-day, on the way back to Söul. He is happy – Capt. Rossamsohn of the "Chong Riong" says "That little boy always laughs." Papa and mama were quite seasick, but Sherwood enjoyed the rocking. There are 400 Pyong Yang soldiers upon the Chong Riong going to help quell a rebellion that has arisen in the South; Sherwood was a great 구경 for them – Every one from the General down had to come and see him.

Tuesday July 10, 1894.

Again dear little Sherwood has had a long siege of sickness – dysentery, from the night he reached Söul, June 12, to July 6th he passed blood in his stools nearly every day. June 20th he only ate twice during the day, and then both times vomited it up in one great gush. ~~Papa~~ & Mama were very much concerned about him for many days, but he slowly grew better, and then during the whole time nearly he kept so merry and good natured – he gained the reputation from everybody who saw him of laughing the most ~~for~~ a baby of any they'd

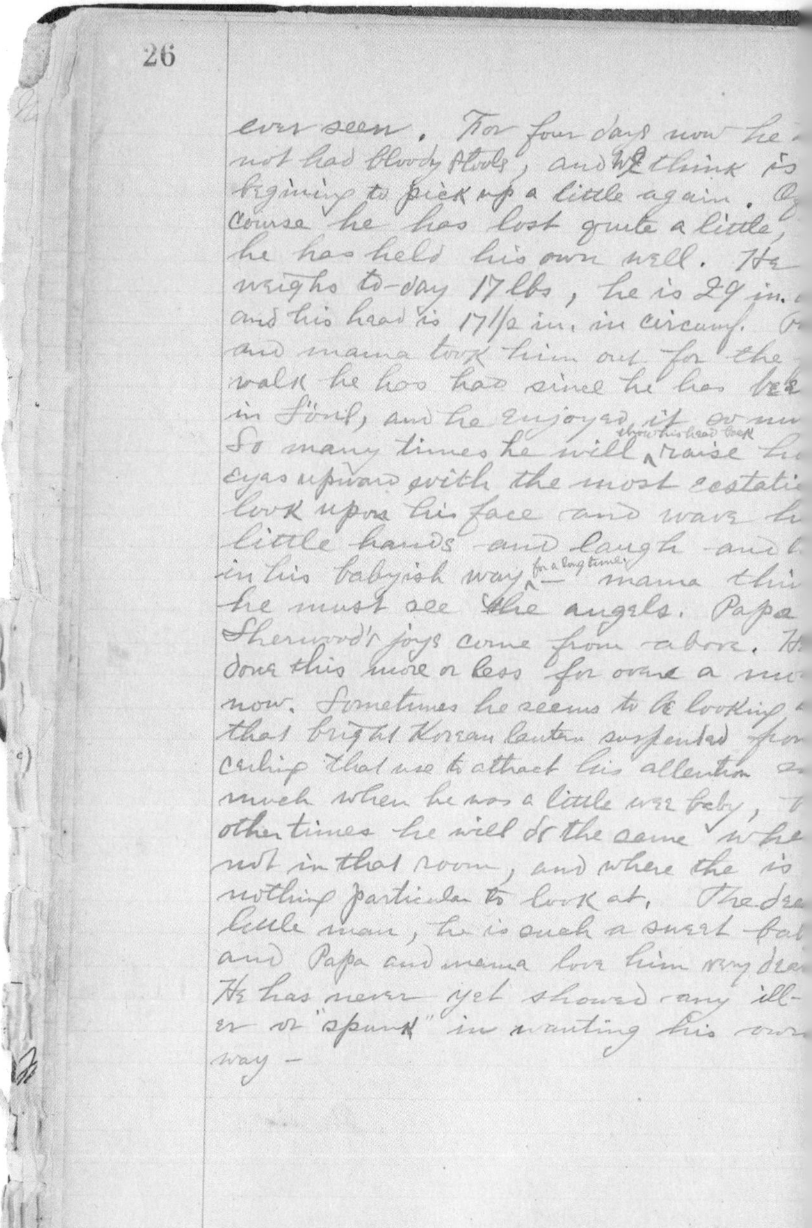

26

ever seen. For four days now he
not had bloody stools, and we think is
begining to pick up a little again. Of
course he has lost quite a little,
he has held his own well. He
weighs to-day 17 lbs, he is 29 in.
and his head is 17 1/2 in. in circumf.
and mama took him out for the
walk he has had since he has be
in Söul, and he enjoyed it ev
So many times he will [throw his head back] raise hi
eyes upward with the most ecstati
look upon his face and wave hi
little hands and laugh and
in his babyish way [for a long time] — mama thi
he must see ~~the~~ angels. Papa
Sherwood's joys come from above. He
done this more or less for over a m
now. Sometimes he seems to be looking
that bright Korean lantern suspended from
ceiling that use to attract his attention s
much when he was a little wee baby,
other times he will do the same whe
not in that room, and where the is
nothing particular to look at. The dea
little man, he is such a sweet ba
and Papa and mama love him very dea
He has never yet showed any ill-
er or "spunk" in wanting his ow
way —

Friday, Aug. 10, 1894.

A merry heart doeth good like medicine. Prov. 17:22.

"'Only a baby!' So little a life,
That no one can tell how amid the world's strife—
The whirr of the loom—where our lives take their form,
This little gold thread should have weaved in its charm!
Yet into those nooks
Where secrets are kept
By laugh and by looks
He wordlessly crept;
And smiled away furrows from faces grown old,
Made warm nestling places in natures grown cold."

Little Sherwood is 9 mos. old to-day; he weighs 18 lbs, is 30 in. long and his head is 17 3/4 in. in circumf. His 3rd wee pearl has just made its appearance, the 2nd left incisor, upper, the two central ones are not through yet, but he seems to be cutting all four of these at once. He has been quite well the last month, though it has been very hot several days of 104° in the shade, with the coolest place in the house 92° His papa put up the tent, up on the school yard where there is more breeze and much purer air than here, and we all go up there to sleep. Mama fixed his bed larger, and cooler, and so that the misquitoes seldom get in now, and he sleeps very well—often right through from 8 p.m. to 5 a.m., but sometimes awaking for one feeding at about 1 o'clock. He sleeps with just his flannel band, his napkin and gingham nightdress. One night he rolled

out of his little bed upon the groun[d]
and either did not awake or soon go[t]
to sleep again for no one heard h[im]
when Sylvia got up in the mo[rn-]
ing and found he was not in h[is]
bed, she looked to see if he was
with mama, and was quite alarm[ed]
when she could not see him; finally
she found him down between his be[d]
and the side of the tent - apparently
none the worse for making his
bed upon mother earth except fo[r]
some musquito and flea bites. After
awaking somewhere between 5 & 6 a. m
Sherwood will lie talking, and laughing for an hour in his bed, we th[en]
take him up and down to the ho[use]
where he gets his morning bath
and then through the hot day he
has no clothes on at all in th[e]
house except his napkin. At
3 p.m. when it is the hottest he an[d]
his mama both get in mama's b[ig]
bath tub, and take a nice cooling bath
spending often a half hour - Sherwo[od]
enjoys this very much splashing and k[ick-]
ing the water to his hearts content - [he]
can float with mama just steadying h[is]
head a little, and taking hold of the si[de]
of the bath tub with his little hands he ha[s]
stood all alone for a few seconds. He is
growing real strong again - he creeps so[me]
but mostly backwards so far - he
doesn't seem to like to get on his knees
but he loves to stand on his feet, and
if one holds his hands he will walk
across the room stepping rather high
but one foot out after the other in
proper order.

After his bath, he is dressed - his band, napkin & thin dress only, and is carried out to some fine shade trees near Mr. Hulbert's house, where he sits on an oil cloth upon the ground, pulls grass, plays with grass-hoppers, or watches Mr. Hulbert's little dogs in their frolics. Little Helen Hulbert comes out and plays with him sometimes which he enjoys very much, he also likes watching baby Ruth Noble & baby Madeline Hulbert. He went over to play with little Miss ~~May~~ Scranton one day, and they were both as good as could be and had a fine time. Mama's hammock is hung under the shade trees, and Sherwood has enjoyed many a nice nap in it at about 5 p.m. He stays up here in the open air until Papa & Mama have had their supper then Papa carries him and he goes with Papa & Mama for a nice walk in the rear of the French Legation. Two little deer belonging to the Legation grounds often run along on their side of the fence keeping with us much of the way. Sherwood likes these very much. In these walks he has made his first acquaintance with the moon and with Lightning. One week Papa was so very busy day and night in the hospital with wounded Korean soldiers, that our walks had to be postponed. These soldiers were mostly wounded the morning of July 23rd when the Japanese took the palace and charge of the city in general. Korea has been influenced by them to delare her independence of China, and the Japs will help fight China - they have had two battles already one upon sea, one upon land, in both of which the Japanese came off victorious.

These are troublous times — Al
the Legations are guarded by soldiers f
their own "men of war", and th
Methodist Compound where we slee
is guarded by American Soldiers each n
So long as the Japanese are victorio
we feel quite safe, as they seem to hav
a mind to do the fair thing, but shou
the Chinese get ahead of them and ma
toward Sŏul, we will no doubt have to leave
upon our Man of War. The British hav
a very large warship at Chemulpo calle
the Centurion. The Americans have
a good sized frigate the Baltimore which w
visited when at Chemulpo.

Amid so much war and rumo
of war, Sherwood has this mont
for the first showed that he ha
a will of his own which he sometim
tries very hard to follow. It show
itself sometimes when one takes away so
thing from him that he wants to play
with, though generally he is not a
all bad about this, and if some other
little thing is given him he gives u
very sweetly. It came out a little
more one day, however, when I determined to have him use a new nipp
— the milk ran out of the old one so easi
that he often mussed his clothes an
bed with it when left alone. But he di
not want the new one — I afterward
tried it myself and concluded that the
milk did come out of it too slow for such a
big boy, but at first it seemed
that it was just a notion with him
and that he would not try to use it.
went without eating all the forenoon
rather than to use it — once when placi

in his mouth when asleep, he promptly rejected it, and then when awaking though very hungry, waking up before he generally did because he had not eaten he would not take it, he cried quite a little, but later sat on the floor and played merrily with his toys another hour, then he was so hungry, he would take the bottle in a sort of desperation and put the nipple in his mouth with his own hand, but it would not more than touch his lips or tongue before he would take it out, he cried hard for mama to help him, but when she would try to put it in his mouth, he would shut his lips so firmly. Mama then set him on the floor and let him cry for fifteen minutes, the hardest he ever cried in his life when he was well, he was not only hungry, but no doubt felt really abused, he would quiet down a little sometimes, and try to notice his rag doll, then he would look up into mama's face, and break out again sobbing. Mama finally took him up and tried feeding him with a spoon to see if it was just stubbornness for wanting the old nipple, but he ate nicely with the spoon, and even drank pretty well, and the smiles soon came back to his face, however, mama was hard hearted, and did not want to give up that new nipple, so his next feeding time she tried it again, but to no avail, and she made him go 12 hours without his old friendly nipple, but he would not use the new one. As he would use a spoon or drink, mama thought she had not excuse sufficient to resist longer, and as she did not care

32

to wean him from the bottle fo
two or three months yet, at his ne
feeding out under the shade-trees she
gave him back his dear old friend, a
through it he drained the bottle w
a good appetite, went to sleep in th
hammock and slept for two hour
and has been the same merry hea
ed child as of yore ever since. Ev
body loves him, Sylvia and Esther
Yonsanie seem to think there is n
baby like him, and my old teacher th
so much of him. His papa often tel
mama that "he is the brightest, p
tiest, and sweetest baby he ever sa
though of course he would not say th
to other folks"

Sherwood doesn't say "Papa" or "Mam
any more lately — he use to say "Pap
so much at Pyong Yang, then after w
came to Söul he would call "Mama, m
ma" many times every day, Mrs. No
often spoke of it; but we have not h
him say either one now for two
or three weeks — he quite often sa
a ke the Korean word for "baby",
that is all we hear now though
jabbers away a great deal — begins to re
some from papers, sings when othe
do, and he loves to play on the organ

Monday, Sept. 10, 1894.

Our little boy is now ten mont
old, the last month has brought h
two more pounds of flesh, three new teeth
and he creeps forward with a sort of a
and a jump wherever he likes to go, an

gets into all sorts of mischief at times, though nothing serious has happened as yet. He now weighs 20 lbs, is 30 1/4 in long, head 18 in. in circumf. he has 4 upper teeth, and two lower ones, the latter we call his "Pyong Yang teeth" the former are all "Seoul teeth" and came through in the following order, first, last month, came the 2nd left incisor, next the first of this month came the Right middle incisor, then after two weeks the 2nd right incisor, followed in a few days by the left middle incisor. He enjoys nibbling a bread crust now, also a chicken bone. He has been pretty well, all the month, had diarrhoea for a few days, then we took him to a picnic, and he was out all day breathing mountain air, and has been well ever since. He lives on condensed milk and oatmeal gruel the most of the time, except barley gruel replaces the oatmeal if his bowels are loose. Only once this month has he suddenly awakened from a sleep with a cry, and then cried for a full half hour evidently in acute pain in his stomach or bowels, he would not touch his milk, and no change of position or anything that could be done seemed to be of any helps to the dear little fellow. When it was over he went quietly to sleep again without eating, and was all right the rest of the night. This happened 2 or 3 times last month, it is hard to tell its cause, whether colic or what, sometimes it seems as if he had worms, he rubs his nose so much, and has a funny hacking little cough when he awakes often, and his abdomen is so large, however that is not nearly so large as it was last month, so it may have been from the dysentery, as also his coated tongue.

This last month, he has said both "Papa" and "Mama" a gr deal, though he probably hardly kno to whom the names belong, as he doesn hear them called much, he knows perfectly well when either his papa or mama calls "Sylvia" who will answer to the call. Sylvia stands up in a corner sometimes, and he will s there alone for her. With something to lean on to he can stand anywhere, and he is begining to pull himself up by things.

He continues to be the same good-natured merry-hearted boy. He lov to play with children so much, at the picnic he was called "that good baby", never cried once except when another chil struck his face with a cup, and when he f out of a hammock. He enjoys one the picture books sent by the Liberty S.S. (scrap pictures pasted on paper muslin) he tires least of it of any plaything he has had he will sit on the floor for a long time leafing over its enjoying the pictures, pointing his fore fin at the eyes, or at a bright color or flower th he likes. That cunning little fore-finger ha become a great pointer this last month, most always uses the right hand, and will stick that finger out with the othe closed and point at any one coming, or at bright light or at any thing he takes a notic and say oh! oh! He also loves to use his right thumb and forefinger to leaf ov quickly any thick book, he seems to like th noise, and the sensation it gives his thumb, looks so cunning about it, and can do it quite as deftly as anyone. He seems to ha a great love for books, and seldom tears them,

Sherwood is the only baby in the house now, Aunt Esther had a dear little boy that only weighed 4 lbs, and Sherwood did so like to look at him and take hold of his doll-like hand, but after only 36 hrs in Aunt Esther's room, God took the tiny baby to Himself – Then followed the little funeral, the same day that baby Vinton was buried, and we saw the dear little baby no more. Soon after this baby Ruth Noble went with her papa & mama to Japan, so Sherwood has been the pet of the household for some time now.

"There's not a monarch but would be
Profoundly joyful could he see
He held a sway as firm as thee
O Baby!
To thee, let proud man come, my dove,
He'll learn this truth that's from above,
'He rules supreme who rules by love',
Like Baby."

Wednesday, Oct. 10, 1894

Sherwood has lost a pound during the last month – rather during the last two weeks of it; he has had diarrhoea all the time, and has not been out doors as much as before; his papa left for Pyong Yang the 1st, and we miss him very much. Sherwood now weighs 19 lbs, and is 30½ in. long, his head measures the same as last month. In the last mail we rec'd a picture of Sherwood's Canadian cousin, Harry Wallace Gray, who weighed 24 lbs when 8 mos. old. Grandma's letter came about Sherwood's picture sometime ago – she says, "Annie & Joe went to town this afternoon & when they came home Annie says I have something in my pocket that will make you smile, I guessed it was the picture of our little grandson and sure

enough it was he and his mother. The old s
ing is the mother is pleased if people say the
baby looks like its father, Sherwood mu
look like his papa for we can't see any
his mother's looks in him. We think he
good-looking chap. Mr Sarles said "he
bright". Most everyone remarks that the
mother looks thin, and Mr. Sarles add
"she grows better looking". I hope Sherw
is well and that the Lord will spare his l
that he may come to see us when his p
and ma returns."

During this month Sherwood an
his mama have had some serious tri
with Amahs — his old friend Sylvi
left to be "chemo" in girls' school, a
we made five different trials befo
we were at all satisfied. We now h
Esther's eldest sister, but as she has a
baby of her own the same age as Ruth, s
can not stay nights, and is not able t
of the attention her own baby needs to do nearly
much work as Sylvia, though otherwise
would be the more capable woman of the t
So we have also taken a boy that Doctor hel
to make well in the hospital, and whom he e
pects to take with him to Pyong Yang to help
in the dispensary work. His name is Yom K
Yongie (염금영이) and he is 18 years old —
was converted in the hospital and seems to
a nice gentle boy. Dr. Busteed has trai
him more or less in the dispensary afterno
and mornings he goes to Mr. Noble's sch
and studies Chinese. Kum Yongie sl
here nights and cares for Sherwood if he
needs attention, is also here to build fire
in the morning, and to take Sherwood u
when he awakes early. Since Papa h

been gone Kun Tongie usually takes Sherwood out for his walk at 4 o'clock. Mama has been busy all the month helping Dr. Cutter in the hospital, but she tries to go too when she can get home early enough.

Since the Noble's went to Japan we have been keeping house by ourselves, and now that Papa is away Sherwood generally sits at the table with mama and helps to keep her from being lonesome. He has a little arm chair that fits on one of the other chairs, and so answers for a high chair. He is generally quite a good boy at the table, will amuse himself with a crust of bread, a chicken bone or a spoon with a little butter or sugar on. Sometimes, however, he stands up in his chair and wants to climb upon the table, then mama has to send him away. Mama & Amah have made him a nice warm red flannel night-gown, which keeps him comfortable these cold nights & mornings, mama also crocheted him a pair of warm woolen socks to wear at night. Through the day he has on his little black stockings and brown leather shoes, a knit shirt, flannel petticoat, and a gingham or calico dress.

One day Mama & Aunt Esther took Sherwood over to the E. Gate to see Rachel & Rebekah and Annie & her baby. Sherwood had eaten his breakfast at 7 a.m. and so mama fixed him a bottle of milk to take along and eat after we got there. About 10.30 he wanted it, and Rachel offered to heat it, and unfortunately broke it and lost all the milk — Sherwood had been playing hard ever since we got there, and he must have been hungry with the long ride, but he was very good-natured — he ate some

water only, and we started for home a
fast as we could - he went to sleep o
the way, we reached home at 12 M. a
he was a patient little boy till mama g
his milk ready.

Sherwood does love to go out so muc
and he is so heavy to carry that mama
has sent to get him a carriage fr
Japan like baby Ruth has. They a
not nearly so nice or good as an America
baby carriage, but they do very well and are
much cheaper. We have been trying
get something of the sort all summer
but so far have not been able to.

Yesterday a telegram came from Papa
saying he had reached Pyong Yang safely. W
don't know when he will return but think
before this time next month. Suppose
Sherwood will almost, if not quite, forget t

40

Saturday, Nov. 10th, 1894.

He shall give his angels charge
thee, to keep thee in all thy ways. "

" A happy birthday, dear Sherwood
From papa and from me
With loads and loads and loads of love
And kisses - three times three.

One whole year has rolled around, a
the dear little boy that God sent us a
year ago to-day, now celebrates the fi
anniversary of his birth.

" Behold! what gifts from wonderland
The year has brought, with lavish hand.
The wondrous blue of those sweet eyes.
Came like yourself from yonder skies.
Your feet that are so lovely made
In rose leaves step't han caught their shade
Reflected gold shines in your hair
And pearl shells pink the cheeks so fair.
Beside this wealth from mines beneath,
The year has brought eight pearly teeth.
By powers of some transforming grace
Big thoughts mature the lovely face,
Half spoken words like shadows wait
The catching up of those more late
They'll come soon baby Sherw

Sherwood awoke feeling very well an
happy this morning, he had his bath at
breakfast time as usual, and played about
10.30 when he took his nap awaking befo
noon. He was then dressed in his pretty birth-d
anniversary dress, and Mrs. Appenzeller kindly loan
him her carriage, and he went over to Shinggokai to
his picture taken. He enjoyed the ride there and back
much, and he ... a pretty, good picture ... every body

It certainly looks like him, and it is just his attitude when sitting on the floor, he usually thrusts out one foot that way. The artist made three different negatives, one creeping, and one sitting in a chair, but this one sitting on the floor was the best.

Sherwood had some fine presents and many of them for such a little boy. Grandma Sherwood remembered him with a gold dollar, Mrs. Noble gave him material for a pretty blue flannel dress, "Uncle Pak and Aunt Esther" gave him beautiful pink 토시, or wristlets, lined and trimmed with white fur, Sylvia sent him a white silk handkerchief upon which she had embroidered in pink "슈부귀다남즈 내귀흔 쇠웃흘" which translated means "Long life, riches & precious sons" My precious Sherwood Hall.

Mary made him a pretty pair of 토시 pieced out of many colored silk, Alice made him a very nice pair of 버션, or Korean socks. Papa & Mama gave him a silver cup, gold lined, and Mama also made him the new dress he has on in the picture. It has a cream waist with fancy silk stitching [illegible]

and a scarlet cashmere overdress tri
with cream silk lace over the shoulders. F
looks very well in it, indeed.
Dear little Sherwood, during the past
he has regained the pound he lost last m
so that he now weighs 20 lbs again. Gra
Sherwood thinks that is very little for a
a year old, but he doesn't seem little to u
people out here. He is 31 in. long, and hi
head is 18¼ in. in circumf. He has two new
that have just put in their appearance, a
had two days and one night of feeling fret
with them when they were coming through the g
For 12 hours one day he didn't eat one bottle of m
and that night mama had to be up four ti
with him, and one time he cried for nearly
hours together, he would not take his milk,
scarcely touch hot water with a little medicine in,
no change of position, rocking, or walking wi
him seemed to be of any avail. The next m
my mama found one of the teeth just cut throu
the gum - perhaps if it had been lanced a da
two before it might have saved that night's
Sherwood never creeps now, in fact he
did of any consequence, he doesn't seem to like
get on his knees, but he walks on his hands & f
with his little body humped up in the air, he can
across the floor very quickly that way, and he ju
loves to have some one chase him in the same way
will laugh so heartily. He also lifts himself up
a chair or anything of that sort, and he just beg
sometimes to have some one take hold of his little
to help support him while he tramps majesticall
around and round the room with happiest
of a smile on his face. He is begining to walk
little if we only take hold of one hand, but he is
and is apt to sit down soon or tease to have both
held, he never seems to tire of that. He does
talk anything but "baby talk" yet, but is t

ing to jabber away in that language quite a great deal, will even read letters and papers pointing to the words; he doesn't say 오이, 오이 오이, (the Korean word for cucumber) so much as he did two and three months ago, but says "quioy, quioy, quioy" a great deal, will often stop in the midst of crying and begin to say it, and says it when he awakes in the night sometimes, and is waiting for his food to be fixed, he doesn't say papa or mama now. No one tries to teach him. He still continues very fond of books and will leaf one for half an hour at a time, he enjoys hunting for the pictures in a book and exclaims with "Oh"s & "Ah"s when he finds them, but he also likes a book without pictures especially if it is a large heavy book. He has nearly worn out his first pair of shoes - one day when his Amah was trying to put on a new pair, she wanted him to stiffen his leg and foot and thrust it out toward her, all of a sudden he seemed to get it through his little head what was wanted and did so, also clenching his fists and holding his arms as if he were pulling back a pair of runaway horses, set his teeth together and put on the broadest of grins. Since then he has repeated the part with his fists and mouth several times and he does look so comical. This last month Sherwood has begun to try to put on his hat, to comb his hair etc - one day mama gave him an old tooth brush to play with and he immediately began to brush his hair, as it most resembled his hair brush to anything he knew, another time he found mamas quill pick on the floor, and he tried to pick his teeth as he had seen mama do; he also tries to blow his nose in the handkerchief, and he is begining to make marks on paper with a pencil

44

Aunt Esther wrote this ne
birthday letter for little Sherwood.

Soul Korea.
Nov. 10. 1894.

My dear darling Sherwood.
It is your first birthday I am very glad you came to this world and let me love you. I hope you grow very useful man and do many good things among the heathen like your father and mother. and honor to your parents and obey their teaching and be a gentle and kind. I hope you grow up be best boy. and love God keep his commandment. Will you dear

wrote, "how I long to see our da
ling little Sherwood, — I will not
able to be down for his birth-day, after

Monday, Dec. 10, 1894.

Son of man, behold, I take away from thee
sire of thine eyes with a stroke: yet neither s
mourn nor weep, neither shall thy tears run
And I will cause you to pass under th
and I will bring you into the bond of the covenant. E
A father of the fatherless is God in his h
habitation. Psa. 68.5.

No shade has come between
Thee and the sun;
Like some sweet childish dream
Thy life has run:
But now the stream has reached
A dark, deep sea,
And sorrow, dim and crowned
Is waiting thee. — A.A. Pro

My poor dear little Sherwood! The gr
est loss has come to thee during the last month th
can ever come, and little darling, you know no
about it now, but the time will come when
will feel it, though perhaps never so keenly a
so for you. (Written on "the China" in the To
on a rough s

Just one month ago, on Sherwood's birthday,
papa left Pyong Yang for home — Mr. Moffett h
been quite seriously sick with malarial fever & dysentery
and papa had trouble in breaking up the fever, but finall
it with Warburgh's tincture. About this time papa himself
he was getting the fever — quinine didn't seem to help him,
he had used up nearly all the Warburg's so that there was
a half dose left — this he took and was some better, he th
the next day, though just about that time, the fever thermo
got broken so he was unable to tell very accurately. How
both Mr. Moffett & papa began to realize that tho
their work for the last 5 or 6 weeks had been both interesting
unusually successful, yet they had staid too long for
the safety of their lives in such a dangerous localit
Just outside of the walls, not far from our house lay
thousands of Chinese killed in battle two weeks befor

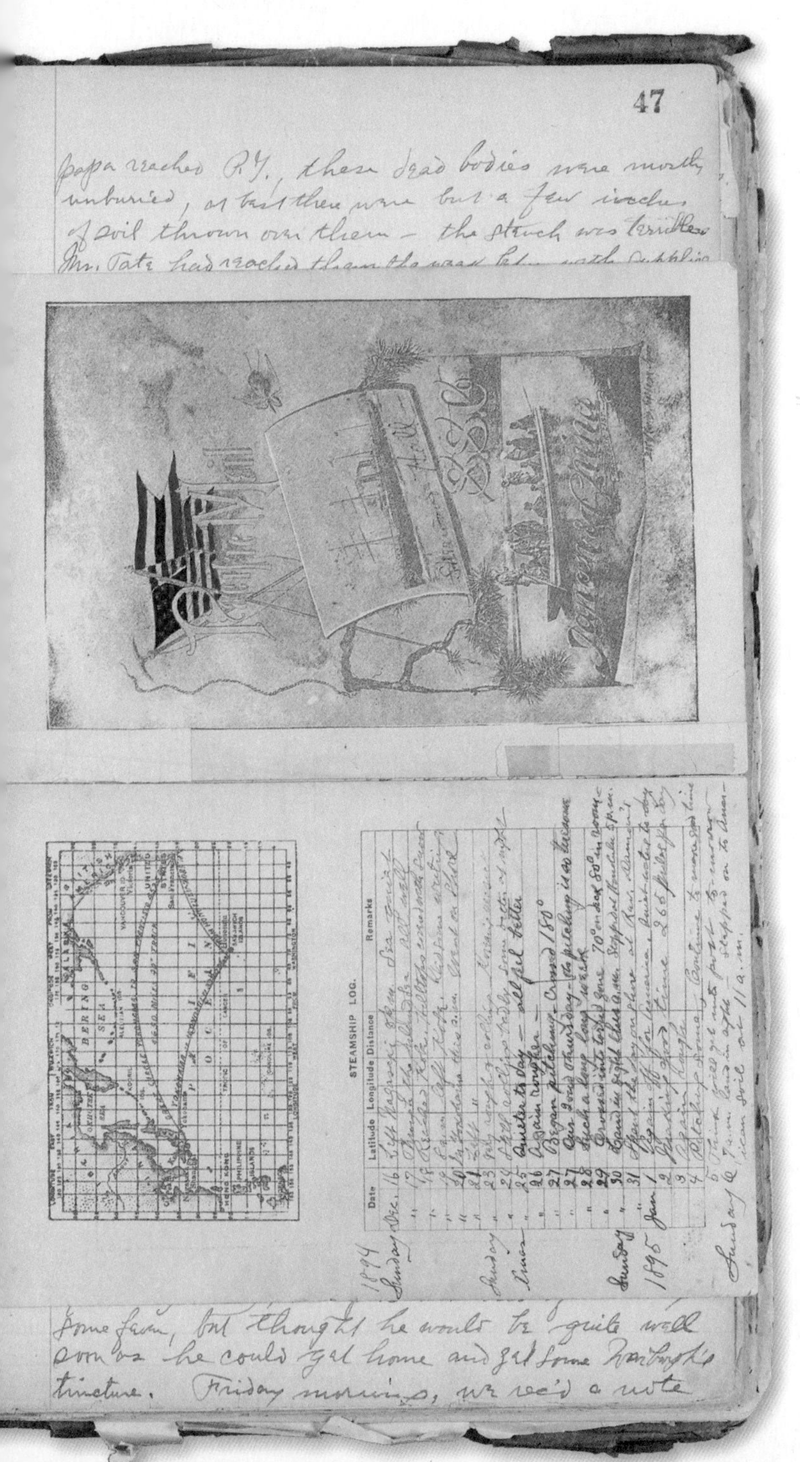
47
papa reached P.Y., these dead bodies were mostly
unburied, at best there were but a few inches
of soil thrown over them — the stench was terrible
Mr. Tate had reached them the week before with supplies
BERING SEA
OKHOTSK SEA
ALASKA
ALEUTIAN IDS.
KOORIL IDS.
VANCOUVER ID.
Victoria
UNITED STATES
San Francisco
Yokohama
Nagasaki
Shanghai
PACIFIC OCEAN
TROPIC OF CANCER
HONG KONG
PHILIPPINE ISLANDS
SANDWICH ISLANDS
CAROLINE IDS.
LONGITUDE WEST FROM WASHINGTON
Pacific Mail
S.S. Co
Japan and China
STEAMSHIP LOG.
1894
Sunday Dec. 16 Left Nagasaki 8 a.m. Sea quiet
" 17 Through the Inland Sea All well
" 18 Reached Kobe. Hilltops covered with snow
" 19 [illegible] Left Kobe. Did some writing
" 20 In Yokohama this a.m. Went on shore
" 21 Left "
Sunday " 23 Very rough & rolling. Korean music?
" 24 Still rolling badly, some better at night
Xmas " 25 Quieter to day — all feel better
" 26 Again rougher —
" 27 Began pitching - Crossed 180°
" 27 Our 2nd Thursday - the pitching is so tiresome
" 28 Such a long long week
" 29 Crossed into torrid zone 70° on deck 80° in room
Sunday " 30 Land in sight this a.m. Stopped at Honolulu 5 p.m.
" 31 Spent the day on shore at Rev. Damon's
1895 Jan 1 Again off for America. Quiet water to day
2 Making good time 265 miles per day
3 Again rough
4 Pitching some, Continue to make good time
5 Think will get into port to-morrow
Sunday 6 7 a.m. land in sight — Stepped on to American soil at 11 a.m.
some fever, but thought he would be quite well
soon as he could get home and get some Warburg's
tincture. Friday morning, we rec'd a note

48

from Mr. Moffatt asking that a chair
sent to the river for the doctor that after
so Mr. Noble kindly went down with
waited till late, but no steamer came
no more word was rec'd till Satu
afternoon when Mr. Jones sent telegr
through Japanese legation that "Messrs Mo
Tate and Hall leave for Tongsan at 4 p.m.
is sick, send doctor and chair to Tongsan to-
and wait" So Mr. Noble & Dr. Bustee
down with a long chair, bedding, food etc,
waited until after midnight but still
signs of the steamer. Early in the
Mr. Noble went down again with like re
In the afternoon Dr. Vinton kindly offere
still no steamer or word from it - he left t
there, so that if they might happen to come
morning they would have something to help
[illegible] with.

All this made a pretty anxiou
ing time for mama, but every one
to think that likely the steamer had
started or that it had gotten stuck on
sandbar and would get off soon. Mo
morning after breakfast they sent
mama to visit the daughter of one of t
Pansa's professionally, and also wis
~~little~~ Sherwood would come with his
that they might see him. Mama wa
getting her medicines ready to go, wh
word came that papa had arrived - Gr
up little Sherwood in her arms she ran
hallway, and there was dear papa lying
in the long chair which had just been
in by the coolies - Mr. Tate took him
and carried him in his arms to the bed
Amah quickly got ready. Papa kissed m
and Sherwood, and he seemed so bright a
happy because he had finally gotten

that at first we did realize how sick he was. It seems the steamer they started out on Sat. eve. struck a rock and went down after they'd been

Delivery Form

IMPERIAL GOVERNMENT TELEGRAPHS

Station Seoul Date 14/11 94 18

Office No. 26

Class 4

No. 1 K

Words 38

Time received 1.35 p.m.

Address Matsui Seoul

Remarks

Given in at Chemulpo Date 14 Nov 94 18 10 / 11 p.m. M.

Transmit following U.S. Missionary Dr. Scranton; Messrs Moffett, Tate, and Hall leave here for Young San at 4 p m. Dr. Hall is sick send doctor and chair to Young San tonight and wait

Jones

to have advice at least, and papa agrees, so Dr. Busteed came, also Dr. Scranton — it seemed likely to the doctors that it was another case of the native Remittent — a

relapsing fever (01 47) like Mrs Lewis
Dr. Allen had been so seriously sick with
and that Dr. Bustead had had such goo
success in his hospital by treating with
cold baths and hypodermics of strychnine
occasionally. And as papa's stomach was so
sensitive that he could scarcely bear food,
seemed impossible for the present at least
for him to take Warburg's tincture — So
cold bath treatment with as much nourishing f
as possible was settled upon — and after th
first cold bath papa felt so much better that
he asked for the next — however, neither see
reduced the temp. of any amount, and aft
the second he was so exhausted, and the shoc
was so much for him (his body 105° the water was 54° it should have been 104° & gradually lowered)
he dreaded another, and Dr. Bustead only gav
him one more plunge bath — after that just gain
sponge baths which seemed to be better.

Mama took care of papa Monday and Mo
night — Tuesday and Tuesday night, and af
that Mr. Noble helped. Monday night pap
was able to help himself to water when it wa
on the chair beside him, but by Tuesday nig
he was perfectly helpless and had to b
waited on like a child. Mama felt so
tired when Wednesday morning came, a
when Mr. Noble came in and kindly offere
to help, Papa told her not to get up, he
would have Mr. Noble place the screen around t
cot, and she must rest a little, and s
she tried to, but somehow a vision of th
little burying ground down on the banks o
the Han would come to her, and the thou
that Papa's dear body might soon lie buried t
made her heart almost break with grief, and she
could only keep from sobbing aloud, because
would make papa feel badly. As soon as
Mr. Noble had put the screen about mama

bed, papa asked him to bring a pencil and paper and he would give him the last expenses of his trip for Mr. Appenzeller the Treas. – All his other accounts he said would be found in his books. When he had finished, he remarked "Now I am ready to live or to die" Mr. Noble said "Oh we will have you with us a long time yet, doctor; and papa answered "I would like to stay and work a little longer if it were God's will, but if not I shall go 'sweeping through the gates' washed in the blood of the Lamb"; then after a few moments silence he added "It is all the blood of Jesus." Poor mama, she tried not to cry aloud, but she wet the pillow with her tears, and she prayed as she never prayed before that God would spare her dear husband. Then she thought what could she do – papa was certainly worse this morning – it was growing to be an effort for him to speak and it was hard to understand him already, she decided as soon as Dr. Busteed came she would ask him to call Dr. Avison and Dr. Vinton with any one else he liked in consultation, and see if nothing more could be done. The evening before mama & Dr. B. discovered some small red dots over papas body and arms, and with the great prostration and some other symptoms they began to suspect Typhus fever, which was confirmed after the consultation. As fresh air is the best disinfectant and tonic for typhus fever it was decided to open the doors and windows, and put plenty of clothing on the bed, and if possible to obtain fresh cows milk for papa to eat – all the missionaries who were taking milk kindly sent the milk man to us with their portion, so we were able to get 2 qts per day. Papa enjoyed it so much – he said it is the "Elixir of life" and he felt sure it was

52

digested as soon as it reached his stom
mama began to feel a little hopeful, fo
papa's strength could only be kept up a
the 10th or 12th day of the fever when th
crisis could be expected he would g
well. His fever kept up in an average
nearly 105° day and night — it varied b
little — sometimes a few tenths of a degree
sometimes above. His speech grew little
little more difficult to understand, a
mama didn't talk to him much fo
she feared it would tire him — he wou
tell her now and then not to feel b
because he didn't talk more. Once
spoke of his Grandfather Bolton, he had bee
that he had broken his hip, and th
remarked he "hoped Grandfather was in He
before now." He asked if his sister Lil
had gotten through her examinations. N
and then as I came near him, he w
try to tell me how much he loved m
and that it was a love that would la
through eternity. He asked after the little
born one, and smiled when I replied "it seem
strong — it moves about so much more than
Sherwood did." Late in the afternoon,
called me to him, and for some time I co
make out what he said — it sounded like
thing about a "shower-bath" then he t
to spell it out letter by letter, and I found
wanted to see little Sherwood, so the ti
brought him in — we had been keeping
out of the room all we could when we fou
papa's disease was contagious. Papa loo
at little Sherwood longingly, but did no
ask for him to be brought very near, seem
to know the danger, and then he motio
to take him away. Dear little man, it seem
pitiful to think you will remember noth

The cause of typhus wasn't then known, or we need not any of us have been afraid of contagion — after he was better and in other details,

What are Kennie's ... Weird

of the loving, longing, look papa gave you that day. Dr. Busteed staid with papa a part of that night, and Mr. Noble the remaining part. Mama moved my cot and Sherwood's bed into the dining-room, which she had taken so much pains to fix up, that, and the kitchen, while papa was gone, thinking he would be so pleased with the looks of things when he came home — Papa and mama had never practically had the pleasure of keeping house alone. Very soon after their return from their wedding trip — papa went to Pyong Yang, and before his return Mr. & Mrs. Noble came and they all kept house together until papa & mama went to Pyong Yang last spring; after their return they boarded with the Nobles until they went to Japan, when papa and mama had a few weeks alone, and liked it so much they decided they'd fix up the shops for a kitchen, and the bedroom for Papa's study and the dining-room, and keep house by themselves. Papa got it only partly fixed before he went to Pyong Yang on his last trip, and mama finished it up after he was gone, but he never saw it, and they never had the pleasure of "keeping-house" anymore.

Thursday morning papa asked for pencil and paper and tried to write, but it seemed just like little Sherwood trying, and he gave it up — This day he was unable to take his milk so well — the paralysis that evidently effected his speech was spreading more and more, and seemed to be involving the muscles of the pharynx, and it was with diffiuculty he could swallow, and quite often the milk would come back again — this soiled his beard so much, that Dr. Busteed suggested it should be cut, so mama asked papa if he would mind if his beard were cut, and he answered slowly but distinctly "It — will — be — good", so Mr. Noble cut it off from the chin alone, making him look like he use to in his College pictures at Queen's University.

He asked for a mirror, and smiled a
he saw the transformation.
Although papa's fever kept so very
all the time his mind wandered but lit
Once to-day looking at the shelf belo
the bed, he said he wanted Mr. B
come and put legs upon it, and put it
doors where there was plenty of air – he w
evidently thinking of his bed. Always, how
as long as he could talk, he would ans
intelligently when a question was put to h
In the afternoon I mentioned to him t
our order had come from San Francisco,
asked "To Chem-Chem-Ch-e-m-u-l-p-o
said "no, they are here in the house", the
asked if I had a room for my Amah yet
knew from my letters to him I had been troub
about this. This was the last day
talked – once he looked at Mama wh
she was near him with such a sorrowful, b
loving look in his eyes and stammered bro
"I – love – you" – mama said "yes, I kn
you dear, you needn't try to tell me, for it ta
your strength you know" It seemed to b
his greatest trouble because he couldn
talk as much as he would like. Durin
the afternoon he tried to tell Mama some
about his last trip to PyongYang – Mama coul
understand all that he said, but he seemed
want her not to regret that he had gone, f
she understood him say quite plainly "I did
for Jesus sake, and he will reward me
These were about the last words
papa uttered. Thursday night, Dr. Scra
stayed with him; Friday morning he w
unable to swallow; Dr. Busteed tried to
a stomach tube to feed him, but papa co
bear it, and didn't want it, so we fed h
by the bowel, and he retained it well

Aug. 26 '93 Papa sat down at our desk in the Appenzeller house before he [illegible] and remarked he felt like writing poetry and wrote the following two verses; when he had finished he said he would fix them up better sometime.

My years are as a tale that's told
The moments they are precious gold
My day of life is almost gone
And I am getting near my home.

Oh blissful thought and can it be
That I will dwell eternally
With Christ and loved ones gone before
Now waiting on the other shore. – W. J. Hall.

day; Dr. Vinton stayed with him that night - it was the 10th day of the fever, and mama felt when she went to bed that night, that it would likely prove the crisis, but she knew Dr. Vinton would lovingly do everything that could be done - it had not been long before that papa had made a little coffin for Dr. & Mrs. Vinton's dear little baby, and had prayed with them and tried to comfort them - little did Dr. Vinton think he would be so soon watching by dear papa's death-bed. About 7 a.m. Saturday, they called mama in, they thought papa was dying; but he lingered through the day - he seemed to like mama to be near him, and hold his hand. During the forenoon he kept his eyes closed, but would open them if mama stooped and said "Doctor" in his ear - and he would press mama's hand in response to questions she would ask. During the afternoon, papa kept his eyes wide open, and looked straight into mama's; his breathing was difficult, and his heart grew weaker and weaker, but he seemed not in pain - Toward evening he seemed to want mama to hold both his hands in hers - his eyes looked so bright, and just at {sunset Sat. Nov. 24th} he breathed his last, his hands in mama's his eyes fixed upon hers. Mama gently closed those loving eyes, then thinking how they could never look into her eyes again, she opened them once more, for one long, last look - they still looked as bright and so clear, it didn't seem as if his dear spirit could have left the body - Mama closed them then for the last time, and left the room; and took her dear little boy in her arms, and prayed to God to help her to be brave and strong for his sake and that of her little unborn baby whose tiny heart even then throbbed beneath her own. God certainly answered mama's prayer, and in a

[Left margin:] ...eral times she repeated these ... "I will love Thee in life, I will love Thee in death, and praise Thee as long as Thou ... And say when the death dew lies cold on my brow, If ever I loved Thee, my Jesus, 'tis now."

56

Sweet Mother! I am here alone,
In sorrow and in pain;
The sunshine from my heart has flown
It feels the drenching rain - Ah me!
The chill, and mould and rain.

Oh, but to feel thy fond arms twine
Around me, once again!
It almost seems those lips of thine
Might kiss away the pain - might soothe
This dull, cold, weary pain.

But, gentle Mother, through life's storms,
I may not lean on thee,
For helpless, cowering little forms
Cling trustingly to me - Poor babes!
To have no guide but me.

Sweet Mother, for this wandering [illegible]
That loftier faith be given
Her broken reeds all swept away
That she may lean on Heaven [illegible]
Grow strong in Christ and [illegible]

Fanny Forester (Mrs. Judson) 1850.

short time she was able to get
gether the last things for laying de
papa out - his wedding suite, his under
collar, cuffs and necktie etc. But th
night, she awoke about 12M. and
great desolateness of it all so overcame h
that she sobbed aloud, and Kum Jongie w
slept in the room to help care for Sherw
came to her, and tried to comfort her -
said "the Tiane (great-man) has gone to heaven,
is with Yasu (Jesus) now, you must not feel ba

The next day was Sunday, a bri
beautiful day. Papa is spending it with Je
Kum Jongie carried Sherwood, and he and M
went out to get some fresh air, that
possible they might not get sick, th
went out along the wall where papa ca
Sherwood the last time he went walkin
with mama just before he left for Pyong Y

At 2p.m. was the hour ap-
pointed to start for the burial gr
The coffin was but just finished a fe
moments before. Dear papa had m
such pretty coffins for each of the fore
or that had died since he came he
he use to be a cabinet-maker, and help
to make coffins when a young boy, bu
now there were none who knew h
to make one for him, and a Chinese
did the best he could at it - it wa
lined with white Korean silk, and
covered with black cloth.

Mama went in a Sedan Chai
carried by four men, and she carri
little Sherwood on her lap. Dea
boy, he enjoyed the ride out in
the country so much, he seem
particularly pleased with the larg
trees. Before we got to

the River Han, he fell asleep, and slept all through the ceremony at the grave. - He did not hear the cold thud of the earth as it fell on dear papa's coffin, and Mr. Noble said "Earth to earth and ashes to ashes."

After the burial mama & Sherwood went to Dr. Cutler's and stopped in Miss Lewis' room for three days, while the rooms at home were being disinfected.

Tuesday afternoon there was a most appropriate and beautiful Memorial service held in the Chapel for Papa. Mama selected the hymns & papa's favorite chapter, and suggested whom she would like to take part in the service, and Mr. Noble lovingly made out the programme. Afterwards when mama wrote him a little note of thanks, he replied "I loved the Dr. more than words would express, any slight service I have done or may yet be permitted to do, is in itself a sweet pleasure"

Memorial Service.
Rev. William James Hall, M.D.
Pai Chai Chapel, Nov. 27, 1894.

Hymn. - No. 979 Methodist Hymnal. - "Asleep in Jesus".
Scripture Lesson. - Isaiah 43. 1-15 } Rev. W. B. Scranton, M.D.
Prayer }
Hymn of Fanny Crosby (solo)
Address. - Biographical. Rev. W. A. Noble
Address. - Dr. Vinton. Dr. Hall as a Medical Missionary
Address. - Rev. S. A. Moffatt
Hymn. - No. 254 Gospel Hymns. - "Consecration" (Papa's favorite)
Address. - Dr. Busteed.
Address. - Rev. Graham Lee.
Hymn. - No. 318 Gospel Hymns. - "My Jesus I love Thee"
Address. - Dr. Hall's Introduction to Mission work and End. Rev. H. G. Appenzeller
Solo "Sweeping through the Gates" Rev. Graham Lee
Benediction.

MEMORAL SERVICE.

REV. WILLIAM JAMES HALL, M. D.

Pai Chai Chapel, Nov. 27th. 1894.

Hymn written by Fanny Crosby on the departure of

Dr. Hall for the Mission field.

Hymn.

WHO WILL GO?

O'er the ruthless rolling ocean,
Where the Prince of darkness reigns,
Holding fast his countless victims,
Crushed beneath his cruel chains;
Oh, the wail of bitter anguish,
Oh, the deep despairing cry,
Send us light or we must perish,
Send it quickly or we die.

To these wretched, starving millions,
Who the bread of life will bear?
At a throne of grace and mercy,
Who will plead with them in prayer?
Who will undertake the journey?
O'er the stormy billow's foam,
Leaving all without a murmur,
Parents, friends, a native home?

Firmly, bravely comes the answer,
From a loyal mission band,
That our blessed Lord is keeping,
In the hollow of his hand;
Firmly, bravely comes the answer,
Even now I hear him say;
Gracious Master Thou hast called me,
And Thy message I obey.

Dearest brother, you are going,
Where you oft may sow in tears,
And the fruit of earnest labor,
Be withheld perhaps for years,
Though you toil amid their changes,
Burning sun and chilling frost,
Not a seed will be forgotten,
Not a single blade be lost.

God be with you on the billows,
God protect you o'er the main,
In his tender loving kindness,
Bring you back to us again;
But if otherwise determined,
And on earth we meet no more,
May we all sing halleujah,
On the bright eternal shore.

I am sure, if my little Sherwood lives, he will be proud of such a papa some day; only the dear Heavenly father can by any means make up what he has lost in the death of this loving father; but God's richest promises are to the fatherless, and, dear little boy, we claim them for you.

To-day, Monday Dec. 10th, finds little Sherwood, his mama, Youlanie & Esther at Chemulpo, awaiting the sailing of a ship that will take them to Japan, there to take the "China," for America. As mama has been out here almost five years, it is so nearly time for her vacation, that she felt she better be taking it now, when she couldn't well be doing much mission work anyhow. She hopes to return in a couple of years, and would be glad to be sent to Pyeng Yang and help continue the work formed there by dear papa. Esther & Youlanie both wished very much to go to America, and Mama is going to take them both. Youlanie will help with the work at home, and study English what time he can get, and Esther, mama expects to send to school at Liberty, and if she does well, she will send her to Medical College, that she may go back as a Medical Missionary to her Korean sisters.

We came down to Chemulpo Friday the 7th, leaving Söul 7 a.m. and reaching Mr Jones' 5.30 p.m. It was a cold day - Sherwood rode in his mama's chair most of the time, but the rest of the time he rode on horseback in front of Mr Appenzeller. On the Wednesday night before little Sherwood had quite a high fever Temp. 104.5°, Pulse 140, Resp. 50, and Mama feared he was going to have typhus fever, but after a few doses of aconite he got much better, and Thursday he seemed all right, also Friday a.m. so Mama and the other doctors thought it likely

due to teething, and we went on to Clam
expecting to leave on a boat sailing Sat. m
but that morning when Mama dressed
wood, she found him all broken out w
measles, so that is what the face m
The boat was too full to accomodate a
passengers; and of course we couldn't well
anyhow, so we staid over at Mr & Mrs. Jones u
Sherwood should be better of the measles, a
until the next boat comes.

Sherwood is 18 mos. old to-day, a
weighs 23½ lbs with his cloak on. He ca
a little cold last night, and has quite a b
to-day, and seems feverish again.

The "Boynton" came in to-day,
if all is well, we shall probably leave t
upon her next Friday morning, Dec. 14th

"'Tis hard to take the burden up
When these have laid it down
They brightened all the joy of life
They softened every frown.
But, oh! 'tis good to think of them
When we are troubled sore;
Thanks be to God that such have been
Although they are no more

More homelike seems the vast unk
Since they have entered there;
To follow them were not so hard
Wherever they may fare.
They cannot be where God is not,
On any sea or shore;
Whate'er betides, Thy love abides
Our God for ever more.

Thursday, Jan. 10, 1895.

In the morning sow thy seed, and in the evening withold not thy hand: for thou knowest not whether shall prosper, either this or that, or whether they both shall be alike good. Eccl. XI, 6.

" We live in deeds, not years; in thought, not breaths;
In feelings, not in figures on the dial.
We should count time by heart-throbs. He most lives
Who thinks most, feels the noblest, acts the best."

For four weeks now little Sherwood has been traveling every day by sea or by land. We rowed out in a sampan to the "Boynton" just four weeks ago to-day, and sailed the next morning before light. It was very rough all the way to Japan — so windy, and the ship rocked and pitched till we were all so seasick, even Sherwood vomited once. The Captain's wife who was on board kindly cared for him quite a great deal during the day, but mama had to do it all at night — could get no more out of Esther + Tonfanie than out of a couple of logs. None of us, except Sherwood, ate anything for over 50 hrs, and drank but very little water — Mama just vomited, and vomited, until it seemed as if there could possibly be no more to come up. Little Sherwood would take a corner of the blanket he wore and try to wipe off mama's lips after she vomited, and then sometimes he would crawl to where the dish sat that mama vomited into, and he would make-be-lieve vomit too, out of sympathy. Mama couldn't cry, because if Sherwood saw her, he would also cry. Oh, but those were two such awful long nights and days, they seemed like a terrible night-mare. Sunday morning early we got into Nagasaki Harbor — in a little restless sleep, that

mama had that night before, she dre
that when we reached Nagasaki the Chi
was there, and would sail at 4 p.m. Sh
mentioned this to the Capt. & his wife
and all were hoping it might be so, bu
as according to Schedule she should leav
Kobe Monday, the hope didn't comfort us mu
However, a little later when the Pilot came
board, the good Captain came running dow
almost out of breath, and said to mama, "
dream is true, the China is just in, an
leaves this afternoon". The same storm th
made us so sick had delayed the China. "
stayeth His rough wind in the day of the East

Mama sent word to the ladies of the W.F.M.S.
dear Mrs. Van Petten, and Miss French soon ca
on board, and they helped to get the freight
baggage transferred, and our tickets purcha
and we were soon on board the Chin
a comfortable state-room. There was no
time to go ashore, but Miss French kin
brought "O Waka San" the little Japanese g
that began to help mama the same time Esther
in the dyspensary, on board, and Esther and
had a nice little visit with her. She was a
to see little Sherwood. When she left Korea
was not yet married. She is doing nicely now
the Girls' School at Nagasaki.

The China is said to be the finest st
ships on the Pacific, and it did seem s
large and beautiful in comparison to th
small cargo boats we had been on of late
We had such a pleasant time saili
up through Japan's Inland Sea. We reac
Kobe Dec. 18th. The hill-tops were cov
with the first snow we had seen. Thurs
the 20th we spent on shore at Yokohama
Sherwood enjoyed so much riding in a jin
Mama spent a busy day, getting checks on the

bank exchanged upon New York banks, securing tickets to San Francisco, Emigration papers for Mr & Mrs. Pak, foreign shoes for Mrs Pak, and foreign clothes for Mr. Pak etc. Miss Griffis of the W. F. M. S. kindly helped us.

The 21st we sailed from Yokohama out upon our long voyage across the Pacific Ocean via of Honolulu. Up to this time we had none of us been a bit sea-sick upon the China — it had not been rough, and Sherwood had ridden about on deck each day in his baby carriage but as we got out from shore the ship began rocking badly, although the sea did not look very rough — there were high winds however. By Sunday it was quite bad, and the Koreans both felt sick and discouraged again — mama felt badly, but it was mostly because she had to carry Sherwood more when she ought not to. However, after a few days the Koreans got use to it, so they had most of the care of Sherwood, and gave mama a rest.

Tuesday, Dec. 25th — Christmas day, the sea is quieter to-day. Beside Sherwood there are only two children on board the China, Willie Hitt and his sister Beatrice, aged 10 & 4, children of Dr. & Mrs. Hitt of Louisville, Ky. but recently from India. Dr. Hitt went out as a Medical Missionary only a year ago, and is returning now on account of health. Both of these children received some nice Xmas presents, and Mrs. Hitt gave Sherwood a little doll. We spent quite a pleasant day: in the evening Social Hall was decorated with the flags of all nations, Xmas wreathes etc and the officers and passengers got up quite a nice little entertainment of music, readings, solos, and stories.

Five years ago to-day papa took mama to the Metropolitan Museum of Art at Central Park and upon their way home first asked her to become his wife. Now just one month ago to-day his dear body was buried from our sight on the

Banks of the River Han. It has been th
saddest Christmas to Mama that she h
ever seen.
" When some beloved voice that was to you
Both sound and sweetness, faileth sudden
And silence against which you dare not cr
Aches round you like a strong disease and
What hope! What help! What music will
That silence to your sense?" —
The next day, just as the passeng
had begun to get use to the rolling motio
of the ship, and to get upon their sea-legs, s
began pitching — this makes one's hea
feel very badly.
The Stewardess, Mrs. Gurgan, is very k
to Sherwood and his mama — she has been a
widow 11 years — was left with a little bo
and a little girl — both babies. They are wit
their Grandma now in San Francisco.
Sherwood is also very fond of the Stewar
Goodchild, a colored man — Sherwood just crie
go to him every time he sees him. The Stew
often carries him to see the Engine working, an
Sherwood enjoys this so much.
Thursday the 27th was repeated — a
we crossed the line (180°) that day — oh, it di
seem as if Friday would never come & the
week of 8 days instead of seven never end. One w
not think that one day would make such
difference, but one reason was because th
pitching still continued, and every one fel
badly. Mama didn't rest well at nig
and she got so tired of the motion of th
boat days.
Saturday, Dec. 29 we crossed th
Tropic of Cancer into the Torrid Zone, an
the next evening at 5 p.m. anchored a
Honolulu. Rev. Damon came on boar
and invited us to spend the next d

at his home, which we did; it made a pleasant rest for us. Uncle Yon Sanie, Aunt Esther & little Sherwood had their first ride in a horse and carriage, and it was mama's first ride for nearly 5 yrs. At Honolulu it is always summer — the grass is now green — Banana's, bread-fruit, cocoa-nuts etc are growing upon the trees — Oleanders and roses bloom in the garden. Rev. Damon's father was a Missionary to the Sandwich Islands, and he was born there, he married the daughter of Revd. Mr. Happer missionary in China, and an active missionary himself — they have three nice children, and a very beautiful home. Their missionary work is now among the Chinese of the Island.

Jan 1 '95 New Year's day, we started on for America once more, reaching there one day a head of schedule time, Sunday morning Jan. 6th. As it had been storming no one was looking for the China a head of time; so Uncle Robert nor Mrs. Jenkins to whom Mama had written, did not meet us, and after getting out of the Customs, we went to the Occidental Hotel; here, however, Mrs. Jenkins found us in the evening, and we went with her to the Deaconess Home in the morning. Miss Murray a missionary returning from Nanking, China went with us — she and Mama had become quite friends upon board the China, and decided they would travel together to Chicago in a Tourist car, and see how they would like it — it is so much less expensive than a Palace car. Mama was busy all day securing her tickets at reduced rates, looking after her freight and baggage, did not get through till 4 p.m. the hour set by Cous. Sherman Darber to go out to his home, and visit with his family, also Uncle Robert Gildersleeve, Cous. Rob. Darber & Cous Chas. Bonny,

met there, so there was quite a reunion. I
was sorry she couldn't take her little boy, but it wo
have required an hour to go to him, and an hou
come back, and there was not time, so Mama d
see her little boy in all day long, from 9 o'clock i
the morning to 9 o'clock at night. Uncle Ro
went back with her to see his little nephew. Gr
Robert Gilchrist was the first Uncle little Sherwood ev
saw, he gave Sherwood a $20 gold-piece.

The next morning, Tuesday the 8th, we lef
Francisco on the 7 o'clock train, bound straight th
to Chicago without change. We took a tourist ca
which only cost us $6 apiece instead of $15 apiece as
Palace car would have done, and there was mo
liberty for Sherwood, and a good chance to lay his na
then we laid in about $6.00 worth of provision a
a few necessary dishes at Smith's Cash Store, and Un
Jon Jamie served us up three hot meals per day,
we lived well on baked potatoes, hot oatmeal & mi
boiled rice, baked apples, salmon, smoked beef, so
crackers, graham wafers, ginger snaps, macaroni
canned peaches and pears, nuts, candy & fruit, a
hot Chocolate. It averaged just 10¢ per me
instead of $1.00 per meal as upon the Palace car.
were never more than 2 other passengers be
ourselves, so we had almost the whole car
our ourselves. Sherwood found him a colo
friend again in the Porter, a good Methodist f
Omaha, and grew very fond of him. Thi
he will be sure to like Joe, at home — t
must inherit a tendency from his mama
like black-men, he never has seemed at all af
of them.

We have been passing rapidly through
Cal, Nev, Utah and Wyoming. We have y
Neb, Iowa, and Ill. to cross, and we will rea
Chicago Saturday 7 a.m.

Sherwood is 14 mos. old to-day, and wei
26 lbs with his cloak on. He does not ta
" weighs 1 1/2 lbs

at all now — "Eh" "Eh" "Eh" has to do to express all he says, or if he wants anything & if that is not sufficient, he points his finger, and when he don't want a thing, he shakes his head very emphatically. He doesn't walk alone yet — has not had much of a chance, as it was so rough on the steamer he could not creep most of the time let alone learn to walk; however, down in the cabin where oftener than not the thermom. registered 82° he would play about on the floor with just his shirt and "didy" on, and here he began to rise up from the floor alone, and stand for a few seconds looking so proudly about upon us all, then the ship would give a lurch and down he would go; but he was soon upon his feet again, he would do this ten or a dozen times some evenings, before tiring. He also learned to crawl up all the steps to the upper deck, and with Lou Janie or Esther behind him to see that he didn't fall, he did it several times even when the ship was rolling pretty well.

Dear little Sherwood, he is growing such a big boy, he slept all alone in his little berth on the steamer, and soon got so he would sleep all night without awaking for his milk. In the morning, the Chinaboy would bring him some fresh cow's milk and a soft boiled egg, then about 11 a.m. he would have his regular bottle of milk and go to sleep for an hour or two, at 4 p.m. he ate a big bowl of chicken soup every day. He still needs an enema each day, and all the way home never soiled but one napkin. On the cars he slept in an upper berth with Aunt Esther, and generally went to sleep by 8 p.m. and would not awake before 7 a.m. = At 8 p.m. the next train starts
For the Poppy Land afar;
The summons clear falls on the ear,
"All aboard for the Sleeping car!"
"But what is the fare to Poppy Land?
I hope it is not dear."
The fare is this — a hug and a kiss,
And 'tis paid to the engineer, — Edgar W. Abbott

Sunday, Feb. 10, 1895.
In Thee the fatherless findet[h]
mercy. Hosea 14,3.

Last night, my darling, as you slep[t]
I thought I heard you sigh
And to your little crib I crept,
And watched a space thereby;
And then I stopped and kissed your brow,
For O! I love you so —
You are too young to know it now,
But sometime you shall know.
Eugene Fiel[d]

Hannah Whitall Smith's daughter once wrote to her "O
be that thee didst ever love me as I love my little Ruth

Cranium 18½ in. circumf.
Height standing 31 in.

To-day Sherwood is 15 mo[nths old and]
finds him at Grandpa Sherwood's, he ca[me]
here Jan. 14th on Aunt Annie's birthday. He
has gained 1½ lbs since he came to Grandpa's
a new tooth — a left lower . He now w[eighs]
26 lbs (with clothes on) he was weighed in the
bushel basket, and sat down in it quietly and
as good as you please all the time Aunt Annie a[nd]
Mama and Tom Annie were at work at it.

From the first since his arri[val]
at Grandpa's he began trying to walk — evide[ntly]
recognizing he had gotten to a stationary house
solid land. He took a few steps alone the fi[rst]
night, and has walked a little every d[ay al]
most. At first his shoes were too sma[ll]
and Joe bought him a larger pair (No. 5) a[nd]
he was so pleased with them, he wanted
Old ones off right away, and the new ones
and since then he has walked much be[tter]
goes alone anywhere he likes, and the last t[wo]
or three days, has walked rather more than
has crept. He does look so cunning walk[ing]
about, he generally waves both hands, and
"hoot, "he" toot" with his mouth, like a little eng[ine]

If mama can keep this picture in mind just as Sherwood looks toddling about with such a proud look upon his merry face, it will be one of the prettiest on memory's walls.

O little feet! that such long years
Must wander on through hopes and fears,
Must ache and bleed beneath your load;
I, nearer to the wayside inn
Where toil shall cease and rest begin,
Am weary, thinking of your road!

His Grandma, for fun sometimes tells him to open his mouth wide then he can walk better, and he will do so, marching off with his mouth so wide open we can see that new tooth, and look away down his throat, and almost see the last bottle of milk he ate. Yes, he still uses his dear old bottle, always to take his morning nap with, and to go to sleep on at night, the rest of the time he drinks from his cup nicely and he eats well at the table t.i.d. The change in milk and diet at Grandpa's instead of curing his constipation as mama had hoped, only made him grow worse — unboiled cow's milk soft-boiled egg, apple sauce, and even a whole raw apple scraped might be eaten, and then with a glycerine enema it was almost impossible for him to have a movement, and it would pain him so and make him cry so hard that it would bring the tears to the eyes of both Grandma and Aunt Annie. Grandma says to mama "you must do something for that child or he will surely be killed", so mama had cream and oatmeal gruel added to the milk, and then sent and got a bottle of "Syrup of Figs" a spoonful of which he takes each night, and he now has a movement each morning without an enema. The fur is clearing off his tongue and he seems much better every way.

Although Sherwood does not talk …
yet, he understands pretty well what …
said to him. Grandma will say "Where …
Sherwood's new shoes?" and he will stick …
out; or, she will say "where is Sherwood's …
and he will point upstairs.

During this last month the …

Jan. 18, 1895. sent to Sherwood a dear little baby s…
She first opened her eyes in this world …
7 a.m. Friday, Jan. 18th. Her name is "…
Margaret Hall" and she weighs 7½ pou…
When Sherwood was first brought to …
her he looked questioningly from bab…
mama with large wondering eyes; th…
he laid his cheek softly against mam…
much as to say "thank you, mama, dea…
he kissed his little sister and stroked he…
lovingly. Each day he asks to see her, and …
first when she cried, he would cry too; …
he will want some one to go and tend her …
once. Sometimes, Aunt Esther will lay little sista…
Sherwood's arms, and that pleases him very m…
No matter whether Grandma, Fontaine, Aunt Esther, or …
takes the baby, Sherwood has never yet shown …
least sign of jealousy.

Dear little man, he doesn't realize …
what a treasure God has given him, b…
she is spared to him he will know m…
and more, as the years go by, what a pr…
gift dear sister is.

March 10, 1895.

Leave thy fatherless children, I will preserve them alive, and let thy widows trust in me. Jer. 49:11.

"What has my darling been doing to-day,
To pay for his washing and mending
How can he manage to keep out of debt
For so much caressing and tending?
How can I wait till the years shall have flown
And the hands have grown larger and stronger
Who will be able the interest to pay,
If the debt runs many years longer?"

Sherwood does not seem to gain any in height of late, but he has added on two pounds of flesh, and has his first molar through. He can climb up and down stairs all alone, and has never gotten but one tumble though he goes up and down many times a day.

One day he went out to Liberty with Im Fanie for a ride — it was the day Esther began going to school, Feb. 25th.

Every day Im Fanie carries him out for a nice walk in the open air, and to see the horses and cows, and little calves — he enjoys it very much and asks for it each day.

Sherwood is growing to be quite a favorite in the household, his grandma has taught him so that he has learned to like to sit on lap — and Aunt Annie rocks him sometimes. He also climbs upon Grandpa's knee sometimes, He has great times playing with Aunt Annie's little dog "Frisky" and with the two cats "Maltese" & "Beauty", and Grandpa's big dog "Prince". They are all very kind to little Sherwood, but at first they didn't enjoy playing with him very much.

(Frisky)

Wednesday, Apr. 10, 1895.

The Lord relieveth the fatherless
widow. Psalms 146-9.

"Around our incompleteness is
completeness."

Sherwood weighs 30 lbs to-day -
head is 19 in. in circumf. As Aunt
says every week she comes home from
he seems to "grow shorter, and shorter." He
really shorter, but as he doesn't gain in h
as does in width, it makes him appear
He has his first four molars now, and
begining to cut his canines, - he quite
with them too - it is harder for him to am
himself long at a time, and he often wa
up in the night crying - Mama hopes
when these are through, her little boy w
not have any more such hard trouble cutting
He seems quite well now, and has
had to have any medicine for constipation
a long time except phosphate of soda in his
He doesn't care to eat much food at the ta
but he never does when he is cutting tee
his old bottle is his best friend, and even
seems to hurt sometime.

He goes out on the stoop and walk
about in the sunshine alone some days, whe
Josanie is too busy to take him out. One
he fell off, and cut his upper lip, the corner of
mouth, also the inside of his mouth bled quite
great deal.

Grandma has taught Sherwood where
eyes, mouth, tongue, teeth, and ears are. She
say "where are Sherwood's eyes?," and he will bring
little forefinger so near his eye that he winks and
for fear it will go in.

This month mama put the money that dear papa left out upon interest; she hopes not to have to touch the principal until her little boy and girl, need it in college expenses.

Mama is quite busy corresponding with different friends who knew papa; she hopes to get a Memorial volume written before next Nov. 24th. Also she has written an appeal that she has sent to some papers and some friends who helped papa to raise the money to buy the property at Pyong Yang, that they might also aid now in building a Memorial hospital upon that property.

Little Sherwood understands almost everything said to him - tell him to carry apples to Grandpa, to pick this up, or stop doing that, he will obey, but he does not talk at all yet. He will sing "by by" to his rag-doll, also if baby Edith cries he will offer her a bite of his cake or apple, or will try to stick her bottle into her mouth - he will also jiggle the carriage she lies in and sing "by, by, by", he does look so sweet and cunning trying to comfort his dear little baby sister.

Grandpa keeps some maple sugar in his vest-pocket for his little grandson, and about once every day Sherwood will climb up for it on Grandpa's knee, sometimes he will sit quite a long time hoping his Grandpa will offer it to him without his asking, but if he don't he will point to the pocket and say "uh, uh, uh" like a little pig, and then he gets it; but Sherwood is not like a little pig in teasing for more - he seldom asks for another piece, and no matter what sweet he is eating, after he has had ~~quite~~ a little he can't be coaxed to take more.

Joe, also, keeps some ginger cookies and sweet crackers on the milk-room shelf behind the door, and generally every day he will ask Joe for one of these.

Friday May 10, '95

Pray one for another. - Jas. V. 16

"Our dear ones Lord, we bring to Thee
And lay them at thy feet;
Content, through yearning hopes and fe[ars]
To hear Thy promise sweet,
That Thou wilt bless the loving faith
Which seeks for them Thy grace,
And finds beneath Thy shadowing wings
Its quiet resting-place."

To-day finds little Sherwood Hall
and one-half years old, and he has a[...]
grown one inch taller, but he weighs
a pound less.

Sherwood loves to be out doors, w[...]
to be out all the time. One morning [...]
thought she would see if he couldn't t[ake]
care of himself pretty well, as she was [...]
and Jon Janie too; but it wasn't long b[efore]
there was a great outcry in the direction [of]
bee-yard. Joe heard it first, and went just [as]
fast as his poor old rheumatic legs c[ould]
carry him and found little Sherwood fig[hting]
the bees with all his might, they had s[tung]
him on head, face and hands a dozen or [...]
times. Joe brought him in, and Aunt Annie
Mamma removed the stingers and bathed
places stung with soda water which g[...]
ma prepared at once, then mamma [gave]
him his bottle of milk and soon rocked [him]
to sleep; when he awoke he felt pretty [well]
and the stings did not swell much;
you could notice the effects of them [...]
a week after.

One day during this last month [...]
Eva came up and brought a new dres[s]

Sherwood a pretty red & white plaid gingham worked in crossstitch about the bottom by Cousin Eva. Mama also has made him two new calico dresses grandma helped. And he has had to have another pair of shoes No. 6 - the others seemed pretty small - they were not worn out yet.

Grandpa and Sherwood have had their pictures taken together. Sherwood was so good - it seemed as if he knew what he went for, and mamma and everyone is so pleased with them, they seem just perfect of both grandpa & Sherwood.

Ninety and One.

Dear Grandpa seems growing more and more feeble now, we fear we can not have him with us much longer. Some day he will be leaving us like dear papa did. He talked to mamma about it one morning lately,

he said he was quite ready and willin
go, he didn't have the evidence t
some people have, but he believed eve
word in the New Testament, about t
salvation our Saviour came to bring, a
he believed He would save him, as h
trust was in Him. Mamma a
him if he would like not to have h
to Canada this summer, he said he th
she better make preparations to go, and
see how he was later, perhaps he'd
feeling better soon.

Wednesday, July 10, 1895.

Not knowing the things that s
befall me there. - Acts 20:22

" I see not a step before me,
As I tread on another year;
But the past is in God's keeping
The future His mercy shall clear
So on I go not knowing
I would not if I might
I would rather walk in the dark with God
Than go alone in the light
I would rather walk with Him by faith,
Than walk alone by sight."

This morning Sherwood is twe
months old - He weighs 31 lbs.
Uncle Jon Lanie awoke him very
and got him washed and dressed, a
he started with mamma and little S
and Mr. & Mrs. Pok for New York city
after two days he will go on to North
to visit at Uncle Frank's and then
a week or ten days to Glen Buell to
papa's Canadian home.
Sherwood was a good little boy all
way down to the big city of New York w
we reached about 11 a.m. He had a n

time looking out of the car window as he sat beside mamma, and he would point out the horses calling out "back" and the cows saying "möö", and he tries to say "bird" also and he says "see" and "this" quite well, also attempts to say "Kitty", so he has progressed some within the last two months. He has recently grown exceedingly fond of horses and could spend all his waking hours out in the barn watching them, and when he finds the picture of one he is delighted. He calls them all "Back".

June 27th, the 3rd anniversary of mamma's wedding day, dear Grandpa Sherwood left us for his Heavenly home; only the Sunday before he helped Grandma sing one of his favorite hymns "When I can read my title clear to mansions in the skies." Grandpa could not really sing any more than mamma can, but this hymn, and "On Jordan's stormy banks I stand", and "O for a thousand tongues to sing" he use to often "sing at", in a peculiar style of his own on Sunday evenings — sometimes with little Sherwood on his knee, and mamma can remember when he use to hold her on his knee and sing them long ago. It had always been Grandpa's desire to never be sick long or make any one much trouble to take care of him, but to die easily and quickly; and his death was as near as could be what he had hoped for. Just a week before he died Cousins Polly & Horace Crary of Binghamton called upon him and when they went away he walked out to the gate with them; that was the last time he was out of the house, though he walked on the stoop a few times after that; on Monday of the week he died, he said to Grandma, "I do not believe I will live

the week out" — and we could
he was failing each day. Grand-
made him some chicken soup that
relished, and Mamma got him so
unfermented grape juice, — and
ate, a cup of milk three times a day
one in the night, but he didn't fe
hungry he said. Some of Uncle Wa
folks came in to see him every day —
Wednesday morning Frank & Em drove
Thursday Uncle Lee & Aunt Harriet Lar
came over, and Grandpa visited a li
with them; about 1 p.m. he took hi
nourishment and lay down to sleep.
about 4 o'clock he awoke and Uncle
helped him walk out to his chair, and
Walter gave him a big fish that Cousin
caught for him, he said it was a large on
he thought it would taste nice for a chang
That morning he had tried to read from
Christian Herald a story he was interest
but he felt too weak; so in the aftern
Mamma read it to him, and he sa
he understood it all. After awaking th
time he complained of feeling so weak —
he had been dreaming of starting a l
mowing machines to work, and it tire
him all out. Towards evening he sp
of wishing that he "felt more lively,
he might praise the Lord." After e
his usual nourishment and taking t
medicine to help him sleep, he lay down
about 8 p.m. awaking again about 10.
Grandma heard him, and went to
he said he had "slept good" — he
raised himself up and was sitting on t
of the bed as he was accustomed to do
last two months often, to breathe easier.
said now as you are sitting up you fe

take your food and medicine as it is almost time for it — so he took it all right — then Grandma said "don't hurry to lie down, I will sit up with you a little while if you wish, but he replied he thought he better lie down, so he did, Grandma covered him up, and went back to her couch in the sitting room when she thought she heard him make a little noise like snoring, she went quickly to him, but his spirit had gone, his body had never moved a bit — Grandma called Mamma at once, and Mamma will never forget the picture of Grandpa lying there on his left side with his knees drawn up a little as he was accustomed to lie when sleeping and one hand up to his face with two fingers on his brow like he often did when praying, he looked just like a child sleeping so naturally, but it was the sleep from which none awake to weep, and he had reached the place where as he use to sing

"No chilling winds or poisonous breath
Can reach that healthful shore;
Sickness and sorrow, pain and death,
Are felt and feared no more."

The funeral service was held Sunday afternoon, but mamma's little boy can read about this and a sketch of Grandpa's life in mamma's scrap-book when he grows older.

Little Sherwood will probably forget his Grandpa just as he has his papa, but they will not forget him, and they will be watching and waiting for him to come home too by and by. And mamma prays that her little boy may grow up a Christian man and follow Jesus as they tried to do, and then he will not dread death any more than they did. "O death

where is thy sting? O grave where is th[e]
victory? The sting of death is sin + + Bu[t]
thanks be to God, which giveth us the vict[ory]
through our Lord Jesus Christ. Therefore +
ye steadfast, unmovable, always abou[nding]
in the work of the Lord forasmuch as [ye]
know that your labor is not in vain in t[he]
Lord. I Cor XV 55–57 —

Little Sherwood missed Grandpa, [when]
asked where he was, he would go and [look]
in the bed, shake his head, and then c[ome]
out and point at his empty chair wi[th]
such a grave look on his little face — [we]
all miss him so much, but especial[ly]
dear Grandma who has lived with him f[or]
over 36 yrs now — she is so lonely — mam[ma]
didn't like to go away so soon and leave her, [but]
grandma felt with her that it was her duty to [go to]
papa's people who have waited for her so long, a[nd]
about 2 weeks we started.

Saturday Aug. 10, '95 At Glen Buell

But we all, with unveiled face ref[lecting]
as in a mirror the glory of the Lord, are chang[ed into]
the same image from glory to glory. II Cor. III

"When a child is born, how soon [they]
say he resembles his Father! When [we]
are really born again, how soon peo[ple]
say if we are genuine, "he is lik[e]
his Father in Heaven."

Here little Sherwood is in his pa[pa's]
own home — Grandma Hall has given [him]
a little cup that she gave papa before he [was]
five years old. It is inscribed, "They that seek me [early]
shall find me." — — — And here [are]
picture frames, brackets, and even beds
that dear papa made, and the shop th[at]

he fixed up over the woodhouse where he use to work. He was so fond of carpentry and cabinet making work. There is much to remind us of him here all the time. Papa's dear father and mother, brothers and sisters, were all so glad to greet his babies and their mama. Nearly every one speaks of how much Sherwood looks like his papa, though some thinks he looks like Uncle Clifford, but then, they say he looks like his brother Jimmy. Every one calls dear papa "Jimmy" here, and every one admired and loved him so much. Though Grandpa's farm is quite a distance from any village yet people drive from miles around to see "Jimmy's wife and babies", over one hundred came the first two weeks.

Sherwood has not gained in weight any since his last birth-day, but he has added a few words to his vocabulary, or rather he says surely what last month was not much more than an attempt to say, but now he will pronounce after you "back" "Kitty," "birds" "boss" "tate, tate", pie, and mama, And he uses them correctly whenever there is occasion. He still goes to sleep with his bottle — goes lugging it off up stairs so good naturedly, and is soon in the "land of Nod", and after a 2 hrs sleep will awake, climb down from the bed himself, and come down stairs alone. He most always tells, also, when he wants to go to the closet — he says like the little Korean children "she! she! she!" Mrs. Forth gave him a journal that had many pictures of horses in — and Aunt Esther cut them out — and she and Uncle Fontaine pasted them in a pink & blue muslin book that mama made, and he is just delighted with them — will amuse himself pointing to each one, and

where he use to go to ... mama in writing over Dear papa's memoirs. Mama also saw the high school in Athens which he attended

shouting out "back" for a long time, and will beg for the book, sometimes when has another, he will show he is satisfied with it, but will keep saying back" until he gets his "back book" w contains 24 pages of nothing but horse

While in Glen Buell mama quired somewhat into Sherwood's lineage papa's side, and found she could trace back four generations on the Hall side four generations on the Bolton side. As has the Sherwood genealogy quite fully out she thought it would be nice write what she could of the Hall genea in Sherwood's journal, and the Bol genealogy in Edith Margaret's journal, then altogether someday the can read quit little about their ancestors.

Four generations ago there lived the county of Armagh, Ireland a G Hall, he married Margaret Boyd, they had a pleasant home on a f leased for ninety-nine years, se miles from Cady. Belfast, twenty-t miles away was their nearest seap George Hall and his wife were Presbyterians, no doubt were of that good Scotch-Irish, from whom so many of our best men, especially missionaries, trace their de To them were born three children James, Boyd, and Sarah. Geo Hall died early, and after his death James, the eldest son, run the fa he married Jane Foster, Sarah ma Robert Gray and emigrated to Canada, went to Belfast to see them off, a was sorry he had not planned to g with them — a little later he go. The mother, Margaret Boyd married a Mr. Sturgeon, he died, and she married a Robinson, after whose death, she came to Canada with her Sturgeon boys, one of whom, Robert Sturgeon, aged 82 we met in Glen Buell. (She had an epithelioma on her face in her old age, and her son James had one on his hand, but it was not the cause of death in either case.) To James Hall and wife who lived on the old-homestead in Ireland were born George, Sarah and Boyd, and believing they were likely to have a large family, the sequel proved they were right for they had twelve children, they wrote to Boyd then in Canada to come home and they would see about selling out their right in the homestead and they would all go back to Canada together where there was more room for large families. Boyd came, and they sold their lease to a Mr. Anderson. Boyd married Elizabeth Baird (still living in '95 aged 87) and the two brothers with their families came to Canada in 1831. Boyd was a carpenter and stopped with his wife at Brockville for nearly a year. James came to Glen Buell and put up a shanty where he and his family lived, later Boyd and wife joined them and they lived together in the same house for about two years. James was a mason and in 1842 he built him a stone house, which is yet in good repair, and only recently passed out from the Hall family. Here they brought up to manhood and womanhood seven sons and three daughters. George, the eldest, (Grandpa Hall) remembers of helping to carry stone to build the house.

George was born on the old homes[tead]
in Ireland in 1826, Jan. 26th, [illegible]
Apr. 7 1859 he married Marga[ret]
Bolton born Jan. 16 1835, the el[dest]
child of Jno. Bolton of New Dublin. [The]
young couple settled not far from
the homestead at Glen Buell, [on]
some land given Grandpa Hall [by]
his father. There was a log house [on]
the place where they made them[selves]
comfortable and cozy, and here
on Jan. 16, 1860 Sherwood's papa [was]
born. He was named William a[fter]
his mother's Grandfather Bolton, a[nd]
James after his Grandfather H[all].
Before little William James was [a]
year old he went with his father [and]
mother to visit his Aunt Susan Se[ymour]
at Kitley, and here with his cous[in]
Seymour who was about the same age, he w[as]
baptised by the Rev. Mr. Evans of the [Pres]-
byterian church of Toledo. Papa
walked when he was sixteen m[onths]
old, but talked before. He use some[times]
to eat the plaster from the walls of [the]
log house, and when remonstrated w[ith]
by his mother would reply "Why, ma[ma, it]
is good." Like most little boys he [some]-
time got into mischief; one day wh[en]
his father and mother had gone away, [he]
and his sister Alice, two years younger, [p]
a live hen of every feather, and once [when]
Alice was away her brother hung her [doll].
Another time he put a cat through the s[tove]
door into the fire, but poor pussy escap[ed with]
her life through an open lid. Papa wa[s]
always a rather delicate child grand[ma]
says, and they did not send him
to school until the Spring after

was seven years old. He learned quite well — grandma still has a card signed by his teacher showing he was promoted from the 2nd to the 3rd reader before he was nine years old.

As mama likes to have papa's memoirs written and published in a book, his little son can refer to that for further incidents in his childhood, and boyhood life.

The other day we all went over to see Great Grandfather Bolton, he is ninety years old — his hip fell out of joint a year ago, and he broke his leg, and has been confined to his bed ever since, but he looks healthy and well yet. Sherwood and Edith both sat on the bed by him and he talked to them. Great Grandfather's mother he said lived to be 102 — she was a Martha Elliott from Vermont of Dutch descent. (b. July 3 1777 d. Mch 8, 1879) Papa remembered her very well. She was said to be 107 yrs old when she died, but unless the wrong date for her birth was given mama that must have been a mistake. Great Grandfather's Uncle Abram Bolton cut down a tree when he was 100 yrs old, and he lived to be 108.

Great Grandfather Bolton lives in the same house where Grandma Hall was brought up and married — it is built of stone, and is much like the one on the Hall homestead. Two bachelor uncles, Henry and William, and an unmarried Aunt, Sarah, live with their father, Uncle William the baby of the family acts as his nurse now, since his hip was injured. The same day we visited there, we called at Benjamin Bolton's upon a great, great

Nancy Higgison

great Aunt Nancy Bolton. She is a most beauti[illegible]
Sherwood also saw his great great
Elizabeth Baird Hall, the wife of [illegible]
Uncle Boyd Hall. There is an ent[illegible]
in Papa's journal kept in 1884 tha[illegible]
of the death of this Uncle Boyd — Papa [illegible]
very fond of him.

Sherwood has more great uncl[illegible]
aunts than he has uncles and aunts. [illegible]
visited us that were anywhere near, [illegible]
we returned the visits of most.

Aunt Caroline Bradley was home
the West with a little girl not much [illegible]
than Sherwood. She is a dear sweet wo[illegible]
one of Grandma Hall's youngest sisters. [illegible]
sister Aunt Jane Rowsom lives not [illegible]
away and came to see us several tim[illegible]
and we spent a day there. She us[illegible]
live with Grandma Hall a great deal w[illegible]
Papa was a little boy, and mama has [illegible]
picture taken of her when a young wom[illegible]
and Papa and Aunt Alice when children, on e[illegible]
side of Aunt Jane. Aunt Jane is the one [illegible]
use to make apple dumplings for papa [illegible]
he was so fond of. We had some for dinne[illegible]
day we were there. She has three [illegible]
children, Rebecca the eldest teaches [illegible]
Brockville, and Stanley are ho[illegible]
Papa named Stanley, he is a boy [illegible]
fourteen or so. Grandma Hall's pa[illegible]
belong to the Church of England.

Wednesday eve. July 31, the good pe[illegible]
of Glen Buell made a reception in th[illegible]
of the wife of the man they all loved [illegible]
much. Sherwood can read the address [illegible]
welcome in mama's scrap-book. Th[illegible]
following Sunday evening we held [illegible]
Korean service — Yondanie read f[illegible]
his Korean testament, Sherwood [illegible]

dressed in his Korean suite of many colors, and when Rev. stood him up in the pulpit for all to see he was so good and slowly turned about, as though to give them a good chance. Mama told them a little about how Korean boys dress, and then she spoke experiences in opening work at PyengYang. Aunt Esther sang "There is a happy land" in Korean, then in good English told the story of her conversion. Every one was delighted with the service, and they took up a collection of $12.00 which they gave mama to apply towards Aunt Esther's expenses. A similar service was repeated at Lyn, and at Athens, netting $11, and $10. towards the same purpose. We were asked to go to three other places, but mama had to refuse, as it tired her so, and was hard on all — and the other places were difficult to get to.

We were at Grandpa Hall's a little over five weeks, and then spent most a week at Aunt Alice's in Brockville. Every place we went we met papa's dear friends. Mr. & Mrs. Gilroy were so glad to have us with them for a little while — papa thought so much of them both, and they are fine people. God has given us many warm friends in Canada.

At N.Y. city, Sept. 27, '95.

Sunday, Nov. 10, 1895.

As thy days, so shall thy strength
Deut. XXXI

{ Better for Nov. 10 '96 and not that tear.

Another year is dawning!
Dear Father, let it be
In working or in waiting
Another year with Thee!

Another year of leaning
Upon Thy loving breast,
Of ever deepening trustfulness
Of quiet, happy rest.

Another year of progress,
Another year of praise
Another year of proving
Thy presence "all the days."
F. R. Havrg

Mama's little son is two y
old to-day. How much he has p
through since one year ago to-
if we could have foreseen it all the
how we would have shrunk fro
A blissful lack of wisdom,
'Tis blessed not to know;
He holds me with His own right hand
And will not let me go,
And hushes my soul to rest
On the bosom which loves me s
My heart shrinks back from trials
Which the future may disclose,
Yet I never had a sorrow
But what the dear Lord chose
So I send the coming tears back,
With the whispered word "He Knows
M. G.

Mama has been so busy since getting back at Grandma Sherwood's that she has not had time to write in Sherwood's journal, and she must just mention now how Aunt Lillie and Uncle John came down to Brockville to see us off on a Canadian Steamboat "the Passport" early in the morning of Sept. 5th. Grandma Hall sent Sherwood a pretty dark blue cap, and Aunt Alice gave him a new apron as parting presents.

We passed through the Thousand Islands before noon — it was delightful, as was also our trip along the Northern Shore of Lake Ontario to Toronto — we stopped an hour and a half at Kingston where dear papa used to attend college, and mama saw Dr. Kilborn there, brother to papa's dearest friend, Omar Kilborn M.D., now in Shanghai China, driven from Western China by the riots. We reached Toronto the morning of the 6th, and changed to an American boat that took us across the Lake to Lewiston; we were detained sometime by the Custom House officers who declared Aunt Esther & Uncle Yousanie were Chinese and they couldn't come on U.S. ground. We took train to Niagara Falls, there we all went in a carriage to see this grand sight. Sherwood seemed to notice the falls, as we crossed the Bridge to the Canadian side he would point towards them. It was just about noon and both Sherwood and little sister Edith took their bottles and went to sleep in the carriage, while mama, Esther & Yousanie donned rain coats etc and went down under the falls.

Before 3 p. m. we started on
Buffalo, and from there took the
R. R. to Uncle Charles'. We we
travelling from 6 a. m. to 6 p. m.
were on three different boats an
different trains that day; but the ch
were very good — better on the boats
on the cars for long distances.

Uncle Charley & Aunt Maggie —
Cousins Lena, VerNooy, Arthur & Fra
were all delighted to see us and
had a delightful visit there f
one week. One evening repeated
Korean service in their M. E. Church

Sept. 13 we went to Hornellsville
Cous. Rob. Bonney met us with a car
and took us to his house where w
had another pleasant visit. While
Sherwood went with us through a
silk factory and a shoe factory,
was interested in the machinery.

The next day we went on to
hamton, where Cous. Horace Crary m
us and took us to his elegant ho
here we were made most welcome
comfortable; went out riding, an
eral relatives called upon us. Cous. Hor
gave little Sherwood a five dollar bill
Polly Crary gave him four pair of cashm
stockings, and gave mama all the
material for a new dress of beautiful
Henrietta cloth, and ten dollars besi
These proved to be mama's birthday prese
this year. Sept. 19th found us
Scranton, Pa. at Cous. Seth Bonney
Mama celebrated her birthday by goin
in a coal mine 300 ft. "underneath the
where they dig dusty diamonds all the year a
She also went through the largest foun

in the world, that night.

Sept. 21st found us at Cease Mills with Mrs. Noble, and Sherwood renewed his acquaintance with little Miss Ruth. She has grown to be quite a big girl, and says a few words — She is very fond of a doll, and played with our big Korean rag-doll all the time we were there. Sherwood use to torment her so when he found it teased her, by pretending he was going to take it away from her, she would run crying to her mother to take her part. The 24th we went on to Wilkes Barre where we saw Dr. Stockel, mama's old college-mate, and her sister Mrs. Dr. Butler. They both thought mama had two fine babies. Here Sherwood went through the Lace factory. The night of the 25th found us in Jersey City at Cous. Marietta Sherwood's. We had a good visit there, and we shall never forget their kindness. One day we went over to New York, and Mr. Garber, the artist, a friend of papa's took some pictures of his babies free. Saturday night the 28th found us safe home on the dear old farm again. Little Sherwood had been perfectly well during all the time we were gone, except for now and then a bad night from cutting eyed double teeth. He did not gain in weight any while in Canada, and not much in height. He is very active — all the time on the go except when he is asleep. He generally takes a couple hours nap every day, and sometimes soon after getting to a new place he will sleep four hours. He still has his bottle.

Feb. 18 '97. Baby sister Edith got mamma's ink bottle and spilled it all over, and then took her little fore-finger and painted her brother's picture black. This is the 4th ink bottle she has spilled recently and mamma has spanked her soundly.

Sherwood & Baby Edith.

The second anniversary of Sher
birthday finds him 34 inches t
and he weighs just 34 pounds
pound to the inch. So during the yea
has gained in weight 14 lbs, b
only 3. inches in height — howev
mama measured him lying down —
way he now measures 36 inches, a
of 5. His head now measures 1
a gain of one inch, and beside t
8 incisors he had a year ago he h
cut in the following order four mola
four canines (cuspids) two molars (sec
so that he now has 18 instead
8 teeth. A year ago he walked on
hands and feet now upon his
only, and since that first p
of shoes he was wearing out the

has had five more pairs, the first two of which he outgrew, the next he wore out, and the last two he has yet — they are No, 6's a year ago he wore 4's. Then he did not say any words, now he has quite a vocabulary. Back, whoa-back, Kitty, birds, this, by-by, boss, bee, bite, tutetute, pia, mămă, bow-wow, goose, Joe, and Joe's Chair, pig, cake supper, — dark, Ai, Joe's boots, drink. He calls a ball a "boet" and Fontaine "Llah" and he pronounces mămă like the Canadians do "mă mă," Joe sounds half way between "Cho" and "Dew" — he pronounces pig like an Irishman would, and his "Auer" means either breakfast, dinner, or supper, as the case may be — it evidently comes from the prolonged sound of the last syllable when Grandma calls "din-ner" or "sup-per" when mama is up stairs. "Llah" also probably has a similar origin as mama has been in the habit of calling to Uncle Fontaine as "Fon tan nah"; in saying goose he generally says only "goo", he seemed to have picked it up himself, the first time mama ever noticed him saying it was upon our return home the first day the Japanese screen was put up in our room, he pointed to the white storks upon it and called them goo, and when he saw white turkeys, or the picture of geese or ducks he does the same — mama never taught him to say it, but perhaps some one in Canada did, but they only had ducks at Grandpa Halls. He has only lately begun to say dăk for dark and "dout" for "drink", and "hok" for hot, first he called hot "ha" He calls any kind of a sore or a pain a "bite", and if its is his own, and it hurts very bad he calls it a "bee bite".

he was stung again at Grand
and perhaps he remembers yet that
time he played with the bees. He
As "bite" is the only verb he u
he does not make many senten
and they are very simple such
"bow-wow bite". "Kitty bite" "Dah
He tries to say more, one mo
when I was dressing, and he had
awakened and called "Dah" I s
"Dah is eating breakfast" and
said "Dah" then made his mouth
like he does when eating, and th
said "buzz", or "Sonsanie is eating b
When mama was gone away to New Y
for a week he would say "mā mā
tute, whoa-back" meaning th
his mama had gone away on the
and the horses would bring her
and he generally says it now wh
ever mama is away anywhere. Grandma
ably taught it to him in the first pla
He recognizes the walk of mama,
and Ai, and will tell which on
is coming by the sound. Mama
often hears him calling "Joe" in
his sleep, like he use to "bac
He reads great long stories now
from letters or papers. He uses a
spoon and a fork well at the table
he eats nearly all kinds of food—
very fond of rice, drinks a great de
of water, and is fond of apples and pears
all kinds of meat he calls "paeg". He can say "pear" a well whether he ge
While Ai was here he had a tame rabbit,
was the first Sherwood has seen, an
later he noticed a picture of one on his b
and came running to show it to his Grandma
saying "Ai" "Ai". He is very quick at recogniz
pictures and photographs.

Grandma gave Sherwood a silver dollar for his birthday present, and mama let him have for the first the little black wooly dog that Dr. Busteed gave him his first Xmas; by squeezing the bulb attached to the string about the dog's neck he can be made to walk and prance about. Sherwood enjoyed both of his presents, he always is very fond of money, loves to get a hold of it in his hand; and of course the toy dog pleased him. He was quite good too to let his little sister play with it. Since his return from Canada, Sherwood is not nearly so good to Edith Margaret as he use to be, he seldom asks to kiss or to hold her now, and he is quite apt to jerk anything away from her that he wants, and he has been known to deliberately slap her, to push her over, and to step on her fingers, and mama has had to whip him for it. It has only happened a few times, however; and a great many times he is quite willing to give up to her anything to amuse her or keep her from crying. He has a great notion every night after supper of saying "bye, bye" and nothing will do but that mama must sit down and rock him, he will not let any one else; and at first he didn't like to have little sister sit upon mama's lap too, but now he don't mind. Quite often he will wake up in the night with tooth ache (from cutting new teeth) or with the leg ache which he has begun to have, and ask to be taken to mama's bed where he stays till he goes to sleep. He has

quite a little temper of his o
and sometimes when things do
go to suit him he will throw
himself down on the floor and s
He is generally quite easily div
however, and is pretty good to m
he knows what "whip" means
well and seldom needs it, on
sometimes when he don't like
be dressed, or is bad to little sister
doesn't behave well at the table.
wears drawers now, and mama
some nice warm red flannel pant
for him this winter – he is pre
good to use them, but forgets h
self sometimes, of course.

Altogether mama's son is
pretty good little boy for his age,
mama feels sure he will gro
better and better as he becomes ol
and wiser. He is quite good lo
these last pictures, taken by Mr. Ga
do not do him justice – they a
not clear, and not very well finis
The one taken upon dear Grandpa's
is better.

Sherwood's hand,
2 yrs.
34 lbs, 34 inches – (1914)

34 in.
2
1 68 in = height & inches grown
only 5 ft 8 in!

Friday, Jan. 10, 1896.

Till we all come in the unity of faith, and of the knowledge of the Son of God, unto the measure of the stature of the fulness of Christ.
Eph. 4:13.

"Little by little all tasks are done;
So are the crowns of the faithful won,
So is heaven in our hearts begun.
With work and with weeping, with laughter and play,
Little by little, the longest day
And the longest life are passing away—
Passing without return, while so
The new years come and the old years go."

Another New Year has begun, and to-day finds Sherwood 2 yrs, and 2 mos. old. He has his other two 2nd yr. molars now, so has his whole set of first teeth, twenty in number. Lou Sarie made him a New Year's present of a little tooth-brush, and he likes to have it used, and tries to use it himself. He has had a pretty hard time as usual getting these last two teeth through, been restless a number of nights, and has not eaten very well. He has lost one pound since his birthday so weighs but 33 now, mamma has noticed his hands seemed thinner, he has grown an inch in height and measures 35 in. standing now. He loves to be weighed and measured, and is so good and patient through it all no matter how long we are about it. In Mr. Earle's store he weighed 36 lbs, so perhaps we don't weigh correct with our scales.

At Christmas time, Sherwood went to the Xmas service Sunday morning with Aunt Annie and mamma, and he was so good never did one thing out of the way, and didn't go to sleep either — he enjoyed the music very much. He also liked the ride there and back, he is quite as fond of horses as ever, and he says "Prince orse" and "orse Nat" now, as Grandma's black horse is named Prince, and the bay one Janette.

Uncle Frank's boys sent some of their

nice toys for Sherwood's and Edith's
Christmas, there was a big box f
but mamma gave some to Uncle Wal
children and kept some to give them
another time. Christmas morning be
Sherwood came down stairs Jonsonie ga
him a dollar, when he got out
the dining room there was a ti
& wagon, a train of cars and a nice mu
picture book for him, and he was deli
as the tin horse was painted black he
it "dsa Prince", the cars he still
the tut-tute, as the engine has the
of a clock on he calls it the "cock tute"
The picture book is of animals, and he h
learned to know and say "bear", "lion
"monk" (for monkey). He calls the sheep "ma
the zebra and all that look like horses
calls horses and several that resem
pigs have to go under that name.

He has added quite a number
new words to his vocabulary. Besides
mentioned above he now says "light",
baby, cow, hot'ado, hello, shoes, meat
mine, milk, bottle, yes, no, book, fork, house
He combines "black dark" and sometimes
"black dark bite" he has only lately begun to be
little afraid of the dark, don't know of any ca
He also says "pig meat", and "cow meat", "co
"cow mek" "candle mek" "Prince bow-wow
black dog. When the baby wore one of his gr
aprons one day, he would point to it and s
"no, no, mine"; "bee-book", "horse-book", tw

2nd 30 words

He has just begun to call himself "Sherud" and he cal
"Lellie", or "baby-Lellie", he says also "baby's doll"
The first snow he saw he called "m
and when he went out and saw some sn
flakes that came flying toward him he cal
"bees" and when a lot came down a

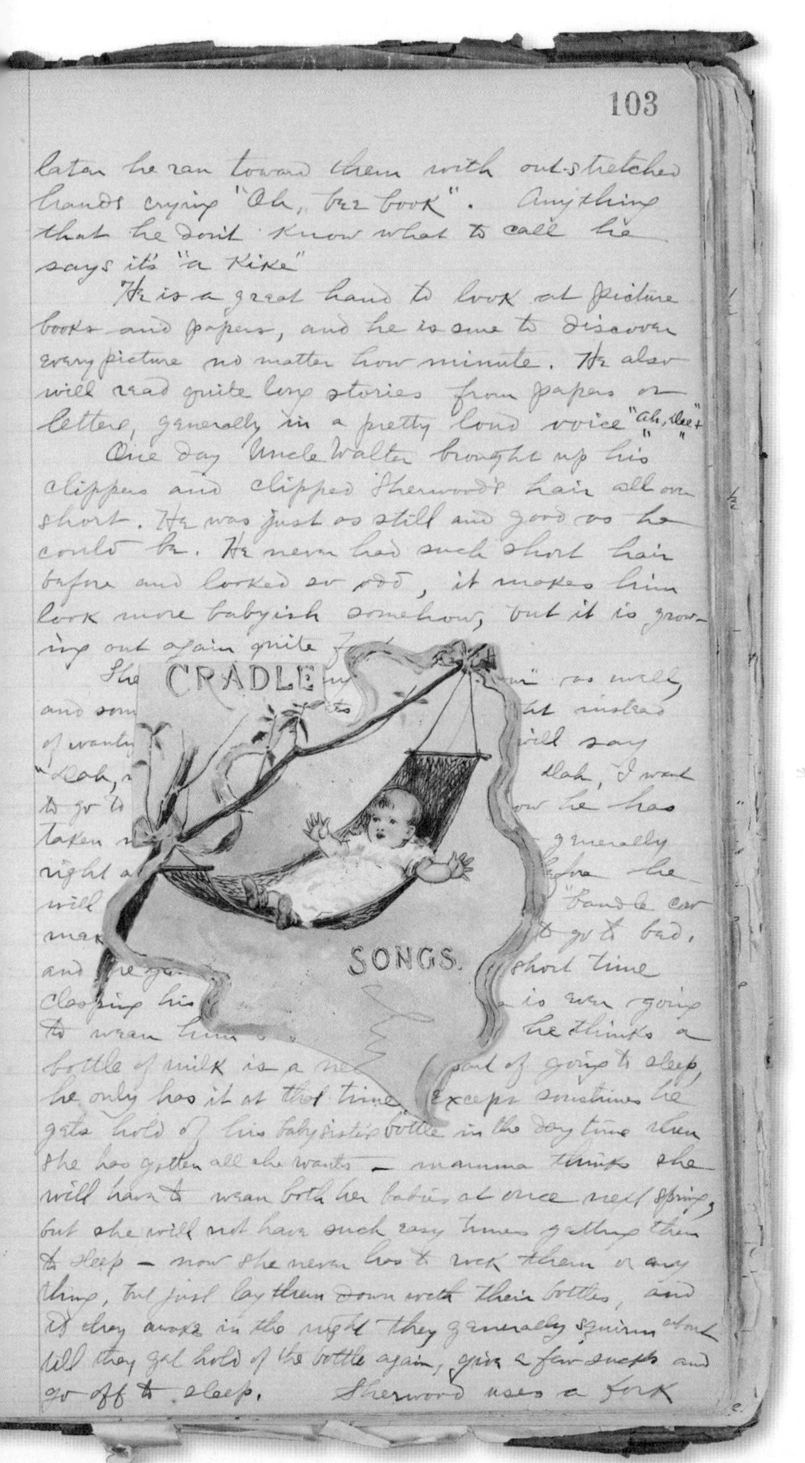

later he ran toward them with out-stretched hands crying "Oh, bee book". Anything that he don't know what to call he says it's "a kike"

He is a great hand to look at picture books and papers, and he is sure to discover every picture no matter how minute. He also will read quite long stories from papers or letters, generally in a pretty loud voice "ah, dee t" " "

One day Uncle Walter brought up his clippers and clipped Sherwood's hair all over short. He was just as still and good as he could be. He never had such short hair before and looked so odd, it makes him look more babyish somehow, but it is growing out again quite fast.

She … "…our" as well, and som… …st instead of wanti… …will say "Dah, … dah, I want to go to … …ow he has taken … generally right a… …fore he will … "bandle car" mak… …& go to bed, and he … short time sleeping his … is ever going to wean him … he thinks a bottle of milk is a ne… …art of going to sleep, he only has it at that time except sometimes he gets hold of his baby sister's bottle in the day time when she has gotten all she wants — mamma thinks she will have to wean both her babies at once next spring, but she will not have such easy times getting them to sleep — now she never has to rock them or any thing, but just lay them down with their bottles, and if they awake in the night they generally squirm about till they get hold of the bottle again, give a few sucks and go off to sleep. Sherwood uses a fork

and spoon at the table now very w
and has for several months, except w
he don't seem to care to eat, then he pl
too much. He is most fond of soups and sp
victuals so far. He will eat a little bread
but never a large piece, like a boy of his age or
to. He eats some cake & pie, and a little meat,
not often care for potatoes. He often asks
a drink of milk at the table and generally on
between meals, and will drink a cupful of
his main living still seems to be milk e
if he has 20 teeth.

In looking at the picture of himself & g
he will point to grandpa's vest pocket and t
make his mouth go like "eating", as he see
still remember how Grandpa use to give
candy. He also notices the cane, which he ca
In looking over O'Neill quarterly which he likes
well, he will pick out the brush & combs, button
and other toilet articles that look like "mama's",
then he will find those that look like Dad's
always calls that bookcase & desk that is adverti
with soap, mamma's no matter where he
the picture. He continues to express him
by gestures wherever he can. When he
pictures of flowers, he always smells of them
he asks for water it is generally by going thro
the motions of drinking it. To-day he asked
to show him his picture (that I posted in
journal on the 2nd anniversary of his birth) by a
placing his open hand over his waist
is in that picture; and then when he
mama to show him the lock of hair, he put
fingers on top of his head and motioned to his
He calls the hot-water-bag "mamma's pig" and
and sister often have fine times playing with it
when he sees a picture anywhere advertising one
points to it and exclaims "mamma's pig."

One day he had a little china doll that he tried to make stand up — mamma took it and tried too, and gave it back to him saying it could-n't stand up, but he kept on trying and shortly mamma heard him exclaim and she looked up and there sure enough the doll was standing, he gazed at it very complacently saying "Sherwd" "Sherwd", and mamma patted her little "Sherwd" on the head for accomplishing what she thought couldn't be done.

Only since he was 2 yrs old, has Sherwood voluntarily kissed his mamma, and he only rarely does it now — but is always prompt enough to kiss when asked.

Sherwood has bowed his head for some time when the blessing is asked at the table, and lately he begins to try to ask it himself. He bows his head, shuts his eyes tightly, and murmurs some make-believe words. Recently mamma had him kneel with her when praying in her room, and he was so quiet and reverent, and seemed almost to understand what was being done.

Friday Apr. 10, 1896

The children which God hath graciously given thy servant. — Gen. 33-5

The loveliest gems of "our" house
Are the children "as" you see
And I cannot tell how precious
My two darlings are to me.

If I tell you of two diamonds,
Larger than have yet been found,
And of deeper, richer lustre
Than the gems the world around,

A tiny fraction of the value
Of their sweet young lives to me,

Can but dimly be imagined,—
Mine for all eternity.
Mattie Wilcox Nor

Sherwood is 2 yrs. 3 mos. old
Mamma went down to N.Y. city over
week ago to speak to a young ladies m
band in Dr. Cuylers church in Brooklyn
Also she is going to put out the
dear papa left us, and take a mortga
5% on some property in the upper part o
city. Lawyer Skidmore on Pine St. lda
do the business and is very kind. He also
put mamma's will for her. Of course,
of mamma's death the money would go
her children, but if they should be yet
mamma thought she would like to say wh
be their guardians, so she has appointed
Frank Sherwood, and Dr. Omar Kilborn,
she thinks will try do just what ma
would like to have done by her children.
left a bequest of $400 toward the Memori
for papa, providing she has not contribu
much during her life time for it. Everythi
is to be divided equally between Sherwood and
Uncle Charles and Uncle Frank are the execu

Sherwood and Edith are both always real
when Mamma is away from them. She wo
liked to have taken Sherwood with her this t
but couldn't very well. Sherwood is a
so many words to his vocabulary that
can scarcely keep track of them now.
some time he has called reading "ah-de
when both he and Edith make-believe rea
of papers or books it is all "ah-de, ah
Sherwood calls Annie "Jan" now, so he has a
for all as he calls Grandma "Ba ba" —
what the little Scranton girls call their
mother. Besides these he says "big,

all dirty, (shoe & eugh) snow, rain, wolgk (water) gingk wolgk - fall down, sky, hard, see eat, drink it up, potatoes, slippers, medicine, flower all gone, down stairs, up stairs, bed, sleep, happy day, go away, whip baby's hands, go to ? bety (birdy) mamma written up stairs, elbow, go out doors, in the house, baby cry, gobble turkey, chickie, calf, deer

Friday, July 10, 1896.

Blessed is he that considereth the poor: the Lord will deliver him in time of trouble. Psa. XLI, 1.

The sweetest lives are those to duty wed,
Whose deeds, both great and small,
Are close-knit strands of an unbroken thread
Where love ennobles all.
The world may sound no trumpets, ring no bells,
The book of Life the shining record tells.

Thy love shall chant its own beatitudes
After its own life-working. A child's kiss
Set on thy sighing lips shall make thee glad:
A poor man served by thee shall make thee rich;
A sick man helped by thee shall make thee strong;
Thou shalt be served thyself by every sense
Of service which thou renderest.
Mrs. Browning.

Mamma is away from her dear little Sherwood to-day; she is the examining physician for the Christian Herald Fresh-air children this summer, and lives at Mt. Lawn, Nyack, attending to any that may be sick while there. Dr. Klopsch, the manager, did not think it would be proper for her to have her own children with her, but gives

her the privilege of staying over Sa
Sunday with them every two or th
weeks. It was pretty hard for ma
to make up her mind to be separated fr
darlings so much, but she felt it
be best for this summer — She can
them again with her at 12 | 6.45 th
fall in the I. M. M. S. work. Then she
they are all safe and will get goo
at Grandma's with uncle Jon Lanie to
and all, and it might be better for
than to be at Nyack. Last night
Many as 30 of the children at Mt. Lawn
taken sick with vomiting, and mam
had a great time going around to atten
all and didn't get to bed till 2 a. m
of the caretakers were no good to help,
mamma and the matron had to do m
the cleaning up and all. Mamma is
tired to-day — and her L. tendo Achilles
given out as it sometimes does when she is
feet too much.

Mamma has been home once
ready to see her own babies — She
her work in New York June 22nd, and
examined quite large parties of children
day, as many as 95 once, for the week,
this filled the time up quickly, and
stay 10 days, there were Monday, Tues.
that no children had to be examined,
mamma went home unexpectedly
with Chas. Gregory to his house, and then
to grandma's — found the house all clo
went in through the kitchen, and f
Sherwood taking his afternoon nap o
Grandma's bed, went up stairs and fo
the baby fast asleep in the crib, a
Grandma was also taking her nap.
waked up first — Both were so glad to see m

Sherwood still continues to lose in flesh — only weighs 32 lbs — Before mamma went away she took Sherwood with her for a little visit to White Lake and Bethel — were gone 4 days, and mamma hoped the change would do Sherwood good — but he ate so little while he was away, and would scarcely touch milk. However, when he got home again his appetite was some better, but mamma thought it best to continue the chocolate emulsion of cod-liver oil which he had begun before — he is a real good boy to take it. It is possible he misses his "bandle milk" as the 1st of May mamma began to wean both her babies — first by not putting any milk in their bottles — just giving them empty, after all the milk they would each drink at night. But Sherwood had begun to lose before that — he didn't seem to mind it — never asked for milk to be put in his bottle but once or twice; and then when he went with mamma to Bethel mamma didn't take the bottle at all, and he went to sleep the first two nights without asking for it, but the 2nd morning when he awoke he wanted it, and after that scarcely ever asked for it again — so it was not so hard to wean him as mamma had feared it might be. At the same time mamma had told Mrs Lanie not to give the bottle to Edith any more, so after Sherwood came home there were no more bottles — the first for two years. It seems so strange not to have to clean them any more. But it also seems very good; and mamma thinks it will be best now that hot weather comes again —

Sherwood always wants to g
sleep lying close by mamma in
when she is home, then often he
asleep Uncle Jordanie removes him
own crib where he generally sleeps
whole night through - Sometimes
to tell he wants to "shee"; and he very sel
wets the bed, or his drawers, any more
ma thinks he can wear pants this
surely alright, he is such a good boy

When mamma goes away St
will say "Sherwood no cry - soo
Sherwood go on Tute-tute." He tal
great deal now, more than ma
can write down! He is begining al
to like to have stories read to him,
he grew very excited over that of "Litt
Riding-hood" one day - he would sa
wolf - bite Baba - poor Baba".
great interest in the pictures - inter
thing in them - the flowers, butterflies,
dishes, "Pom make cook", the crow, "Baba
Etc - everything there was to be seen.

Uncle Frank, Aunt Kit and Co
Pelt and Clare are coming to spe
three weeks at Grandma's this
mer - in fact suppose they are
now. as they intended to start with
They live in the city of Cohoes now, an
boys are very anxious to get into the c
No doubt they'll all have a real good
Then Aunt Lilbe and Cousin Rebecc
Canada are going to visit us too.
will go home again when they are
Just one year ago to-day we st
visit Uncle Frank and the Canadian
It seems strange to note Sherwood wei
one pound more to-day than he did then
worries mamma that he gains so little in

of late — but perhaps it is because he is developing mentally. Mamma thinks it would be good if he could have an entire change and live in a different place for a while, and she is going to see if Dr. Klopsch may not let her children come to the C.H.C.H. after a little, — he said in the first place that after he knew all the caretakers he might see fit to change his mind about having some children here of those connected with the institution: so unless Sherwood is doing much better the next time mamma goes home she will see if Dr. Klopsch will not let them come. It seems most a pity when mamma is doing so much for other people's children she can not do a little for her own even here — with Dah to care for them it would take very little of her time, and mamma would be quite willing to pay for their board; but Mr. Klopsch seems to fear people might not understand it, and would think the C.H.C.H. was taking care of children whose parents could do it for them. So perhaps after all, it would be wiser to hire their board at a neighbors just across the way, if mamma does conclude to bring them when next she goes home.

112

Tuesday, Nov. 10, 1896.

O God, thou art my God; early w
seek thee. Psa. 63, 1. { See poem quoted fr
on last birthday, an
and this poem the

"The leaves are fading and falling, the winds are co
The birds have ceased their calling, but let me tell you my
Though day by day, as it closes, doth darker and colder g
The roots of the bright red roses will keep alive in t
And when the winter is over the boughs will get new
The quail come back to the clover, and the swallow to the
The robin will wear on his bosom, a vest that is brigh
And the loveliest way-side blossom will shine with
The leaves to-day, are whirling, the brooks are all dry and
But let me tell you my darling, The Spring will be s
There must be rough, cold weather, and winds and rains s
Not all good things to-gether, come to us here, my ch
So when some dear joy loses, its beauteous summer,
Think how the roots of the roses, are kept alive in

From a poem on "November" in Barnie's 3rd re

Sherwood's third birthday anniversary –
spent at Grandma Sherwood's like his second,
this time he was there alone while his m
and sister were down in New York where all wer
28th & took up the work at 1212 E. 45th St, but the 28
Oct. mamma started to attend the Gen. Ex. mee
the W. F. M. S. at Rochester, and she took Sherwood
stopped on the way at Liberty and left him
dear Grandma, and there he has been ever since
from there mamma gets very good reports o
little boy. Grandma writes he is just as g
as he can be, he sleeps with grandma, a
makes company for them all. Grandma plans
come down to the city and bring him back to m
and sister just before Thanksgiving. Mamma
a little story book called "Mamma's helpers" for S
birthday, and Aunt Annie had his hair cut at M
Grandma gave him a new pair of shoes, and Jo
him a pair of mittens. It was a nice su

113

day, grandma wrote and Sherwood played out of doors, and altogether enjoyed his birthday very much. Here is the first letter little Sherwood ever sent his mamma. Two years ago this time mamma remembers a similar one that his dear little hand wrote for papa in Pyong Yang.

Sherwood has not gained so much physically this year as last, but has developed more mentally. He only weighs the same (34 lbs) his head measures 19 3/4, a gain of 1/2 inch, and he measures 37 1/4 inches, or a gain of 3 1/4 inches in height. So he is quite a great deal more slender than a year ago, one can even notice _that_ in comparing the pictures of his hand. It worries mamma some to think he is no heavier than a year ago, but then he seems well, and looks well, and now since he has been wearing pants, he really looks rather stout and chunky — strangers always speak of him as being a "sturdy, healthy looking boy." He has been in pants now since Sept. and seems "every inch a little man," though he is "only a baby after all" when one comes to think that only to-day he is 3 yrs old.

He seems to be rather incl
to a religious turn of mind even thus
For over a year he has always heard so
of Church, and dearly loves to go, and
for some time he has been praying "Now I
and Grandma says he seldom forgets
her house when he goes to bed, that is he
always thinks of it without being reminded,
once he said it all through alone, but gener
likes it to be repeated to him a line or two a
time, and he follows. He has several tim
asked "Where is God", and once when
reply was "In Heaven", he thought a minu
then asked "God died?" evidently associati
he had heard about his papa having died, and gone to
It was quite some time before he lost that idea
later he would say when thinking upon the
"God didn't die", "God is in my heart, and Go
where papa is." He frequently announces
he wants to go to Heaven, though he never
wants to die. He will say "Someday, I go to
or "Next week I go to Heaven, I come back
One time he said to his grandma "I'd li
go to Heaven" and then suddenly added "but, I
fall down."

Feb. 10th Sherwood was 38 1/4 in. high.

May 10th, 1897

This is the covenant that I will make with them after those days, saith the Lord, I will put my laws into their hearts, and in their minds will I write them. Heb. X 16

"Leaning on Thee in childlike faith
To Thee the future I confide
Each step of life's untrodden path
Thy love shall guide."

Sherwood, At 3 1/2 years.

Six more months have passed and gone since mamma has had time to write in Sherwood's journal, and now he is three and one-half years old, and the above is a good picture of him at this time, he has changed very little from his last birthday in appearance, however. He weighs only a half-pound more, though he he has

gained nearly three inches in heig
He now is three feet four inches t
his head measures twenty inches in c
ference, and he weighs thirty-four and
pounds. Mamma bought him th
brown suite of pants, coat & vest a
Christmas time, just before he, an
mamma went with Grandma up
Cohoes to visit uncle Frank and fa
We spent a week there, and Sherwo
enjoyed it immensely, his cousins
and Clare are so good to him. He of
asks to go back to uncle Frank's aga
Though Sherwood has changed so li
in six months, it is interesting to tu
back back and compare this last
with the one taken upon Grandpa's
just 2 yrs ago this time. Before t
were taken it seemed as if the other
much like him yet, but now one
easily notice how much more ma
he has grown - the other looks lik
baby face, and this like a manly
boy. Each is perfect in its way to ma
ma's fond eyes.
Sherwood and Edith sometimes p
to-gether quite a long time very nic
and again they'll not agree at all, b
quarrel and even fight. Sherwood is p
the first one to cry out enough, and co
to mamma for protection from hi
vigorous little sister. He loves her
the same though - one night wh
he and Edith had been sleeping to-gethe
in the crib mamma for some reason
Edith in bed with her - he awoke in
night and feeling for her thought she
lost and began to cry, mamma asked him
what was the matter, and he said "Ja

find the baby, bu-hu, bu-hu". Sometimes when he hurts her or does anything wrong he will quickly say "I didn't mean to - I forgot" or "I won't do that any more, not of it". One time he was talking about seeing a bad boy on the street, and when asked what made the boy bad, he said he guessed "he had no mamma to whip him!"

Sherwood doesn't say his prayer as well as he use to - often forgets to pray, and sometimes when reminded says he is too tired, or he will pray by and by. One time, soon after Grandma went home after her six weeks visit with us, evidently thinking she would be lonesome, he put in his prayer "Don't let Baba cry". One day when playing, he suddenly said "now I am going to pray" and he kneels down before his little chair and said "Jesus, Saviour" then words seemed to fail him, and after a little pause he said "I am done", and went on with his playing again - he was so sober and grave over it, that it hardly seemed like a play prayer, he has not so far repeated it. Looking out of the window one evening into the dark he remarked "I guess God make the dark come". Once he asked "Why, God let the rain come?" and was quite satisfied with the answer "to give the trees, and grass and flowers a drink, and a nice bath."

For two months, during Feb. & March, Sherwood went to a sort of a Kindergarten on 45th St. a couple of blocks from us. He liked it very much at first - didn't even want to come home - he only went mornings from 9.30 to noon, then took a nap in the afternoon. He called it going "to school" and he felt quite important over it. He played with blocks and putting little pegs in holes, and also sewed on little perforated cards twice a week - he liked this very much, also

he made a couple of chains of st
& bright colored paper. He seemed to
his teacher a Miss Norman, and she a
called him a good boy – but she nev
took time from the other children, who
mostly trying to get through the primary
and ready to enter school, to teach him
regular Kindergarten rhymes & song
games. He would just sit & pa
in his little chair, and never hardly
until he came home. Mamma
rather disappointed that he didn't learn
and was thinking about taking him out
all of a sudden he stopped himself, a
Ma couldn't coax him to go again. b
that when asked he always said "I like
to Kool."

A card sewed by Sherwood at the Kindergar

No one has tried to correct Sherwood yet
forms of speech he uses – he will ask "
Go up stairs see Clifford?" or "Can me
me pick papers all up?" He kn
what "untie" means, but when he wa
ask to have a thing tied up, he will
"untie it up." It has not been
now that he has used the word
"ess" as he calls it. Before this he
replied with a complete sentence wh
asked anything he wanted to give an aff
ative reply to.

May 20th mamma's work at the Home for medical missionary Students closes, and she is going to take Sherwood to Phila, and attend the alumni meetings of her college the 20th & 21st. He looks forward with great pleasure to seeing "mammas Kool & mamma's teachers" After that he will go to Baltimore with mamma to say "good-bye" to aunt Esther who has just finished successfully her first year in medical college there, and then they'll return to Liberty to dear grandma and the baby, where they expect to spend the summer till it is time to start for Korea.

Mamma has decided to take up her work in Korea again — that is what she hoped to do when she returned if the W. F. M. S. saw fit to send her, and as they seem quite willing to do so, and the mission in Korea very anxious to have her come back, she feels that is what God would have her to do. She has prayed if it is not God's will that he should hedge up that way, and open the way at home but that way is wide open at both ends, while the home work seems hedged up. The work mamma has had all the winter has been very hard and was made so unpleasant for her by Dr. Dowkontt, who was the one who got her to take it up in the first place, but who later decided he wanted it himself, and though the Board of managers insisted upon mamma's staying yet they allowed Dr. Dowkontt & family to remain as guests of the house, and he took every occasion he could to make things disagreeable for mamma — so that as there is not much of a chance for improvement mamma only felt called to stay in that work until the lady managers could

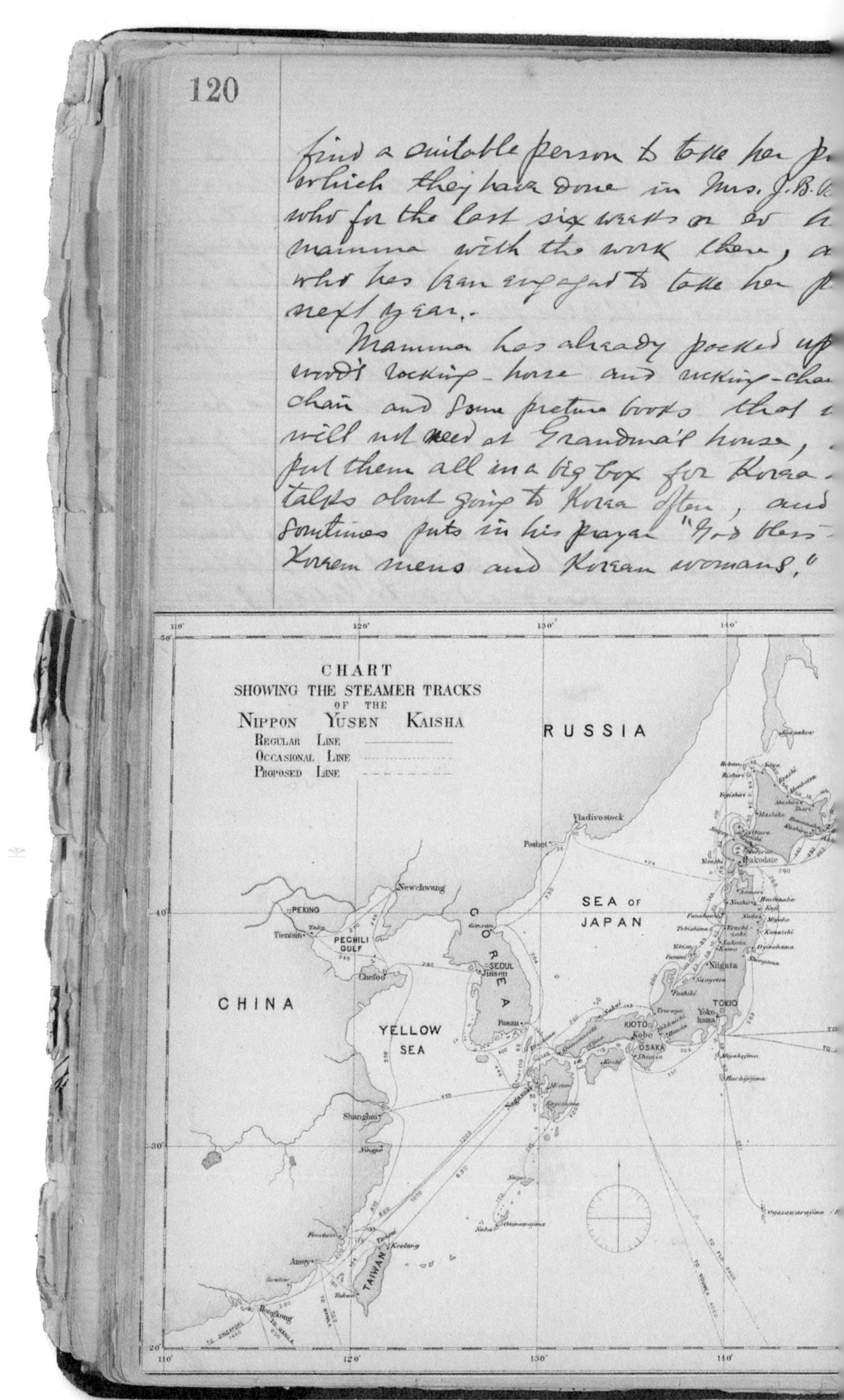

120

find a suitable person to take her
which they have done in Mrs. J.B.
who for the last six weeks or so
mamma with the work there,
who has been engaged to take her
next year.

Mamma has already packed up
's rocking-horse and rocking-
chair and some picture books that
will not need at Grandma's house,
put them all in a big box for Korea.
talks about going to Korea often, and
sometimes puts in his prayer "God bless
Korean mens and Korean womans."

121

Wednesday, Nov. 10, 1897. At Chemulpo, Korea (Inchun)

Even a child is known by his doings whether his work be pure and whether it be right. Prov. xx—11

" One small life in God's great plan;
How futile it seems as the ages roll,
Do what it may or strive what it can
To alter the sweep of the infinite whole!
A single stitch in an endless webb,
A drop in the ocean's flow and ebb,
But the pattern is rent where the stitch
is lost,
Or marred where the tangled threads have
crossed,
And each life that fails of the true intent
Mars the perfect plan that the Master
meant."

This is Sherwood's birthday—four years old to-day. It seems like quite a coincidence that he should have arrived in Korea, the land of his birth, upon the same day he first came, but such is the case, as we just arrived per S.S. Hego at 9 a.m. and landed from the sampan at 10 o'clock—just the same hour Sherwood put in appearance four years ago to-day. But this time there was no loving papa to greet him. Mr. Jones was there to meet his wife & baby girl who traveled with us all the way from St. Paul. U.S.A, and Mrs. Dr. Follwell was down from Pyong Yang to meet her sister Dr. Lillian Harris, and Misses Paine & Frey from Seoul to meet Miss Pearce both of whom were also in our party from St. Paul and are W.F.M.S. missionaries to help in the work in Seoul. We all came to Steward's Hotel (except the Jones who live in Chemulpo

to await the going of the river steam[er]
Seoul the night of the 11th —

So much has happened [in the]
six months that has just gone by [since]
mamma last wrote in this journa[l]
ought to be briefly reviewed, but no dou[bt]
things that ought to be noted will be omitted
less important things may be told. It is
mamma can't get time to write oftener,
no doubt twice a year will be all sh[e can]
do now.

We reached Grandma's house [about]
the first of June from our Southern tr[ip]
mamma couldn't spend as much [time]
as would have been pleasant bec[ause]
she had so much to do to get ready [to]
return to Korea. Besides all the [other]
things there was papa's book which
mamma had been unable to touch f[or a]
whole year now with the other [work she]
had taken up, and this fall she m[ust]
finish it and attend to its publicati[on before]
going to Korea. So for six weeks s[he]
worked steadily away at the ma[nu]
script and July 15th went down [to]
New York to arrange for its publishing
staid nearly a month — commenced [the]
reading, and done a little Post Graduate [work]
and a lot of shopping for Korea. [Grandma]
and Dah took care of Sherwood & Ed[ith while]
mamma was gone; though Dah [was not]
as good help as he was, and worried
grandma by his doings. He has de[cided]
not to return to Korea with us as he p[romised]
to do when Mamma brought him to Ame[rica]
so mamma told him he must get [work]
elsewhere as quickly as possible, for [she]
did not need him now — was only [keeping]
him, that he might help her on [the]

way back to Korea — if she had known he was going to do this way she would not have brought him up from N.Y. at all, but had him took the work there she found for him in May. He asked Mamma to get him work again in the city, but as he absolutely refuses to do cooking or washing & ironing the only work he knows how to do, mamma was unable to get him any-thing and he was all summer on mamma's hands at an expense of $4 per week and was a great deal more trouble and anxiety than he was worth. However, later he repented, and began to do better, and became willing to do any work mamma could find for him, and then she got him a nice situation in the family of Rev. G. B. Sandford.

Edith was with Grandma during the month of May, and she learned then to say "Gamma" instead of Baba, but after Sherwood came home he still stuck to Baba. Grandma tried many times to get him to say Grandma, but he didn't seem to be able — she would try to catch him, when he would say "I can't say it" she would say "what can't you say?" and he would reply "I can't say you." But one night along the last of June he suddenly found he could say it by repeating it very fast in a sort of an explosion — he could say Gam-ma Gam-ma Gam-ma! and since then he has called her so.

Sometimes when mamma is praying he will ask her to pray aloud, and once when she had finished he said "You forgot to pray for Joe and Colbert." Without any one drawing his attention to it, he noticed Colbert didn't go to church with us, and asked why, and said he was going to ask him to go. Mamma was afraid if he did, Colbert, who is a R. Catholic, might

think he was put up to do so, but he w
One time he said he would like
"God's garden" – mamma don't know
he ever heard that expression either.
He never likes to ask any one for
things except mamma. One time
needed his hair cut, and mamma k
forgetting to ask Uncle Walter to bring
hair clippers – so one day at the table
both Grandma & Walter were there, he sa
mamma "Don't forget to tell gamma
Uncle Walter to fetch his clippers,"
was quite an indirect way of asking
Sept. 6th we left the dear old
nest and turned our faces Westwar
the Far East. It was hard to say "g
bye" to the dear ones – the M. E. Chu
had made us a nice farewell mee
Sherwood & Edith was dressed in Korean clothes
and gave Mamma for Papa's
memorial in Korea $ and Cousin Polly Gray
sent $50. Mamma had quite a talk
Joe one day about being and out and one t
she had talked to him before she went to
before and he claimed he was just as go
Christian as those who had their name
the Church book – but this time he was a
touched and he almost promised he wo
to church and give his name in on p
He always speaks of his good habits, and m
told him she feared he thought he was go
his own strength only, and claimed no c
of his Saviour's, but he said no, he fe
Lord helped him, and that he believed
prayer, and hoped to go to Heaven. Late
one of mother's letters he told her tell mamm
he had prayed "Now I lay me down to slee
the "Lord's prayer" for over 30 yrs. Dea
black Joe, it seemed so pathetic, that
ma just had to cry over it.

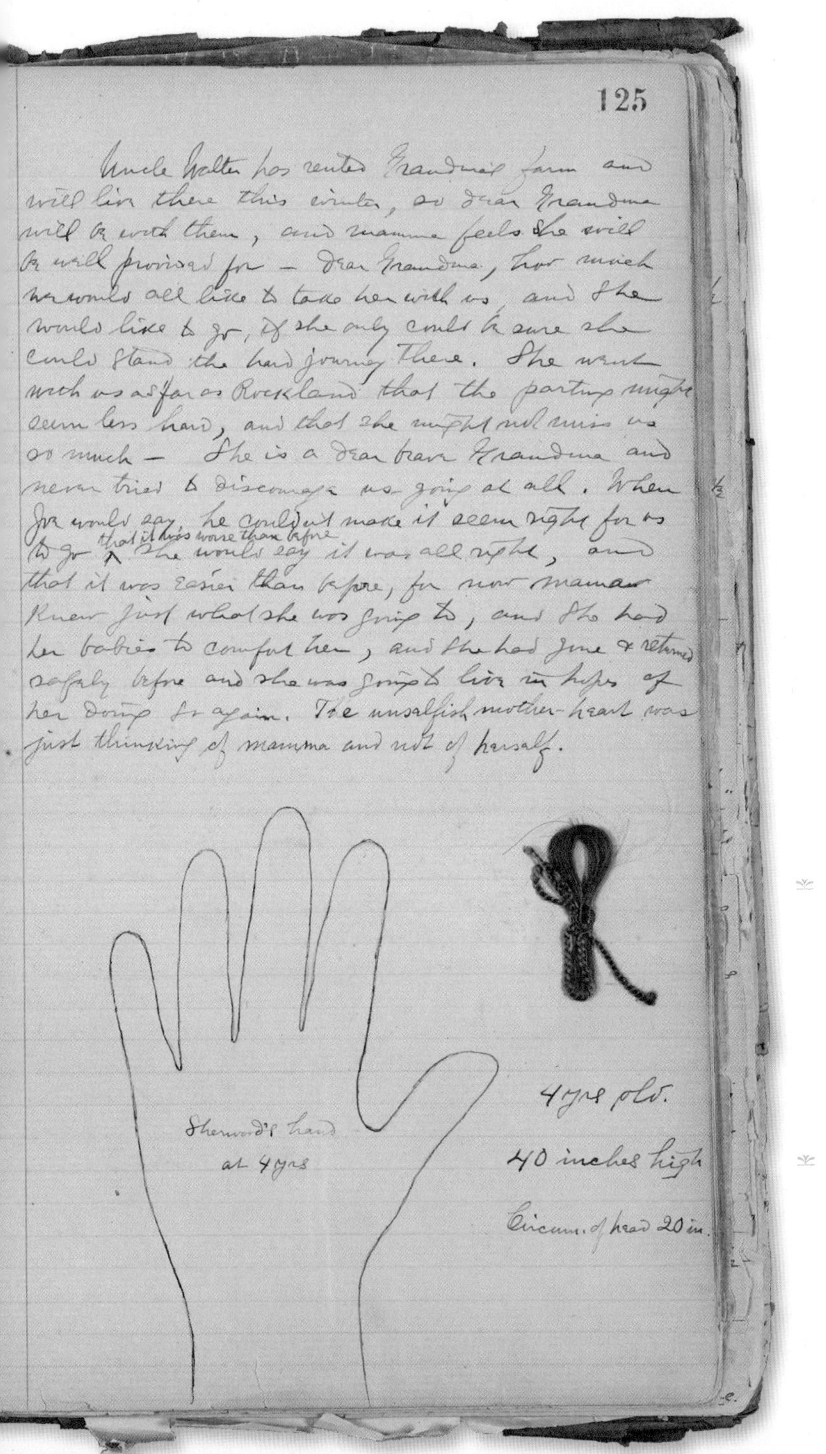

125

Uncle Walter has rented Grandma's farm and will live there this winter, so dear Grandma will be with them, and mamma feels she will be well provided for — dear Grandma, how much we would all like to take her with us, and she would like to go, if she only could be sure she could stand the hard journey there. She went with us as far as Rockland that the parting might seem less hard, and that she might not miss us so much — She is a dear brave Grandma and never tried to discourage us going at all. When Joe would say he couldn't make it seem right for us to go that it was worse than before she would say it was all right, and that it was easier than before, for now mamma knew just what she was going to, and she had her babies to comfort her, and she had gone & returned safely before and she was going to live in hopes of her doing so again. The unselfish mother-heart was just thinking of mamma and not of herself.

Sherwood's hand at 4 yrs

4 yrs old.

40 inches high

Circum. of head 20 in.

So we were off, and we ... as far as Utica the first night ... we had to wait till next day to make ... nections, but we spent the time plea... at Mr. Jones' home. Sherwood ... Jones got on nicely — he thought She... a pretty nice little boy — they took a... morning walk together. Later we c... at Mrs   sister of Dr. B. H. Jo... who was mamma's teacher in the Po... at the Manhattan Eye & Ear Hospital.

The next evening we were in Ogdensburg at ... home of Dr. Mary Bryan one of mamma's ... mates, and the next day there w... a missionary meeting here, and S... & Edith were in Korean costume and ... gave an informal talk on her work in ... Sherwood & Edith had a nice visit her... Dr. Bryan & her sister & niece were ... kind to them and made them feel ... at home, & Dr. Bryan helped ma... dress & undress them, and care for t... so it made it very easy for her. Sh... not get as much help anywhere else ... the way to Korea. The last m... ing we were t... Dr. Bryan too... the children's p... in their Korean ... and she sent ... me some copies ... which gives ... idea how t... looked at th... time. The D... said she migh... some better one... later.

Sherwood at 4 years

We went from Ogdensburgh up the St. Lawrence to Brockville on the Island Bell — Sherwood enjoyed it very much. Uncle Will Gray was down to the wharf to meet us and we were soon at Aunt Alice's. Little cousin Harry who is just a little older than Sherwood had swung himself to sleep in the patent swing waiting for us, but he soon awoke. He is larger than Sherwood now, though two yrs ago when we were here, Sherwood was the larger. The children had great times playing, but quarreled at some. Cousin Harry was pretty good though, and let Sherwood & Edith play with his playthings. Cousins Maud & Allan have grown very much, and will be quite grown up the next time we see them.

We spent about 18 days in Canada — mostly at Grandpa Hall's. Aunt Alice & Cous. Harry were over with us and stayed a week. We had a good visit at Aunt Jane Ransom's. Aunt Jane & Cous. Effie helped mamma care for Sherwood & Edith quite a little, but one day Sherwood who was very fond of chasing Aunt Jane's ducks, got into the duck pond and got his feet wet, his apron soiled and his nice new straw hat all spattered. They both enjoyed going with Aunt Jane to feed a little calf also.

Mamma's birthday we spent at papa's dear friends' Mr. & Mrs. Gilroy. We also made pleasant visits at Uncle Boyd Hall's, Mr. Pourisse's where the children saw a young fox, and at Mr. Percival's. At both of these places they paid a great deal of attention to the children — at Mr. Pourisse's we had our first maple syrup of which the children are very fond.

One day we had a nice visit at Great Grandfather Bolton's — he is still confined to his bed with his broken hip, but is cheerful and contented. He is 92 yrs old and he talked to Sherwood of papa, and also sang some with Uncle William.

Just the last day before Mamma le[ft]
Buckville Mrs. Gilroy took her and [Esther]
to Mrs. Nash's who very much wanted a
from them — we had a nice time — Esther
and Mr. Nash a very old man, swung to
in the patent swing. They live in a very
old stone house which is nice and room[y]
very comfortably fixed up. Mrs. was
fond of dear papa — she told us much abo[ut]
him. Once when they were at Camp meeting,
said she was taken with a very severe headache
old trouble with her, and had to leave the prayer
one night — the next morning when her he[ad]
seemed splitting open — papa looked in at the
door, and said "How is your head Mrs. Na[sh]
She said how did you know there was any[thing]
the matter, he replied Mr. Winter had said
would not have left the prayer meeting for anyt[hing]
She told him "yes, it was very bad" and papa
back to his tent and prayed for her. Then
boy gave him some nice trout, and
took them with him, and again put
his head in Mrs. Nash's tent door asked [the]
same question, and she said that a s[hort]
time after he had left, her head had
stopped paining, and she had remarked to he[r]
sister that her headache was quite gone. P[apa]
said "Praise the Lord." and then gave her
nice fish telling her he thought they'd
good for her — He also told her they were giv[en]
him, that she might not mistake that he had bought
on purpose. So she told him she would hav[e]
them prepared and invited him to enjoy
with her, which he did. She said
often came to see her in her home, a[nd]
she thought as much of him as of an
Sept. 27 we left Buckville on the C.
was changing at Carlton Junction 2 a.m.
then on to St. Paul reaching there 8.45 a.m.

Then we spent a pleasant day with Mrs. Jones & Margaret Jane at the home of her uncle. In the evening we started on for Uncle David Powell's in Victor, S. Dak. reaching there 11 a.m. Sept. 30. Sherwood was taken sick in the night – vomited – and was feverish & drowsy all the way to Letcher, where Uncle David met us, and we drove 10 miles across the Prairie to his home. Mamma put Sherwood right to bed, and gave him a dose of physic the first medicine he had needed since he left Grandma's. His throat was some sore, and as Mamma didn't have the spray with her, Sherwood learned to gargle his throat quite well. By morning he was much better and after another day – quite himself again. [this trouble was probably due to eating too many grape seeds] He seemed to have been tired out. He was so hungry for butter-milk that Auntie Powell had to churn almost on purpose for him – and oh, how he did enjoy it – drinking great big glasses full at a time.

Sherwood had a good time in Dak. – cousin Jason showed him picture books and toys he had had ever since he was a little boy like Sherwood, and a scrap-picture book mamma had made him and some book marks that he had kept all these years till he was a grown man, now 24 yrs old – the picture-book was in perfect condition though made over 20 yrs ago – it was made on paper-muslin pinked about the edges – leaves of blue & black alternate – the outside of black & tied with a pink ribbon. Mamma wishes Sherwood might take a lesson from this and take such good of his playthings. He does do pretty well, and used to be quite careful till he learned to be more destructive from little sister, but she is getting over it now as she grows older. Auntie Powell gave Sherwood a nice picture plate to remember Ella by. Cousin Nira gave Edith a

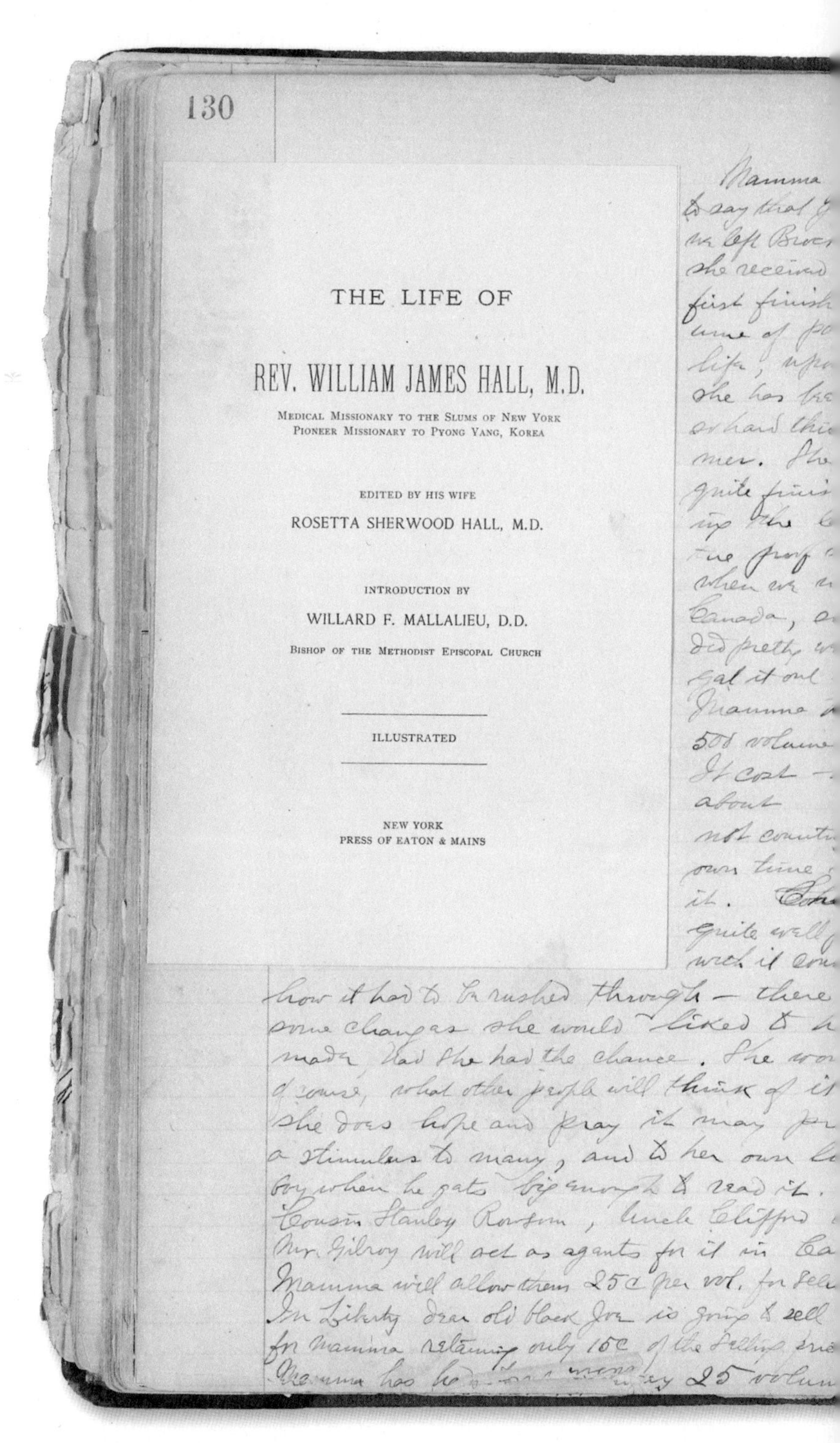
130

THE LIFE OF

REV. WILLIAM JAMES HALL, M.D.

MEDICAL MISSIONARY TO THE SLUMS OF NEW YORK
PIONEER MISSIONARY TO PYONG YANG, KOREA

EDITED BY HIS WIFE
ROSETTA SHERWOOD HALL, M.D.

INTRODUCTION BY
WILLARD F. MALLALIEU, D.D.
BISHOP OF THE METHODIST EPISCOPAL CHURCH

ILLUSTRATED

NEW YORK
PRESS OF EATON & MAINS

Mamma
to say that
we left Broo
she received
first finish
ume of pa
life, upo
she has bee
so hard this
mer. She
quite finis
up the
the proof
when we
Canada,
did pretty
get it out
Mamma
500 volume
It cost
about
not countin
own time
it.
quite well
with it con
how it had to be rushed through — there
some changes she would liked to h
made, had she had the chance. She won
of course, what other people will think of it
she does hope and pray it may pr
a stimulus to many, and to her own li
boy when he gets big enough to read it.
Cousin Stanley Rowson, Uncle Clifford a
Mr. Gilroy will act as agents for it in Ca
Mamma will allow them 25c per vol. for sell
In Liberty dear old black Joe is going to sell
for Mamma retaining only 10c of the selling pric
Mamma has [illegible] 25 volum

and providing she sells all the rest, she can clear about [blank]. The first $100 of which she proposes to use towards papa's memorial.

Oct. 6th we met Mrs. Jones & Gretchen, Dr. Lillian Harris & Miss Pearce (new missionaries for Korea) in St. Paul, and we journey to-gether in a tourist car to Vancouver. There were only 4 other people in the car — one little girl of about six who played nicely with the children — mamma's babes & Mrs. Jones baby don't get on well together at all — and mamma's babies are quite as much to fault as Gretchen this time, as she has improved since last winter when she visited us in N.Y. while Sherwood & Edith have rather gone backward. Just the day before we arrived at Vancouver mamma discovered that the little six yr. old girl was just getting over the whooping cough. If her parents had told of it — it would have been better for her not to have played with the little children, as it is a bad time for them to get it now just as it is coming on toward winter.

Sherwood enjoyed the C. P. R. pretty well especially after we reached the Rockies. He would sit looking out of the window quietly for a long time enjoying the magnificent scenery. Later on he liked to look for the Indians, and saw some with some wild geese to sell. It was so cold that there were not many at the Stations.

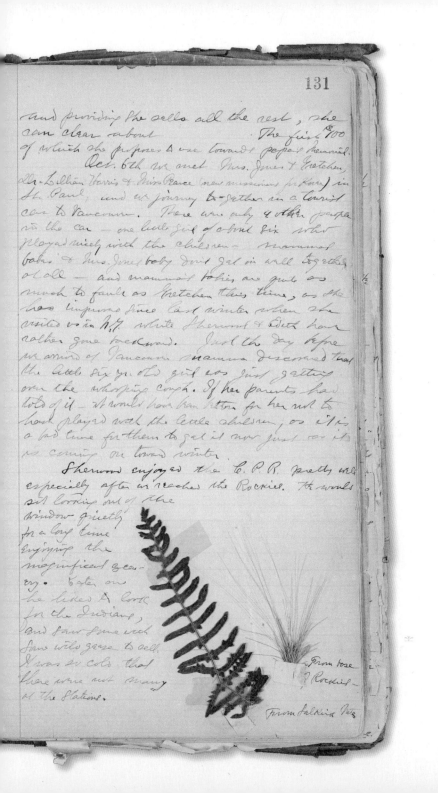

From base of Rockies —

From Selkirk Mts

CANADIAN PACIFIC RAILWAY CO'S S.S. EMPRESS OF INDIA. 6,000 TONS. 10,000 H.P.

We stopped at the Commercial Hotel,
Vancouver over Sunday. Edith was se[illegible]
didn't go to the table, but Sherwood enjoyed
pretty well.

Oct. 11th we sailed on the Emp[ress]
of India. There were 16 missionaries,
baby 3 mos. old, and Sherwood, Edith & Gretche[n]
were also about 10 other children — and [illegible]
[illegible] gers, [illegible]. We enj[oyed]
[illegible] & evening as it was s[illegible]
[illegible] the children are se[illegible]
[illegible] saloon about one [illegible]
[illegible] fast & lunch, and t[illegible]
[illegible] — so mamma [illegible]
[illegible] when the first g[illegible]
Often they are aslee[p]
[illegible] not made no troub[le]
[illegible] that mam[ma]
[illegible] from her dinne[r]
raisins generally &
[illegible] some paper, and lea[ve]
them on the camp stool beside Sherwood
on the lounge, and when he awakes he
reaches for them and enjoys them very m[uch]
Sometimes mamma brings figs, but Sherwoo[d]
seem to like them though sister does.

The second day out when we tried to [get]
up in the morning we were each sea-[sick]
so we staid in bed all day — Sherwoo[d]
Edith not vomiting quite so often as mam[ma]
but unable to retain anything for 24 h[ours]
the following morning Sherwood felt [illegible]
awhile after his breakfast, but he mana[ged]
not to vomit, and by noon he was g[etting]
on his sea-legs and was well and [illegible]
the rest of the voyage. He was real [illegible]
eating with a good appetite all the time
and mamma is quite sure he mu[st]
have gained though he has not b[een]

Fellow Mis. Passengers

While Sherwood was seasick he remarked "it seems if the ship is going up a side-hill."

weighed since he left Canada when he weighed 34 lbs. There was a little boy 7 or 8 yrs old on board that Sherwood played horse a great deal with — he got off at Yokohama, and Sherwood missed him from there on to Nagasaki.

Every night Sherwood puts in his prayer about God not letting the ship fall down in the water — in fact he has prayed it almost each night since he saw Dr. Joseph sail away from N.Y. last winter.

Oct. 28th we left the good Empress at Nagasaki — Sherwood has asked more than once to return to her, so he must have enjoyed her very much. He was given a cap band with H. R. S. Empress of India on in gold thread as a souvenir of having run in the races they had on deck one day. Mamma put it around his sailor cap that cousin Will gave him, and he likes it very much.

We had to stop about 10 days at Nagasaki waiting for the Jap. steamer Higo to take us to Korea. The first three or four days Sherwood seemed quite well, but on Nov. 4th came down with what is probably whooping-cough contracted from the little girl on the cars. He was better on the 6th so we left that evening on the Higo Maru. Were seasick the next day. Monday we spent at Fusan — took lunch with Rev. & Mrs. Ross — which seemed very nice as we don't enjoy the food on this Jap. steamer — the Japanese don't seem to know how to cook so well as the Chinese, and then the Capt., Steward, & all the officers are Japanese. All try to be very kind. The three children are all there are on this boat first class. We started on again Mon. eve. Got along well till Tues. noon, when it became very rough — choppy, and

[Left margin, vertical:] From temple of the Bronze Horse — Nagasaki

[Inserted note:]
[Sh]erwood (Pertussis)?
[Ex]posed Oct. 6 – 9th
[on] St. Paul to Vancouver
[Nov.] 4th after not [be]ing well for 2 days [wa]s seized with [c]oughing at lunch time & vomited. That night was restless & feverish.

5th	a.m.	p.m.
Temp.	99.8 —	100.4°
Pulse	150 —	130
Resp.	36	28

[6th] A.M. 98.4°
P. 112
R. 32
[P.]m. sailed on the [Hig]o Maru. Had no

Sherwood & Mamma both threw up the[ir]
lunch — Sister was asleep and didn't g[et]
lunch, but she threw up an apple t[hat]
she teazed mamma for when she awoke
all lay down with our clothes on — outside
and all, and felt so badly that we n[ever]
took them off all night long. In th[e]
morning we knew we were near o[ur]
and we felt better — washed, straighten[ed]
up and took quite a breakfast. About
the Steamer stopped in the outside harbor,
we took a Sampan the long row to sho[re]
landing 10 a.m. as before noted.

Mamma gave Sherwood four
kisses when they got on land, an[d]
began to teach him for the first how
she is. He can say "four years old" a[nd]
but generally forgets — will say "I don't kn[ow]"
some-times "five" as he knows that nu[mber]
best often imitating the pop-corn seller
crying 'Pop-corn only five cents.'

Mamma also gave Sherwood a s[mall]
bamboo arm chair, and a box of building [blocks]
which already he can build quite pretty thing[s]
He enjoys them very much.

One day when mamma was compla[ining]
of tobacco smoke, Sherwood said — "Ma[mma]
why don't God make mens not smoke."
Mamma said He would if they'd only ask T[him]
to, but they don't ask.

Sherwood has written several letter[s]
back to Grandma Sherwood, and one to Gra[ndpa]
He remembers them, and Aunt Annie, ...
& ... always in his prayers and occasi[onally]
other friends.

Mamma does pray and hope that [her]
little son will grow up good, that h[e]
will begin now, for as the text say[s]
a child is known by his doings" — That

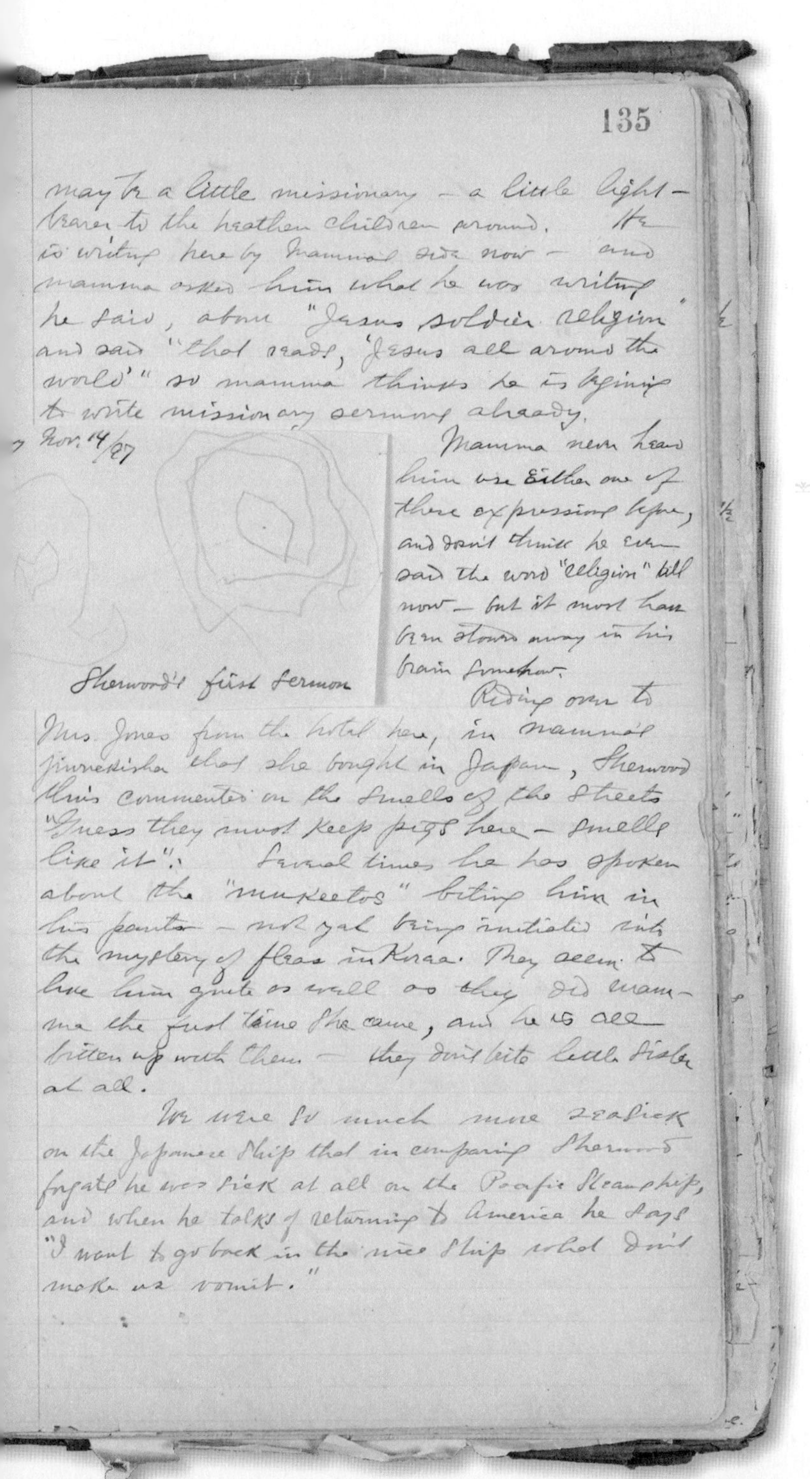

135

may be a little missionary — a little light-bearer to the heathen children around. He is writing here by mamma's side now — and mamma asked him what he was writing he said, about "Jesus soldier religion" and said "that reads, 'Jesus all around the world'" so mamma thinks he is begining to write missionary sermons already.

Nov. 14/87

Mamma never heard him use either one of these expressions before, and don't think he ever said the word "religion" till now — but it must have been stowed away in his brain somehow.

Sherwood's first sermon

Riding over to Mrs. Jones from the hotel here, in mamma's jinrikisha that she bought in Japan, Sherwood thus commented on the smells of the streets "Guess they must keep pigs here — smells like it". Several times he has spoken about the "muskeetos" biting him in his pants — not yet being initiated into the mystery of fleas in Korea. They seem to like him quite as well as they did mamma the first time she came, and he is all bitten up with them — they don't bite little sister at all.

We were so much more seasick on the Japanese ship that in comparing Sherwood forgot he was sick at all on the Pacific Steamship, and when he talks of returning to America he says "I want to go back in the nice ship what don't make us vomit."

March 10, Thursday – 18

Söul,

"Thou shalt remember all the
which the Lord thy God led thee. – Deut.

" Sometimes above the path I tread,
The clouds hang dark and low;
But thro' the gloom, or thro' the night
My heart no fear can know,
That close beside me walks a Friend
Who whispers low, "Until the end."

Sherwood has now been 4 mos.
Korea, most of which time has been s
in Söul – he is begining to talk of g
Pyong Yang when the grass gets green and the
come out. If the money comes for us to go,
Mamma hopes it may before two more month
The New Home at E. Gate is not complete
is the new building here, so the W. F. M. S. worker
all here on the old place at present – Dr.
& Miss Lewis at the Hospital, Misses Paine & Frey
former wash-house, Miss Rothweiler in her old room
Harris & Miss Pierce in Mrs. Scranton's old room, mamma
the Children in the old Chinese School-room, while
little guest house mamma use to occupy here,
Kitchen and dining room. Within 2 or 3 mos
will no doubt be quite a scattering, as Miss Paine (
Dr. Cutler) will go home to America, Miss Rothweiler
Dr. Harris expect to go to the E. Gate, and mamma and
want to go to Pyong Yang, but at present we
form one household meeting t.i.d. in
dining room. The expenses are shared – ma
paying two shares – ~~fuel~~ has cost over 60 yen
mamma's room alone (aside from fuel) – Expenses have also been great
far, averaging $56.23 per share, a month, from Dec. to May
for Mamma, and one share for Edith & Sherwood $11
Until the begining of Feb. both Sherw
Edith were pretty well in Söul, – a little

that their Amah took them with her to a Korean house (Joseph Apache's) to get her hair pulled out even across her forehead and there they were exposed [illegible] Sherwood had the [illegible] ase, mamma [illegible] them again [illegible] was not as [illegible] n, he came

16th [illegible] time, [illegible], but [illegible] Edith— [illegible] but [illegible] weeks, [illegible] ly ill [illegible], considered [illegible] being [illegible] high for [illegible] it meant [illegible] disease [illegible], but [illegible] se has [illegible] was very [illegible] oyed carworthy [illegible] and we [illegible] at church [illegible] was relief [illegible] more. [illegible] few hours [illegible] ys, and [illegible] gh just [illegible] mma does [illegible] ay prove [illegible] to all [illegible] s. Twice, [illegible] mamma, as it were from the very jaws of death, and this time it was almost more than mamma felt she could expect. But God is merciful and good, so good.

Rubeola followed by (?)

Feb. 5th 6 p.m. Temp 103.8° — 6.30 Santonin gr ½, Calomel ", Syr. figs 3ii
" 9.30 T. 99.8° P. 145 Perspiring — 6.30 Aconite, Gelsemium, Camphor & Bryonia
6th 7 a.m. T. 102.4° P. 138 Santonin & calomel [illegible]
10.30. 100.4° P. 120 — 8 a.m. good stool
1.30 p.m. 99.8° 128 — 11 " slept for 2 hrs. Brown liquid stool, bile & mucus [illegible]
7th 7 a.m. 100.4° { Felt nauseated — was given some nuts 4 p.m. yesterday. Now gave another dose syr. figs
8 p.m. 99.8° P. 96 Had stool with bile 8 p.m.
8th Seemed alright to-day — was exposed to cold some this afternoon & coughed a little.
9th Nose running — eyes sore. Face spots [illegible]
1 p.m. tired & sleeping R. 36 P. 180
8 " sleeping, perspiring T. 101.5 R. 28 [illegible]
10th Broken out with measles T. 102.5°
Exposed Jan 28. but had " before
11th Still more broken out — 8 p.m. T. 98.5° P. [illegible]
12th Rash fading — feels well R. [illegible]
13th Rash all gone — Had sponge bath & change of clothes before hot fire 7 p.m.
14th Seems all well — was out too much in afternoon & got over-tired — Couldn't sleep well — complained bitterly of being so tired
15th Didn't want to be dressed. Complained of [illegible] ears a little & of stomach sore. Had good [illegible] formed stool, but gave another dose of syr. figs at noon.
12 m. T. 102° P. 160 1 gr. Quinine
7 p.m. 102.2° P. 168 & 1 dose of Cold & fever tablets (?)

The children have a very good ti
working - she is industrious, and
Christian, baptized Nettie - but she ha
faculty for playing with or amusing th
scarcely none for coaxing them to do
they ought to if they don't want to, and s
really seems to aggravate them. Howeve
does her other work so well mamma has
loath to part with her, not feeling sure
do any better. It is pretty hard li
two such little children in a family l
none of them mothers, but each thinkin
the more, she knows how children
to behave - However, there has bee
real trouble, only mamma has a fe
that most of the ladies think she
make ~~make~~ her children mind as well
they ought - mamma wishes they di
better, but they are such mere babes yet,
little or no pride for their reputations, and
dining-room where almost alone, they come
with the other ladies, they sit in low chairs
a little table by themselves, and often
to wait until the whole eight ladies are
upon, before they get anything, and it
easy for them to get into disorder in
case; then being in low chairs they can
out so easily, and being always alone, they
advance any in table etiquette, but rather go b
Mamma feels if they were in high-chairs at
table with us all, they would do better -
the table don't seem to be large enough.
will be good when we can get in a little
of our own - The ladies pay very little at
to the children in any way - Miss Rothweiler
the most of any. However they are children th
care for petting, and I suppose that is one rea
But so far, we have gotten on very happily t
and our pleasant relations do not seem to be st

Sherwood doesn't pick up Korean very fast – the amah is young, and she learns English of the children faster than they do Korean of her, and they don't see much of other Koreans. I did want them to play with Miss Lewis's two little Korean girls, but she seems to think her girls most too good for mamma's babies to play with. So they play mostly with Mr. Appenzeller's children. Sherwood and Mary especially are great friends, and are together much of the time. They get on very nicely – Mary is older and she has her way, Sherwood giving in very meekly. One day Mary told Sherwood to sit in a certain chair – he objected, so she said she would go home & started out – Sherwood cried – then she came back and asked him if he would do it, and he sat down just where she said smiling sweetly on her through his tears.

Speaking of Korean both the children already use the Korean exclamation "I-ko" they call their rubbers 신 and say "thank you" in Korean, also 어서 어서 "hurry" and 조심하오 "be careful". Sherwood may say some other words that ~~I~~ don't come to mamma's mind now, but as stated before, he has picked up very little so far – playing as he has with American children altogether.

In English, mamma can't keep track of his vocabulary any more. He is dropping more and more of his baby words & pronunciations. Mamma almost regrets it, and when Dr Cutler tries to teach him to say a word like grownfolks she feels almost like telling her to stop – mamma almost never, so far, has corrected the speech of either of her darlings – they don't use much "baby talk" for they have not had it used to them, but what little they naturally say in a baby way, sounds so sweet to mamma's ears, she likes to hear it. Miss Rothweiler likes to ask Sherwood "How much do you love your mamma?" and hear him say "Berry lots." He says "outside up" for inside out and "Knocks" for knots, also "Knock" for lock.

"undress" for both dressing & undressing

Christmas night he said "I'll kiss, if day don't come again to-morrow." Since new year he has begun to say "Excuse the proper times and places. He seldom and sometimes reminds mamma when
He begins to use his imagin also reason quite a little. So ago, he told about a wonderful glass he had bought for Edith, and that she very careful of. Later he said he didn't buy it only "sunk" about it. He asked "Can lions bite God?" and then seemi thinking a little farther - partly answering question in his own mind, he asked "has G bleed?" then reasoning a step further asked "If I didn't have any bleed then woul lions bite me?" Another time he aske the girls in the school here have no when told that most of them had heathen who don't know about God he said "Why don Know about Him, God made them didn
One time when he must have felt a hungry he said "Mamma look at the c it is dinner time - the hands are just this (V) sticking up his fore & middle fingers close to-gethe sure enough it was 5 min: after 11, he had observed that the two hands were always about position when we went to dinner, which is goo observation for a little four year old to make ma
He continues quite fond of his fine horse he received in New York a year ag Often brushes him off, combs out his mane and sometimes has him say his prayers, a God to help him be a good horse. Sherman the idea that to be good is pleasing to Go when he is a good boy he will say "How is Once after telling he was going to be good a God happy, he came running to mama said "I heard God ha! ha! ha!" (ma

happy gurgling laugh for the ha, ha, ha) When told that if he would ask Jesus to live in his heart He would keep all the bad out he prayed once "Come here in my heart, Jesus" and for several days he had the sense that He came, and he really was better. After hearing about Grandma's broken arm, he prayed every night "Help Grandma's arm get well - make the bone grow on" and he generally asks God to help "all the folks in the hospital to get better, and help everyone to hear about God and about Jesus." One day after seeing some prisoners in the chain-gang, and being told about them, he suggested that "someone ought to preach to the prisoners.

He is quite a hand to suggest answers to his own questions, as one day he said "How does God make mammas? does he do like this? (working his hands so) like the men's make coal balls?" A bit later sitting down in his little rocking chair he mused - "God makes little babies - and He makes mammas all the same."

(from Sherwood's friend Dr. Harris)

...ining brightly this
...ning and Florence is
... her to see little John
... and stay to dinner
... him - So I must
... to get her ready.
... sends a sweet smile
... and Edith and also
... love this little
... can carry to you
I want to thank you
writing me such a
kind letter. Tell ma-
I shall be home soon
love to her and Edith
a lion's share to yourself.
Lovingly,
Lillian Harris.

{ Dear Grandma wrote this nice letter to Sherwood which mamma copies here.

Dear Sherwood, I was so glad to get a nice letter from you. I am glad you are trying to be a good boy and mind your ma. I do hope you will be good and not make your ma uneasy. I am glad you think of me and kiss my picture. I like to look at your picture - yours in Korean clothes is nice.

I think of you so much - I pray God he will make you well when you are sick, and that you will be spared to come to America when your mamma returns.

You must write me again.

Grandmother.

Apr. 17th '98.

142

Thursday, Nov. 10th, 1898

All things are of God. - II. Cor.

"Perhaps there are tenderer, sweeter things
Somewhere in this sun-bright land
But I thank the Lord for his blessings
And the clasp of a little hand.

A little hand that softly stole
Into my own that day
When I needed the touch I loved so
To strengthen me in the way.

It seemed to say, in a strange, sweet way
"I love you, and understand."
And calmed my fears, as my hot heart-
Fell on that little hand.

Again Sherwood's birthday
come around, and this time it fin
five years old. He is 2½ in. taller th
year, but his head has gained scarcely a 1/4 in. in
and he weighs 41 lbs.

5 yrs old
41 lbs, 42 ½ in.
head 20¼"

It is 9 mos. since mamma has written in this journal — and nine very busy months they have been, and that has been the easiest part. For another great sorrow has come to us in the early part of them, and our precious one, the "little comforter" God sent us in our first great sorrow, was removed from our loving arms before we even got settled in our new home at Pyong Yang. Sherwood said when he first heard that God took her, that he thought it was "because papa wanted her so much."

Sherwood misses his little sister, and longs for her presence — he often asks "how long it will be before Jesus comes, and Edith will live again." He has several times said "Oh, if Edith were only here I would love her so much, and be so kind to her and never quarrel with her again."

After she was dressed for the last time in her dainty white clothes, he went with mamma to see her — he seemed to realize that it was only her body and that her spirit had gone — he picked some white clover blossoms and placed in her hands, he seemed a bit chary of touching her, but he kissed her forehead then, and again when we saw her for the last time in the pretty white casket after the beautiful service — he made no remark about it at the time but later several times when describing anything very cold he would say "it was as cold — as cold as Edith's forehead."

Though he did not see her buried, as her dear body was laid to rest by papa's on the banks of the Han, yet he understands about that. He calls it "planted" and he associates it with rising again from the dead, and was surprised to find that the Koreans who don't know Jesus "planted" their dead too.

Nine months is most too long a time to give a proper review of, especially when

mamma has been so occupied with o
work than watching her little boy.
yet she finds quite a little time to be w
there are the meal times, and she alway
and reads to him after dinner when he lies down
his nap – then while he is sleeping mam
the dispensary patients; he often awakes
she is through & sometimes comes in and see
of the work, but he is very good to go out when
If mamma goes walking or calling he a
goes with her, and we have our jinrickisha
and have enjoyed a number of nice rides
bs he takes a nap, he doesn't go to bed v
so spends a good part of the evening with
ma. He has learned a new prayer
he says without the prompting that alw
necessary in "Now I lay me down to sleep",
yet quite frequently chooses to say that – but
he says in such a sweet devout tone
"Jesus tender Shepherd hear me
little lamb to-night,
ness be Thou near me
p till morning light."
ow adds an impromptu p
s God to bless his various f
se to go through the list
night. Once he said as usual "God bless
and then said without anyone telling "Oh, I don't ne
for him any more" and never did again. When a
sick or goes away on the sea he more frequ
remembers them in prayer. He has
learned a nice morning prayer
for a long time at first he said without
ing, but of late he has not been saying
so much, and when he does it has grown
"Now I lay me" he waits for the prompting at the beg
each line. It is "Now I awake, and rise from slee
I pray the Lord my life to
In all I do from morn till
I pray the Lord to lead me

CHILD'S EVENING PRAYER.

Jesus, tender Shepherd, hear me;
Bless Thy little lamb to-night.
Through the darkness be Thou near me,
Watch my sleep till morning light.

All this day Thy hand has led me,
And I thank Thee for Thy care;
Thou hast clothed me, warmed and fed me;
List to my evening prayer.

Let my sins be all forgiven,
Bless the friends I love so well;
Take me when I die to heaven,
Happy there with Thee to dwell.

in saying grace at meals
— he always says
"God is good, and we thank him for this food
… Give us this day our daily bread" or
"give us our daily daily bread"
summer while took quite an
… things grow, especially
he had seen planted. One
shower, the sun came out again
the wind, and mamma heard
… on the stoop say "The grass
head and says "Thank you God
rain, and the flowers shake
the corn, and say "Thank
… us hatch out."
… asked "Did God paint the
and the sky?" One time he said
God's thoughts", and it does seem as
little fellow did oft times — Oh, that
always.
He has been looking forward and count-
days to his birth day now for over
… — first it was so many Sun-
…, and then so many days — he
… to get quite an idea of time. A
before, one of the patients hearing he
cat, brought one — quite a nice
white cat not quite grown, that is fairly
— he first wanted to call it "Dr. Scranton"
"Mr. Bunker", but mamma said she didn't think
… gentleman would be complemented by it, and
settled on "Silver moon" suggesting it him-
he had long been wishing for a kitten or "some
to pet and had frequently prayed for the same
"Silver-moon" his birth-day present from God.
bright silver dollar from Grandma Sher-
… Susan embroidered a pink Korean silk
with Chinese characters in green …
… etc, Ruth gave him a little Japanese …

My dear boy: how I love you; hope you wont forget me & the rest of your friends - Your baby cousins are well: & we have four nice Kittens; I wish you had one & Ruth one, we have a white one & a black one. Now, these verses I send is for your Mama & Mrs Noble to read. Your Bro. can keep them if he wants them in Aunt Maryanns …

… all the news now … seeds come up Joe … tell me how much … would like to know … — Grandma

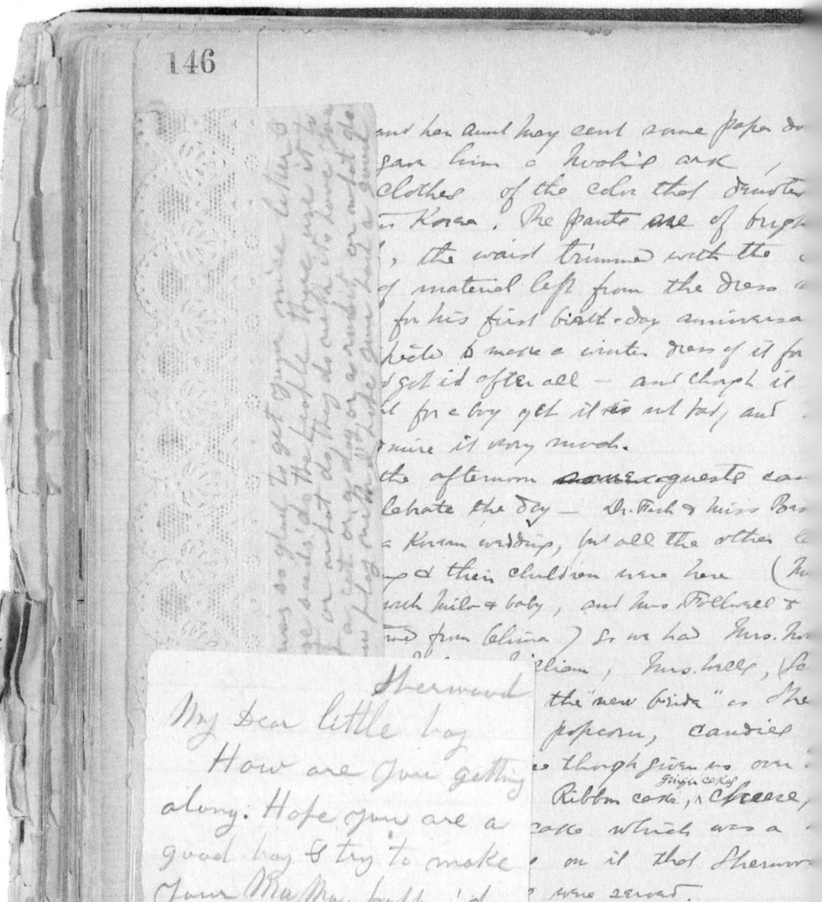

146

Sherwood
My Dear little boy
How are you getting along. Hope you are a good boy & try to make your Ma Ma. happy; do you like your new house – do you learn to talk Korean any. I suppose you sleep with your ma ma now dont you! Are you still lonesome without your little sister! You have been gone one year! Now I hope God

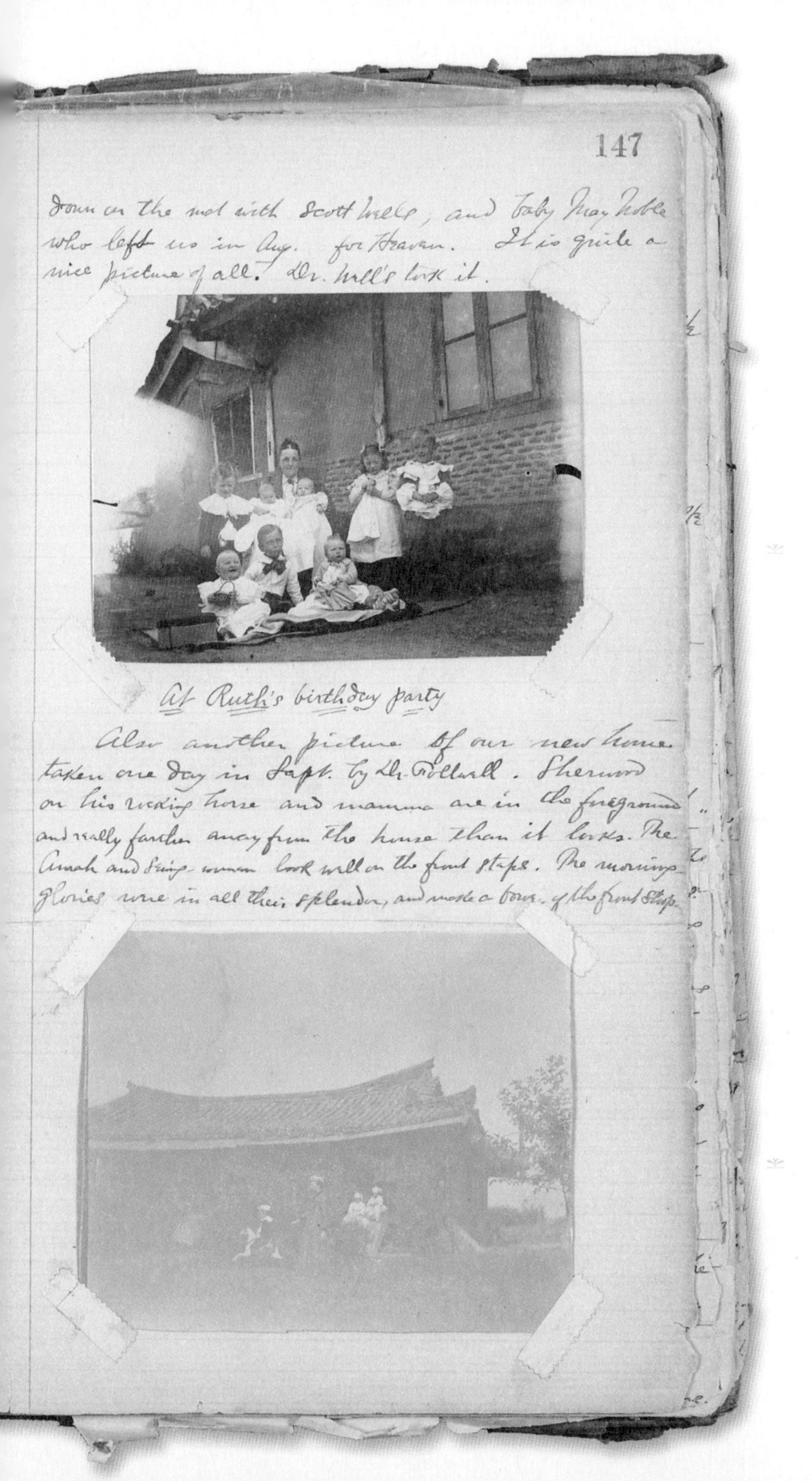

147

down on the mat with Scott Wells, and Baby May Noble who left us in Aug. for Heaven. It is quite a nice picture of all. Dr. Wells took it.

At Ruth's birthday party

Also another picture of our new home taken one day in Sept. by Dr. Follwell. Sherwood on his rocking horse and mamma are in the foreground and really farther away from the house than it looks. The Amah and sewing-woman look well on the front steps. The morning-glories were in all their splendor, and made a bower of the front steps.

146

... pot, and her aunt May sent some paper dolls — mamma gave him a ... and suit of clothes of the color that ... in Korea. The pants are of bright red silk plush, the waist trimmed with the same, is made of material left from the dress mamma made him for his first birth-day anniversary. ... had expected to make a winter dress of it for Edith, but Sherwood got it after all — and though it looks pretty bright for a boy yet it is not bad, and the Koreans admire it very much.

In the afternoon ~~some~~ guests came to help us celebrate the day — Dr. ... & Miss ... had gone away to a Korean wedding, but all the other ladies ... and their children were here ...

Sherwood

My dear little boy:

How are you getting along. Hope you are a good boy & try to make your Mamma happy; do you like your new house — do you learn to talk Korean any. I suppose you sleep with your mamma now dont you! Are you still lonesome without your little Sister?

You have been gone one year: ...

147

Down on the mat with Scott Wells, and baby May Noble who left us in Aug. for Heaven. It is quite a nice picture of all. Dr. Wells took it.

At Ruth's birthday party

Also another picture of our new home taken one day in Sept. by Dr. Follwell. Sherwood on his rocking horse and mamma are in the foreground and really farther away from the house than it looks. The ... and ... look well on the front steps. The morning glories were in all their splendor, and made a ... of the front steps.

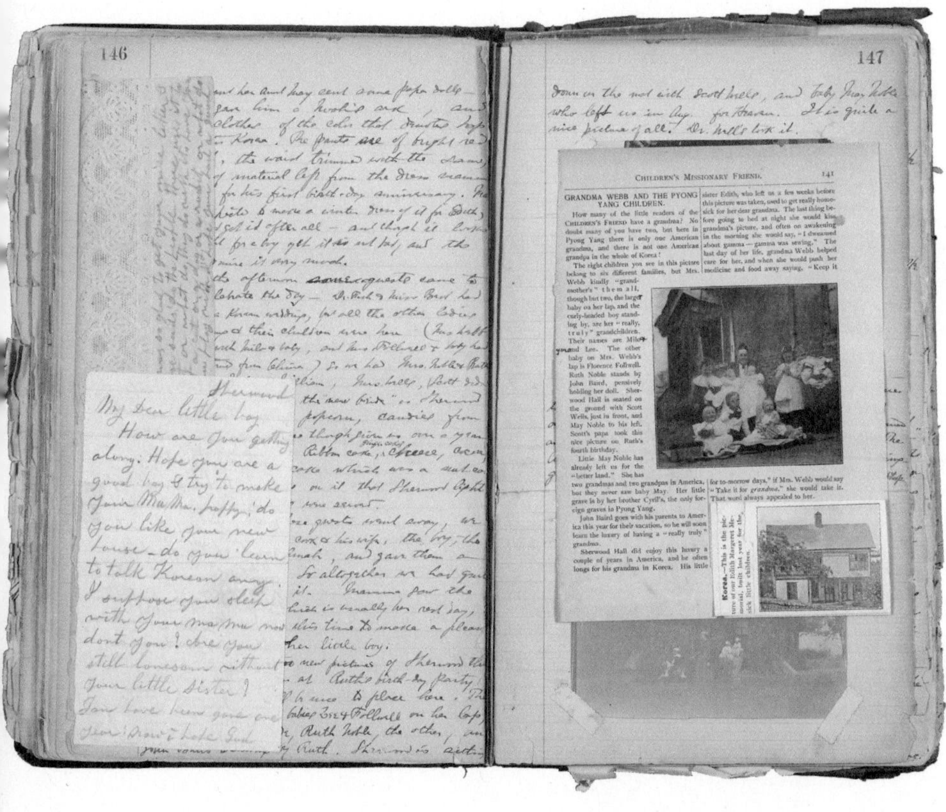

146

147

CHILDREN'S MISSIONARY FRIEND. 141

GRANDMA WEBB AND THE PYONG YANG CHILDREN.

How many of the little readers of the CHILDREN'S FRIEND have a grandma? No doubt many of you have two, but here in Pyong Yang there is only one American grandma, and there is not one American grandpa in the whole of Korea!

The eight children you see in this picture belong to six different families, but Mrs. Webb kindly "grandmother's" them all, though but two, the larger baby on her lap, and the curly-headed boy standing by, are her "really, truly" grandchildren. Their names are Milo and Lee. The other baby on Mrs. Webb's lap is Florence Follwell. Ruth Noble stands by John Baird, pensively holding her doll. Sherwood Hall is seated on the ground with Scott Wells, just in front, and May Noble to his left. Scott's papa took this nice picture on Ruth's fourth birthday.

Little May Noble has already left us for the "better land." She has two grandmas and two grandpas in America, but they never saw baby May. Her little grave is by her brother Cyril's, the only foreign graves in Pyong Yang.

John Baird goes with his parents to America this year for their vacation, so he will soon learn the luxury of having a "really truly" grandma.

Sherwood Hall did enjoy this luxury a couple of years in America, and he often longs for his grandma in Korea. His little sister Edith, who left us a few weeks before this picture was taken, used to get really homesick for her dear grandma. The last thing before going to bed at night she would kiss grandma's picture, and often on awakening in the morning she would say, "I dreamed about gamma — gamma was sewing." The last day of her life, grandma Webb helped care for her, and when she would push her medicine and food away saying, "Keep it for to-morrow days," if Mrs. Webb would say "Take it for *grandma*," she would take it. That word always appealed to her.

Korea.—This is the picture of our Edith Margaret Memorial, built last year for the sick little children.

Sherwood is quite observing, ma thinks — more so she is [illegible] she is — one reason perhaps is, he can [illegible] better. He noticed Grandma Webb's wrinkles (she has not many) and asked if all grandma's [illegible] "cuts" in their face like Grandma Sherwood & Webb's. The room we occupied while Mr. Nobles when we first came to Ryors [illegible] an ingrain rug on the floor, and a screen like was in our room at home, also the bed not in a bedstead but just made up on the [illegible] like we had ours fixed. at Grandma's [illegible] put it back against the wall in the day time the screen in front. Though mamma was not [illegible] with the similarity, Sherwood noticed it at [illegible] and declared it was just like our room [illegible] Grandma's. When Dr. Cattle visited us, [illegible] a shirt-waist of white stripes with red, [illegible] was just like a doll dress Aunt Annie use[illegible] and gave to Edith — Sherwood noticed it [illegible] and said it was like Edith's doll's dress [illegible] a panel picture entitled "inspiration" [illegible] hangs near mamma's desk are some angels floating down and dropping roses [illegible] lady sitting in the evening twilight. Sherwood [illegible] at it carefully and asked "Is Edith [illegible] like them? Then as he often does, he [illegible]ed himself and said "I guess she has a [illegible] white dress like that of Jesus in the [illegible] of the Korean Church" evidently having [illegible] the one of Christ's ascension which [illegible] him with cloud like robes about him.

He has quite an idea of the f[illegible] of words to ideas. He doesn't like chic[illegible] bones to be called "drum sticks". Also when mamma spoke of the wall as a fence he [illegible] "You mustn't call *that* a fence, it is [illegible] of stone and its a wall — fences are ma[illegible] wire —" where he ever learned so mu[illegible]

Chitte Balbe
Nov 5 - 1898

Dear Sherwood,

I have thought of you very often, and now I am going to write you something about this place and also about the gold they stamp out of the rock in the mill here. First I hope that you and your Mama are real well. That Ruth is a very sweet playmate to you. Please give her and her parents my best wishes.—

This little town is situated at the bottom or foot a hill which is surrounded by other hills & these are again surrounded by other hills

420 It is nothing but hills & hills with

... many questions about the gold-mines where Mr. Bunker's work is. He rec'd a nice letter from Mrs. Bunker recently telling more about it — He is very anxious to visit the gold mines.

Sherwood often talks about Heaven or asks questions about it — and thinks it is so good that we will never be sick anymore or cry there, but he says "I don't want to go to Heaven till I get a big man, and get tired."

Susan was piecing a quilt for herself, and he wanted to sew too, and started a quilt for Ruth's doll, he pieced 3 blocks, but hasn't finished it yet. Mamma began her first quilt just before she was 5 yrs old too — and she began going to school the summer after she was five, so she has been telling Sherwood for some time.

that after he is five years old he must
to study his lessons; and he had quite an ide
what it meant for he knew "Wendy &
Appenzeller study lessons" and he has
looked forward to it. As mamma is writin
about 3 weeks after Sherwood's birth day, she
add that rather to her surprise he has kep
his interest in his lessons, and as yet it
not grown an old thing as mamma feared it
There seems no good time in the day that ma
can regularly get for these lessons except right
supper which doesn't seem the best time for
little boy to study, but he asks for it, and d
...a forget it one night — he don't even
...r Sunday night. He works away at it
...'s lap at her desk always a half hou
...s an hour before he gets tired. Ma
...t him start in Korean rather
..., because it is quite as simple, an
...sy to write — At least mamma th
...ld get his eyes and muscles tra
rather more easily and quickly with Korea
that he would learn English more rapidly late
Course one lacks the pleasant helps in learning
that there are for learning English, but so far
has gotten on quite nicely. He has learn
recognizes at sight, anywhere, the following
or words 어, 가 (go), 오 (come), 고, 고
이 (this), 다 (all), 보 (see), 소 (cow) 어, and
he makes fair attempts at writing them, tho
he tires at this more quickly than the other
...dy. He enjoys hunting new words best of
... will go over page after page in que
the one he has just learned — quickly finding every
often seeing them before mamma. At morn
and at Church he searches through the Korean Bi
hymn-book finding all the words he knows. If
keeps on, it will not be so very long before he can
morning lesson with us — As Korean is more perfectly phone

Sherwood's first attempts at writing Korean

"mother"

The word "mother" in Korean the first time Sherwood wrote it alone

Winter of 98-99

어머니 "mother"

...nounce its words more easily than Eng-
...linese, though as in English one may not understand them.
...y fond of having stories read to him –
...n one or more every day when he lies
...p, and he never lets off from a
...not even these short winter days.
...counts on a long Bible story,
...ntirely often to 3 chapters in
...tory of Jesus" which is most
...is the best mamma has. Quite
... him right straight from the
...y subject that he may have
...n from seeing the pictures in
..., or has heard of in some way.
... for the Stoning of Stephen, of the Story
..., the story of Creation, of the flood, etc.
... recently his Bible lesson was on
... Abraham's prayer, and though he
... much attention at the time, it evident-
...im, for that night there was a
... city near the river, that we could see
...s the first sight of the kind he had seen
...t was filled with pity for the poor
... then lose their homes, and when he
... Koreans had no fire engines or any such
... fire like they have in America, he said
... it out", so he did, adding just before
he opened his eyes "I believe". Then he looked out
again and reported the fire much smaller, and
mamma thought it was too.

He misses Mary Appenzeller very much, and for months hardly a day passed without his speaking about her + but he is getting quite fond of Ruth Noble now – and while Ruth was gone to Seoul for a month, he thought John Baird pretty nice. He is very fond of company – cannot content himself alone at all hardly – except now with his Kitty he does make out to skip a day now and then without teasing either for Ruth to come here, or him to go there.

...should all be so glad to see him. He and his little sister are warmly remembered by our little ones. They
had such good times together last winter. Your Re-
positories I sent by Bro. Moffett and I doubt not you have
them by this time. May God bless you. Remember me to
Susan. I miss her in our work here. Very love to Sherwood and
believe me. Sincerely Yours, H. G. Appenzeller

...boy was out the floor and howled for him. He wants mamma to read over and over times to him.

Wednesday May 10, 1899.

All things whatsoever ye w
that men should do to you, do ye ev
to them. Mat. VII, XII.

We cannot make bargains for Bliss
Nor catch them like fishes in a
And sometimes the things our life mis
Helps more than the things whi
For good lieth not in pursuing
Nor gaining of great nor of small;
But just in the doing, and doing
As we would be done by, is all.
— Alice Cary

Time passes so quickly and mamm
so busy that she can only touch up
some of the changes that come to
Last Dec. mamma took a little
leaving Sherwood with R
like it very well, when
s really gone and he
at night — but he
s a pretty good boy, a
receive mamma back h
time however that mam
along; so in March
mamma went again. She
by boat to a point
ey lives; then went over
pack-pony. He enjoyed it
place we stopped at, and
he night after leaving the
strip-hens" in the room with
d picked the first "grand
n.
he enjoyed himself playing
ren — At Nampo
black pigs that were

ADVERTISE IN THE JOURNAL,
JAMESTOWN'S HOME NEWSPAPER.
Read Daily by Thousands of the People You Want to Reach

Dear mamma I want you to come back quick
I want to stay up until Mrs. Noble goes to bed
Next time you go away I want you to tell me before you go.
I'll be very glad to hear the stories you will tell me about where you went.

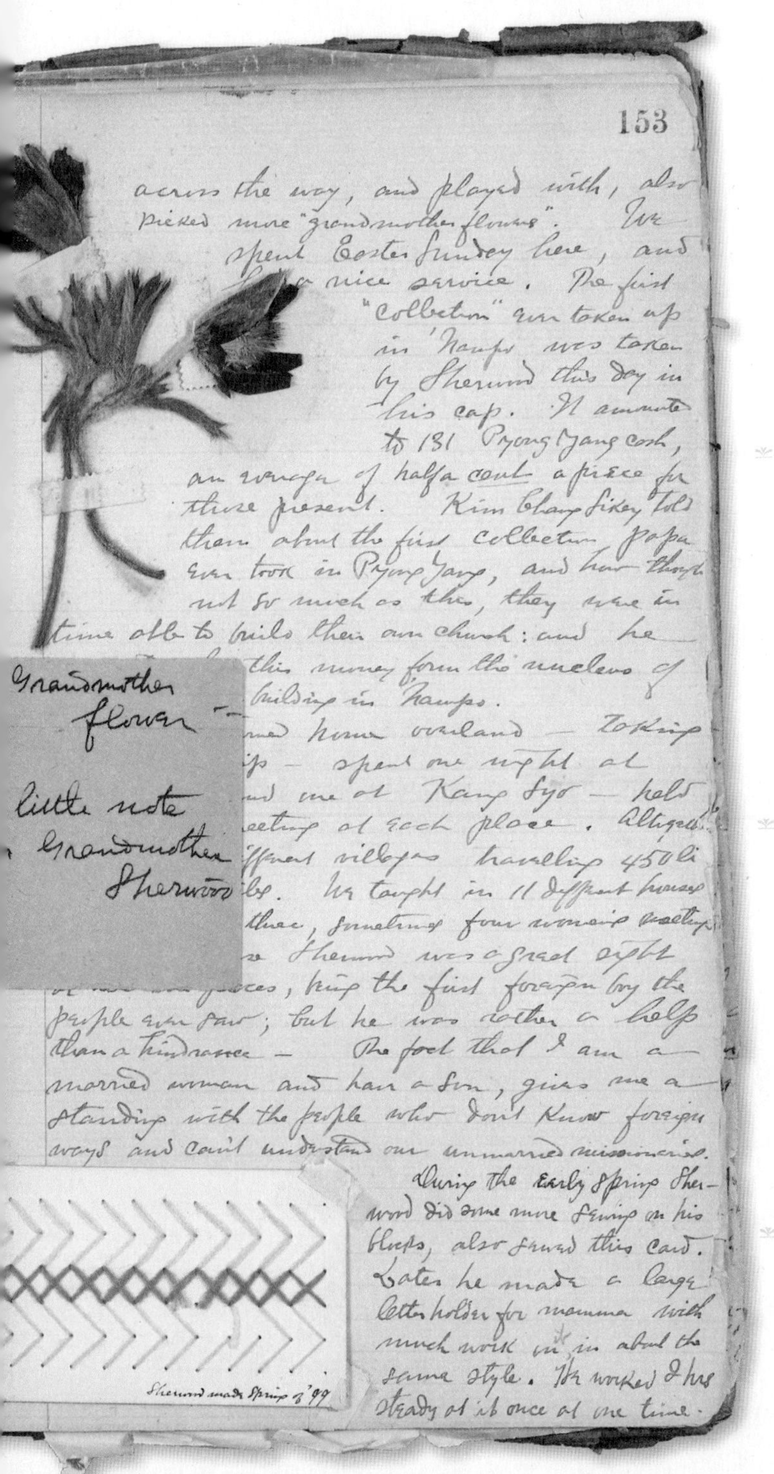
153

across the way, and played with, also picked more "grandmother flowers". We spent Easter Sunday here, and [had] a nice service. The first "collection" ever taken up in Nampo was taken by Sherwood this day in his cap. It amounted to 181 Pyong Yang cash, an average of half a cent apiece for those present. Kim Chang Sikey told them about the first collection papa ever took in Pyong Yang, and how though not so much as this, they were in time able to build their own church: and he [illegible] this money form the nucleus of [illegible] building in Nampo.

[illegible] home overland — taking [illegible] — spent one night at [illegible] and one at Kang Syo — held [illegible] meeting at each place. Altogether [illegible] different villages travelling 450 li [illegible]. We taught in 11 different houses [illegible] three, sometimes four women's meetings [illegible] Sherwood was a great sight [illegible] places, being the first foreign boy the people ever saw; but he was rather a help than a hindrance — The fact that I am a married woman and have a son, gives me a standing with the people who don't know foreign ways and can't understand our unmarried missionaries.

During the early spring Sherwood did some more sewing on his blocks, also sewed this card. Later he made a large letter holder for mamma with much work on it in about the same style. He worked 2 hrs steady at it once at one time.

"Grandmother flower" —
little note [illegible] Grandmother Sherwood

Sherwood made Spring of '99

The first of May just one year
the time we first arrived at Pyong Y
we left together with Mr. Noble, Dr. &
Follwell & Florence to attend Annual mee
in Seoul. We went down to Nampo o
a boat — were three days getting th
and were detained in a Korean i
5 more days, but finally got off o
the Steamer for Chemulpo, where we s
a couple of days at Mrs. Jones' and the
went up to Seoul. Sherwood enjoy
very much meeting and playing
the children again. He said he wasn't
of Mary Appenzeller because her curls partly c
her face — but he was very bashful with
at first because he said "her face showed so
She had her hair combed back & tightly braided.

Sherwood also had the pleasure of
rides on the Seoul Electric R.R. which began ru
while we were there, but a riot soon put a sto
it.

Before we came down from Pyong Yang
tried to fill some of Sherwood's teeth, his first lo
bicuspids and his upper mid. incisors have deca
spots in — he was very patient, but mam
didn't have very good success, at least the fil
didn't last. At Nampo in biting a piece
hard bread one day, he lost his first too
the R. lower mid. incisor, and a month lat
mamma pulled its mate. While in Seoul
dentist put some better fillings in the decay
spots which will make his teeth last
till the new ones are ready to come

One day when not feeling very well
Sherwood said "I feel like a "joint" the
had been knocked on his forehead with a stone
He always calls a giant a "joint" an
mamma has never corrected him. Instea
of saying "little by little" he always says "by

by little". He said "How does Summer come? By little, by little like the sun rises"? Also he asked "Do I get big by little by little?"

Mamma is kept so very busy with her work, she can't get much chance to note her little boy's sayings and changes. I expect some day like Livingstone she will feel like writing as he did "I often ponder over my missionary career + + + and though conscious of many imperfections, not a single pang of regret arises + + except that I did not feel it my duty, while spending all my energy in teaching the heathen, to devote a special portion of my time to play with my children. But generally I was so much exhausted with the mental and manual labor of the day, that in the evening there was no fun left in me. I did not play with my little ones while I had them, and they soon sprung up + + + and left me conscious that I had none to play with."

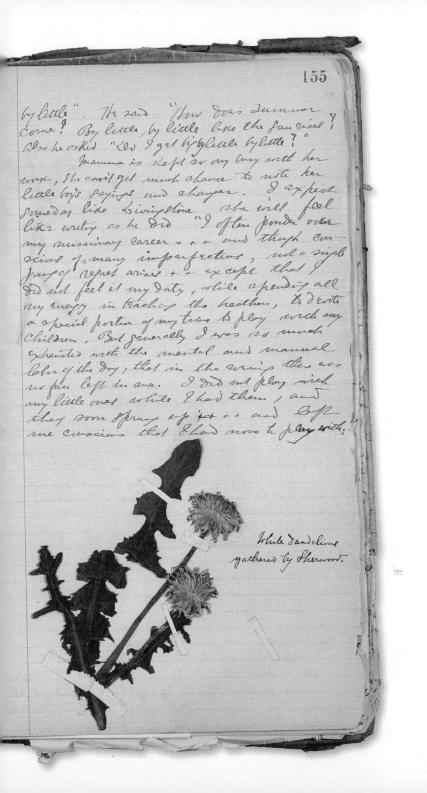

White dandelions
gathered by Sherwood.

156

Friday, November 10th, 1899.

My days are swifter than a wea[ver's]
shuttle. Job. vii, 6.

"He sat on my knee at evening,
The boy who is "three and thre[e]
And the clear blue eye from his sun-bro[wn]
Smiled happily up to me.
I held him close as the twilight f[ell]
And called him "my dear little so[n]
Then I said: 'I have wondered for many [a]
Where it is that my baby's gone

I'd a baby once in a long while gone,
Whom I rocked just as I do you.
His hair was as soft as yellow silk,
And his eyes were like violets blue
His little hands were like pink-tipped fl[owers]
See, yours are so strong and brown.
He has slipped away and is lost, I fea[r]
Do you know where my baby's gone.

Did my voice half break as the thoughts woke
Of the sweet and sacred days
When motherhood's first joys were min[e]
Was a shade of regret on my face?
For close round my neck crept a sturdy
And the boy who is "three and three
Said, 'The baby – he went to Boyland,
And – didn't you know? – he's me

"Old Father Time" has rolled
Nov. 10th around to Friday once m[ore]
and "my dear little son" is six ye[ars]
old. He measures 3 feet 9 in. in h[eight]
has gained 2 3/4 in, and he weighs 46½ lb.

We celebrated by a little afternoon tea-party to which all were invited big and little. The birthday cake was a walnut one frosted, and with 6 candles on which Sherwood lighted, and later blew out. We had also other cake and crackers and candy and pop-corn. Also what Sherwood enjoyed very much some fire-works.

This year what with the usual work and trying to build the Edith Margaret Children's Ward, mamma has been too busy to pay much attention to the sayings or doings of her little lad, for though often interesting or amusing at the time, mamma soon forgets them with so many other things to think of.

Just one or two things by way of samples. Sherwood knew that Mrs. Folwell milked their cow, and last summer when he first heard the Nobles had a cow he asked "Who nurses their cow, Mr. Noble or Mrs. Noble?

Mrs. Swallen has kindly allowed Sherwood to come at the time she teaches her own children Sundays, and he has learned quite a number of Bible verses. Last July after learning Jno. 3.16 he asked mamma to explain about "perish" and "everlasting life", and later said he feared he might not go to heaven. Mamma said Why, it says "whosoever believeth" — you believe Jesus don't you? He replied "Yes, I believe, but I don't always mind him." Evidently he feels faith and works should go to-gether.

A few months ago, mamma remarked after hearing Sherwood recite some of his verses, that when she was 5 yrs old she didn't know any Bible verses, and he said. "I think I'll make a good humjun" (husband) when I get big." When I laughed, he said "I can't say that word right, if little boys can't say humjun when they are little can't they when they get big?" He often talks as if he thought he was going to be "mamma's humjun" when he gets big, he never seems to think of being anyone else's.

158

The next week after Sherwood's birth...
we set out upon another country trip...
all went by pack-pony this time. We
went 300 li or 100 miles north, and the...
were so short we had to be four whole days
and traveled after dark at that sometimes. The i...
we staid at over night were not good, but better th...
those we happened to strike on our way back. ...
were glad to get to our destination Koksan wh...
Mr. Bunker established Mr. C in mission work a...
where later mamma persuaded his wife "Josa...
and little daughter Lucy to join him. They ...
quite a nice home here very pleasantly sit...
We brought our boy with us, and he cleaned ...
a room for us where with our cots we were comf...
He also gets our meals for us and we spen...
a pleasant and profitable 10 days there. Sherwo...
Lucy made good playmates. We got six other
girls to come in every day and started a day sch...
that has since grown to ten with a good average a...
ance. We also were invited to call at a ...

"3+3"

...ho a catechism or ...
...evening meetings ...
...interested in the...
...ings. Our last Sunda...
...es as drains of bean...
...to give up their fetish...
...and selling wine. ...
...s where so many of...
...that almost every ho...
...given up to supplying t...
... . It is a discouragin...
...to the present there ha...
...but Mr. & Mrs. C feel
...think it will not be so lo...
...interested Sherwood very
...gie, was the day ...
...ines. Mamma will ...
...kie's letter to Sherwood her...

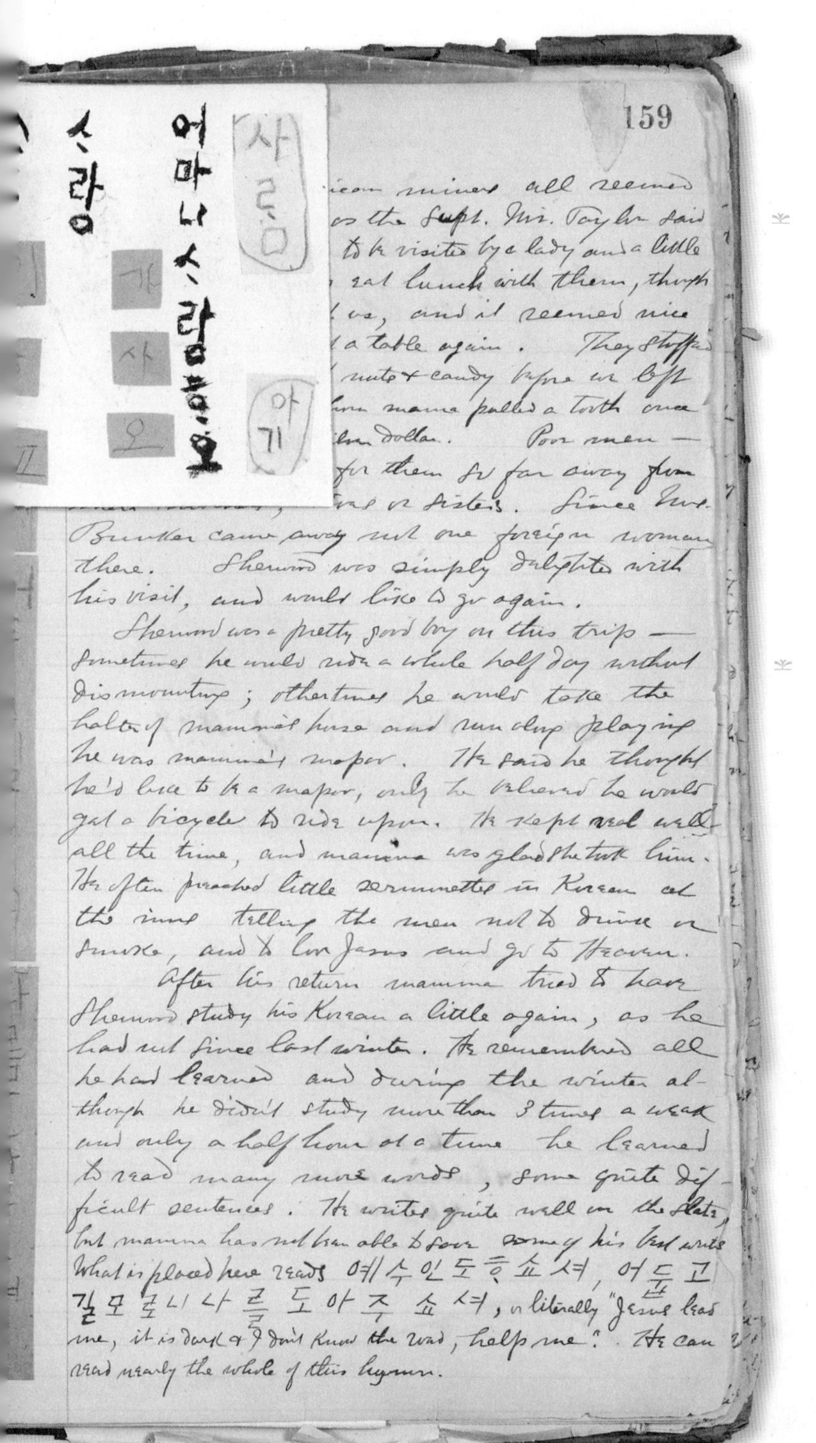

159

...ican miners all seemed
...as the Supt. Mr. Taylor said
...to be visited by a lady and a little
...eat lunch with them, though
...d us, and it seemed nice
...d a table again. They stuffed
... nuts & candy before we left
...hen mama pulled a tooth once
...ilver dollar. Poor men —
... for them so far away from
... ers or sisters. Since Mrs.
Bunker came away not one foreign woman
there. Sherwood was simply delighted with
his visit, and would like to go again.

Sherwood was a pretty good boy on this trip — sometimes he would ride a whole half day without dismounting; othertimes he would take the halter of mamma's horse and run along playing he was mamma's mapoo. He said he thought he'd like to be a mapoo, only he believed he would get a bicycle to ride upon. He kept real well all the time, and mamma was glad she took him. He often preached little sermonettes in Korean at the inns telling the men not to drink or smoke, and to love Jesus and go to Heaven.

After his return mamma tried to have Sherwood study his Korean a little again, as he had not since last winter. He remembered all he had learned and during the winter although he didn't study more than 3 times a week and only a half hour at a time he learned to read many more words, some quite difficult sentences. He writes quite well on the slate, but mamma has not been able to save some of his best writing. What is placed here reads 예수인도ᄒᆞ쇼셔, 어둡고 길모로니 나를 도아 쥬 쇼셔, or literally "Jesus lead me, it is dark & I don't know the road, help me". He can read nearly the whole of this hymn.

160
(On Dr. Alice Fish's wedding-day) 1899
6 yrs –
45 inches high
46½ lbs

Thursday May 10th, 1900.
At Chefoo, China

The fear of the Lord is clean enduring forever, the judgments of the Lord are true and righteous altogether. More to be desired are they than gold, yea than much fine gold. Psa. 19, 9 & 10

We are here to be perfected;
Only Christ our needs can see:
Rarest gems bear hardest grinding,
God's own workmanship are we!

Sherwood and mamma landed here May 1st, mamma had planned to go to Tientsin for her vacation, but just before taking the boat at Chemulpo got word from Dr. Benn that it would be better not to come at this time on account of the epidemic of malignant scarlet fever they are having, so mamma decided to go to Shanghai instead, and did not intend to stop at Chefoo only long enough to get the first boat, because she is feeling very much
is where she and papa
she feared the associations of
feel her loneliness all the
ch a beautiful place, and
rtable, and Sherwood
py with sea, and sand,
and star-fish, that it
away so soon, and
over 10 days. We will
n the Genkai Maru, the
came here on 8 years ago.
his place is like heaven,
am mamma has always
few boarders at this house
eats 8 o'clock dinner
the drawing-room (he calls
9.30 p.m. He of course
-nap or he couldn't do this

livette, Wilbur and
Gertrude.
rdially invite Sherwood
their little tea party
morrow Feb. 22. 1900 at
o'clock

160 162

He affords considerable amusement for Mrs.
and Mrs. Watts Jones and her sister Miss Badgely w
his unsophisticated manners. It took hi
long time to learn the names of the two lady g
and he spoke of them as "her" but now he
calls them by name. He always has trouble w
"Mr." & "Mrs." and he is apt to call Mr. Price "t
man Mrs. Price"

He digs in the sand making roads & w
all the day most — or collects tiny stones or plays
plays in the poultry yard. Twice he has gone
little picnics with some of the C. I. M. school chi
After dinner he enjoys going in the drawing-roo
with the ladies, and he gets Miss Badgely to p
"I see something red" or the color game he likes so well.
When 3 other children were here they played hide the thimb
The last few evenings the ladies have told stories and
asked Sherwood to tell some, he makes quite a bra
tempt, but his stories are pretty short ones, and
in them unless he makes up one as he goes along. Th
ite one is about a little girl who went to get eggs
her mamma and after getting in the chicken-house
two rattlesnakes. Then he will generally go on and t
his mamma use to play with milk snakes when she
little girl.

Sherwood has written nice letters to Grandm
to Ruth since coming to Chefoo. To-day the Ch
finished him a pretty pair of low brown leather sh
which he will appear in to-night at dinner with
velvet pants and a cream cashmere blouse. The
[illegible] iven Edith in Canada, but it was nev
[illegible] til now for her brother. This wi
[illegible] ur last evening here.

Sherwood Hall.
from Ruth.

A

AR SHERWOOD
AM GLAD
U ARE
MING HOME

Saturday, Nov. 10th, 1900.

My son, forget not my law; but let thine heart keep my commandments: for length of days, and long life, and peace, shall they add to thee. Let not mercy and truth forsake thee: bind them about thy neck; write them upon the table of thine heart: so shalt thou find favour and good understanding in the sight of God and man. Trust in the Lord with all thine heart; and lean not unto thine own understanding. In all thy ways acknowledge Him, and He shall direct thy paths. — Prov. iii, 1-6.

"A child went merrily for a play
But a thought, like a silver thread
Kept winding in and out all day
Through the happy golden head —
"Mother said: 'Darling, do all that you can
For you are a part of God's great plan.'"

He knew no more than the twinkling star,
Or the cloud with its rain-cup full,
How, why, or for what all strange things are,
He was only a child at school;
But he thought: "'Tis a part of God's great plan
That even I should do all that I can."
— Margaret Sangster

Sherwood has been looking eagerly for- ... months now to when ... — older than any other ... He and mam- ... little party in which ... an attractive feature for the ... all the eggs used in the ... blowed out, and yesterday ... gelatine. There were part ... een, and others were left white. ... a nice walnut cake, ... candy scattered over it, and ... nut candy, and salted pea-nuts

... In 3 days at school, at ... a dozen little envelopes ... mamma wrote the invitation ... — Please come and help

THANKSGIVING.

MAMMA

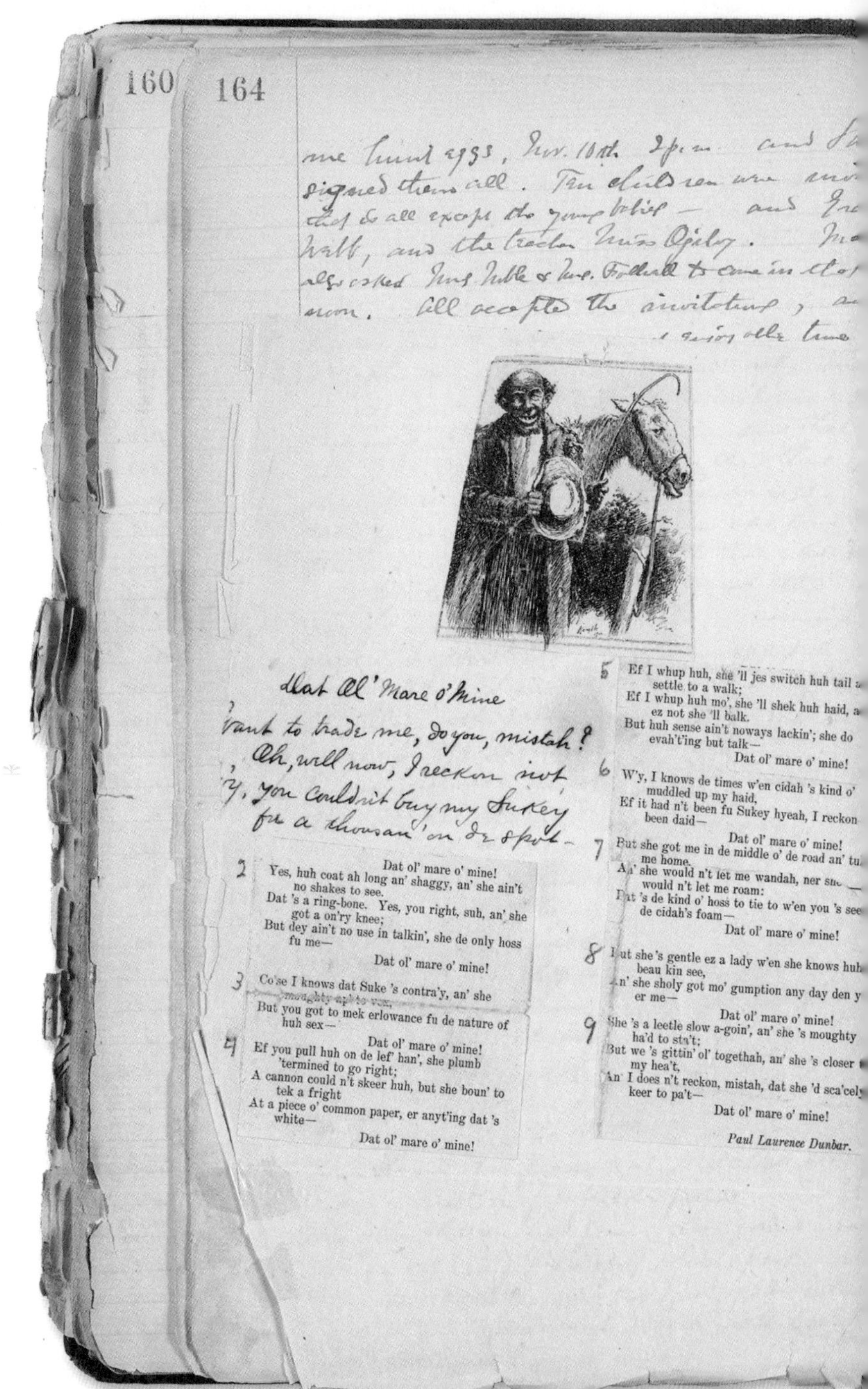

160 164

me lunch eggs, Nov. 10th 2 p.m. and [illegible] signed them all. The children were [illegible] that is all except the young babies — and [illegible] Webb, and the teacher Miss Ogilvy. [illegible] also asked Mrs. Noble & Mrs. Follett to come in at [illegible] noon. All accepted the invitation, [illegible] [illegible] time

Dat Ol' Mare o' Mine

[illegible] want to trade me, do you, mistah?
Oh, well now, I reckon not,
[illegible] You couldn't buy my Sukey
fu a thousan' on de spot—
Dat ol' mare o' mine!

2 Yes, huh coat ah long an' shaggy, an' she ain't no shakes to see.
Dat 's a ring-bone. Yes, you right, suh, an' she got a on'ry knee;
But dey ain't no use in talkin', she de only hoss fu me—
Dat ol' mare o' mine!

3 Co'se I knows dat Suke 's contra'y, an' she moughty apt to vex,
But you got to mek erlowance fu de nature of huh sex—
Dat ol' mare o' mine!

4 Ef you pull huh on de lef' han', she plumb 'termined to go right;
A cannon could n't skeer huh, but she boun' to tek a fright
At a piece o' common paper, er anyt'ing dat 's white—
Dat ol' mare o' mine!

5 Ef I whup huh, she 'll jes switch huh tail a[nd] settle to a walk;
Ef I whup huh mo', she 'll shek huh haid, a[n'] ez not she 'll balk.
But huh sense ain't noways lackin'; she do evah't'ing but talk—
Dat ol' mare o' mine!

6 W'y, I knows de times w'en cidah 's kind o' muddled up my haid,
Ef it had n't been fu Sukey hyeah, I reckon [I'd] been daid—
Dat ol' mare o' mine!

7 But she got me in de middle o' de road an' tu[rned] me home,
An' she would n't let me wandah, ner she would n't let me roam:
Dat 's de kind o' hoss to tie to w'en you 's see[in'] de cidah's foam—
Dat ol' mare o' mine!

8 But she 's gentle ez a lady w'en she knows huh beau kin see,
An' she sholy got mo' gumption any day den y[ou] er me—
Dat ol' mare o' mine!

9 She 's a leetle slow a-goin', an' she 's moughty ha'd to sta't;
But we 's gittin' ol' togethah, an' she 's closer [to] my hea't,
An' I does n't reckon, mistah, dat she 'd sca'cely keer to pa't—
Dat ol' mare o' mine!

Paul Laurence Dunbar.

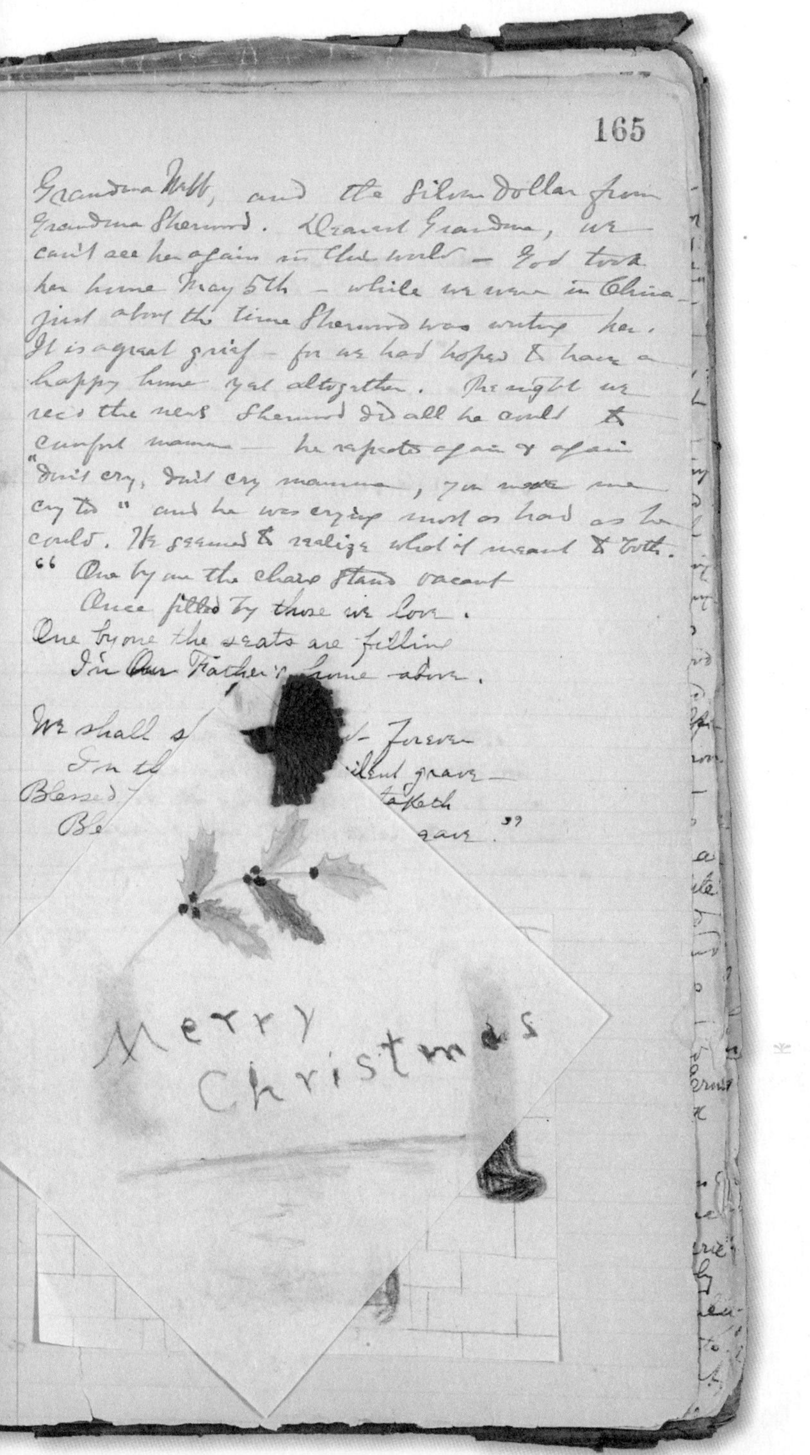

165

Grandma Webb, and the silver dollar from Grandma Sherwood. Dearest Grandma, we can't see her again in this world – God took her home May 5th – while we were in China just about the time Sherwood was writing her. It is a great grief – for we had hoped to have a happy home yet altogether. The night we rec'd the news Sherwood did all he could to comfort mamma – he repeats again & again "don't cry, don't cry mamma, you make me cry too" and he was crying most as hard as he could. He seemed to realize what it meant to both.

" One by one the chairs stand vacant
Once filled by those we love.
One by one the seats are filling
In Our Father's home above.

We shall s… – forever
In th… silent grave –
Blessed … taketh
Be… gave."

Merry Christmas

160

166

The boy and girl

The boy and

have an apple

have and apple

an egg

an egg

1900
Christmas.
Made during
"busy hours" at school
a surprise for mama.

Christmas day, all
Yang missionaries
children were in
take dinner at
Noble's. After din
the first Christm
in Pyeng Yang.
children made
gay paper garlands
lanterns to decor
and there were
nice presents
the children.
was more than p
be presented with a
tiger that seemed
perpetual motion a
of the tree. "Santa
there to give out th
and altogether it wa
success. Miss Agi
a nice little progra
for the children to sing,
also recited "That Old

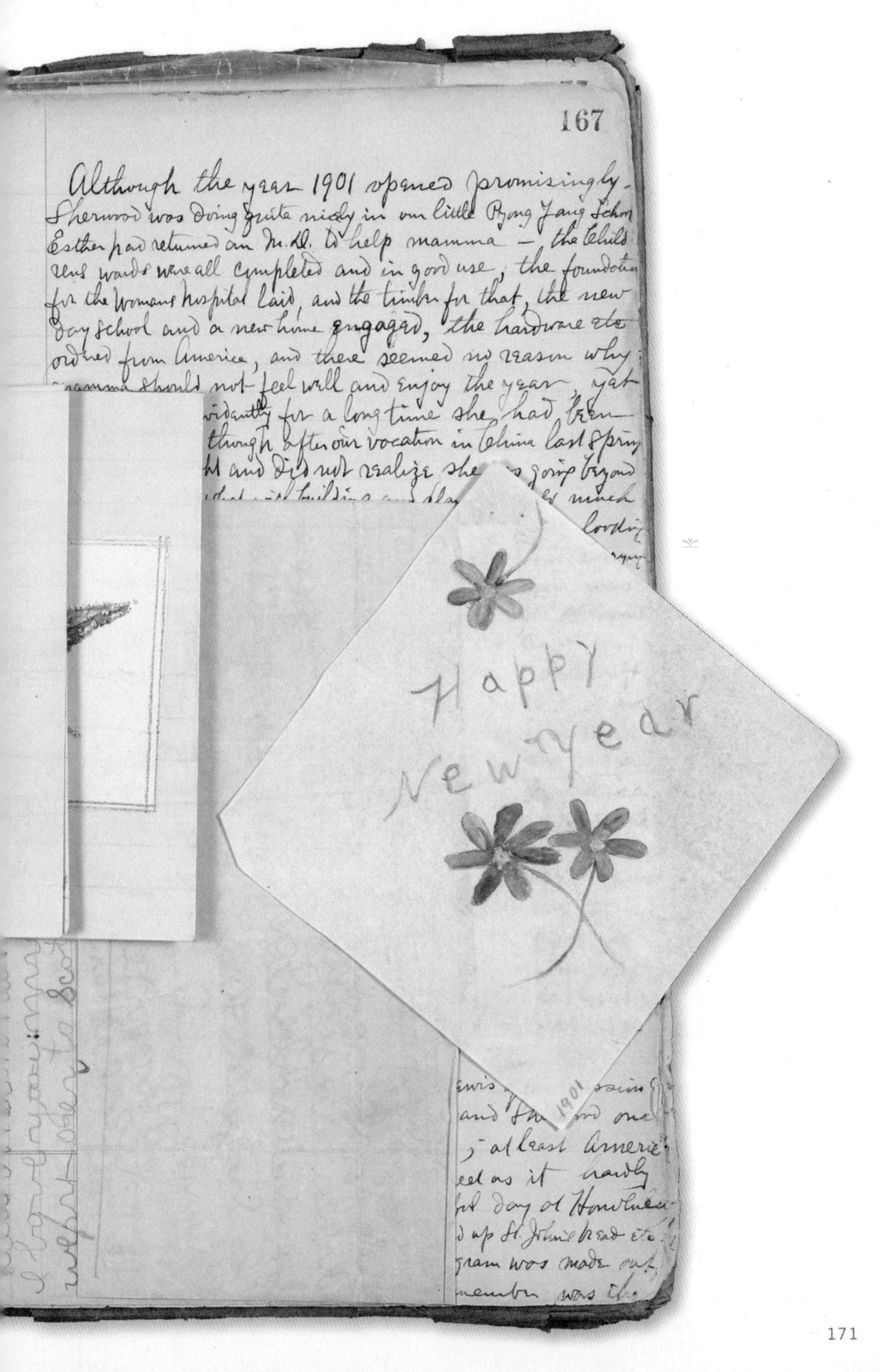
167
Although the year 1901 opened promisingly -
Sherwood was doing quite nicely in our little Pyong Yang School
Esther had returned an M.D. to help mamma - the Child
rens wards were all completed and in good use, the foundation
for the Womans hospital laid, and the timber for that, the new
day school and a new home engaged, the hardware etc
ordered from America, and there seemed no reason why
mamma should not feel well and enjoy the year, yet
Happy New year
1901

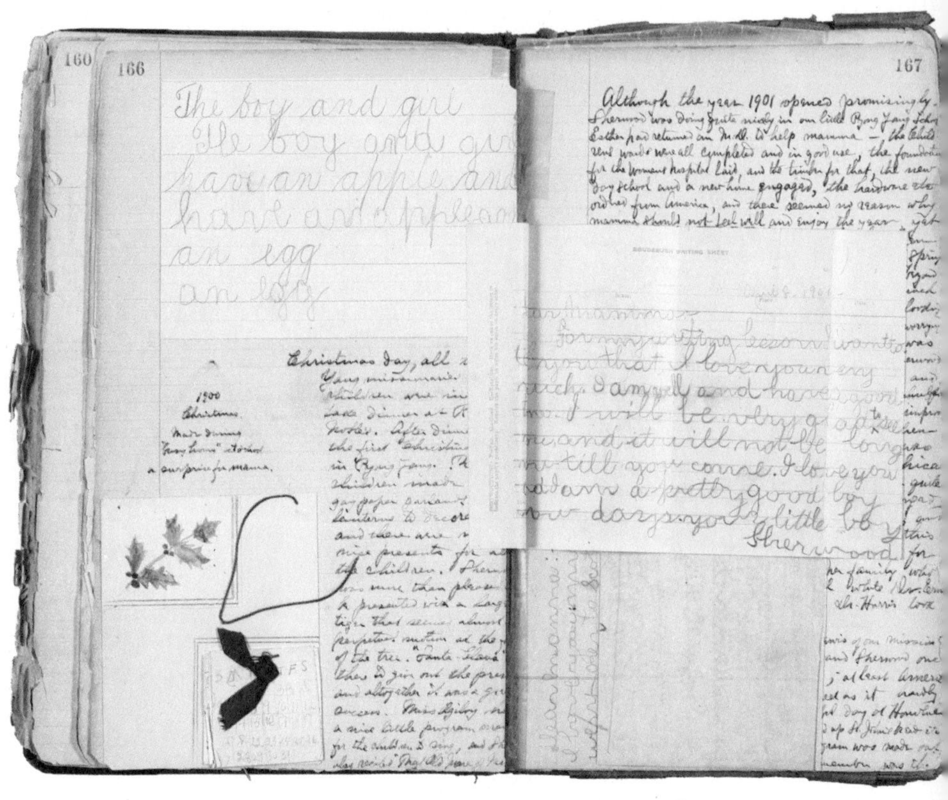
166
The boy and girl
an egg
Christmas day, all
1900
Christmas
a surprise for mamma.
167
Although the year 1901 opened promisingly.
mamma should not feel well and enjoy the year
Sherwood

166

The boy and girl
The boy and gi[rl]
have an apple and
have and o[...]

the children. Sherw[ood]
was more than please[d]
& presented with a large
tiger that seemed almost
perpetual motion at the f[oot]
of the tree. "Santa Claus"
there to give out the pres[ents]
and altogether it was a gre[at]
success. Miss Ogilvy [...]
a nice little program [...]
for the children to sing, and [...]
also recited "That Old [...]"

167

Although the year 1901 opened promisingly. Sherwood was doing quite nicely in our little Pyeng Yang School, Esther had returned an M.D. to help mamma — the Childrens wards were all completed and in good use, the foundation for the Womens hospital laid, and the timber for that, the new day school and a new home engaged, the hardware etc. ordered from America, and there seemed no reason why mamma should not feel well and enjoy the year, yet she did not. — Evidently for a long time she had been overtaxed and though after our vacation in China last Spring she felt all right and did not realize she was going beyond her strength [...]

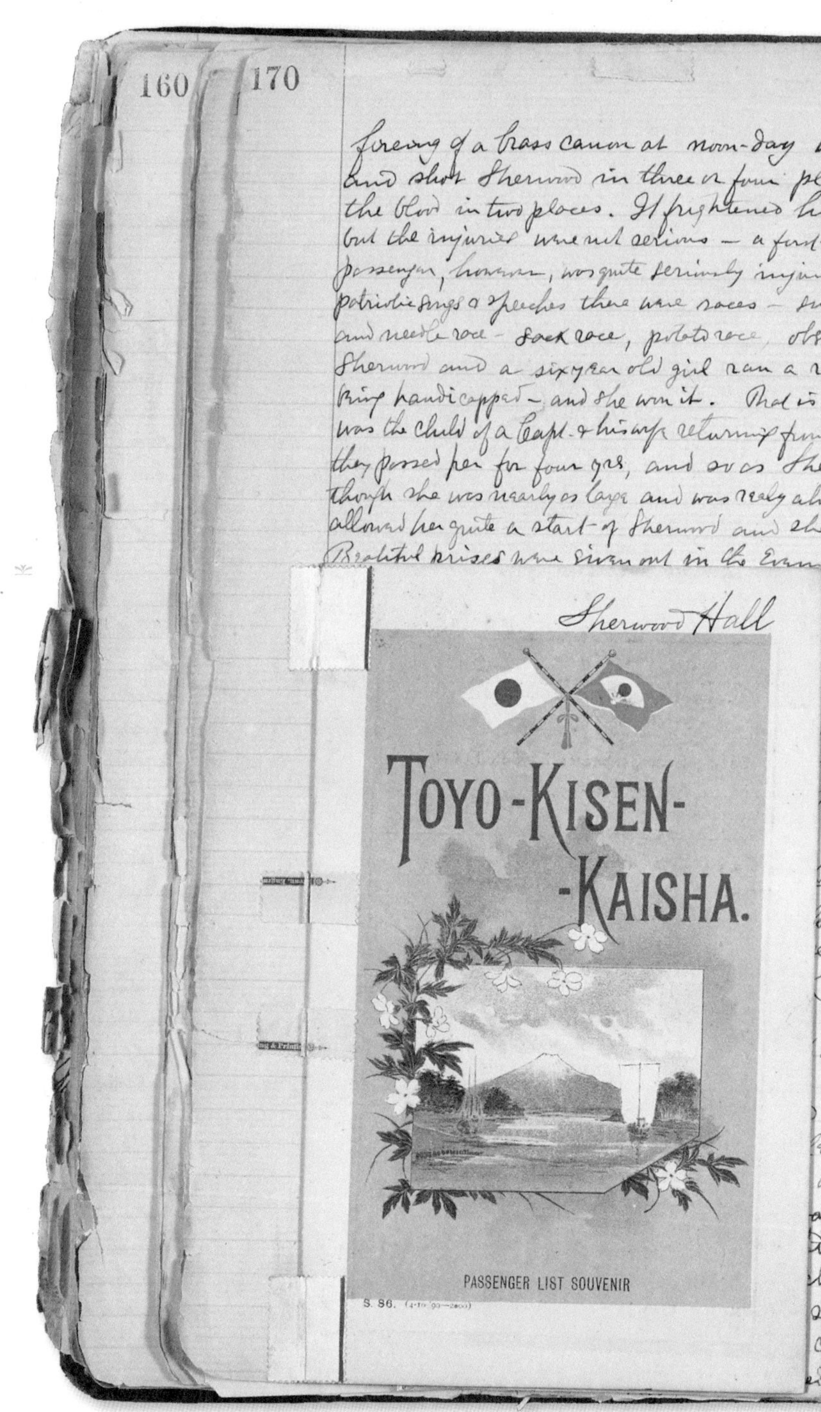
160
170
Sherwood Hall
TOYO-KISEN-
-KAISHA.
PASSENGER LIST SOUVENIR
S. 86.

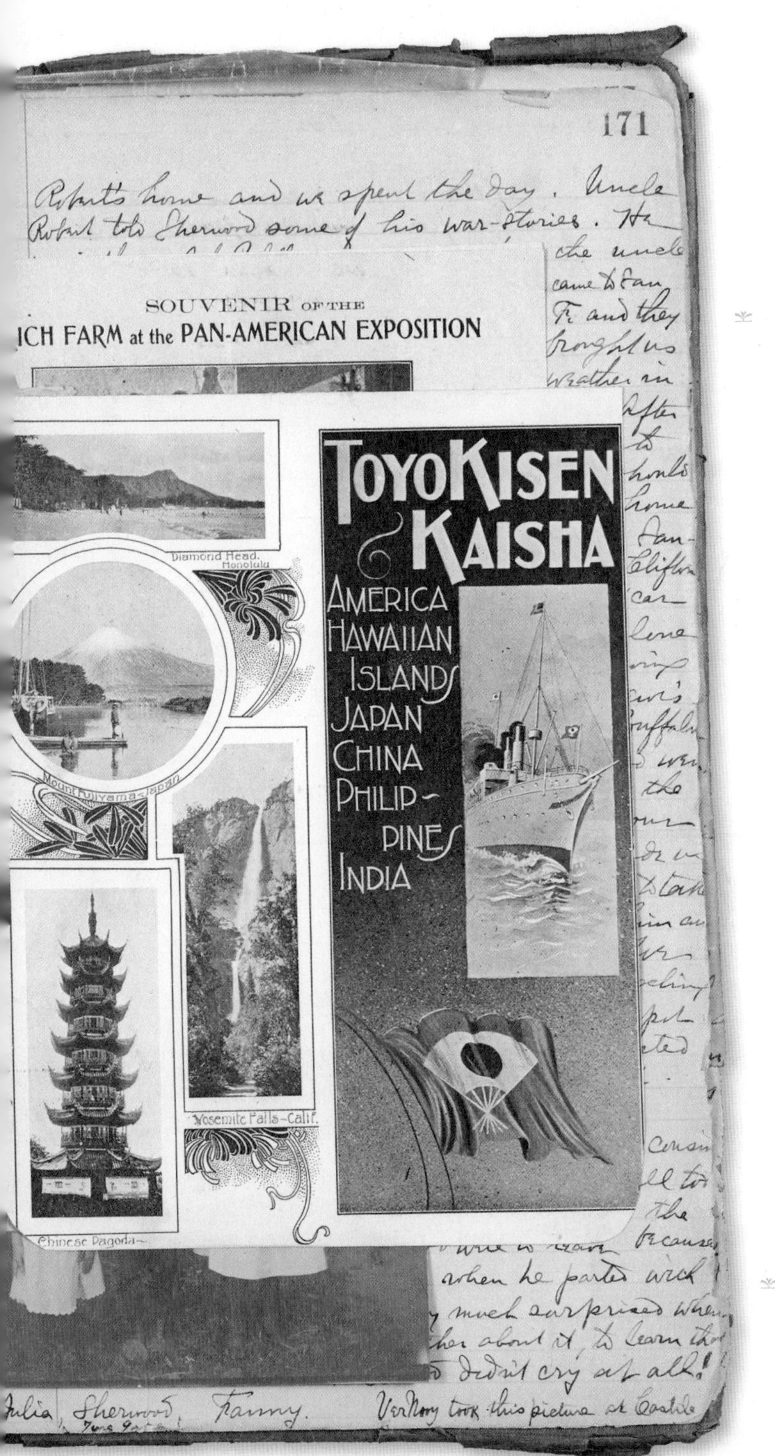
171
Robert's home and we spent the day. Uncle
Robert told Sherwood some of his war-stories. He
SOUVENIR OF THE
ICH FARM at the PAN-AMERICAN EXPOSITION
TOYO KISEN KAISHA
AMERICA
HAWAIIAN
ISLANDS
JAPAN
CHINA
PHILIP-
PINES
INDIA
Diamond Head. Honolulu
Mount Fujiyama-Japan
Yosemite Falls-Calif.
Chinese Pagoda
when he parted with
much surprised when
didn't cry at all!
Julia, Sherwood, Fanny.
VerNooy took this picture at Castile

170-171의 스크랩

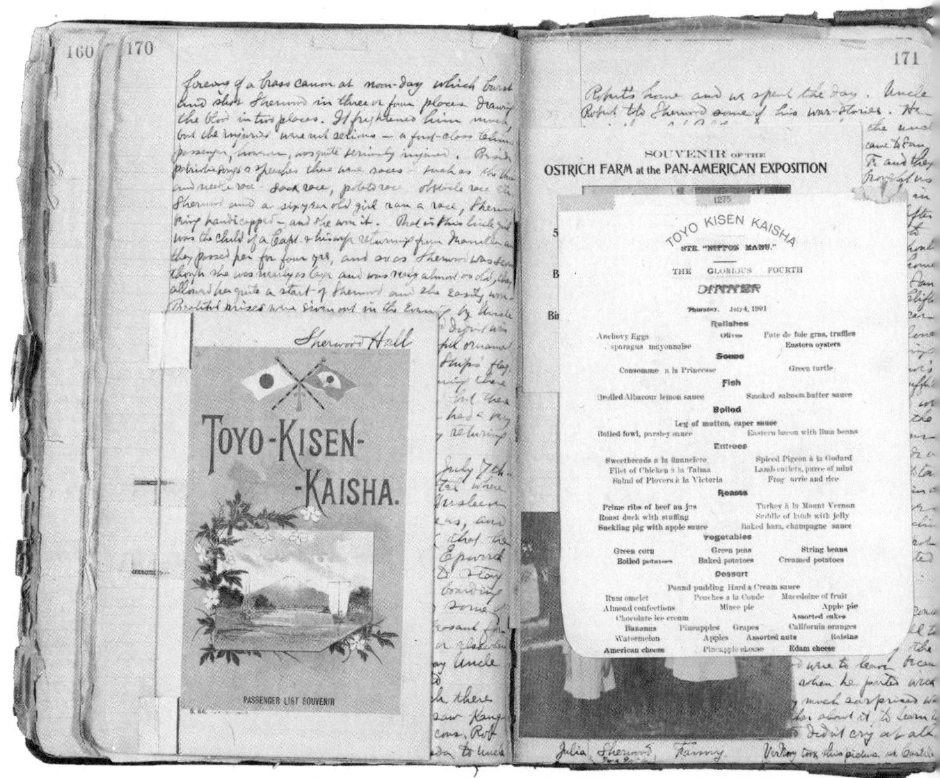

160
170
171
Sherwood Hall
TOYO-KISEN-KAISHA.
PASSENGER LIST SOUVENIR
SOUVENIR OF THE
OSTRICH FARM at the PAN-AMERICAN EXPOSITION
TOYO KISEN KAISHA
THE GLORIOUS FOURTH
DINNER
Thursday, July 4, 1901
Relishes
Anchovy Eggs
Olives
Pate de foie gras, truffles
Eastern oysters
Soups
Consomme a la Princesse
Green turtle
Fish
Smoked salmon butter sauce
Boiled
Leg of mutton, caper sauce
Boiled fowl, parsley sauce
Eastern bacon with lima beans
Entrees
Spiced Pigeon à la Godard
Roasts
Roast duck with stuffing
Suckling pig with apple sauce
Vegetables
Green corn
Green peas
String beans
Boiled potatoes
Baked potatoes
Creamed potatoes
Dessert
Mince pie
Apple pie
Assorted cakes
Bananas
Pineapples
Grapes
California oranges
Watermelon
Apples
Assorted nuts
Raisins
American cheese
Pineapple cheese
Edam cheese

170
171
SOUVENIR OF THE
OSTRICH FARM at the PAN-AMERICAN EXPOSITION
50
Big
Birds.
Seven,
Eight
and
Ten
Feet
High.
WEIGH 250 TO 450 POUNDS.
TOYO-KISEN-
-KAISHA.
PASSENGER LIST SOUVENIR
TOYO KISEN
KAISHA
AMERICA
HAWAIIAN
ISLANDS
JAPAN
CHINA
PHILIP-
PINES
INDIA

160 172

Mamma never touched my
journal from Nov. 10th 1900 until Nov. 10,
and as there is so little space left
it now she thinks it is best to
insert some of our letters to sh
how Sherwood spent his birthday
Christmas etc and not undertake
write much. Sherwood and mam
were separated for eight long m
except for about a 10 days visit in
when she came to get some winter clothes a
to attend the New York Branch Annual me
on her way back to the Sanitarium.

173
CALIFORNIA 1901
FIFTH
INTERNATIONAL CONVENTION OF THE
EPWORTH LEAGUE
SAN FRANCISCO
JULY 18th-21st incl.
Sanitarium, Castile, N.Y.,
Aug. 19th.
My Dear Sherwood,
Just a line to let you

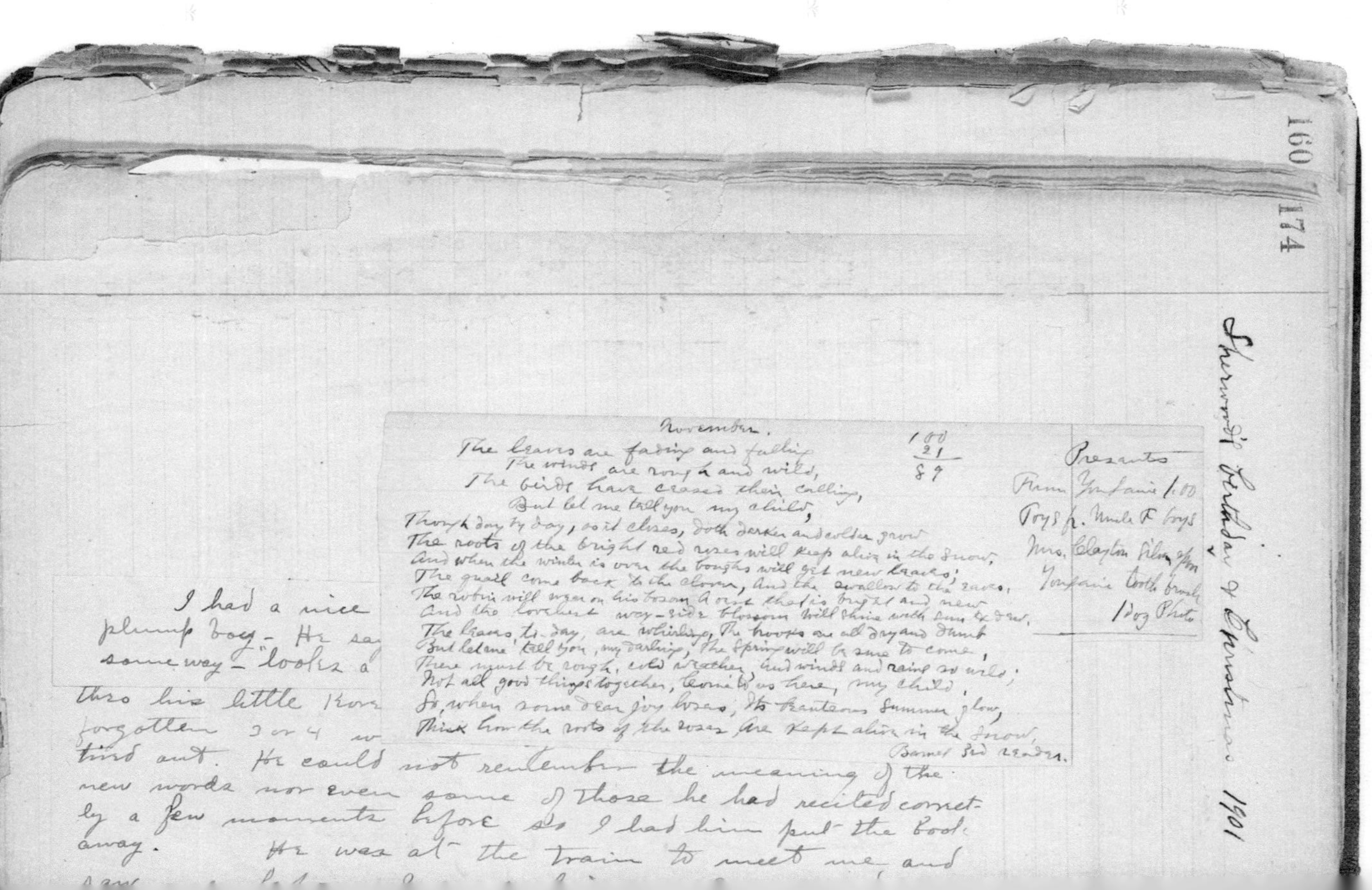

160 174

Sherwood's birthday & Christmas 1901

November.

The leaves are fading and falling,
The winds are rough and wild,
The birds have ceased their calling,
But let me tell you my child,
Though day by day, as it closes, doth darker and colder grow
The roots of the bright red roses will keep alive in the snow,
And when the winter is over the boughs will get new leaves;
The quail come back to the clover, and the swallow to the eaves,
The robin will wear on his bosom a vest that is bright and new
And the loveliest way-side blossom will shine with sun & dew.
The leaves to-day are whirling, the brooks are all dry and dumb
But let me tell you, my darling, the Spring will be sure to come,
There must be rough, cold weather and winds and rains so wild;
Not all good things together, come to us here, my child;
So, when some dear joy loses its beauteous summer glow,
Think how the roots of the roses are kept alive in the snow,

Barnes 3rd reader.

1 00
21
89

Presents

From Grandma 1.00
Toys fr. Uncle F. Toys
Mrs. Clayton Film
Grandma tooth brush
1 Dog Photo

I had a nice
plump boy- He sa[...]
some way - "looks a[...]
thro his little [...]
forgotten 3 or 4 w[...]
tired out. He could not remember the meaning of the
new words nor even some of those he had recited correctly a few moments before so I had him put the book
away. He was at the train to meet me and

175

The only letter Sherwood wrote in his own hand to mamma during their 8 mos. of separation.

Johnstown N.Y.
Mar. 7 1902.

Dear Mamma,
I thought it was time for me to write you a letter. aunt Jen, Belle and Uncle Amos came last week, and four people from Gloversville. Belle and I had a very good time. We played horse and had some fun with the blocks. I cannot think of any more so will close.
Sherwood.

JOHNSTOWN Y. W. C. A.

4 O'CLOCK SERVICE.

The missionary meeting last Sunday afternoon was of special interest. Master Sherwood Hall, who recently came to this country from Korea with his mother, who is a medical missionary, was present and told us some interesting facts concerning the people, also showed pictures and articles of wardrobe worn in Korea. Several papers on the people and their customs were read during the service.

... him, as she was to talk on Korea, Kit... she could & Sherwood was willing to go, + ... home & they were delighted with him. ... the ladies of St. Paul's Lutheran Church ... and now they want him to take his ... d go there this Wed evening + he is going.

160 1 176

Examples of how Sherwood uses the Queen's English
"That book is very inestrating." "Eminately is
the first camera they ever saw." "Don't interrupt
One rainy night at Batum "When I awoke it was pitching
novel way of expressing "it was pouring". "He needs some corp-
ishment" – Telling his mamma one d
a story Dr. Cutler had read him he said "they
little girl a box-chatter, Dr. Cutler says they
child that talks a good deal a boxchatter." "
he got things twisted a little. On the Glenlo
number of terms have been applied to h
he is not used to and he comes and as
ma What does "rude" mean or i
the same as "cheat"? "What does Tommy
mean when she says "I'll tan you"?"

On a street car in N.Y. city
turn he quite convulsed mamma a
how sat near and overheard by remarking
young woman sitting opposite – "Mamma d
think she is nice looking – I don't
face is nice, but her skin is nice.

3. Sherwood and Mama left Liberty on the early morning train for Brooklyn. When we bade Jo and

[illegible] -bye" the evening before, it
if we were sure we were
five yrs work in Korea;
btful on account of the
the Pyeng Yang mis-
n both Sherwood and
, about our going on to
might be back again
e all packed up and
emed right and the
go together.
e blue wool cap that he got
window this morning. He
It cost us 10¢ to open the
get out the blue duck hat
took lunch at Mrs. Vail's
his Bunny there which he
brought with him in a box that Aunt Em gave him.

Later we went over to Brooklyn and were rec'd most kindly by mamma's old school-mate Mi[ss] Temperance Gray who has given $20 to Mama towards Sherwood's return expenses to Korea, and gave $50 to our P.Y.S.A. the first year. We spent about 10 days here, and during that time Sherwood enjoyed visiting Prospect, Bronx and Central Parks also a delightful afternoon and evening at Eden Musee where he saw the Coronation of Edward VII, his King. This was very fine indeed.

" Cablegram came from Korea reading

but in spite of this all our missionary friends on this side thin[k] we should go and after meeting Dr. Cut[ler] and talking the matter over with her. and it seeming to be her sense too that we should return together mamma decided it was right, and asked Dr. Cutler to come over to Brooklyn an[d]

160 178✓

go with us in the morning to Atlantic H
to talk the matter over with Mrs. Skidmore
and if she still approved we were ready to
the night boat for Albany to make a farewell
at Uncle Frank's and ~~on~~ on our way to Canad

Aug. 22nd Morning just as we were all ready to go, S
rec'd a letter from Mrs. Skidm
fficially to return to Korea with
3rd. So from that time mam
the matter settled, but as we
to Atlantic Highlands and mamma
pleasant trip for Dr. Cutler we w
taking his Bunny with him.
at Sherwood made pleasant friend
and some other
leasant
and
joyed the trip w

Aug. 23rd ~~Uncle~~ Frank w
We had a good time

Brockville Aug 26th 1902 Off for Canada
full week at

Glen Buell Aug. 27th Alice and Cousin
came to see us.

At aunt Alice Gray's

Sept. 1st Labor day. We turned back to the U.S. again
way we came. Our baggage by some mistake got way
we didn't know it till the following morning, then the
us it would come the next a.m. but it did not. While
for the "Adirondack" of the Peoples line to start from A
Sherwood had quite a scare – he tho't his mamma
away from him – he felt hurt over it for a lo

Sept 2nd Arrived in N.Y. at 10 a.m. without luggage –
a good part of the day and quite a bit of money trying
where it was, and at last Sherwood who was ca
mamma's belt bag, ~~lost~~ lost that with her purse, go
stamps and all. We were up till 2 a
trying to find it, and visiting two police head-
making our last arrangements for sailing the
morning etc. Got no track of the lost bag or bag

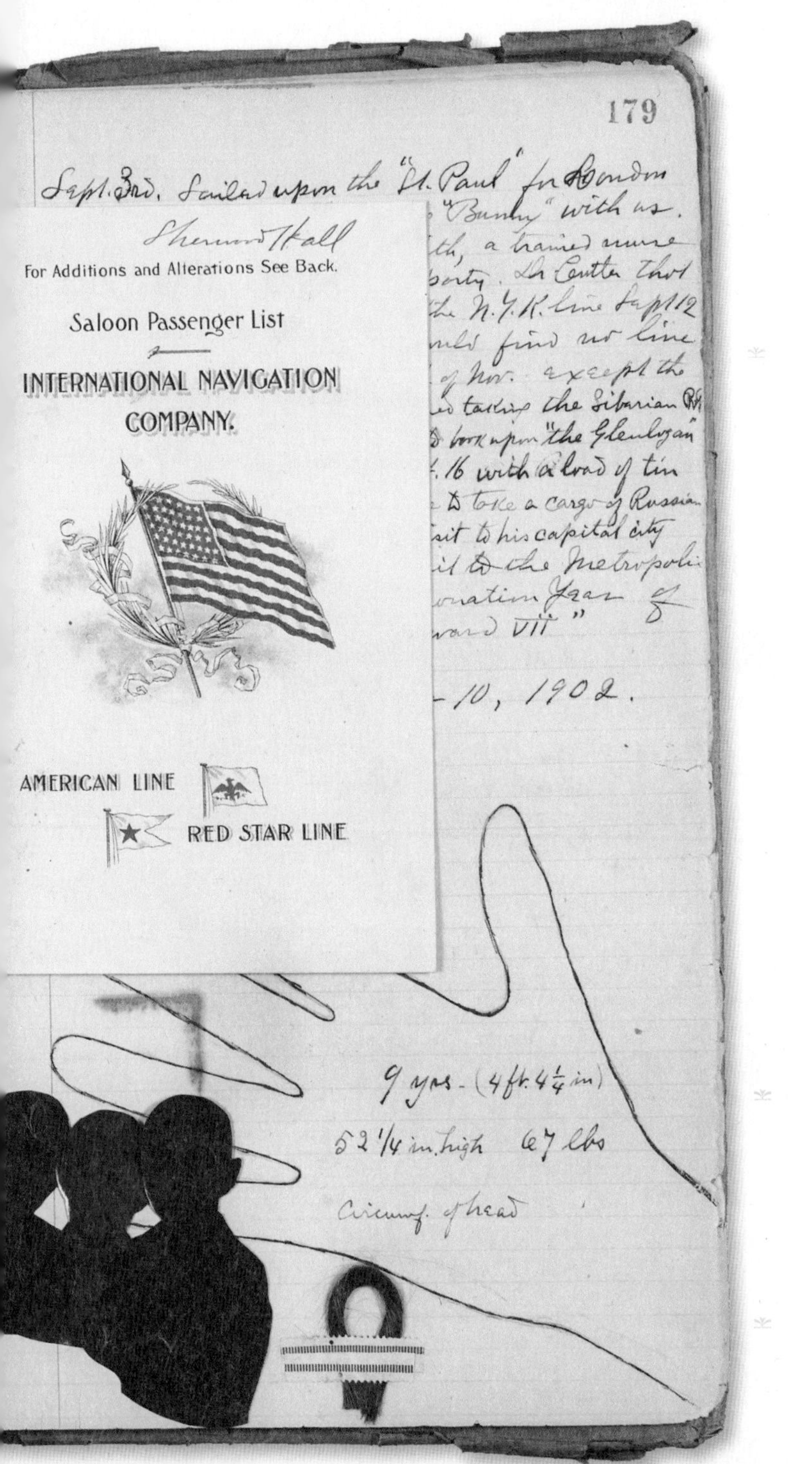
179
Sherwood Hall
For Additions and Alterations See Back.
Saloon Passenger List
INTERNATIONAL NAVIGATION COMPANY.
AMERICAN LINE
RED STAR LINE
Sept. 3rd. Sailed upon the "St. Paul" for London
9 yrs - (4 ft. 4¼ in)
52¼ in. high 67 lbs
Circumf. of head

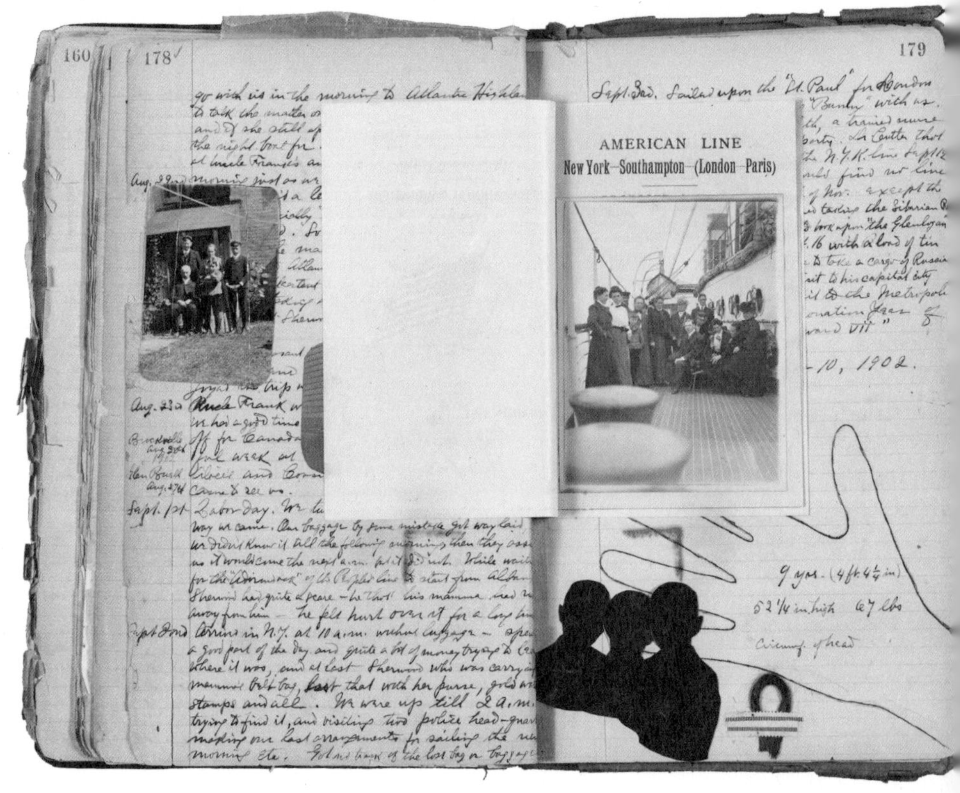
160
178
179
AMERICAN LINE
New York–Southampton–(London–Paris)

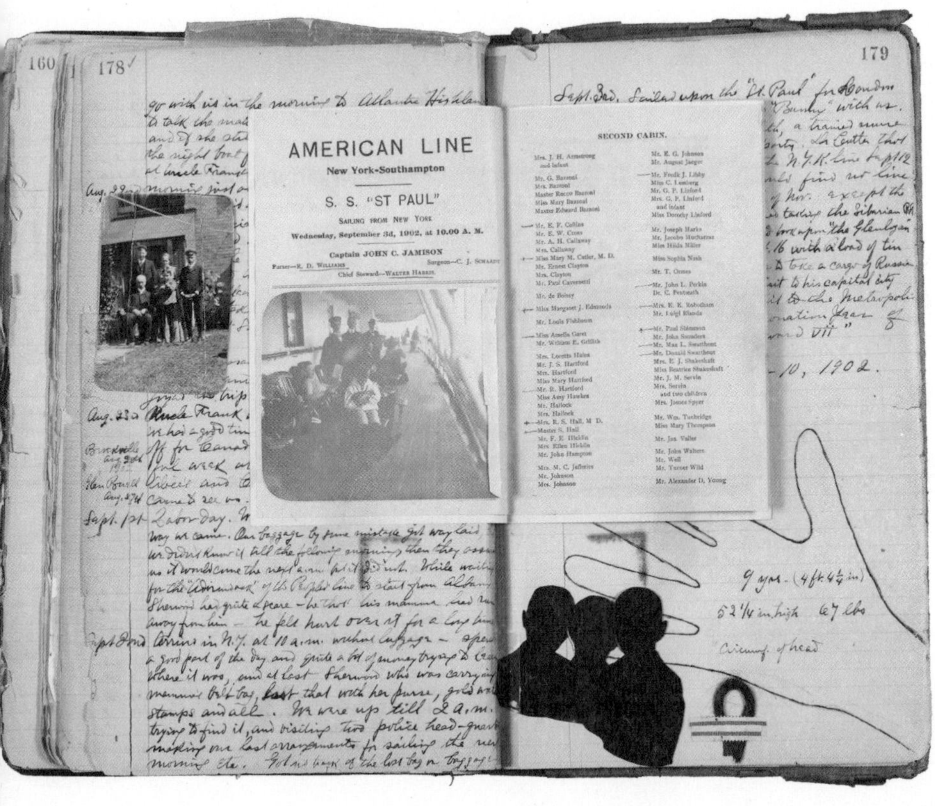
160
178
179
AMERICAN LINE
New York-Southampton
S. S. "ST PAUL"
SAILING FROM NEW YORK
Wednesday, September 3d, 1902, at 10.00 A. M.
Captain JOHN C. JAMISON
Chief Steward—WALTER HARRIS
SECOND CABIN.

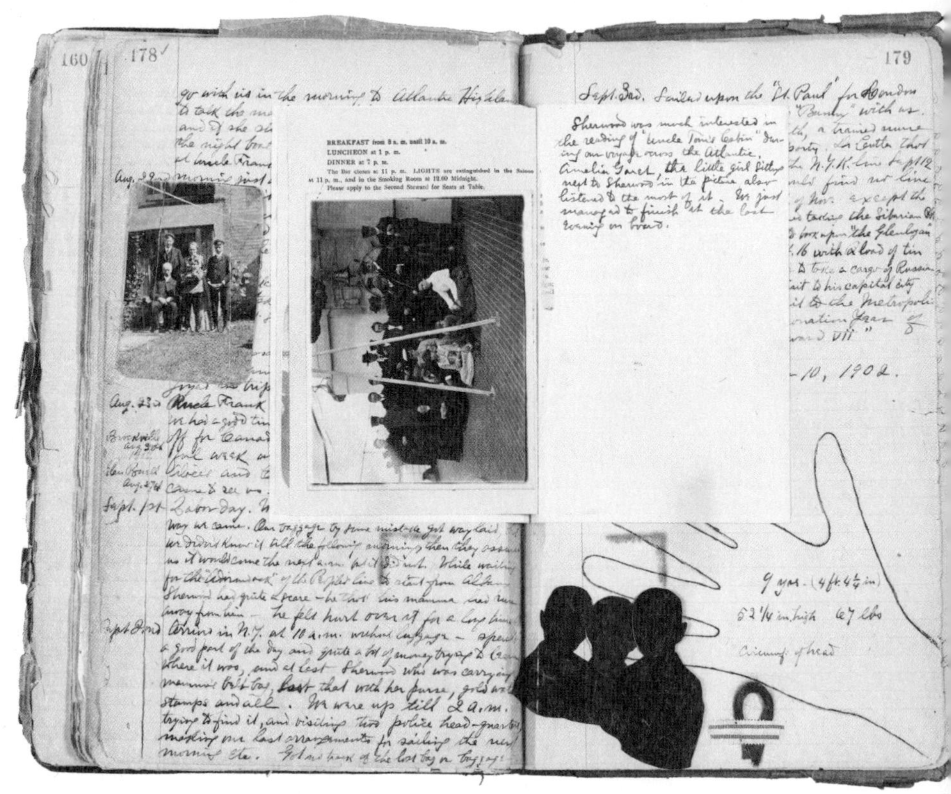
160
178
179
BREAKFAST from 8 a. m. until 10 a. m.
LUNCHEON at 1 p. m.
DINNER at 7 p. m.
The Bar closes at 11 p. m. LIGHTS are extinguished in the Saloon at 11 p. m., and in the Smoking Room at 12.00 Midnight.
Please apply to the Second Steward for Seats at Table.
Sherwood was much interested in the reading of "Uncle Tom's Cabin" during our voyage across the Atlantic. Amelia Garet, the little girl sitting next to Sherwood in the picture also listened to the most of it. We just managed to finish it the last evening on board.

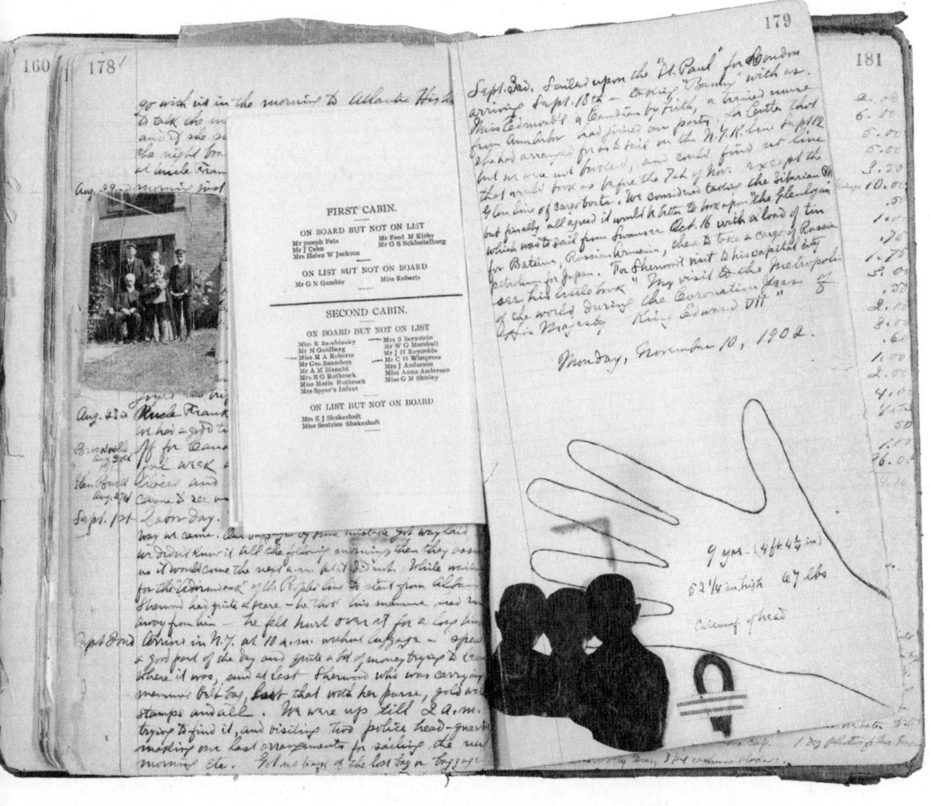
160
178
179
181
FIRST CABIN.
ON BOARD BUT NOT ON LIST
Mr Joseph Fels
Mr J Cohn
Mrs Helen W Jackson
Mr Fred M Kirby
Mr G S Schloetelborg
ON LIST BUT NOT ON BOARD
Mr G N Gamble
Miss Roberts
SECOND CABIN.
ON BOARD BUT NOT ON LIST
Miss R Bacchinsky
Mr M Goldberg
Miss M A Roberts
Mr Geo Saunders
Mr A M Bianchi
Mrs E G Rothrock
Miss Marie Rothrock
Mrs Spyer's Infant
Mrs B Bernstein
Mr W G Marshall
Mr J H Reynolds
Mr C H Wimpress
Mrs J Anderson
Miss Anna Anderson
Miss G M Shirley
ON LIST BUT NOT ON BOARD
Mrs E J Shakeshaft
Miss Beatrice Shakeshaft
Monday, November 10, 1902.

160 180

Sherwood's expenses.

1st year

1st outfit of baby clothes
Horlick's food
Cream and oatmeal
Condensed milk
Pepsin (& postage on it) & other medicines
1 piece of toweling for napkins
1 1/2 doz Arnold's Knit "
1 " inside " "
1 piece Korean cloth for napkins
3 Arnold's Knit bands 1.20 2 Knit night drawers
Worsted for crocheted socks
3 doz photos small
1st short clothes & making
2 pr. Shoes nos 3 & 4
3 prs stockings
Nursery pins & stocking suspenders
Nursing bottles & nipples
Hired help in Korea

Presents,
From Mrs. Jones 1 crocheted hood
" " Scranton 3 prs baby socks
" different Korean friends 6 " Korean baby socks
" Mrs. Moore hood & long cloak
" Mrs. Junkin crocheted powder sacket
" Mrs. Reynolds 1 long white dress.
" Joe for Christmas $1.00
" Mrs. Noble " Baby blanket
" Miss Lewis & Dr. Cutler Baby Elephant & dog
" Xmas tree Knit ball
" Dr. Busteed black-dog (mechanical)

r.	Birthday anniversary dress	2.00
	Baby Carriage fr. Japan	6.00
	Condensed milk	5.00
	Horlick's food	5.00
	Syrup of Figs & Phosphate of sodium	3.50
	3 dresses, 4 aprons, 2 waists 1 hat & muffler in Chicago	10.00
	1 pr. shoes No. 5	.50
	4 prs. stockings	1.00
	3 pr. Shirts gray wool fr. San Francisco	.75
	2 pieces Birdseye diaper	1.75
	1 doz Knit diapers	3.00
	1 pr brown leather Shoes 5 1/2	.50
	2 pr. good heavy shoes No 6.	2.00
	Gingham dresses & aprons & sewing	3.00
	2 cotton shirts at Liberty	.60
	4 pairs muslin drawers	1.00
	1 doz photos, Birthday in Korea	2.00
	1 " " with Grandpa	4.00
	Crib 3.25 Chamber chair 1.25	4.50
	Nursing bottles & nipples	.50
	Silver cup & napkin ring (marked)	1.00
	Hired help in America	96.00
		154.10

Presents

Birthday, from Grandma 1.00
" " Mrs. Noble Light blue flannel dress
" Mrs. Scranton crocheted cap & mittens
{ " Yontaine & Esther fur lined wristlets
" Mary – silk wristlets, Alice, Korean baby socks.
" Sylvia – white silk hood embroidered Korea }
From Mrs. Junkin white Saxony mittens
2 pr. crocheted nightsocks from Mrs. Hulbert
1 night dress from Miss Lewis also 2 night shirts
Heavy overcoat fr. Henry Appenzeller – had also been worn by Allen boy.
1 Gingham dress from Aunt Emma, embroidered by Cous Eva.
1 child's coat trimmed with Angora fur from Mrs Junkins
From Uncle Robert in San Francisco $20 gold piece
" Cous. Mr. Sherwood Binghamton $5.00. Mr. Webster 5.00
Grand ma Hall blue felt Turk's cap. 1 doz photos fr Mr. Gerber
Cous. Polly Cray 3 prs cashmere stockings.

160 182

3rd yr

3 prs red wool drawers
1 black wool drawer leggins
1 pr arctic rubbers no 6 1/2
1 pr brown Saxony mitten
1 pr. Shoes no. 7
1 " rubbers no 8
1 bottle Syrup of Figs
3 prs drawers size 3 @ 29c (muslin)
Mouth organ
Stocking supporters
1 large sized bottle Syrup of Figs
2 pr. drawers
2 Ferris waists @ 35
2 pr drawers
1st suite of clothes (with pants size age 4) (Sailor waist size age 3)
2 prs pants, age 5
1 Shirt waist
1 pr. Shoes & 1 necktie
1 bottle Syrup of Figs
2 bottles chocolate emulsion cod-liver oil
Hired help $100 (1/2 of cost) Board July, Aug & Sept $6.00 106.
122

Presents, Birthday Grandma silver dollar,
Christmas from Josie tooth-brush, Toys & books
From Mrs. Clayton "5 Points" silver spoon. From Joe, ...
" Velt - coat & cap

4th yr - That is from 3rd birth-day to 4th
Birthday presents, from grandma a new pair of shoes
" " " Aunt Annie, hair cut ...
" " " Joe pr. mittens, from ...
Christmas, from Miss Botner toy watch & chain, ...
rocking-horse. Candy & nuts from Jamie Interman & ...
1 gloss cap & leather purse & colored hdkf from Joe. ...
1 Victoria Jubilee hdkf. from Aunt Jane. $1 from Grandma
$1 from Grandma Sherwood - 1 china plate from Auntie Powell - ...
from Mamma -

Suite of clothes - brown 5 yrs	1.98 (?)
1 Rocking horse	2.98
Blue overcoat 5 yrs old	2.98
Tuition at Miss Naumann's school for Feb.	2.00
" " " " " " Mch	2.00
2 gingham aprons	70
1 blue sailor suite	1.00
1 Yellow blouse	69
2 Shirt waists	58
To Mrs. Barnth for care	4.00
1 cap at O'Neils	75
3 cheap caps	75
1 pr Shoes 8½ c J.Y.	1.50
1 " " heavy Liberty	1.00
Medicine	50
1 nice Straw hat, Bloomingdale's	1.50
1 thin blue-black wool sailor suite	1.98
1 thick wool " pants	50
1 brown " " 50 2 prs knit drawers 50	1.00
1 blue calico waist	45
Syr. Fig. 40 Choc. emulsion 75	1.15
Trav. ex. food, fruit etc in U.S.	1.50
At Commercial Hotel	70
Food from St. Paul to Vancouver	52
Tips	1.75
Toys in Japan	.73
S.S. ticket Van Couver to Nagasaki	80.75 (?)
Jinrickishas in Japan	.50
Board for 9 days in "	2.50
Steamer ticket to Chemulpo	7.00
	$124.94

160 184

Nov. 10th 97 to Nov. 10 '98.

Board at Stewards
Freight, duty & expenses enroute
1 chair bamboo
1 pr. Shoes no 10 at Russian store $1.50 repair in
1 " goloshes " " " "
1 " Shoes from N. Y. no. 10
2 prs wool stockings" Elastic 20
Syr Figs. & medicine
2 caps (cheap) tin N. Y. 1 in Japan
Coolie hire for rickshaw 25c
1/18 of Household stores, fuel etc
1/18 Chicago order
" San Fran order
1/18 English order
1/18 Dec Household acct
Kept no account after going to Pyeng
While at Uncle Frank's – Shoes repair 15c
Cough Med. 20, cap 35, Suit 3.50
Rubbers? 15 – waist 25, Overshoes 1.00
Shirt & drawers 50, writing book 10
Shoes 75c, pants 39c suspenders 15
Rubbers 15 total

185
A lock of
hair on
birthday
Sept. 10th
1906-
This "first-teen"

160
186
188

HOLIDAY GREETINGS
NINTH YEAR

160
May this Season be
sorrow free.

Journal of Sherwood Hall
from birth in Seoul, Korea, Nov. 10, 1893
until able to write for himself Nov. 10, 1902
[illegible] glimpses of his first term, 1906

Sent by Dr. Sherwood, at the
request of Pastor Scott of Liberty, N.Y.
thru' Miss [illegible] who bro't it across
the Pacific in the U.S.A. evacuation
boat "Mariposa", and mailed from
[illegible], Calif., arriving at
[illegible], Dec. 7th, 1940.

2부

번역본

셔우드 홀 육아일기
1893.11.10-1902.11.10

그가 우리에게 약속하신 것은 이것이니
곧 영원한 생명이니라(요한1서 2:25)

[앞표지 덧싸개]

셔우드 홀의 육아일기.
1893년 11월 10일 출생부터 혼자 글을 쓸 수 있게 된 1902년 11월 10일까지.
그리고 1906년 사춘기의 첫 모습.
얼 스콧(Earl Scott) 목사의 요청으로 런드(Lund) 양이 미국으로 가져왔고
미 세관에서 우편으로 보내왔다.

[앞표지]

셔우드 홀의 육아일기
1893.11.10-1902.

[앞날개]

《닥터 윌리엄 제임스 홀 목사의 생애》
-뉴욕 슬럼가의 의료선교사, 한국 평양의 개척 선교사
-그의 아내 로제타 셔우드 홀 박사 편집
-윌라드 F. 말랄리우 감리교 감독의 서문
-뉴욕시 5번가 150번지 이턴 & 메인즈 출판사에 주문할 수 있음
-가격 $1.50(우송료 포함)

이 역사(책)은 조선이라는 나라에서 일어난 사건, 생활 및 관습을 생생하게 묘사하고 있다.
따라서 한국인의 모든 것에 관심 있는 대중에게 사랑하는 홀 의사의 생애에 대한
기록으로서의 가치와 더불어 두 배의 기쁨을 줄 것이다. -〈크리스천 헤럴드〉
이 책을 진심으로 추천한다. 이 책은 젊은이들의 마음에 거룩한 삶을 살며 영혼을
구원하고픈 진지한 열망을 고무시키는 데 크게 기여할 것이다. -〈코리안리포지터리〉
말랄리우 감독은 홀 박사를 영웅이자 순교자라고 말한다. 그의 《생애》는 그가 평범한 의무를
넘어선 일을 하고 있다는 것을 전혀 의식하지 못했으며, 그의 행복은 부름 받은 임무가 있는

곳에 있었다는 것을 보여 준다. 이 이야기가 전해지는 곳마다 선이 행해지지 않을 수 없다.
-〈크리스천 애드보케이트〉
이 책은 자기 부인과 사랑에 관한 단순한 이야기로 우리를 고양시키는 홀 박사의 삶에 대한 기록 외에도 한국의 관습과 그 민족에 대한 가치 있는 서술이다. -〈우먼즈 미셔너리 프렌드〉
이웃을 위한 힘든 투쟁과 고귀한 봉사에 대한 감동적인 이야기. *** 400 페이지가 넘는 이 책은 잘 편집되었고, 영웅적인 세계 선교사들의 도서관에 더해질 것이다.
-〈메디컬 미셔너리 레코드〉

1 **[시병원 광고]**
대개 하나님이 세상을 사랑하사 그 외아들 예수 그리스도 씨를 주어 무릇 믿는 자는 망함을 면하고 길이 삶을 얻을 것이요 믿지 않는 자는 길이 죽고 영혼을 구하지 못하느니라
죄를 사하여 주시리라
시병원(施病院)
경대정동미국호의원(京大貞洞美國胡醫員)

2 **셔우드의 옷**
"오, 어머니로서 할 수 있는
가장 달콤한 일은
앙증맞은 옷을 만드는 것이다."

첫 배내옷(5번) 첫 긴 드레스 2번 포대기(2번) 담요(2번)
담요(2번) 치마(2번) 긴 속치마(1번) 흰 속치마(2번) 긴 속치마(1번) 흰 속치마(2번)
첫 짧고 흰 드레스(4번) 첫 체크무늬 드레스(4번) 첫 짧은 드레스(2번)
첫 잠옷(2번) 짧은 드레스 망토

3 첫 앞치마들 2번 첫 짧고 흰 플란넬 속치마(2)
첫 짧은 플란넬 속치마(2번) 겨울 앞치마(1) 겨울 앞치마(2)
셔우드 생일 기념 드레스 2번째 잠옷
노블 부인이 준 생일 선물 드레스 2벌 소매 없는 앞치마(2)
꽤맨 블라우스(4) 드레스 위에 입는 블라우스(2) 크레이프 플란넬 블라우스

4 "셔우드는 파란 플란넬 옷이 많다. 시카고에서 재단한 옷감을 가져왔고, 젠켄스(Jenkens) 부인이 재단된 회색과 흰색 바탕에 갈색 줄무늬가 쳐진 옷을 주셨다. 앙고라 털로 테를 두른, 흰색과 회색이 섞인 두꺼운 외투도 주셨다."

잠옷(2) 겨울 앞치마(1) 여름 바지(2)와 윗도리(1) 1898

역동적인 진화

다른 조건들이 같을 경우, 당신의 위대함은 당신의 친할아버지와 당신의 나이 차와 정비례한다는 것을 알게 될 것이다. 그 차이가 50년이 채 되지 않는다면 당신이 탁월하게 될 가능성은 거의 없다.
홀트 앤 코(Holt & Co) 출판사에서 출간한 이 책의 저자인 시카고의 캐스퍼 베드필드(Casper Bedfield)는 누구든지 역사 속에서 위의 말이 틀린 예를 하나라도 찾아서 자신에게 보여 준다면 1,000달러를 주겠다고 했다. 그는 역사상 가장 위대한 인물 10명의 아버지들의 평균 나이가 그들의 유명한 아들들이 태어났을 때 55세가 넘었었다는 사실에 주목했다.

"너의 친할아버지(Grandpa Hall)가 태어난 해 1826년, 셔우드 홀이 태어난 해 1893년, 67년 차이."

5 "우리는 하나님을 믿는다."

6 "내가 태어난 집" 1899년 여름.

[일기 원본 7–8쪽 없음]

9 그가 우리에게 약속하신 것은 이것이니 곧 영원한 생명이니라(요한1서 2:25).

미스바

우리가 서로 떠나 있을 때 주께서 나와 너를 살펴 주시기를.

오늘 하루를 감싸는 믿음의 작은 울타리를 지어라,
그 공간을 사랑스러운 행동으로 채우고 그 안에 머물라,
내일을 둘러싸고 있는 담 너머를 쳐다보지 말아라,
하나님께서 너를 견디도록 도우시리라, 기쁨이든 슬픔이든.
미국 주일학교 협회
성서공회(Bible House), 뉴욕.

10 1893년 11월 10일, 금요일, 오전 10시

그의 평생을 여호와께 드리나이다(사무엘상 1:28)

"갓 태어난 아기, 부드러운 분홍빛 아기.
눈 깜짝할 사이에 두 세상을 접했네."

사랑스럽고 조그만 사내 아기가 여기 있다. "우리 아가." 엄마가 아기에게 첫인사를 했다. 아기는 한국의 10번째 달 10일[1] 10시에 태어났다. 엄마가 바랐던 바로 그날, 셔우드 외할아버지[2]의 생일날 태어난 것이다. 외할아버지는 오늘로 89세가 되셨다. 아기는 9파운드의 큰 사내아이이고 이름은 셔우드 홀(Sherwood Hall)이다. 아기는 아주 참을성이 많은 것 같다. 이때껏 딱 한 번 울었을 뿐인데, 자기 폐가 건강하다는 사실을 알리기에 적당한 만큼만 울었다. 그 후로는 하루 종일 아주 조용했다. 아기는 예쁘게 생기지는 않았다. 아기치곤 긴 코에 '전형적인 남자아이' 모습이다. 성장하면서 얼굴이 더 예뻐지리라 믿어 의심하지 않는다. 아기 셔우드는 진짜 파란 눈을 가졌는데, 한국인 눈처럼 동양적으로 눈꼬리가 살짝 올라가 있지만 엄마 눈에는 너무나 아름답게 보인다. 입은 아주 예쁘고, 귀도 잘생겼다. 지금은 이마가 약간 좁아 보이지만 크고 둥근 두상을 가지고 있다. 그리고 손톱은 더할 나위 없이 예쁘다. 아빠처럼 손가락이 길지만 손은 엄마 손을 더 닮은 것 같다. 아기는 마른 편이며, 키가 크고 예쁜 몸매다. 발은 장미 꽃잎을 물들인 것처럼 예쁘다. 하지만 어느 아기인들 이런 예쁜 발을 가지지 않았으랴? 루이스(E. A. Lewis)[3] 양이 셔우드의 첫 목욕을 시켰다. 이 작은 '하나님의 미소의 화신'에 얼마나 감사한지.

11 11월 12일, 일요일 – 아기 셔우드가 오늘 처음으로 미소 지었다. 아주 착한 아기다. 아빠는 거의 하루 종일 아기를 책장 위 아기 바구니에 뉘여 놓고 있다. 그레이트하우스(C. R. Greathouse)[4] 부인이 아기를 보러 오셨다. 에스더 이모가 아기를 씻겨 주었다.

11월 26일, 일요일 – 엄마가 처음으로 셔우드를 씻겼다. 셔우드의 주치의 커틀러(M. M. Cutler)[5] 박사가 방문하셨다.

11월 30일, 목요일, 추수감사절 – 아기 셔우드에게 긴 흰색 드레스와 분홍색 테를 두른 예쁜 모직 아기 겉옷을 입혔다. 지금까지 셔우드는 자그마한 연하늘색 배내옷을 입고 있었다. 오늘 이후부터 당분간 아빠는 집에 계시지 않을 것이다. 아빠는 내일 평양으로 떠나신다. 셔우드는 1파운드가 늘었고, 생후 4일째부터 앓았던 황달도 거의 다 나았다. 이 기간 동안 셔우드는 변비가 너무 심해서 매일 관장을 해주어야 했다. 이 외에는 달리 힘들게 하는 것 없이 건강하게 잘 자라고 있다.

"아기 셔우드에게 첫 목욕을 시켜 준 루이스 양"

12월 25일, 월요일, 크리스마스

재난은 티끌에서 일어나는 것이 아니며 고생은 흙에서 나는 것이 아니니라(욥 5:6)

"하지만 슬픔은 이기적이다. 나는 모르겠다.
왜 내가 항상 다른 사람들보다 더 많이 아파야 하는지.
하지만 나는 안다. 그들을 위해서도 나를 위해서도
하나님은 최선을 다하신다는 것을."[6]

셔우드는 아빠가 떠난 바로 그날부터 아프기 시작했다. 그리고 한 달간 심하게 아팠다. 급성 위염에 걸린 것 같다. 엄마는 식이요법을 했고, 음료를 많이 마셨다. 그리고 작고 사랑스런 우리 아기에게 엄마 젖이 잘 맞도록 최선을 다했다. 처음에는 엄마 젖이 잘 맞는 것
12 같았으나 어린 아기의 장이 극도로 예민한 단계에 접어들면서부터 엄마 젖이 너무 기름졌던 것 같다. 그래서 12월 1일부터는 하루 24시간 동안 약간의 보리차와 젖 두세 번밖에 먹지 못한 것 같다. 생후 6주가 되었을 때 아기 몸무게는 태어날 때보다 조금 덜 나가게 되었고, 이웃들은 우리 아기가 이 세상에 오래 있지 않을 거라고 생각하기 시작했다. 이즈음 아빠가 집에 오셨다. 아빠도 같은 생각으로 두려워하면서 때때로 아기가 그를 주신 하나님께로 돌아간다는 생각을 엄마가 받아들일 수 있도록 애써 말해 주셨다.
아빠가 함께 계신다는 것, 그 자체가 엄마는 물론 아기에게도 큰 도움이 된다는 사실이 곧 입증되었다. 책임을 나누고 짐을 가볍게 해주는 사람이 있으니 어린 셔우드는 금세 눈에 띄게 좋아졌다.

아기가 아팠던 기간 중 후반기 기록
12월 13일-새벽 2시부터 14일 새벽 2시까지 젖 한 번 먹은 것 빼고 모두 토했다.
12월 14일-오후 1시까지 음식을 받아먹었으나 다음 날 새벽 2시까지 아무것도 먹지 못했고, 보리차조차 마시지 못했다.
12월 15일-새벽 4시에 먹은 젖을 토했다. 10시에 보리차를 먹였다. 정오에 우유와 물을

조금 주었다. 4시에 먹은 것은 모두 토했다. 밤 10시와 자정에 먹은 것은 토하지 않았다.
12월 16일-6시에 먹은 것을 모두 토했다. 10시와 자정에 먹은 것은 소화해 냈으나 4시에 먹은 것은 모두 토했다. 7시에 먹은 것은 토하지 않았다. 지난 사흘간 20개의 비스무트(Bismuth)와 췌장 효소(Pancreatine) 분말을 먹였다. 약으로 인해 대변 색깔이 검게 변했고, 하루 한 번밖에 변을 보지 못했다. 주사를 주지 않으면 이것마저도 누지 못한다. 아기가 변을 보고 싶어서 안절부절못하면서도 변을 보지 못할 때 젖을 먹이면 토할 것이 분명하다.
밤 9시-보리차를 마셨고, 잠을 자고 싶어 했다.
정오-물.
새벽 2시-물과 우유.
새벽 6시-물과 우유.
12월 17일-오전 9시 보리차.
오전 10시-물과 우유. 조금 토했다. 다시 변을 보기 어려워진 것 같다. 11시에 관장제(enema) 4드램[7]을 주었다. 그 후에는 잠을 자고 싶어 했고, 오후 2시까지 잤는데, 변을 보지 못했다. 불편해서 다시 잠을 깼다. 한 번 더 관장을 해주고, 변을 보기 전에 젖을 주었다. 모두 토했는데, 산(acid)이 약간 올라왔다.
오후 5시 30분-젖을 주었으나 모두 토했다.
저녁 7시-보리차, 그전에 변을 조금 보았다.
저녁 9시-물과 우유를 받아들였다.
새벽 1시-물과 우유를 받아들였다.
12월 18일-새벽 5시, 물과 우유를 받아들였다.
오전 8시 30분-칼로멜(Calomel) 분말과 관장.
오전 9시-젖을 거의 다 토했다.
오후 5시-글리세린(Glycerine)을 사용해서 관장을 계속 해주었다.
후에 커다란 변이 나왔다. 분말 3봉지를 주었다. 밤에 잘 잤다.
12월 19일-다시 토했다. 다시 변을 보고 싶어 불편해하는 것 같았다. 관장을 해주자 변이 잘 나왔다. 산성기가 있었다. 저녁 내내 잤다. 밤 9시에 젖을 먹였더니 3시 30분까지 잤다.
12월 20일-오전 6시에 일어나서 변을 보고 싶어 했다. 뜨거운 물을 주지 않았다.
오전 7시까지 울었지만 변을 볼 수 없었다. 글리세린을 사용해서 관장을 해주었다.
커다란 변이 나왔다. 젖을 먹은 후 잠들었다. 오후 3시 30분이 넘을 때까지 괜찮았지만 그 시각 이후 저녁 내내 잘 쉬지 못했다. 오후 5시에 관장을 해주었지만 가스만 나왔다.
저녁 8시-잠을 자지 못해서 한 번 더 관장을 해주었더니 아주 큰 변이 나왔다. 젖을 먹고 바로 잠이 들었다. 밤에 잠을 잘 잤다. 새벽 1시와 오전 6시에만 젖을 먹였다.
12월 21일-아침 먹은 후 관장을 하니 초록색 변이 나왔다. 산성변이었다. 오전에 잠깐 잤는데, 나머지 시간과 저녁에는 거의 자지 못했다. 장이 불편한 것 같았다.
오후 5시에 한 번 더 관장을 해주니 초록색 변을 보았다. 점액이 아주 많았다.

물에 펩신(Pepsin)을 타서 워든 비스무트 우유(Worden's Milk of Bismuth) 10 미님[8]과 함께 주었다. 젖을 줄 때마다 조금씩 토했는데, 7시에 먹은 젖은 거의 다 토했다.
12월 22일-셔우드는 조금 나아진 것 같다. 아빠가 집에 돌아오셨다.
12월 23일-셔우드는 하루 종일 아주 잘 지냈다. 물에서 잠이 들었다.
빨리 통통해지라고 아빠가 아기를 깨워 젖을 먹게 했다. 이 작고 사랑스러운 아기는 밤새 아파서 꼬박 12시간 동안 다시 잠을 자지 못했다.
12월 24일-다시 나아졌다.
12월 25일-보리차와 엄마 젖 그리고 펩신을 먹고 변을 아주 잘 보았다.
12월 26일-홀릭스(Horlicks)[9] 식품을 주기 시작했다.

오늘 셔우드는 알렌(H. Allen)[10] 댁 남자 아이들로부터 크리스마스 트리를 보러 오라는 초대를 받았다. 하지만 그 댁에 갈 수 있을 정도로 회복된 것은 아니었다. 모두들 셔우드를 기억하면서 장난감을 보내왔다. 다른 아기들은 다 참석했다.
셔우드는 크리스마스 선물을 아주 많이 받았다. 무어(R. E. Moore)[11] 부인께서 아름다운 외투와 모자를 주셨고, 레이놀즈(W. D. Reynolds)[12] 부인은 예쁜 드레스를, 노블(W. A. Noble)[13] 부인은 멋진 담요를, 김 부인과 노 루시(Lucy No)는 버선 한 켤레씩을 주셨다. 그리고
13 버스티드(J. B. Busteed)[14] 박사님은 검정털 점핑 강아지를 주셨다.
앓고 있는 우리 아기에게 아주 즐거운 크리스마스였다. 아기는 밤과 아침에 계속 관장을 받아야 한다.

1894년 1월 10일-셔우드가 태어난 지 2개월이 되었고, 몸무게는 10파운드다. 이제는 엄마 젖과 홀릭스 식품을 번갈아서 잘 먹고 있다. 아빠는 오늘 다시 평양으로 출발하셨다. 8주에서 10주 동안 못 오실 것이다.
보모가 셔우드를 잘 돌보고 있어 엄마에게도 큰 도움이 되고 있다.

하지만 그녀에게도 어린 아이와 남편이 있기 때문에 밤에는 우리 집에 머물러 있을 수 없다. 그래서 그녀는 낮에 많은 일을 힘들게 해야 한다. 아빠가 출타 중일 때는 자주 앓는 셔우드를 11시나 12시까지 돌보기도 하고, 새벽 5시나 6시쯤 다시 오기도 한다.
보모는 아기 빨래와 다림질을 하고, 불을 살피고, 집안일도 한다.
하지만 아빠는 이번에 떠나면서 밤에도 함께 있어 줄 수 있는 사람을 한 명 더 구하는 게 좋겠다고 하셨다. 지난 번 출타할 때 그렇게 했더라면 엄마와 아기에게 큰 도움이 되었을 텐데 하면서 그때는 왜 이 생각을 못했는지 안타까워했다. 엄마가 지치고 잘 쉬지 못하면 그 영향이 아기에게 미치게 마련일 뿐 아니라, 가녀린 몸집의 충성되고 착한 보모는 다가오는 봄에 우리와 평양에 갈 수 없으므로 평양에 함께 갈 수 있는 사람을 미리 구해서 보모가 없을 때 도울 수 있도록 훈련시켜 놓는 게 좋을 것 같다.

1월 29일 – 오늘부터 노 씨의 죽은 동생의 아내인 '실비아'(Sylvia)가 와서 일을 하기 시작했다. 이 불쌍한 여인을 좋아하게 되리라는 생각이 든다. 진실로 실비아는 이 세상에 아무도 없는 외톨이다. 부모님은 모두 돌아가셨고, 남편도 최근 사망했으며, 유일한 자식인 어린 딸도 우리 여학교에서 발생한 화재로 사망했다. 실비아는 종종 슬퍼하면서, 번 돈을 줄 사람도 없는데 왜 벌어야 하느냐고 말한다. 하지만 그녀는
18 남편 장례를 치르면서 아빠에게 10불의 빚을 졌으므로 적어도 그만큼의 돈은 벌려고 한다. [일기 원본 14–17쪽(15–16쪽 없음)][15]
그 금액을 모으게 될 쯤이면 셔우드와 우리 집안일에 흥미를 갖게 될 것이고, 다시 한 번 '인생은 살만한 가치가 있다'고 느끼게 될 것이다.

그녀는 기독교인이므로 평양에서도 많은 도움이 될 것이다.

1894년 2월 6일, 한국 설날 - 이제 셔우드는 11파운드가 나간다. 변비에 걸린 것만 빼면 꽤 건강하다. 셔우드는 웃기도 하고 옹알이를 하며 거의 하루 종일 아주 밝다. 오랫동안 바구니에 누워서 예쁜 자기 손가락을 가지고 노는데, 마치 엄마가 우리 아가 손가락을 좋아하는 것만큼 자기 손가락을 좋아하는 것 같다. 우리 아기는 또 바구니 옆에 파란색 리본으로 묶여 있는 반지를 가지고 노는 것을 좋아하는데, 바구니에 부딪혀 딸랑 소리가 나도록 그것을 손으로 친다. 가끔 이렇게 30분가량 놀기도 한다. 우리 아기는 또 천장에 달린 한국식 등 아래 누워 있는 것을 좋아한다. 이 등 밑에는 작은 밀랍 아기 인형이 달렸는데, 셔우드는 그것을 한참 동안 쳐다보면서 귀엽게 웃으며 말을 건다. 엄마의 한국어 선생님도 셔우드에게 매우 친절하고, 셔우드도 선생님을 좋아한다. 선생님의 부인이 셔우드에게 예쁜 버선을 두 켤레 보내 주셨다. 하나는 비단으로 만든 것이고, 하나는 모직으로 만든 것인데, 둘 다 비단실로 수놓여 있다.

1894년 3월 10일 - 셔우드는 4개월이 되었다. 몸무게 12파운드,
키 24인치, 머리 둘레 16인치다. 지난 달 며칠 동안 무척 아팠는데,
지금은 다시 많이 좋아졌다. 아직도 관장을 해야 하지만, 외할머니[16]의
19 제안으로 3주 전부터 작은 '요강'을 사용하고 있다. 이 방법은
기저귀를 채우는 것보다 쉽고, 셔우드가 그 위에 앉아 있는 모습은
아주 그럴싸해 보인다. 셔우드가 낑낑 소리를 내면서 자기가 신고 있는
작은 빨간색 양말을 내려다보고 있는 동안 보모가 셔우드의 웃옷을

붙잡고 등을 받쳐 준다. 종종 너무 힘들어 눈물을 흘리기도 하지만, 우리 아기는 아주 용감한 꼬마 사내다. 그렇게 긴 시간이 지난 다음에는 기분이 좋아진다.

요즘 셔우드는 2주가 넘도록 커다란 헝겊으로 만든 인형의 얼굴을 쳐다보는 것을 좋아한다. 인형을 쓰다듬고 옹알옹알 인형에게 말을 거는데, 어떨 때는 정말 재미있게 인형을 가지고 논다. 이 헝겊 인형은 한국 사내아이 옷을 입고 있다. 보모는 인형을 셔우드의 '형'이라고 부른다. 우리 아기는 또 엄마의 선생님이 주신 한국 딸랑이를 흔들면서 노는 것을 좋아한다.

오늘이 셔우드의 생일[17]이기 때문에 데리고 '나가'(out)[18]고 싶었지만 비가 왔다. 우리 아가는 사흘 전에 처음으로 외출해서 노블 목사님이 잔디 씨 뿌리는 것을 보고 왔다.

3월 12일 – 셔우드가 어린 맥스 스크랜턴 양을 방문해서 그 아이를 보며 옹알이를 했는데 아주 사랑스러웠다.

3월 17일 – 거의 10주 만에 아빠가 돌아오셨다. 셔우드는 노래를 불러 주는 사람이 다시 온 것을 아주 좋아했다. 셔우드는 아빠와 함께 즐겁게 놀면서 곧잘 아빠의 수염을 잡아당긴다. 아빠는 자기 아들에 대해 아는 것이 거의 없다. 그사이 우리 아기는 예쁘게 많이 변했으며 지금 아주 건강하고 행복하다. 그리고 아빠와 즐겁게 지내고 있다.

1894년 4월 10일

어린아이에게 끌리며(이사야 11:6)

"'겨우 아기'라고요! 아, 모르셨나요!
저 작은 발이 아무도 갈 수 없는 곳을 걸을 것이며
저 부드러운 손가락이
선율을 타며
말로 표현할 수 없는
달콤한 음악을 만들 거라는 것을!
아기의 손이 머무는 곳에 가슴줄 불협화음이
마술처럼 새로운 조화로 넘치게 되는 것을,
아기의 가느다란 목소리로 부르는 달콤한 멜로디 속에
가정의 화합이 이루어진다는 것을."

셔우드는 오늘로 5개월이 되었다. 모습 그대로 정말 사랑스러운 아들이다. 이사벨라 버드 비숍(I. B. Bishop)[19] 부인은 "외모가 아주 지적인 아기"라고 하셨고, 그레이트하우스 장군은 이렇게 잘 웃는 아기를 본 적이 없다고 하셨다.

셔우드는 지금 13파운드 반이다. 통통하지는 않지만 엄마 젖에 오트밀죽과 하이랜드 농축 크림을 약간 보완한 것으로 잘 자라고 있다. 최근 크림이 너무 시어져서 이글 브랜드 연유를 사용하기 시작했다. 외할아버지 농장에서 나오는 질 좋은 우유와 크림을 조금만 먹을 수 있어도 아주 잘 자랄 텐데……. 외할머니는 당신이 셔우드를 보고 뽀뽀할 수 있을 때까지 엄마가 대신 매일 뽀뽀를 해달라고 적으셨다. '올드 블랙 조'(Old Black Joe)[20]는 셔우드에게 미화 1불을 보내 주었다. 매기[21] 외숙모는 사랑스러운 어린 조카가 먼 이교도 국가에서 태어나리라고는 생각지도 못했다면서 모두 놀랐지만 기쁘다고 적으셨다. 프랭크[22] 외삼촌은 "아기가 자기 국적을 잘 모를 것 같구나. 우리를 대신해서 사랑스러운 아기 셔우드에게 뽀뽀해 주렴. 아무렴 그 애도 선교사가 되겠지"라고 말씀하셨다. 템피 그레이는 셔우드의 눈이 동양적으로 치켜 올라갔는지, 그리고 머리를 땋을 것인지 알고 싶어 했다. 셔우드의 어린 사촌 모드 그레이[23]는 셔우드가 백인 아기가 아닐까 봐 걱정된다면서, 만약 그렇다면 가족으로 인정하지 않을 거라고 했다.

21 우리 셔우드는 정말 착한 아들이다. 나쁜 버릇이 하나도 없다. 안고 걸어 달라거나 흔들어 달라고 울지도 않고, 엄지손가락이나 다른 그 무엇도 빨지 않는다. 기저귀를 더럽히지도 않고, 매일 아침 큰애처럼 한국 요강을 사용한다. 하루에 아침, 점심, 저녁, 취침 전, 이렇게 네 번씩 규칙적으로 젖을 먹고 밤에는 한 번 이상 깨는 적이 거의 없다. 깨는 시간은 자정과 새벽 2시 사이이고, 반 시간 정도 젖을 먹고는 아침 6시나 7시까지 잔다. 젖 먹는 시간 사이에 한 번씩 오트밀과 연유를 먹는다. 셔우드는 지금 만들고 있는 짧은 드레스를 입고 평양에 가서 어린 개척선교사가 될 준비를 하고 있다.
셔우드가 곧 짧은 드레스를 입게 되어서 긴 아기옷을 입은 첫 사진을 찍어 주었다. 혼자 찍은 사진은 실제보다 통통하게 나왔고, 그 애의 표정을 담고 있지 않았다. 그래서 사진을 더 뽑지 않았다. 엄마 무릎 위에 앉아 있는 사진은 아기의 머리 위치가 좋지 않기 때문에 인물만큼 잘 나오지 않았고, 손도 움직였다. 그래도 아빠와 엄마 그리고 친구들은 이 사진이 우리 아기와 가장 비슷하게 나왔다고 생각했다. 셔우드가 웃지 않고 있을 때 흔히 짓는 특별한 작은 표정을 담고 있기 때문이다.

"오, 어머니로서 할 수 있는 가장 달콤한 일은
아기의 앙증맞은 옷을 만드는 것이다."

[긴 옷을 입은 셔우드]

[로제타와 5개월 된 셔우드]

22 1894년 5월 10일, 목요일

네가 사는 날을 따라서 능력이 있으리로다(신명기 33:25)

주어진 사명을 마칠 때까지 우리는 죽지 않는다. – 화이트필드(Whitefield)

오늘은 셔우드의 6개월 생일이다. 아기는 이날을 평양에서 보내고 있다. 그동안 우리 아기는 정말 많이 자랐다. 3주 전 서울을 떠날 때의 그 아기라고 아무도 알아보지 못할 정도다.

우리는 2주 동안 제물포의 존스(Jones) 부인[24] 댁에 머무르면서 평양으로 가는 증기선을 기다렸다. 그곳에 있는 동안 화창한 날에는 여선이[25] 셔우드를 안고 오랫동안 산책을 했다. 셔우드는 양호한 상태에서 여행을 시작했다. 출발 후 곧 태풍을 만나 33시간 동안 정박해야 했다. 금요일 정오부터 화요일 정오까지 바다에 떠 있었다.

모두 심하게 배멀미를 했지만 셔우드는 이리저리 흔들리는 것을 재미있어했다. 그래서 우리 아기에게는 이때의 정박이 오히려 도움이 되었다. 잘 놀고 잘 자고 잘 먹었다. 실비아는 너무 아파서 아기를 돌볼 수 없었다. 하루는 아빠와 엄마까지 너무 아팠다. 다행히도 사랑스럽고 착한 아기는 이미 일본인 선원들과 한국인 선원들 사이에서 친구를 많이 만들었고, 친절한 한국인(일본인들을 위한 통역)이 잔잔한 바다에 다다를 때까지 셔우드를 잘 돌보아 주었다.

셔우드는 이제 발그레한 혈색이 돌고 포동포동하며 힘도 세졌다. 엄마 아빠뿐 아니라 다른 사람들 눈에도 건강해 보인다. 키 26인치 반, 머리 둘레 17인치이다. 이곳에서는 몸무게를 잴 방법이 없지만 적어도 16파운드 이상 나갈 것 같다. 셔우드는 이제 뽀뽀하는 법을 배우기 시작했는데, 우리 아기는 정말 작은 사랑꾼이다. 첫 이가
23 두 개 나기 시작했고, 다다(dada), 파파(papa)라고 말을 하는데, 어떨 때는 엄마('a ma')라고 하기도 한다.

셔우드는 어제 처음으로 누워서 낮잠을 자다가 자고 있던 2피트 높이의 상자에서 굴러 떨어졌다.

그날 무려 1,500명의 여인들과 아이들이 평양에서 처음 보는 외국인 아기 셔우드를 보러 왔다. 오늘은 누구라도 오기 두려워할 상황이 이곳에서 있었음에도 150명이 넘는 사람들이 열 명 또는 스무 명으로 조를 지어서 들어와 5분에서 10분쯤, 때로는 좀더 머무르다 갔다. 모두에게 셔우드가 큰 구경거리라는 것이 밝혀졌다.

오늘 아침 일찍 아빠의 조사 창식[26]과 마펫(S. Moffet)[27] 목사의 조사 한 씨[28]가 감옥에 갇혔다는 소식이 왔다. 다른 기독교인들은 매를 맞았다고 한다. 잠시 후 아빠의 남학교 교사 오 씨[29]가 우리 집

마당에서 감옥으로 끌려갔다. 셔우드와 엄마는 몇 시간 동안 홀로 남겨졌다. 당시 아빠는 감옥에 있는 불쌍한 사람들을 방문하고 감사를 만나러 갔다가 급히 서울로 전보를 치기 위해 전신국에 가 계셨다. 에스더와 실비아는 에스더의 작은 집에 들어가 꼼짝 않고 있었다. 하지만 우리는 구경하러 온 여인들과 아이들 때문에 계속 바빴다. 그들은 이 집에서 일어난 일들을 눈치 채지 못했고, 아기의 모든 것에 관심이 많았다. 모두가 셔우드를 보고 "곱소"라고 했다.

6개월 생일을 맞은 나에게

녀석, 애살맞은 장난꾸러기
너의 넓고 훤한 이마
너의 경이로운 눈빛,
마치 "다음은 뭐죠?" 묻는 것 같은.
아직 네가 남자(he)인지 여자(she)인지 모르겠고
네 옷도 그걸 말해주지 않아. 그래, 그 말이 맞아
모두들 그냥 "아이"(it)라고 부르는 것이.
나에게 말해 봐. 너는 누구의 놀라운 신동이니?

모두들 너를 나라고 해, 나라고!
사실 인물이 그렇다고 입증하네
(내가 부정할 수 없는 사실이야)
그럼 첫 작품이 최고지.
나도 '앙증맞고', '귀엽고', '달콤'했을까?
나도 "구-구", "구-와" 옹알거렸을까?
그리고 발가락을 꼼지락거리고 발을 차 댔을까?
그리고 잘했다고 우쭐댔을까? 그런가요, 사랑하는 어머니?

너의 머리 깊숙한 곳에
무슨 생각이 숨어 있니, 아무도 모르는 무슨 생각이?
모두 덧이불로 꼭꼭 덮어놓았니?
고무 반지, 새로운 발가락?

방금 나온 네가 살던 삶에 대한 여운이
아직도 그 안에 있는 거니?
그 모든 움직임은
뾰족한 핀으로 콕 찔려서 생긴 거니?

너는 여덟 살이 되고 싶어
안달하는 건 아니겠지?
그 엉뚱한 변덕스러움으로
너의 이름 '아기'를 싫어하는 건 아니겠지?
아, 아가야, 이 자리에 머무는 것에
만족하지 못하는 것이 안타깝구나. 그렇구나.
이제부터 앞으로 자라고 또 자라면
네가 무엇이 될지 그 꿈을 꼭 잡고 있거라!
- 에드윈 L. 사빈

셔우드는 평소처럼 6시에 목욕하고 깊이 잠들었는데 갑자기 성난
황소가 땅을 차며 포효하는 것 같은 요란한 소리가 들려 그만 잠에서
깨버렸다. 나이 많은 김 포도대장(Captain Kim)이 잔뜩 화가 나서 오늘
오후 이 집에 두고 갔던 서류를 내 놓으라고 했다. 그는 서류를 두고
24 간 뒤 곧바로 하인을 보내 그 종이를 돌려달라고 했으나 아빠는 그것을
가지고 있는 것이 좋을 거라는 생각에 내주지 않았었다.
아빠가 나가서 포도대장을 진정시키려 했지만 하필 그 자리에 여선이 있었고 포도대장은 감히 아빠에게는 손대지 못하고 여선에게 달려들어 상투를 잡고 발로 차고 때렸다. 그리고 자기 부하들을 시켜 그를 감옥으로 데리고 가라고 명령했다. 그때 재빨리 아빠가 그 종이를 내주었고, 그는 여선을 그냥 두고 떠났다. 조용해지자 셔우드는 다시 잠이 들었다.

5월 14일 – 잇몸에서 이가 나오고 있지만 아직 보이지는 않는다. 셔우드는 이제 무른 변을 본다. 평양에 온 후로는 한두 번 정도 관장을 했을 뿐이다.

5월 17일 – 셔우드 몸이 좋지 않다. 제물포에서처럼 산책하고 싶어 한다. 우리는 셔우드를 데리고 기자묘(箕子墓)에 가서 하루 종일 있었다. 기자는 기원전 1122년 한국 문명을 창시한 사람이다. 오늘 셔우드의 작은 진주를 볼 수 있었다. {이 이는 1899년 남포에서 빠졌다.}[30]

5월 22일 – 셔우드가 조금 좋아졌다. 셔우드는 이제 "파파", "엄마"(A–ma)라고 똑똑하게 말한다. 두 번째 이가 나오는 것이 보인다. 셔우드는 오늘 처음으로 아주 재미있어하면서 종이를 두 쪽으로 찢었다. 하지만 이제 종이를 찢으면 안 된다는 것을 배워야 한다. 엄마는 요즘 매일 여덟 명에서 열아홉 명 정도의 환자를 돌본다. 그리고 진료가 끝나면 아빠와 창식 아저씨와 함께 셔우드를 데리고 긴 산책을 다녀온다. 이렇게 산책을 하니 셔우드의 볼이 다시 발그레 혈색이 돈다. 오늘 아주 즐거웠다.

5월 26일 – 두 번째 이가 거의 다 나왔다. 셔우드에게 석회수를 탄 우유를 주기 시작했다. {이 이는 5년 후 서울에서 빠졌고, 곧바로 앞니 영구치가 나왔다.}[31]

25 1894년 6월 10일, 일요일

네가 물 가운데로 지날 때에 내가 너와 함께할 것이라(이사야 43:2)

"깊은 요람에서 흔들흔들
나는 평화롭게 잠을 자네
물결 위에서 안전한 쉼을 얻네
오 주님, 당신은 구할 능력이 있으시니
주님은 나의 간구를 외면치 않으시니
당신은 참새가 떨어지는 것도 아시니
나의 잠은 고요하고 평화롭도다
깊은 요람에서 흔들흔들." - 엠마 윌라드(E. Willard), 1832년

셔우드는 오늘 황해에 있다. 서울로 돌아가는 길이다. 아기는 기분이 좋다. 청룡호의 테슨손(Tessensohn) 선장도 "이 아기는 항상 웃네요"라고 말한다. 엄마와 아빠는 배멀미를 심하게 했지만 셔우드는 배가 흔들리는 것을 즐거워했다. 청룡호에는 남쪽에서 일어난 폭동[32]을 진압하기 위한 평양 군인 410명이 타고 있었다. 셔우드는 그들에게 좋은 구경거리가 되었다. 장군 이하 모두가 보러 왔다.

1894년 7월 10일, 화요일

어린 셔우드가 다시 오랫동안 아팠다. 이질이었다. 서울에 도착한 6월 12일 밤부터 7월 6일까지 거의 매일 변에서 피가 나왔다.

6월 20일에는 종일 두 번밖에 먹지 않았고, 먹을 때마다 한꺼번에 다
토해버렸다. 엄마, 아빠는 여러 날 동안 정말 걱정을 많이 했다.
셔우드는 천천히 회복되었고, 그후로는 명랑하고 순하게 지냈다.
셔우드를 보는 사람들은 하나같이 여태껏 본 아기들 중 가장 잘 웃는
26 아기라고 했다. 이제 변에서 피가 안 나온 지 나흘이 되었다. 우리는
셔우드가 다시 조금씩 자랄 거라고 생각한다. 셔우드는 살이 많이
빠졌지만 평소 체중을 유지하고 있다. 오늘 몸무게는 17파운드이고,
키는 29인치, 머리 둘레는 17인치 반이다. 엄마, 아빠는 서울에 도착한
후 처음으로 셔우드를 데리고 산책을 했다. 아기가 아주 좋아했다.
자주 머리를 뒤로 젖히고, 기뻐 어쩔 줄 모르는 얼굴로 눈을 높이 치켜
뜨고, 손을 움직이면서 오랫동안 웃으며 옹알이를 했다. 엄마는 아기가
천사들을 본 것이 분명하다고 생각한다. 아빠는 셔우드의 기쁨은
하늘에서 온 것이라고 한다. 셔우드는 이러한 행동을 대략 한 달 넘게
했다. 셔우드는 갓난 아기일 때 천장에 매달아 놓은 밝은 한국등을
아주 관심있게 쳐다보았었다. 하지만 굳이 그 방에 있을 때가
아니더라도, 그리고 딱히 볼 것이 없는 곳에서도 같은 행동을 했다.
사랑스런 우리 아가, 재롱둥이 우리 아가. 엄마와 아빠는 너를
많이많이 사랑한단다. 셔우드는 아직까지 심술을 부린 적이 없고,
자기 뜻대로 해달라고 '앙탈'을 부린 적도 없다.

27 1894년 8월 10일 금요일

마음의 즐거움은 양약이라도(잠언 17:22)

"'겨우 아기'라고요! 쪼끄만 생명이
세상의 투쟁에서,
윙윙 돌아가는 삶의 베틀에서
어떤 매력을 풍기며 금실을 짤는지 알 수 없잖아요!
새새틈틈
비밀이 숨겨진 곳에
웃음과 재롱으로
말 없이 기어와
주름 가득 늙은 얼굴에 웃음을 주고
차가워진 가슴에 따스한 둥지를 지어줄지 알 수 없잖아요."

어린 셔우드가 오늘로 9개월이 되었다. 몸무게는 18파운드이고, 키는 30인치, 머리 둘레는 17¾ 인치이다. 세 번째 작은 진주가 보이기 시작했다. 두 번째 이는 왼쪽 윗니였고, 중앙의 두 개는 아직 완전히 나오지 않았지만 네 개가 한꺼번에 나오는 것 같다. 지난 달 며칠은 무척 더웠지만 셔우드는 잘 지냈다. 그늘에서도 104°(화씨)가 넘었고, 집에서 가장 시원한 곳도 92°였을 정도로 무더웠다. 아빠는 학교 마당에 텐트를 쳤다. 그곳이 집보다 바람이 잘 들고 공기도 더 좋았다. 우리는 텐트에서 잤다. 엄마가 아기 침대를 더 크고 시원하게 만들어 주었기 때문에 모기도 이제 거의 들어오지 못한다. 그래서 아기는 아주 잘 잔다. 가끔씩 새벽 1시쯤 젖을 먹기 위해 깰 때도 있지만 주로 저녁 8시에서 새벽 5시까지 깨지 않고 잘 잔다. 셔우드는 가벼운 플란넬 띠, 기저귀 그리고 체크 무늬 잠옷만 입고 잔다. 어느 날 밤
28 셔우드가 침대에서 바닥으로 굴러 떨어졌는데, 잠에서 깨지도

앉았는지 아니면 금방 다시 잠이 들어버렸는지 여하튼 아무도 아기가
떨어지는 소리를 듣지 못했다. 실비아가 아침에 일어나서 아기가
침대에 없는 것을 발견하고 혹시 엄마와 같이 있는지 찾아보다가
아기가 없자 정말 놀랐다. 마침내 셔우드가 아기 침대와 텐트 구석
사이에 있는 것을 발견했다. 다행히도 다친 데 없이 땅 위에서 잔
것뿐이고, 몇 군데 모기와 벼룩에게 물린 자국밖에 없었다. 셔우드는
5시와 6시 사이에 잠에서 깨면 자기 침대에 누워서 한 시간 동안 혼자
말을 하고 웃기도 하면서 논다. 그런 후 우리는 아이를 데리고 집으로
가서 목욕을 시키고, 더운 날 집 안에 있을 때는 기저귀만 채워 준다.
가장 더운 오후 3시에는 엄마가 아기를 데리고 커다란 욕조에
들어가서 반 시간 정도 시원한 목욕을 한다. 셔우드는 마음껏 물을
튀기고 물장구를 치며 아주 좋아한다. 엄마가 붙잡아 주면 머리를
꼿꼿이 한 채로 물에서 조금 뜰 수 있다. 그리고 작은 손으로 욕조
옆을 잡고 혼자서 몇 초 동안 서 있기도 한다. 아기는 다시 튼튼하게
잘 자라고 있다. 셔우드는 조금 기기도 하는데, 지금까지는 주로
뒤로만 긴다.
이 아이는 무릎으로 기는 것을 좋아하지 않는 것 같다. 대신 발로
서 있는 것은 정말 좋아한다. 손을 잡아 주면 발을 높이 들어 한 발씩
제대로 순서에 맞추어 내밀면서 방을 가로질러 걸을 수 있다.
29 목욕 후 아이는 옷을 입는다. 띠와 기저귀를 차고 얇은 옷만 입는다.
그리고 헐버트 댁 가까이 있는 시원한 나무 그늘로 옮겨진다.
그곳에서 셔우드는 땅 위에 펼쳐진 기름천 위에 앉아서 잔디를
뜯으며 메뚜기랑 놀거나 헐버트 씨의 작은 강아지들이 장난치는 것을
쳐다본다. 가끔씩 어린 헬렌 헐버트가 나와서 셔우드와 노는데,

셔우드는 헬렌과 노는 것을 아주 좋아한다. 또 아기 루스 노블과 어린 매들라인 헐버트를 쳐다보는 것을 좋아한다. 하루는 어린 맥스 스크랜턴 양에게 놀러 가기도 했다. 둘 다 더할 나위 없이 착했고 즐거운 시간을 가졌다. 엄마의 해먹이 나무 그늘 아래 달려 있다. 때로 셔우드는 5시쯤 이 해먹에서 낮잠을 잔다. 그리고 아빠와 엄마가 저녁 식사를 하는 동안 해먹 안에서 바깥 공기를 쐰다.

식사 후 아빠가 아기를 안고 엄마와 프랑스 공사관 뒤까지 산책을 한다. 공사관에서 키우는 작은 사슴 두 마리는 종종 우리와 먼 거리를 유지한 채 담을 따라 달린다. 셔우드는 이 산책을 아주 좋아한다.

이렇게 산책하는 동안 셔우드는 처음으로 달을 알게 되었고 번개도 알게 되었다. 한 주는 아빠가 부상당한 한국인 병사들 때문에 병원에서 밤낮으로 너무 바빴기 때문에 산책을 미뤄야 했다. 이 병사들 대부분은 일본인들이 궁궐을 점령하고 도시를 장악했던 7월 23일 아침[33]에 부상을 당했다. 한국은 일본의 영향력 아래 중국으로부터의 독립을 선언했다. 이제 일본은 중국과의 투쟁을 돕게 될 것이다. 일본과 중국은 이미 두 번의 전투[34]를 치렀다. 한 번은 바다에서, 한 번은 내륙에서 싸웠는데 두 번 다 일본이 승리했다.

30 지금은 불안한 시절이다. 영사관들은 모두 자국 '군함들'에서 파견된 군인들의 경호를 받고 있다. 그리고 우리가 머물고 있는 감리교 구역은 미국 군대들이 매일 밤 지키고 있다. 우리는 일본이 승리하는 한 안전하다고 느끼고 있다. 일본인은 공정하게 일을 처리하려는 태도가 있는 것 같기 때문이다. 하지만 중국인들이 그들을 앞질러 서울에 진군하게 되면 여지없이 우리는 우리 군함으로 가야 한다. 영국은 제물포에 '센추리온'이라고 부르는 아주 큰 전함을 정박시키고 있다.

미국인들에게는 제법 큰 구축함 '볼티모어' 호가 있는데, 우리는
제물포에 머물 때 그 배를 방문했었다.
그렇게 많은 전쟁 중에서, 또 전쟁의 소문 중에서 셔우드는 이번 달에
처음으로 자기도 의지가 있다는 것을 보여 주었다. 때로 셔우드는 자기
뜻대로 하려고 무척 애를 쓴다. 가령 자기가 가지고 놀고 싶어 하는
것을 누군가 빼앗을 때 이 같은 모습이 나타나곤 하는데, 그렇다고
아주 심한 것은 아니고 대신 다른 것을 주면 순순히 포기한다. 그런데
하루는 좀더 강하게 자기 의지를 드러냈다. 내가 셔우드에게 새
젖꼭지를 사용하기로 한 날인데, 낡은 젖꼭지에서는 우유가 너무 쉽게
나와서 젖병을 물린 채 아기 혼자 놔두면 종종 옷과 침대를 적시곤 했기
때문이다. 하지만 셔우드는 새 것을 원치 않았다. 나중에 내가 한번
새 젖꼭지를 시험해 보았더니 과연 셔우드처럼 큰 아기가 사용하기에는
우유가 너무 천천히 나왔다. 그러나 처음에는 아기가 그냥 새 젖꼭지를
사용하기 싫어하는 단순한 행동이려니 생각했다. 셔우드는 새 젖꼭지를
사용하느니 차라리 먹지 않겠다는 듯 오전 내내 아무것도 먹지 않고
31 버텼다. 한번은 자고 있을 때 새 젖꼭지를 물려주었는데 즉시 뱉어
버렸다. 그리고 잠에서 깨 배가 고플 때도 절대로 새 젖꼭지를 빨지
않았다. 먹은 게 없어서 배가 고파 평소보다 일찍 깨면서도 말이다.
이렇게 깨면 조금 울다가 그냥 방바닥에 앉아서 장난감을 가지고
한 시간 동안 잘 놀았다. 그러다가 너무 배가 고프면 절박한 심정으로
자기 손으로 젖병을 다시 잡고 젖꼭지를 입으로 가져갔다. 그러나
젖꼭지가 입술이나 혀에 닿기가 무섭게 뱉어 버리고는 엄마가 도와
주기를 바라면서 크게 울었다. 엄마가 젖꼭지를 다시 입에 물리려
하자 셔우드는 입을 꽉 다물었다. 그래서 엄마는 아기를 그냥 울도록

15분간 마루에 내버려 두었다. 건강한 상태에서 이처럼 심하게 운 적이 없었다. 배가 고프기도 했지만 정말로 학대받고 있다고 느꼈을 것이다. 조금 진정하고 헝겊 인형에게 관심을 주려다가도 다시 엄마 얼굴을 쳐다보며 흐느껴 우는 것이었다. 마침내 엄마는 이렇게 고집 부리는 것이 옛 젖꼭지를 원해서 그러는 것인지 알아보려고 아기를 안고 숟가락으로 먹여 보았다. 그런데 아기는 숟가락으로 잘 받아먹었고, 제법 잘 마시기까지 했다. 그리고 곧 다시 얼굴에 웃음이 피어났다. 그러나 이 매정한 엄마는 새 젖꼭지를 포기하지 않았다. 그래서 다음 끼니 때가 되었을 때 다시 새 젖꼭지를 시도해 보았다. 하지만 아무 소용이 없었다. 엄마는 12시간 동안 아기의 정든 옛 젖꼭지를 주지 않았지만 아기는 새 젖꼭지를 쓰려 하지 않았다. 아기가 숟가락으로 먹고 마시려 했기 때문에 엄마는 더 이상 강요할 구실이 없게 되었다.
32 그리고 엄마는 아직 두세 달 동안은 젖을 떼지 않을 작정이었으므로 다음 끼니 때는 넓은 나무 그늘로 나가 아기의 정든 옛 친구를 다시 주었다. 아기는 그 젖꼭지로 맛있게 병을 다 비운 다음 해먹에서 잠들어 2시간 동안 잤다. 그리고 예전처럼 명랑한 아이가 되었다.

모두들 셔우드를 사랑한다.

실비아, 에스더, 여선이는 우리 셔우드 같은 아기는 세상에 없다고 생각하는 것 같다. 그리고 엄마의 연로하신 선생님도 셔우드를 끔찍이 생각하신다. 아빠는 종종 엄마에게 "셔우드는 내가 본 아기 중 가장 똑똑하고, 가장 예쁘고, 가장 사랑스러운 아이"라고 말한다. 물론 다른 사람들에게는 그렇게 말하지 않지만 말이다.

셔우드는 요새 "아빠", "엄마"라고 부르지 않는다. 평양에서는 자주 "아빠"라고 하곤 했는데…… 그리고 서울에 온 후로도 하루에 몇 번씩 "엄마, 엄마"라고 했는데…… 그래서 노블 부인이 종종 셔우드가 "엄마, 엄마" 소리를 한다고 말씀하셨는데 말이다. 우리는 지난 2, 3 주 동안 한 번도 셔우드가 엄마, 아빠를 부르는 소리를 듣지 못했다. 셔우드는 이제 자주 "아기"라는 소리를 낸다. 한국말로 "베이비"라는 뜻이다. 요즘은 옹알거리는 소리가 많지만 우리 귀에는 "아기"라고 하는 소리만 들린다. 글 읽는 시늉을 하고 다른 사람들이 노래 부르면 같이 부르기도 한다. 그리고 오르간 치는 것을 좋아한다.

1894년 9월 10일, 월요일

우리 아기가 이제 10개월이 되었다. 지난 한 달 동안 셔우드의 몸무게는 2파운드 늘었고, 이가 세 개 더 났다. 그리고 가고 싶은
33 곳으로 엉금엉금 앞으로 기어간다. 아직까지는 별로 심각한 일이 생기지 않았지만 가끔 말썽을 일으키기도 한다. 지금 몸무게는 20파운드, 키는 30¼ 인치, 머리 둘레는 18인치이다. 윗니 네 개, 아랫니 두 개가 나왔다. 우리는 아랫니들을 '평양 이'라고 부르고, 윗니들은 '서울 이'라고 부른다. 치아들은 다음과 같은 순서로 나왔다. 첫 번째 이는 지난달에 나왔고, 두 번째는 왼쪽 앞니, 다음으로 이달 초하루에 오른쪽 중앙 앞니, 그리고 2주 후에 두 번째 오른쪽 앞니, 며칠 후 왼쪽 중앙 앞니가 나왔다. 셔우드는 지금 빵 껍질을 조금씩 씹는 것을 즐기고 있는데, 닭 뼈도 그렇게 씹는다. 며칠간 설사를 하기는 했지만 이번 달에는 건강히 잘 지내고 있다. 우리는 셔우드를 데리고 소풍을 갔고, 아기는 하루 종일 밖에서 지내면서

산공기를 마셨다. 그리고 그 후로 아주 잘 지내고 있다. 변이 묽어져서 오트밀 대신 보리죽을 먹는 때를 제외하면 주로 연유와 오트밀을 먹고 있다. 이번 달에는 단 한 번 갑자기 울면서 깨어나 반 시간 동안 울었는데, 알고 보니 급성 복통이었다. 우유는 입에 대지도 않으려 했고, 자세를 바꾸거나 그 어떤 방법을 취해도 가여운 아기에게는 아무런 도움도 되지 않았다. 고통이 가시자 셔우드는 아무것도 먹지 않고 다시 조용히 잠들었다. 그리고 밤새 괜찮았다. 지난달에는 이런 일이 두세 번 정도 있었다. 유아 배앓이인지 무엇인지 원인을 잘 모르겠다. 때로 회충이 있는 것처럼 보이기도 하는데, 코를 심하게 문지르고 깨어났을 때 자주 이상한 소리를 내면서 잔기침을 하기 때문이다. 복부도 팽창되어 있다. 그렇지만 지난 달만큼 불룩하지는 않고, 혀에 설태가 낀 걸로 보아 이질 때문인 것 같기도 하다.

34 이달부터 셔우드는 "아빠", "엄마"라는 말을 많이 한다. 다른 사람들이 우리를 그렇게 부르는 것을 듣지 못하기 때문에 누가 아빠이고 엄마인지 잘 모르는 것 같지만 말이다. 그러나 아빠나 엄마가 "실비아" 하고 부르면 누가 대답할 것인지 정확히 알고 있다.

가끔씩 실비아가 셔우드를 모서리에 세워주면 셔우드는 혼자 서 있을 수 있다. 무엇이든 잡으면 어디서든 서 있을 수 있고, 이제 막 혼자 잡고서 일어나기 시작했다.

셔우드는 여전히 온순하고 명랑한 아이로 자라고 있다. 셔우드는 아이들과 노는 것을 정말 좋아한다. 소풍을 가면 '착한 아이'라는 말을 듣는다. 어떤 아이가 컵으로 얼굴을 때렸을 때와 해먹에서 떨어졌을 때 외에는 운 적이 없다. 셔우드는 리버티 주일학교에서 보내준 그림책 하나를 특히 좋아하는데, 광이 나는 모슬린 천에 그림을 스크랩해서 붙여 놓은 책이다. 이때껏 가지고 놀던 장난감은 거들떠 보지도 않고 방바닥에 오랫동안 앉아서 책장을 넘겨가며 손가락으로 눈, 색깔, 꽃 등 자기가 좋아하는 것을 가리키면서 그림책을 재미있게 본다. 셔우드의 앙증맞은 검지손가락은 이번 달에 아주 대단한 지시봉이 되었다. 아이는 항상 오른손을 사용하는데, 나머지 손가락은 쥐고 검지손가락만 능숙하게 펴서 다가오는 사람이나 밝은 빛 그리고 자기 관심을 끄는 것들을 "오! 오!" 하면서 가리킨다. 셔우드는 두꺼운 책의 책장을 재빨리 넘길 때는 오른손 엄지손가락과 검지손가락을 함께 사용하는 것을 좋아한다. 책장 넘기는 소리와 엄지손가락에 느껴지는 감각을 좋아하는 것 같다. 셔우드는 아주 살며시 책장을 넘기는데, 누구보다 못지않은 능란한 솜씨로 넘길 수 있다. 셔우드는 책을 아주 좋아하는 것 같다. 그리고 책을 찢지 않는다.

35 현재 셔우드는 우리 집안의 유일한 아기이다. 에스더 이모가 아들을 낳았었는데 몸무게가 4파운드밖에 나가지 않았다. 셔우드는 아기를 쳐다보고 인형 같은 손을 잡는 것을 좋아했다. 하지만 태어난 지 36시간 만에 하나님은 아기를 에스더 이모의 방에서 당신 곁으로 데리고 가셨다. 그리고 조촐한 장례식이 있었다. 그날은 빈튼(C. C. Vinton)[35] 댁 아기가 땅에 묻힌 날이기도 했다. 우리는 사랑스럽던 아기를 더 이상 볼 수 없게 되었다. 곧 이어서 루스 노블의 아기가 엄마, 아빠와 일본으로 갔다. 그래서 셔우드는 당분간 집안에서 귀염둥이가 되었다.

"세상에, 이런 군주가 없다네, 보는 것마다 크게 즐거워하고
목석 같은 당신을 흔들리게 하는

오, 아가!
나의 비둘기야, 잘난 사람 너에게로 오라고 해보렴
그 사람은 하늘에서 온 진리를 배울 것이니
'사랑으로 다스리는 자가 천하를 다스림이라'
아기처럼."[36]

1894년 10월 10일, 수요일

지난 달, 아니, 지난 2주 만에 셔우드는 몸무게가 1파운드 빠졌다. 계속 설사했고, 예전만큼 바깥에 나가 있을 수 없었다. 아빠는 이달 초하룻날 평양으로 떠났으며, 우리는 아빠를 무척 그리워하고 있다. 셔우드는 지금 19파운드이고, 키는 30½인치, 머리 둘레는 지난달과 같다. 지난 번 우편물에서 셔우드의 캐나다인 사촌 해리 윌리스 그레이의 사진을 받았다. 해리는 8개월 때 몸무게가 24파운드였다고 한다. 얼마 전 셔우드의 사진에 대한 외할머니의 편지도 도착했다. 외할머니는 이렇게 말씀하셨다.
"애니[37]와 조가 오후에 마을에 다녀왔단다. 집에 와서 애니가 '내 주머니에 엄마를 웃게 할 것이 들어있어요' 하지 않겠니. 나는 그것이 우리 어린 손자의 사진이라고 짐작했는데, 정말로
36 아기와 너의 사진이었단다. 옛말에 아기가 아빠를 닮았다고 하면 엄마는 기뻐한다고 했는데, 셔우드는 정말 아빠를 쏙 빼어 닮았지 싶다. 엄마 모습이 하나도 없으니 말이야. 셔우드는 아주 잘생긴 녀석이구나. 사레스(Sarles) 씨는 '아주 똑똑하게 생겼군요'라고 했단다. 사람들 대부분이 아기 엄마가 야위었다고 하는데, 사레스 씨는

'점점 더 예뻐지네요'라고 했단다. 셔우드가 건강하기를,
주님이 셔우드의 생명을 지켜주셔서 엄마, 아빠와 함께 돌아와
우리와 만날 수 있기를 바란다."
셔우드와 엄마는 이번 달에 보모 문제로 많은 어려움을 겪었다.
셔우드의 오랜 친구 실비아가 여학교의 '침모'로 떠났고, 다섯 명을
시험해 본 후에야 우리 모두가 만족할 만한 사람을 구할 수 있었다.
지금 에스더의 언니[38]가 새 보모로 와 있다. 하지만 그녀에게도 루스
또래의 아기가 있기 때문에 밤에는 머물 수 없는 형편이다. 그리고 자기
아기도 돌봐야 하기 때문에 비록 그녀가 두 사람 몫을 할 수 있을
정도로 능력 있는 여인이라 해도 실비아가 했던 만큼 일을 할 수 없다.
그래서 우리는 아빠가 병원 일을 잘 하실 수 있도록 도움이 될 만한
소년을 따로 고용했다. 아빠는 이 소년을 평양으로 데리고 가서
진료소 일을 돕게 할 생각이다. 소년의 이름은 '염금영이'(Yom Kum
Yongie)[39]고, 나이는 18세다.
금영이는 병원에서 신자가 되었는데, 착하고 점잖은 소년인 것 같다.
버스티드 박사가 오후에 진료소에서 그를 조금씩 가르치고 있다.
그리고 오전에는 노블 목사의 학교에 가서 중국어를 공부하고, 밤에는
이곳에서 자면서 필요할 때마다 셔우드를 돌보아 준다. 또한 아침 일찍
불을 피우고, 셔우드가 일찍 깨면 아기를 데리고 나온다. 아빠가 떠난
37 뒤로는 금영이가 4시에 셔우드를 데리고 산책을 나간다. 엄마는 한 달
내내 병원에서 커틀러 박사를 돕느라 바빴다. 하지만 집에 일찍 오는
날에는 함께 산책을 나가려고 노력한다.
노블 가족이 일본으로 간 후 집에는 우리만 있게 되었다. 그리고
아빠마저 출타 중이므로 셔우드가 엄마와 식탁에 앉아서 엄마가

외롭지 않게 해주고 있다. 셔우드의 작은 안락의자는 식탁 의자에
딱 맞게 얹혀져 아기들이 앉는 높은 의자로 안성맞춤이다. 셔우드는
보통 식탁에 잘 앉아 있는 편이다. 빵 껍질, 닭 뼈를 가지고 놀거나
숟가락으로 버터 조각이나 설탕을 가지고 잘 논다. 하지만 가끔
의자에서 일어나 식탁에 올라오려 하기도 한다. 그러면 엄마는
셔우드를 제 자리로 돌려보내야 한다. 엄마와 보모 아주머니가
셔우드를 위해 따뜻한 빨간색 플란넬 잠옷을 만들었다. 이 잠옷은
쌀쌀한 아침 저녁에 셔우드를 포근하게 해준다. 엄마는 또 우리 아기가
밤에 신을 수 있게 따뜻한 모직 양말을 뜨개질로 만들어 주었다.
셔우드는 온종일 검정 양말에 밤색 가죽 신발을 신고, 메리야스 셔츠와
플란넬 속치마 위에 체크 무늬 드레스나 옥양목 드레스를 입고 있다.
하루는 엄마와 에스더 이모가 셔우드를 데리고 레이첼(Rachel),
레베카(Rebekah), 앤과 그녀의 아기를 보러 동대문까지 갔다. 셔우드는
7시에 아침을 먹었기 때문에 엄마는 그곳에 도착한 후 먹일 우유를
만들어 갔다. 10시 반쯤 셔우드는 우유를 먹고 싶어 했고, 레이첼은
우유를 데워주겠다고 했다. 하지만 유감스럽게도 우유병이 깨져
버렸고, 우유가 전부 쏟아졌다. 셔우드는 그곳에서 잘 놀기도 했지만
그곳까지 가는 시간이 꽤 오래 걸렸으므로 무척 배가 고팠을 터인데
38 정말 순하게 잘 버티어 냈다. 물만 조금 마셨을 뿐이다. 우리는 서둘러
집으로 돌아왔다. 오는 길에 아기는 잠이 들었고, 우리는 정오쯤 집에
도착했다. 셔우드는 엄마가 우유를 준비할 때까지 잘 참아 주었다.
셔우드는 외출하는 것을 무척 좋아하는데, 안고 다니기에 너무
무거워져서 엄마는 아기 루스의 것과 같은 일제 유모차를 사고 싶어서
사람을 보냈다. 일제 유모차는 미제 유모차처럼 멋지거나 좋은 것은

아니지만 유용하고 훨씬 저렴하다. 우리는 여름 내내 유모차를 구하려 했으나 아직까지 구하지 못하고 있다.
어제 아빠로부터 안전하게 평양에 도착했다는 전보가 왔다. 우리는 아빠가 언제 돌아오실지 모른다. 하지만 내달 이맘때가 되기 전에는 돌아오시리라 생각한다. 셔우드가 아빠를 까맣게 잊어버릴 것 같다.

39 [꽃 그림]

40 1894년 11월 10일, 토요일

그가 너를 위하여 그의 천사들을 명령하사 네 모든 길에서
너를 지키게 하심이라(시 91:11)

"생일 축하해, 사랑하는 셔우드
엄마, 아빠가
사랑을 더하고 더하고 더하여
뽀뽀를 세 번씩 되풀이해서 보낸다."[40]

1년이 지나갔다. 하나님께서 1년 전 오늘 우리에게 보내 주신 사랑하는 어린 아들의 첫돌을 축하하고 있다.

"보세요! 지난해에 신비로운 나라에서
어떤 풍성한 선물이 왔는지.
경이로운 파란색 예쁜 눈,

저 먼 하늘에서 너처럼 왔구나.
사랑스럽게 빚어진 너의 발,
장미꽃잎으로 물들었구나.
금빛 찬란한 네 머리,
진주 조개 분홍빛 고운 볼,
이 부유함에 더하여 저 깊은 광산에서
솟아난 여덟 개의 백옥 같은 이,
변화시키는 은혜의 힘으로
사랑스런 얼굴에 큰 생각이 자라고
늦은 사람을 그림자가 더 길게 따라잡듯이
못다한 말들이 기다리고 있구나."[41]

[첫돌 머리 타래]

셔우드야, 너는 곧 잘 하게 될 거야.
셔우드는 오늘 아침 기분 좋고 행복한 상태로 일어났다. 평소처럼 엄마가 아침 식사를 하는 시간에 목욕하고 10시 반까지 놀다가 낮잠을 청한 뒤 정오 전에 깼다. 그리고 예쁜 돌복을 입었다. 친절하게도 아펜젤러 부인이 자기 마차를 빌려주셨고, 셔우드는 사진을 찍으러 진고개로 갔다. 셔우드는 즐거운 마차 여행을 했다. 그리고 모두들 사진이 잘 나왔다고 했다.

41 [첫돌을 맞은 셔우드]

사진은 정말 셔우드처럼 나왔다. 마루에 앉아 있을 때의 모습과
똑같다. 사진의 포즈처럼 그렇게 한 발을 내민다. 사진사는 원판
음화를 세 개 만들었다. 하나는 기는 것이고, 하나는 의자에 앉아
있는 것이다. 하지만 마루에 앉아 있는 이 사진이 가장 잘 나왔다.
셔우드는 좋은 선물을 많이 받았다. 작은 아이에게는 지나치게 많은
선물이었다. 외할머니는 셔우드를 기억하여 금화 1불을 주셨고, 노블
부인은 예쁜 드레스를 만들 파란색 플란넬 옷감을 주셨다. '여선
삼촌과 에스더 이모'는 흰털로 테를 두른 아름다운 분홍색 토시를
주셨다. 실비아는 직접 수놓은 흰색 비단 손수건을 보내 주었는데,
분홍색으로 '슈부귀다남즈 내귀훈 쇠웃헐'[42]이라고 글자를 수놓았다.
번역하면 '오래 살고, 부귀를 누리며, 아들을 많이 낳기를. 나의 귀한
셔우드 홀'이라는 뜻이다. 메리[43]는 예쁜 비단 색동토시 한 쌍을,
앨리스는 좋은 버선[표기는 '버션'] 한 켤레를 만들어 주었다. 엄마와
아빠는 금테 두른 은잔을 주었고, 엄마는 사진에 입고 있는
새 드레스도 만들어 주었다. 이 옷은 화려한 비단 무늬가 박힌 크림색
42 상의에 주홍색 캐시미어 겉옷이 딸렸는데, 어깨에는 크림색 비단
레이스가 달려 있다. 이 옷을 입은 셔우드는 정말 멋져 보였다.
귀여운 우리 셔우드는 이번 한 달 동안 지난달에 빠진 몸무게를
회복했다. 그래서 다시 20파운드가 되었다. 외할머니는 한 살짜리
남자 아이로서는 너무 말랐다고 생각하시지만 이곳에서는 그리 작아
보이지 않는다. 키는 31인치, 머리 둘레는 18¼인치다. 새 이가 두 개
나는 것이 보인다. 이가 잇몸을 뚫고 나오던 이틀 낮과 하루 밤 동안
셔우드는 아주 힘들어 했다. 하루는 12시간 동안 우유를 한 병도 먹지
못했다. 그날 밤 엄마는 아기와 함께 네 번을 일어나야 했다. 그중

한 번은 거의 3시간을 울었다. 셔우드는 우유를 먹지 않으려 했고, 약을
조금 탄 더운 물도 입에 대지 않으려 했다. 몸의 위치를 바꾸어 주고,
흔들어 주고, 같이 걸어 주어도 소용이 없었다. 다음 날 아침 엄마는
이 하나가 잇몸을 뚫고 나오고 있는 것을 발견했다. 하루 이틀 전에
절개해 주었다면 밤에 겪었던 고통을 피할 수 있었을지도 모르겠다.
셔우드는 이제 기지 않는다. 사실 기는 단계를 거치지 않았다.
이 아이는 무릎을 땅에 대는 것을 좋아하지 않는 것 같다. 그 대신
작은 몸을 공중으로 봉긋하게 올리고서 손과 발로 걷는다. 그런
모습으로 아주 재빨리 방을 가로질러 간다. 그리고 다른 사람이 같은
자세로 자기를 쫓아오는 것을 좋아한다. 그렇게 해주면 정말 재밌어
하면서 웃는다. 셔우드는 의자나 그 비슷한 것을 붙잡고 쉽게
일어선다. 때로는 걸을 수 있도록 손을 잡아 달라고 애원한다.
손을 잡아서 걸음마를 시켜주면 얼굴에 행복한 미소를 지으면서
위풍당당하게 방안을 돌아다닌다. 셔우드는 한 손을 잡아주면 조금씩
걸을 수 있게 되었다. 하지만 아직 무서워하면서 쉽게 주저앉아
버리거나 두 손을 잡아 달라고 조른다. 아이는 걷는 것을 지루해 하는
법이 없다. 셔우드는 아직 '아기 말투' 외에는 별로 하는 말이 없지만
43 그 언어로 옹알이를 아주 많이 하게 되었고, 단어들을 가리키면서
글자와 서류들을 읽으려고까지 한다. 두세 달 전에는 "외이, 오이,
오이"(cucumber의 한국어)라는 말을 많이 했지만 이제는 "구이, 구이,
구이"라는 말을 자주 한다. 울다가도 중간에 울음을 그치고 그 말을
하기 시작한다. 가끔 밤에 깰 때도 그 말을 한다. 그리고 이제는 식사를
기다리는 동안 아빠, 엄마라고 하지 않는다. 아무도 셔우드를 가르치려
애쓰지 않았지만 셔우드는 여전히 책을 좋아하고, 어떨 때는 책 한 권을

반 시간 동안 넘기기도 한다. 책 안에 있는 그림 찾는 것을 좋아하고, 그림을 찾게 되면 "오" 혹은 "아" 하고 감탄한다. 그러나 그림 없는 책도 좋아하는데, 특히 크고 무거운 책을 좋아한다. 셔우드의 첫 번째 신발이 거의 다 닳아서 어느 날 보모가 새 신발을 신겨 주며 셔우드가 다리와 발을 펴서 내밀어 주기를 바랬다. 갑자기 아이는 자신이 어떻게 해야 하는지 머리에 떠올린 것 같았고, 곧 그렇게 해주었다. 그러면서 주먹을 꼭 쥐고, 도망치는 말의 고삐를 당기듯이 몸을 뒤로 젖히면서 팔을 구부린 채 이를 드러내고 활짝 웃음을 지었다. 그 후로 셔우드는 여러 차례 주먹을 쥐고 웃음 짓는 것을 반복했다. 그 모습을 보면 절로 웃음이 났다. 지난 달 셔우드는 모자 쓰기, 머리 빗기 등을 시도했다. 하루는 엄마가 가지고 놀라고 오래된 칫솔을 주었는데 셔우드는 그것으로 바로 머리를 빗기 시작했다. 아이가 이해하기로 칫솔은 머리빗과 가장 비슷한 것이었던 것이다. 또 한번은 엄마의 누비이불 바늘을 마루에서 찾아내서 엄마가 하는 것처럼 자기 이를 쑤시려고 했다. 손수건에 코를 풀려고 하기도 했다. 그리고 연필로 종이에 끄적거리기 시작했다.

44 에스더 이모가 어린 셔우드에게 친절한 생일 축하 편지를 써주었다.

[에스더가 어린 셔우드에게 보낸 편지]

한국, 서울
1894년 11월 10일

내 사랑하는 셔우드,
오늘이 너의 첫돌이구나. 네가 세상에 와 주어서, 그리고 내가 너를 사랑할 수 있게 해주어서 정말 기쁘단다. 앞으로 꼭 필요한 사람이 되어서 너의 아버지, 어머니처럼 그리스도를 모르는 사람들 가운데서 훌륭한 일을 많이 하고, 또 부모님을 공경하고, 부모님의 가르침에 순종하여 점잖고 친절한 사람으로 자라길 바란다. 또한 착한 아이로 자라서 하나님을 사랑하고 그분의 명령을 지키길 바란다. 꼭 그렇게 해주겠니? 하나님께서 너의 이 아름다운 생일을 축복하시고 너에게 어려운 것들을 이해할 수 있는 지혜를 주시기를 기도드린다. 너의 부모님과 나는 너를 끔찍이 사랑하며 네가 좋은 사람으로 성장하기를 바라고 있단다. 오, 우리는 너를 정말로 사랑한단다. 아직은 네가 읽을 수 없으니 너무 많이 쓰지는 않을게. 사랑을 전하며,
박(여선) 삼촌과 에스더 이모로부터.

실비아도 한국말로 친절한 편지를 써주었다. 일부를 번역하면 다음과 같다. "오늘이 아기의 첫돌이네요. 가서 아기를 직접 보고 싶지만 다른 사람 집에서 바쁘게 지내고 있습니다. 셔우드는 제가 낳은 아기는 아니지만 저는 그 아이를 제 아이처럼 사랑하고 있습니다. 그래서 좋은 것들을 많이 주고 싶습니다. 하지만 그럴 능력이 없어서 그다지 좋은 것은 아니지만 사랑을 담아 이 비단 손수건을 보냅니다. 아가야, 너의 어머니는 아빠가 네 생일에 집에 안 계셔서 외로우실 거야."

오늘 우리는 얼마나 아빠를 그리워했는지 모른다. 아빠는 마지막 편지에서 다음과 같이 적었다. "우리 사랑하는 아들 셔우드가 정말 보고 싶구려. 하지만 결국 나는 셔우드의 생일날 갈 수 없을 것 같소." [일기 원본 45쪽은 내용 없음]

46 1894년 12월 10일, 월요일

인자야 내가 네 눈에 기뻐하는 것을 한 번 쳐서 빼앗으리니 너는 슬퍼하거나 울거나 눈물을 흘리거나 하지 말며(에스겔 24:16)
내가 너희를 막대기 아래로 지나가게 하며 언약의 줄로 매려니와 (에스겔 20:37)

그의 거룩한 처소에 계신 하나님은 고아의 아버지시며(시편 68:5)

"너와 해 사이에
가리우는 것이 없으니,
어린아이의 달콤한[44] 꿈처럼
너의 생이 지났으니,
이제는 시내가
깊고 어두운 바다에 닿았으니,
슬픔은 희미해지고 왕관이
너를 기다리고 있네." -프록터(A. A. Proctor)

불쌍한 우리 셔우드! 지난 달 너는 세상에서 가장 소중한 것을 잃었단다. 너는 어려서 지금은 그 상실에 대해 아무것도 모르겠지만 시간이 지나면 느끼게 될 거야. 비록 내가 너로 인해 아픈 것만큼은 아니겠지만 말이다. (열대 지역의 거친 바다를 항해하는 '차이나호' 안에서 기록함.)
바로 한 달 전 셔우드의 생일날, 사랑하는 아빠는 평양을 떠나 집으로 향하셨다. 마펫 목사가 말라리아로 인한 열과 이질로 아주 심하게 아팠기 때문에 아빠는 그 열을 내리는 데 어려움을 겪으셨고, 결국에는 와버그 팅크제를 사용해야만 했다. 이때쯤 아빠에게도 열이 있었으나 키니네는 도움이 되지 않았다. 와버그 팅크제가 거의 동이 나서 아빠는 정량의 절반 정도를 복용했고, 조금 나아졌다고 생각했다. 다음날에는 체온계가 고장나서 체온을 정확히 잴 수 없었다.
이즈음 아빠와 마펫 씨는 지난 5-6주 동안 평양 사역에 많은 노력을 기울이셨고, 특별히 성공적인 결과를 거두었음에도 생명의 안위가 위험한 지역에서 너무 오래 머물렀다는 사실을 깨달았다.

47 아빠가 평양에 도착하기 2주 전에 있었던 전쟁에서 사망한 수천 명의 중국인 시신이 우리 집에서 멀지 않은 성벽 밖까지 널려 있었다.

[1894년 12월 21일 차이나 호 티켓][45]

"1894년 12월 16일, 일요일-오후 5시 나가사키에서 출발. 바다는 잔잔함.
17일-내해를 지나감. 모두 괜찮음.
18일-고베 도착. 산꼭대기가 눈으로 덮여 있음.
19일-오전 8시 고베 출발. 편지를 조금 씀.
20일-오전에 요코하마 도착. 해안으로 감.
21일-요코하마 출발.
12월 23일, 일요일-파도가 매우 거칠어 배가 흔들림. 에스더와 여선이 멀미를 함.
24일-여전히 배가 흔들림. 밤에는 좀 잔잔함.
25일, 크리스마스-오늘은 좀 잠잠해짐. 모두 좀 나아짐.
26일-다시 파도가 거칠어짐.
27일-배가 요동함. 경도 180도 선을 지남. 두 번째 목요일. 속이 울렁거려 피곤함.
28일-긴긴 한 주간이 지남.
29일-열대 지역(Torrid Zone)을 지남.
12월 30일, 일요일-오전에 땅이 시야에 들어옴. 오후 5시 호놀룰루 정박.
31일-해변에 있는 데이먼(Damon) 목사 댁에서 하루를 보냄.
1895년 1월 1일-미국으로 다시 출발. 오늘 바다는 잔잔함.
2일-배가 잘 가고 있음. 하루에 265마일.
3일-다시 파도가 거칠어짐.
4일-배가 좀 흔들림. 계속 잘 가고 있음.
5일-내일 항구에 들어갈 것 같음.
1월 6일, 일요일-오전 7시에 육지가 시야에 들어옴. 오전 11시에 미국 땅을 밟음."

이 시신들은 매장되지 않은 채 버려져 있었고, 그나마 잘 처리했다고 할 수 있는 것도 몇 인치 두께의 흙을 뿌려놓은 것이 고작이었다. 악취는 끔찍했다. 테이트(L. B. Tate)[46] 목사가 보급품을 가지고 일주일 전에 도착했고, 모두들 마펫 목사가 더 위독해지기 전에, 그리고 주위

상황이 더 심각해지기 전에 집으로 출발하는 것이 낫겠다고 결정했다. 그러나 서울로 가는 말을 구할 수 없었다. 증기선을 탈 희망도 희박했을 뿐 아니라 증기선이 있다 하더라도 나루터까지 횡단하기도 어려울 거라고 생각했다. 그렇지만 모두들 온종일 걸려서 강 나루터에 내려가 형편을 살펴보니 다행히도 일본인 병사 600명을 이동시키는 배가 있다는 것을 알게 되었다. 열병과 이질을 앓고 있는 병사들을 태운 배였다. 평양에서는 죽은 중국인 병사들이 살아 있을 때보다 더 많은 사람들을 죽이고 있었다. 아빠, 마펫 목사, 테이트 목사는 11월 14일 수요일에 제물포에 도착하는 이 배의 선실을 잡았다. 사랑하는 아빠는 이 여행 동안 배멀미를 하지 않았고 상태도 조금 좋아졌다. 하지만 배가 땅에 닿자마자 구토, 고열과 오한으로 다시 앓기 시작했다. 아빠가 탄 배가 도착하기 전에 서울로 가는 강 증기선이 막 떠났기 때문에 모두들 하루를 기다렸다가 다음 배를 타기로 했다. 그러나 안타깝게도 토요일 저녁이 될 때까지 서울로 가는 증기선이 없었다. 아빠의 병세가 더욱 악화되었지만 모두들 아빠가 육로 여행은 견딜 수 없으리라 생각했으므로 증기선을 기다릴 수밖에 없었다. 엄마는 그 주 내내 매일 밤낮으로 아빠가 돌아오기를 애타게 기다리고 있었다. 화요일 평양에서 육로로 온 이(Ni) 씨가 아빠의 손편지를 가지고 왔는데, 아빠가 그 편지에 자신이 그 편지보다 먼저 서울에 도착할지도 모른다고 적으셨기 때문이다. 또 수요일 밤에는 다른 그룹과 함께 평양에서 온 오 씨가 금요일에는 분명히 도착할 거라는 아빠의 손편지를 가지고 왔기 때문이다. 아빠는 이 편지에서 미열이 조금 있기는 하지만 집에 돌아와 와버그 팅크제를 복용하면 곧 회복될
48 거라고 하셨다. 금요일 아침 우리는 마펫 목사가 보낸 전갈을 받았다.

금요일 오후 아빠를 위해 강으로 가마를 보내 달라는 내용이었다. 고맙게도 노블 목사가 가마를 준비해서 강으로 나갔다. 그러나 늦도록 기다려도 증기선은 오지 않았다. 다음 날 토요일 오후가 되어서야 존스 목사가 일본 영사관을 통해 보낸 전보를 받았다. "마펫, 테이트, 홀 씨가 4시에 용산을 향해 떠남. 홀 박사가 위독하니 오늘 밤 용산으로 의사와 가마를 보내고 기다리시오." 노블 목사와 버스티드 박사가 긴 의자, 침구, 음식 등을 가지고 내려가서 자정이 넘도록 기다렸다.

[존스 목사가 제물포에서 서울로 보낸 전보]
수신: 서울 날짜: 1894. 11. 17. 17:00
발신: 제물포 날짜: 1894. 11. 17.

미국 선교사 스크랜턴에게 전송함: "마펫, 테이트, 홀 씨가 4시에 용산을 향해 떠남. 홀 박사가 위독하니 오늘 밤 용산으로 의사와 가마를 보내고 기다리시오." 존스.

하지만 여전히 증기선은 보이지 않았다. 아침 일찍 노블 목사가 다시 가 보았지만 결과는 같았다. 오후에는 친절하게도 빈튼 박사가 가겠다고 나섰다. 여전히 증기선은 오지 않았고, 증기선에 관한 소식도 없었다. 빈튼 박사는 가마를 나루터에 두고 돌아왔다. 아침이 되기 전에 도착하더라도 도움을 받을 수 있도록 해둔 것이었다.

기다리는 동안 엄마는 무척 초조했다. 하지만 모두들 증기선이 아직 출발하지 않았거나 모래톱에 걸렸다가 곧 빠져 나올 거라고 생각하는 듯했다. 월요일 아침 식사를 마치자 어떤 판서의 딸을 왕진해 달라는 요청이 들어왔다. 아기 셔우드도 엄마와 같이 오면 좋겠다고 했다. 엄마가 약을 준비해서 막 떠나려 할 때 아빠가 도착했다는 소식이

왔다. 어린 셔우드를 팔에 안고 엄마는 복도를 달려 나갔다. 가마꾼들
이 막 복도로 긴 의자를 들여왔고, 그 위에는 사랑하는
아빠가 누워 있었다. 테이트 목사가 아빠를 일으킨 후 팔을 부축하여
보모가 재빨리 준비해 둔 침대로 옮겼다. 아빠는 엄마와 셔우드에게
키스했다. 드디어 집에 도착했으므로 기쁘고 행복해 보였다. 우리는
49 아빠가 이렇게 심각하게 아픈지 몰랐다. 토요일 저녁에 출발한
증기선은 출항한 지 세 시간 만에 바위에 걸려 침몰했다고 한다.
아빠는 안전하게 구출되었지만 아빠의 약 상자, 책, 옷가지 등은 모두
떠내려 갔다고 한다. 밤새 시끄럽고 지저분한 여관에서 지내야 했기
때문에 아빠는 잠을 이루지 못했고, 밤 중 내내 위독했다고 한다.
아침에 그분들은 보트를 구해서 가능한 한 빨리 집으로 가는 것이
현명한 방법이라고 판단했다. 하지만 썰물 때라 물살을 거슬러야
했으므로 다시 하루 낮과 밤을 강 위에서 지낼 수밖에 없었다. 그날
아침 강가에서 마펫 목사가 말씀을 읽고 아빠와 함께 기도했다고
한다. 그러자 아빠는 다시 힘을 냈고, "주님을 의지하는 것이 얼마나
달콤한지요"라고 말한 후 잠드셨다고 한다. 참으로 오랜만에 푹
주무셨다고 한다.
여선은 토요일 하루 종일 아빠를 위해 맛있는 닭백숙을 만들었다.
그리고 일요일에 다시 닭을 고아서 그릇에 담아 가지고 왔다.
아무것도 들지 못하던 아빠가 이번에는 무우 반찬과 함께 국을 조금
드셨다.
아빠는 엄마에게 "건강할 때 아내와 집이 얼마나 큰 기쁨인지 알고
있었지만 이제는 새로운 경험을 하게 되었구려. 아플 때 아내와 집이
얼마나 큰 위로가 되는지 말이오"라고 말했다.

엄마가 아빠의 열을 재어 보니 105°였다. 모두들 아빠의 병세에 대해
이야기를 나눈 후 버스티드 박사를 부르는 것이 좋겠다고 했다. 아빠는
엄마가 뉴욕에서 아빠의 고열을 치료하여 낫게 한 적도 있고 누구보다
엄마를 더 신뢰한다고 했지만 우리 모두는 될 수 있는 한 여러 의사
선생들의 조언을 받아 보는 것이 나을 거라 생각했고 아빠도 이에
동의했다. 그래서 버스티드 박사가 왔고, 스크랜턴(W. B. Scranton)
박사도 오셨다. 의사 선생들은 이 병을 이곳 풍토병으로 열이 올랐다
50 내렸다 하면서 고열이 반복되는 회귀열(임병)[47]로 본 것 같다. 루이스
양과 알렌 박사가 심하게 앓았던 것과 같은 병처럼 말이다. 버스티드
박사는 그 병을 냉수욕과 피하 스트리크닌 주사로 적절히 처방해서
고친 사례가 많았다. 그러나 아빠는 위가 너무 예민해져서 아무 음식도
못 드셨기에 와버그 팅크제를 전혀 삼키지 못했다. 그래서 우리는
냉수욕 치료를 하면서 가능한 한 영양을 섭취시키기로 결론을 지었다.
첫 번째 냉수욕을 마친 후 아빠는 훨씬 좋아졌다며 다시 냉수욕을
시켜 달라고 했다. 하지만 열은 내리지 않았고 두 번째 냉수욕 후에는
기운이 너무 빠졌을 뿐 아니라 몸의 온도 차가 너무 심해서 충격이
컸으므로 아빠는 다시 냉수욕 하는 것을 두려워했다. 아빠의 체온은
105°였고 물의 온도는 54°였다. {104°였고 점차 열이 내렸다.}[48] 그래서
버스티드 박사는 냉수욕이 아닌 전신욕만 한 번 더 하게 하셨다. 전신욕
후에는 스펀지 목욕만 했고, 이로써 한결 수월하게 잘 견딜 수 있었다.
엄마는 월요일과 화요일 이틀 동안 밤낮을 지새면서 아빠를 돌보았다.
그 뒤로는 노블 목사께서 도와주셨다. 월요일 밤에는 아빠 혼자서도
옆 의자 위에 있는 물을 마실 수 있었다. 하지만 화요일 밤부터는
전혀 움직일 수 없었고, 어린 아이처럼 마냥 기다릴 수밖에 없었다.

수요일 아침이 되자 엄마는 아주 지쳐 버렸다. 그때 노블 목사가 오셔서 기꺼이 도와주겠다고 하자 아빠는 엄마에게 더 이상 일어나지 말라고 하시면서 노블 목사께 엄마 침대 주위에 병풍을 쳐 달라고 했다. 그러면서 엄마는 좀 쉬어야 한다고 했다. 그래서 엄마는 좀 쉬려 했지만 어쩐지 엄마 눈앞에 한강 둑에 있는 작은 매장지[49]가 환상으로 나타났고, 사랑하는 아빠가 그곳에 곧 묻히게 될 거라는 생각이 몰려와 엄마의 가슴은 슬픔으로 찢어지는 듯 했다. 엄마는 소리 내어 흐느껴 울지 않으려고 안간힘을 썼다. 그렇게 하면 아빠가 마음 아파할 것이기 때문이었다.

51 노블 목사가 엄마의 침대 주위에 병풍을 치자마자 아빠는 노블 목사께 연필과 종이를 가져다 달라고 하여 재정부장 아펜젤러(H. G. Appenzeller) 목사께 보낼 마지막 여행 경비 지출 내역을 적어 주었다.
그리고 다른 모든 회계장부는 아빠의 책들 사이에 있다고 알려주셨다.
이 일을 마친 후에는 "이제 나는 살거나 죽을 준비가 되었습니다" (Now I am ready to live or to die)라고 말씀하셨다.
노블 목사가 "오, 우리는 당신과 오래 살 것입니다, 의사 선생님"이라고 하자 아빠는 이렇게 대답했다. "하나님의 뜻이 그렇다면 저는 이곳에 머물면서 일을 조금 더 오래 하고 싶습니다. 하지만 그렇지 않다면 저는 어린 양의 피로 씻겨진 '천국 문을 거침없이 지나'갈 것입니다."
그리고 몇 분간의 침묵이 흐른 뒤 아빠는 "예수의 피밖에 없습니다"라고 덧붙이셨다. 불쌍한 엄마, 엄마는 소리 내어 울지 않으려고 애썼지만 엄마의 베개는 눈물로 젖었다. 엄마는 그 어느 때보다도 간절히 하나님께 사랑하는 아빠를 남게 해달라고 기도드렸다.
그리고 나서 이 상황에서 엄마가 할 수 있는 것이 무엇인지 생각했다.

아빠는 오늘 아침 눈에 띄게 위중해졌으며, 한 마디 말을 하기도 힘들어하셨고, 하는 말을 알아듣기도 이미 어려워졌다. 버스티드 박사가 도착하자 엄마는 곧 에비슨(O. R. Avison)[50] 박사와 빈튼 박사 그리고 버스티드 박사가 견해를 묻고 싶은 모든 분들을 불러서 더 이상 할 수 있는 것이 있는지 상의해 달라고 부탁했다. 이날 엄마와 버스티드 박사는 아빠의 몸과 팔에 난 작은 붉은 반점을 발견했고, 심한 탈진 등 다른 증세들을 종합해 볼 때 발진티푸스일 거라고 생각하기 시작했다. 그리고 여러 의사 선생들의 진찰 후 아빠의 병명이 발진티푸스로 확인되었다. 신선한 공기가 발진티푸스에 가장 좋은 소독제였고 강장제였기 때문에 침대 위에 따뜻한 이불들을 덮고 문들과 창문들을 모두 열어놓기로 했다. 그리고 가능하면 아빠가 마실 신선한 우유를 구해 보기로 했다. 우유를 마시고 있던 선교사들이 모두 친절하게 우유 배달부를 우리에게 보내 자신들의 몫을 주었고, 그래서 우리는 매일 2쿼트의 우유를 얻을 수 있었다. 아빠는 우유를 정말 맛있게 드셨다. 아빠는 그것을 '생명의 묘약'이라고 불렀다.

52 {그 당시 우리는 발진티푸스의 원인을 몰랐고, 아빠가 목욕하고 옷을 갈아입은 후에는 전염을 걱정할 필요가 없는 줄 알았다.}[51] 아빠는 우유가 아빠의 위에 닿자마자 소화가 된다고 확신했다. 엄마는 약간의 희망을 갖기 시작했다. 열이 가장 심하게 나리라고 예상되는 10일째나 12일째까지 버텨 주신다면 아빠는 좋아질 수 있을 것이기 때문이다. 아빠의 열은밤낮 평균 105° 정도로 지속되었다. 십 분의 몇 도 정도만 오르락 내리락 할 뿐, 별 차도가 없었다. 아빠가 하는 말들은 점점 더 알아듣기 어려워졌다. 그리고 엄마는 더 이상 아빠에게 말을 많이 하지 않았다. 말을 거는 것이 아빠를

피곤하게 할까봐 두려웠기 때문이다. 아빠는 가끔 엄마에게 아빠가 말을 더 이상 하지 않은 것으로 상심하지 말라고 일러주셨다. 한번은 아빠의 볼턴[52] 외할아버지에 대해 말씀하셨는데, 할아버지의 둔부가 골절되었다고 들었다면서, “지금 할아버지가 천국에 계시기를 바란다”고 하셨다. 아빠는 누이동생 릴리[53]가 시험을 통과했는지 물었다. 엄마가 아빠 가까이 갈 때면 종종 얼마나 엄마를 사랑하는지, 아빠의 사랑은 영원할 거라는 말을 해주려고 애를 썼다. 뱃속에 있는 아기에 대해서도 물었는데 엄마가 “아기는 아주 건강한 것 같아요. 셔우드보다 훨씬 많이 움직여요”라고 대답하면 미소를 짓곤 했다. 오후 늦게 아빠가 엄마를 불렀는데 한동안 엄마는 아빠가 무슨 말을 하시는지 알아듣지 못했다. “샤워 뭐”라고 하시는 것 같았는데 엄마가 잘 알아듣지 못하자 아빠는 한 글자 한 글자 철자를 말하기 시작했다. 그제야 엄마는 아빠가 ‘셔우드’를 보고 싶어 한다는 것을 알아차렸고, 보모가 셔우드를 데리고 들어왔다. 우리는 아빠의 병이 전염성이라는 것을 알고 난 후 될 수 있는 한 셔우드를 방에 들여놓지 않았었다. 아빠는 어린 셔우드를 간절하게 바라보셨다. 하지만 그 아이를 더 가까이 부르지는 않았다. 그 위험성을 아는 듯했다. 그렇게 한참을 간절한 눈빛으로 쳐다본 후에는 셔우드를 데리고 나가라는 몸짓을 했다. 사랑하는 우리 아가, 아빠가 너를 바라보았던 그 사랑이 담긴 간절한 눈빛에 대해 네가 아무것도 기억하지 못할 것을 생각하면
53 얼마나 애처로운지 모르겠다. 그날 밤 얼마 동안 버스티드 박사가 아빠와 함께 계셨고, 노블 목사는 저녁 시간에 아빠를 지켜 주셨다. 엄마는 엄마 침대와 셔우드 침대를 식당으로 옮겼다. 엄마는 아빠가 안 계시는 동안 식당과 부엌을 고치느라 고생했지만, 아빠가 집에

돌아오셔서 부엌을 보면 정말 기뻐하시리라 생각했기에 열심히 고쳤다. 엄마와 아빠는 사실 가족끼리 지내는 즐거움을 가져 본 적이 없었다. 신혼여행에서 돌아오자마자 아빠는 평양으로 가셨고, 아빠가 돌아오기 전에 노블 목사 부부가 들어오셨다. 그리고 노블 목사 가족은 지난 봄 엄마, 아빠가 평양에 갈 때까지 우리와 지냈다.

우리 가족이 평양에서 돌아온 후에는 노블 목사 가족이 일본으로 갈 때까지 다시 함께 지냈고, 그 댁이 떠난 후에야 엄마, 아빠는 그때 단 몇 주 동안 가족끼리 지낼 수 있었다. 그리고 그렇게 지내는 것이 정말 좋아서 엄마, 아빠는 창고를 고쳐 부엌으로 사용하기로 했고, 침실을 수리해서 아빠의 서재와 식당으로 사용하면서 우리 집을 가져보기로 했다. 평양으로 떠나실 무렵 아빠는 집 일부분만 고쳐놓고 가셨으며, 그동안 엄마는 집수리를 마무리 했는데, 이렇게 아빠는 새로 단장된 집을 보지도 못하고, 단란한 '살림'을 누려보지도 못하고 아파서 누워 계신다.

목요일 아침 아빠는 연필과 종이를 달라고 하고 무언가를 쓰려고 했다. 하지만 그것은 마치 어린 셔우드가 글씨를 쓰는 것 같았고, 아빠는 글쓰기를 포기했다. 그날은 우유를 잘 들지도 못했다. 결국 마비가 와서 아빠는 점점 더 말을 할 수 없게 되었고, 인두근육에도 영향을 끼쳐 음식을 삼키기도 힘들게 되었다. 아빠는 우유를 자주 토했다. 토한 우유는 아빠의 턱수염을 더럽혔고, 버스티드 박사는 수염을 깎는 게 좋겠다고 하셨다. 엄마는 아빠에게 턱수염을 깎아도 되겠냐고 물어 보았다. 아빠는 천천히 그러나 분명한 어조로 "괜-찮-아-요"라고 대답했다. 노블 목사가 턱 윗부분까지 수염을 말끔히 잘라 주셨다. 그러자 아빠의 모습은 퀸스대학교에서 찍은 학창시절 사진과

비슷해졌다. 아빠는 거울을 가져다 달라고 하셨고, 거울에 비친 모습을
54 보고 미소 지었다. 고열이 지속되었지만, 아빠는 정신을 놓지 않았다.
오늘은 리(G. Lee)[54] 목사가 오셔서 침대 뒤에 있는 책장을 보면서
책장에 다리를 달아 공기를 쐴 수 있도록 밖으로 옮기면 좋겠다고
하셨다. 아빠의 침대를 생각하고 그러신 게 분명하다. 말을 할 수
있으면 모든 질문에 올바르게 대답했다. 오후에 엄마는 아빠에게
우리가 주문한 것이 샌프란시스코에서 도착했다고 말씀드렸다.
아빠는 "제—제—제-물-포-에?"라고 물었다. "아니, 여기에, 집에
왔어요"라고 엄마가 대답했다. 그러자 아빠는 보모가 쓸 방이
준비되었냐고 물었다. 아빠는 엄마가 보낸 편지에서 우리가 보모
문제로 어려움을 겪고 있다는 것을 알고 계셨다. 이날은 아빠가 말씀을
하신 마지막 날이었다. 한번은 엄마가 아빠 가까이 있을 때 아주
슬프고도 사랑에 찬 표정과 눈으로 엄마를 바라보면서 떠듬떠듬
"사-랑-해-요"라고 말씀하셨다. "그래요, 알고 있어요, 여보.
말할 필요 없어요. 말하면 기운이 빠질 거예요"라고 엄마가
말해드렸다. 하고 싶은 말을 다 할 수 없다는 사실이 아빠를 가장
힘들게 하는 것 같았다. 오후에 아빠는 엄마에게 평양 방문에 대해
이야기해 주려고 애를 쓰셨다. 엄마는 아빠의 이야기를 다 알아들을
수 없었지만 아빠가 그곳에 갔던 것에 대해 엄마가 후회하지 않기를
바라는 듯했다. 그리고 엄마는 아빠가 아주 분명하게 "나는 그 일을
예수님을 위해 했다오. 그리고 주님은 나에게 상을 주실 거예요"라고
하는 말을 알아들었다. 이 말은 사랑하는 아빠가 남기신 마지막
말씀이 되었다.

{1893년 8월 26일 – 아빠는 아침 식사 전에 이곳 아펜젤러 댁 서재에 있는 책상에 앉아서 시를 쓰고 싶다고 하셨다. 그리고 아래 두 절의 시를 지었다. 시 쓰기를 마친 후에는 언젠가 더 좋게 고쳐야겠다고 하셨다.

"나의 세월은 마치 동화 같았습니다.
값진 황금 같은 순간들이었습니다.
나의 이생의 날은 거의 다 지나가고
본향에 더 가까이 다가가고 있습니다.

오, 생각만 해도 더없이 행복한,
영원히 함께 거한다는 생각,
저 편에서 기다리고 계신 주님과
먼저 가신 사랑하는 분들과 함께." – W. J. 홀}[55]

목요일 밤에는 스크랜턴 박사가 아빠와 함께 계셨다. 금요일 아침이
되자 아빠는 아무것도 삼키지 못하셨다. 버스티드 박사가 위관으로
영양을 공급하려고 했으나 아빠는 견디지 못하셨고, 위장에 튜브 넣는
것을 원치 않았다. 그래서 장을 통해 음식을 제공했다. 그리고 그것을
그날은 잘 유지하셨다. 금요일 밤에는 빈튼 박사가 아빠와 함께
55 계셨다. 열이 난 지 열흘째 되는 날이었다. 엄마는 그날 자러 가면서
위기가 온 것 같다는 생각이 들었다. 하지만 엄마는 빈튼 박사께서
사랑하는 마음으로 할 수 있는 모든 것을 다 하시리라는 것을 알고
있었다. 아빠가 빈튼 박사의 어린 아기를 위해 작은 관을 만들고

박사 부부와 함께 기도하면서 그분들을 위로하려고 애썼던 것이 불과 얼마 전 일이었다.[56] 그런데 이렇게 빨리 빈튼 박사가 아빠의 임종을 지켜보게 되리라고 어찌 생각이나 하셨을까. 토요일 아침 7시쯤 의사 선생들은 엄마를 방으로 들어오라고 하셨다. 모두들 아빠가 죽음을 맞고 있다고 생각했다. 하지만 아빠는 그날 하루를 버티셨다. 아빠는 엄마가 가까이서 손을 잡아주는 것을 좋아하는 듯했다. 정오까지 계속 눈을 감고 계셨는데 엄마가 몸을 숙이고 아빠 귀에 대고 "닥터" 하고 부르자 대답으로 엄마의 손을 꼭 잡아주셨다. 오후에는 눈을 크게 뜨고 엄마의 눈을 똑바로 쳐다보았다. 힘들게 숨을 쉬셨고, 심장은 점점 약해졌다. 하지만 고통스럽지는 않은 것 같았다. 저녁이 되자 엄마가 두 손을 잡아주기를 바라시는 것 같았다. 아빠의 눈은 아주 밝아 보였다. 그리고 11월 24일 토요일 해질 무렵, 아빠는 마지막 숨을 쉬셨다. 아빠의 두 손은 엄마의 두 손을 잡고 있었고, 아빠의 눈은 엄마의 눈을 바라보고 있었다. 엄마는 부드럽게 사랑스러운 두 눈을 감겨 드렸다. 그러고 나서 아빠의 눈이 엄마의 눈을 다시는 볼 수 없을 거라는 생각에 아빠의 눈을 한 번 더 뜨게 했다. 마지막으로 오랫동안 볼 수 있도록. 아빠의 눈은 여전히 밝고 맑아서 아빠의 사랑스러운 영혼이 그 몸을 떠나간 것처럼 보이지 않았다.

{엄마가 그날 사랑하는 아빠의 이마에 맺히는 '죽음의 이슬'(death-dew)을 닦아줄 때 엄마의 마음속에 찬송가 <내 주 되신 주를 참 사랑하고>(My Jesus I Love Thee)의 다음 구절이 계속 떠올랐고, 엄마는 이 노래를 몇 번 큰 소리로 반복해서 불렀다.

"살아 있을 때나 죽을 때나 당신을 사랑합니다.
내게 숨쉴 수 있도록 허락하실 때까지 당신을 찬양합니다.
내 이마에 차가운 죽음의 이슬이 맺힐 때 말하겠어요.
나의 주님, 지금 이 순간 당신을 가장 사랑합니다."}[57]

엄마는 마지막으로 아빠의 눈을 감겨드리고 그 방을 나왔다. 그리고
사랑하는 어린 아들을 안고 와서 하나님께 아들을 위해 자신이 더
용감하고 강해질 수 있게 도와달라고 기도했다. 그리고 아직 복중에
있는 어린 아기를 위해 기도했다. 그때 엄마의 심장 아래 있던 그
아이의 작은 심장도 요동쳤다. 하나님은 엄마의 기도에 확실히 응답해
56 주셨다. 그리고 단시간에 엄마는 아빠의 입관 준비를 할 수 있었다.
아빠의 결혼식 양복, 속옷, 목회자용 컬러(collar), 커프스, 넥타이 등을
꺼내 입히면서. 하지만 그날 밤 엄마는 자정 12시에 잠에서 깨었고,
걷잡을 수 없는 외로움이 몰려와서 큰 소리로 흐느껴 울었다.
셔우드를 돌보기 위해 와 있던 금영이가 엄마에게 와서 엄마를 위로해
주려고 애쓰면서 "대인께서는 천국에 가셨습니다. 그분은 지금
예수님과 함께 계십니다. 슬퍼하시지 마세요"라고 말했다.
다음 날은 눈부시게 아름다운 일요일이었다. 아빠는 예수님과 함께
이날을 보내고 계실 것이다. 셔우드는 금영이에게 안긴 채 엄마와
신선한 공기를 쐬러 나갔다. 우리에게 병이 들지 않기를 바라면서
아빠가 평양에 가시기 전 셔우드를 안고 마지막으로 산책하던
그 담길을 따라 걸었다.

{사랑하는 어머니! 저는 홀로 여기 있습니다.

슬픔과 고통 속에 있습니다.
햇살은 제 가슴에서 사라졌습니다.
아, 저는 휘몰아치는 비를 느낍니다!
이 한기, 곰팡이, 비.

오, 나를 감싸 안으시는 당신의 정다운 팔을
다시 한 번 느껴 볼 수 있다면,
당신의 입술이 이 고통을
키스로 닦아주실 것만 같은데, 달래 줄 것만 같은데
이 무디고 차갑고 무거운 고통을.

하지만 다정한 어머니, 인생의 풍파를 거치면서
제가 당신께 의지하지 않을지도 몰라요.
힘없이 움츠린 어린 것들이
저를 신뢰하며 매달리기에.
불쌍한 아기들에게는 저밖에 다른 인도자가 없기에!

사랑하는 어머니, 당신의 방랑자가 기도합니다.
드높은 믿음을 주시기를,
상한 갈대가 모두 온전히 치유되고
제가 천국만 바라볼 수 있도록,
제 마음이 그리스도와 천국 안에서 강건해지도록.
-패니 포레스터(저드슨 부인), 1850}[58]

장지로 떠나기로 약속된 시간은 2시였다. 떠나기 바로 몇 분 전에
관이 완성되었다. 아빠는 이곳에 오신 뒤로 사망한 모든 외국인을
위해 예쁜 관들을 만들어 주셨었다. 아빠는 소년 시절 가구공이었고,
관 만드는 것을 도왔기 때문이다. 하지만 지금 아빠를 위해 관을
만들 수 있는 사람이 없었다. 그래서 어떤 중국인이 최선을 다해 관을
만들어 주었다. 관은 흰색 한국 비단으로 테두리가 쳐져 있고, 검은
천으로 싸여 있었다. 엄마는 무릎에 셔우드를 앉히고 네 명이 드는
가마를 타고 갔다. 천진한 아이는 가마 타고 시골길을 가는 것을
참 즐거워했다. 특히 커다란 나무들을 좋아하는 것 같았다. 한강에
57 닿기 전에 셔우드는 잠들었고, 묘지에서 장례식이 진행되는 동안 계속
잤다. 그래서 셔우드는 사랑하는 아빠의 관 위에 흙이 떨어질 때
'쿵' 하고 났던 그 차디찬 소리를 듣지 못했다. 노블 목사님은 "흙은
흙으로, 티끌은 티끌로"라고 말씀하셨다.

장례식 후 엄마와 셔우드는 집을 소독하는 동안 커틀러 박사 댁으로 갔고, 사흘간 루이스 양의 방에서 지냈다.

화요일 오후, 예배당에서 아빠에게 가장 잘 어울리는 아름다운 추도 예배가 드려졌다. 엄마가 찬송가와 아빠가 좋아하던 말씀을 골랐다. 그리고 예배 순서를 맡아주실 분들을 제안했고, 친절하게도 노블 목사가 프로그램을 만들어 주셨다. 후에 엄마는 노블 목사께 짧은 감사의 말을 써서 보냈는데, 그분은 "저는 말로 표현할 수 없을 정도로 홀 박사를 사랑합니다. 제가 해 드렸던 일과 앞으로 할 수 있도록 허락해 주실 봉사는 저에게 큰 기쁨입니다"라고 답하셨다.

추도 예배

닥터 윌리엄 제임스 홀 목사

배재 예배당, 1894년 11월 27일

찬송 감리교 찬송가집 979장 〈예수 안에 잠들다〉(Asleep in Jesus)

성경 말씀 이사야 43:1-15 　 W. B. 스크랜턴 박사

기도 　 W. B. 스크랜턴 박사

패니 크로스비(Fanny Crosby)의 찬송[59]

연설 – 약력 소개 　 W. A. 노블 목사

연설 – 의료 선교사로서의 홀 박사 　 빈튼 박사

연설 – 　 S. A. 마펫 목사

찬송 – 복음성가 234장 〈헌신〉[60](아빠가 좋아하신 찬송)

연설 – 　 버스티드 박사

연설 – 　 그래함 리 목사

찬송 – 복음성가 314장 〈내 주 되신 주를 참 사랑하고〉

연설 – 홀 박사의 선교 사역: 시작과 끝 　 H. G. 아펜젤러 목사

독창 – 〈천국문을 지나〉[61] 　 그래함 리 목사

축도

58 엄마는 언젠가 우리 아들이 한국과 미국의 친구들로부터 받은 친절한 위로의 편지들을 전부 읽을 수 있도록 일기장에 베껴 놓으려 했다. 그러나 편지가 너무 많아서 그냥 그대로 다 보관해 두기로 했다. 어느 분이 "누구보다 우리는 그분을 사랑하였습니다"[62]라고 썼듯이 모두들 아빠를 많이 사랑했단다. 또 어느 분은 "당신의 거룩했던

남편이 그 짧은 일생 동안 베푼 선행은 다른 이들이 같은 시간에 이룬 것의 3~10배의 행적입니다"[63]라고 하셨다. 힐리어(W. C. Hillier) 영국 총영사는 "이 선교지에서 그리도 헌신적이고 성실했던 사역자의 죽음은 그분의 동료 선교사들에게 만회할 수 없는 상실이지만 다른 길을 걸어가고 있는 여러 친구들에게도 깊은 슬픔이 될 것입니다. 그중 제가 한 사람인 것을 자랑스럽게 여깁니다"라고 쓰셨다. 마펫 목사는 "진실로 그분은 주님을 섬기는 일에 충실함이 어떤 것인지를 당신에게 풍성한 유산으로 남기셨습니다. 때에 따라 사용되고 때에 따라 거두어진다는 그분의 목회에 온전한 증거가 되셨습니다"라고 하셨다.

59 윌리엄 홀 목사 추모예배

1894. 11. 27. 배재채플
윌리엄 홀 박사가 선교지로 떠날 때 패니 크로스비가 지어 준 시

누가 가겠느냐?

어둠의 왕자가 군림하는
저 험하고 도도한 바다 건너,
수많은 희생자를
무자비한 쇠사슬로 잡아 가두는 바다 건너.
저 비통한 분노의 곡성,
저 깊은 절망의 울음소리.
우리에게 빛을 주소서. 아니면 멸망이오니,
속히 보내소서. 우리가 죽겠나이다.

이 불쌍하고 배고픈 사람들에게
누가 생명의 떡을 가져다주려나?
주님의 인자와 긍휼의 보좌 앞에서
누가 이들과 함께 기도하려나?
누가 이 길을 가려나?

거센 풍랑을 지나
부모와 친구와 고향을
소리 없이 모두 남겨두고?

충성스런 선교단에서
굳세고 용감한 답이 왔네,
축복의 주님이
손에 붙들고 있는 사람이.
굳세고 용감한 답이 왔네,
이렇게 말하는 사람이,
"자비로운 주님, 당신께서 부르셨으니
당신 뜻을 따르옵니다."

사랑하는 형제여, 당신이 가는군요,
눈물로 씨를 뿌려야 하는 곳으로.
열심히 일한 열매가
오랫동안 맺히지 않을지도 모르는데,
그들의 변하는 모습에 수고하고
불볕과 혹한을 견디려 하네.
한 알의 씨도 잊히지 않으리,
한 톨 열매도 빠짐없이 거두리.

하나님이 물결 위에 함께하시기를,
항상 보호해 주시기를,
부드러운 사랑과 자애로
당신을 우리에게로 돌아오게 해주시기를.
하지만 그게 뜻이 아니시라면,
그래서 우리가 이 땅에서 다시 만나지 못한다면,
밝고 영원한 천국에서
할렐루야 찬양하며 다시 만나세.

엄마는 확신한다. 우리 셔우드가 살아 있는 한 언젠가는 이런 아빠에 대해 자랑스러할 거라고 말이다. 하늘에 계신 아버지만이 사랑하는 아버지의 죽음으로 셔우드가 잃은 것을 채워주실 수 있을 것이다.

하나님은 가장 풍성하신 약속을 아버지가 없는 아이들에게 해주셨다. 그리고 사랑하는 어린 아들아, 우리는 너에게 그 약속이 이루어질 것을 확신한다.

오늘은 12월 10일 월요일이다. 우리, 즉 꼬마 셔우드와 엄마, 여선 삼촌과 에스더 이모는 제물포에서 일본으로 가는 배를 기다리고 있다. 우리는 일본에서 차이나호를 타고 미국으로 갈 것이다. 엄마는 거의 5년간 이곳에 있었으므로 휴가 때가 가까워지기도 했고, 지금은 선교 사역을 잘 할 수도 없는 상황이라서 이참에 휴가를 가는 게 좋겠다고 생각했다. 엄마는 2년 후쯤 다시 돌아올 수 있기를 바라고 있다. 그리고 평양으로 발령받아 사랑하는 아빠가 시작하신 사역이 계속될 수 있도록 돕고 싶다. 에스더와 여선은 모두 미국에 가기를 원했고, 그래서 엄마는 그들과 함께 미국으로 가고 있다. 여선은 집안일을 도우며 시간 나는 대로 영어를 배울 것이고, 에스더는 리버티에 있는 학교에 보낼 계획이다. 에스더가 잘 해내면, 엄마는 에스더를 의대에 보내서 의료 선교사로 다시 한국인 자매들에게 돌아오게 할 것이다.

우리는 7일 금요일 아침 9시에 서울을 떠나 제물포에 왔고, 오후 5시 30분에 존스 목사 댁에 도착했다. 날씨가 추웠다. 셔우드는 엄마 가마를 타고 가다가 간혹 아펜젤러 목사 앞에 앉아서 말을 타기도 했다. 여행하기 이틀 전 수요일 밤에 셔우드는 고열이 났다. 체온이 104.8°까지 올라갔고, 심박수 140, 호흡수는 50이었다.

엄마는 셔우드가 발진티푸스에 걸리는 게 아닌지 너무 두려웠다. 그러나 부자(aconite)[64]를 몇 번 복용한 후 많이 나아졌고, 목요일밤에는 완전히 회복되었다. 금요일 아침에도 괜찮아서 엄마와 의사
60 선생들은 이가 나느라 그랬나 보다고 생각했다. 우리는 토요일 아침

출항하는 배를 탈 수 있기를 바라며 제물포로 갔다. 그런데 토요일 아침 셔우드의 옷을 입히면서 엄마는 셔우드가 홍역에 걸렸다는 것을 알게 되었다. 그래서 열이 났던 것이다. 배는 만선이어서 더 이상 다른 승객을 태울 수 없었기 때문에 우리는 어차피 일본으로 갈 수 없었다. 우리는 셔우드의 홍역이 좀 나아지고 다음 배가 올 때까지 존스 목사 댁에서 신세를 지게 되었다. 셔우드는 오늘로 13개월이 되었다.

몸무게는 외투를 입고 23½파운드가 나간다. 지난밤 감기 기운이 좀 있었는데, 오늘은 기침을 심하게 한다. 그리고 열이 다시 나는 것 같다. '보인튼' 호가 오늘 들어왔다. 일이 모두 순조롭게 된다면 우리는 다음 금요일 아침, 12월 14일에 한국을 떠나게 될 것이다.

"모든 짐 지기 버거울 때
이 짐 내려놓으니
삶의 기쁨 충만하네.
찌푸린 눈살 펴지네.
아! 그러나 힘들 때마다
이제는 사라진 짐
생각해 보니 그로 인해
하나님께 감사하네.

이보다 더 좋은 집 없네.
성도들이 들어갔으니
어디서 살든
따르기 그리 어렵지 않네.

땅이나 바다 그 어디든
하나님과 동행하니
어떤 일이 일어나더라도
주의 사랑 영원히 지키시네."[65]

61 1895년 1월 10일, 목요일

너는 아침에 씨를 뿌리고 저녁에도 손을 놓지 말라 이것이 잘 될는지, 저것이 잘 될는지, 혹 둘이 다 잘 될는지 알지 못함이니라 (전도서 11:6)

"우리는 세월이 아닌 행위로 산다. 호흡이 아닌 생각 속에.
시계 바늘이 아닌 감정으로 산다.
우리는 심장의 고동으로 시간을 재야 한다. 가장 잘 사는 사람은 제일 많이 생각하고 가장 숭고한 마음으로 최선의 행동을 하는 사람이다."[66]

4주 동안 어린 셔우드는 해로와 육로로 매일 여행을 했다. 바로 4주 전에 우리는 거룻배(sampan)를 타고 보인튼 호로 노를 저어 갔다. 그리고 다음 날 아침 동이 틀 때까지 항해했다. 일본까지 가는 동안 내내 파도가 거셌다. 바람이 세게 불었고, 배가 이리저리 흔들려서 우리 모두 멀미를 했다. 셔우드도 한 번 토했다. 낮에는 같이 배를 타고 있던 선장의 부인이 친절하게 셔우드를 돌보아 주셨다. 하지만 밤에는 엄마 혼자 셔우드를 돌보아야 했다. 에스더나 여선에게서 전혀 도움을 받을 수 없었다. 이 두 사람은 멀미 때문에 통나무처럼 처져 있었기 때문이다. 셔우드를 제외한 나머지 사람들은 50시간이 넘도록 아무것도 먹지 못했고, 약간의 물만 마셨을 뿐이다. 엄마는 더 이상 올라올 것이 없을 정도로 계속 구토를 했다. 엄마가 토할 때마다 셔우드는 덮고 있던 담요의 모서리를 끌어당겨 엄마의 입술을 닦아 주려고 애썼다. 그리고 가끔 엄마가 토한 접시가 있는 곳까지 기어 가서 안쓰러운 마음에 자기도 토하는 척했다. 엄마는 울 수 없었다. 셔우드가 본다면 따라서 울 것이기 때문이다. 정말로 끔찍한 이틀 밤낮이었다. 무시무시한 악몽 같았다. 일요일 아침 일찍 우리는 나가사키 항구로 들어갔다. 그 전날 밤 엄마는 비몽사몽간에 꿈을
62 꿨는데, 우리가 나가사키에 도착했을 때 '차이나' 호가 그곳에 와 있었고 오후 4시에 출항할 거라는 꿈이었다. 엄마는 선장과 선장 부인에게 이 꿈에 대해 말해 주었고, 모두 그렇게 되기를 희망했다. 하지만 스케줄에 따르면 차이나 호는 월요일 고베 출항하기로 되어 있었다. 이것은 우리에게 그다지 위로가 되지 않았다. 그런데 얼마 후 도선사가 배에 올라오는 것 같더니, 곧 맘씨 좋은 선장이 숨이 턱에 차도록 뛰어 내려와 엄마에게 큰 소리로 말했다. "당신의 꿈이 실현되었어요. 차이나 호가 방금 들어왔고, 오늘 오후에 떠난대요." 우리로 하여금 그렇게 배멀미를 하게 한 폭풍이 차이나 호를 지연시켰던 것이다. "주께서……동풍 부는 날에 폭풍으로 그들을 옮기셨느니라"[67]

엄마는 여성해외선교회(W.F.M.S.)의 숙녀들께 소식을 보냈고, 곧 반 페턴(Van Petten) 부인과 프렌치(French) 양이 와서 화물과 가방을 옮기는 것과 표를 구입하는 것을 도와주셨다. 우리는 곧 차이나 호를

탔고, 안락한 객실로 들어갔다. 해안에 가 볼 시간이 없었지만 프렌치 양이 친절하게 '오와카 양'을 배 안으로 데리고 왔다. 오와카 양은 전에 진료소에서 에스더와 함께 엄마를 도와주던 일본인 소녀였다. 에스더와 엄마는 오와카 양과 짧으나마 즐거운 시간을 가졌다. 그녀는 어린 셔우드를 볼 수 있어서 아주 기뻐했다. 오와카 양이 한국을 떠났을 때는 엄마가 아직 미혼이었다. 그녀는 지금 나카사키에 있는 여학교에서 훌륭하게 사역하고 있다.

차이나 호는 태평양을 운행하는 배 중에서 가장 좋은 증기선이라는 평판을 듣고 있다. 이 배는 최근 우리가 탔던 작은 화물선에 비하면 아주 크고 아름다웠다. 우리는 일본 내해를 항해하면서 유쾌한 시간을 보냈다. 고베에 12월 18일 도착했는데 산꼭대기가 눈으로 덮여 있었다. 우리가 본 첫눈이었다. 20일 목요일, 우리는 요코하마 해변에서 지냈다. 셔우드는 인력거 타는 것을 정말 좋아했다. 엄마는
63 일본은행이 발행한 수표를 뉴욕은행권으로 바꾸고, 샌프란시스코로 가는 표들과 박 씨 부부를 위한 이민 서류들을 확인하고, 에스더가 신을 외국 신발과 여선이 입을 외국 옷 등을 준비하느라 바쁜 하루를 보냈다. W.F.M.S.의 그리피스(Griffis) 양이 친절하게 도와주셨다.

21일, 우리는 요코하마를 출발해 호놀룰루를 경유해 태평양을 건너는 긴 항해를 시작했다. 차이나 호에서는 아직 아무도 배멀미를 하지 않고 있다. 파도도 거세지 않아서 셔우드는 매일 유모차를 타고 갑판 위를 이리저리 왔다갔다 했다. 하지만 해안에서 멀어지자 배가 심하게 흔들리기 시작했다. 비록 바다는 거칠어 보이지 않았지만 바람이 거세게 불었다. 일요일까지 상황이 아주 나빴다. 에스더와 여선이 멀미를 하기 시작했고 기분이 다시 침울해졌다. 엄마는 건강이

안 좋아졌다. 힘든데도 셔우드를 너무 오래 안고 있었기 때문이다.
하지만 며칠이 지나자 에스더와 여선은 항해에 익숙해졌고, 셔우드를
많이 돌보면서 엄마에게 쉴 시간을 주었다.

12월 25일 화요일, 크리스마스다. 오늘은 바다가 좀 잔잔해졌다.
차이나 호에는 어린이가 셔우드 외에 두 명밖에 없다. 윌리
히트(Willie Hitt)와 비아트리스(Beatrice) 남매로 10세와 4세이고, 최근
인도에서 오신 켄터키 주 루이빌 출신의 히트 박사 부부의 아이들이다.
히트 박사는 의료 선교사로 인도에 간 지 불과 1년밖에 되지 않았지만
건강상 이유로 귀국하는 중이다. 두 아이들은 멋진 크리스마스 선물을
몇 가지 받았다. 히트 부인께서 셔우드에게도 작은 인형을 주셨다.
우리는 즐거운 크리스마스를 보냈다. 저녁에는 사교홀을 만국기와
크리스마스 화환으로 장식했고, 승무원들과 승객들은 흥겨운 음악,
낭독, 독창, 이야기를 하면서 즐거운 시간을 보냈다.
5년 전 크리스마스 때 아빠가 엄마를 센트럴 파크에 있는
메트로폴리탄 박물관에 데리고 갔다. 그리고 집으로 돌아오는 길에
처음으로 아내가 되어 달라고 청혼했다. 그런데 불과 한 달 전 이날
64 사랑하는 아빠의 육신은 우리가 보는 앞에서 한강변에 묻히셨다.
이번 크리스마스는 엄마가 지금까지 보낸 크리스마스 중 가장 슬픈
크리스마스였다.

"분명하고도 달콤하게 들리던 사랑스런 목소리가
어느 날 갑자기 사라졌을 때,
그 침묵에 맞서 절대 울지 않으려 해도
새롭고 강한 병마처럼 아프게 둘러싸네.

어떤 희망? 어떤 도움? 어떤 음악이 이 침묵을 깨뜨리고
당신의 감각을 되찾게 할 수 있을까?"[68]

다음 날 승객들은 배가 흔들리는 것에 익숙해지기 시작했고, 배멀미를
하지 않게 되었다. 그런데 엄마는 속이 울렁거리기 시작했다.
이런 증세는 심한 두통을 유발한다.
승무원 그로겐(Grogan) 부인은 셔우드와 엄마에게 아주 친절하시다.
부인은 홀로 된 지 11년이 되었는데, 남편은 어린 아들과 딸을 남겨두고
떠났다고 한다. 두 아이 모두 그때는 아기였고 지금은 할머니와
샌프란시스코에서 지내고 있다고 한다.
셔우드는 굿차일드(Goodchild) 승무원 아저씨를 참 좋아한다.
아저씨는 흑인인데 그분을 볼 때마다 아저씨한테 가겠다고 울었다.
굿차일드 씨는 자주 셔우드를 안고 가서 엔진을 보여 주셨다.
셔우드는 그렇게 해주면 아주 좋아했다.
경도 180도 선을 넘으면서 27일 목요일이 반복되었다. 마치 금요일이
결코 오지 않을 것 같았고, 일주일이 7일이 아니라 8일이 되어 영원히
끝나지 않을 것 같았다. 사람들은 하루가 그렇게 많은 차이를
만들리라고 생각하지 않을 것이다. 하지만 그럴 만한 이유가 있는
것이, 배가 계속 흔들렸고 모두가 아팠기 때문이다. 엄마는 밤에 잘
쉬지 못했고, 배의 요동 때문에 며칠을 피곤하게 지냈다.
12월 29일 토요일, 우리는 북회귀선을 지나 열대 지역으로 들어갔다.
그리고 다음 날 저녁 5시에 호놀룰루에 도착했다. 데이먼(Damon)
65 목사가 배로 와 주셨고 다음 날을 그 댁에서 지낼 수 있게 우리를
초대해 주셨다. 우리는 그렇게 했고 즐겁게 쉴 수 있었다. 여선 삼촌과

에스더 이모 그리고 어린 셔우드는 처음으로 말과 마차를 타 보았고, 엄마도 거의 5년 만에 다시 탄 것이었다. 호놀룰루는 언제나 여름이어서 잔디는 지금 초록색이다. 바나나, 빵나무 열매, 코코아 너트 등이 나무 위에서 자라고 있다. 정원에는 협죽도와 장미가 피어 있다. 데이먼 목사의 아버지는 샌드위치 섬(Sandwich Islands)의 선교사였고, 데이먼 목사는 그곳에서 태어났다. 그리고 중국 선교사 닥터 해퍼(Happer) 목사의 따님과 결혼했는데, 그 부인 역시 열성적인 선교사이시다. 두 분에게는 세 자녀와 아름다운 집이 있다. 이분들은 지금 그 섬의 중국인들을 대상으로 선교 사역을 하고 계신다.

1895년 1월 1일 새해 첫날, 우리는 다시 미국으로 출발해서 1월 6일 일요일 아침, 일정보다 하루 먼저 도착했다. 폭풍이 있었기 때문에 아무도 차이나 호가 시간 전에 도착하리라 기대하지 않았다.

그래서 엄마가 마중 나와 달라고 편지를 썼던 로버트 할아버지[69]와 젠킨스(Jenkins) 부인이 나오지 않으셨다. 세관을 통과한 후 우리는 옥시덴탈 호텔로 갔다. 그런데 그날 저녁 젠킨스 부인이 우리가 그곳에 있다는 것을 알아내셨고, 다음 날 아침 우리는 부인과 함께 디커니스 홈으로 갔다. 중국 난징에서 귀국한 선교사 머레이(Murray) 양이 우리와 같이 갔다. 엄마와 머레이 양은 차이나 호 안에서 아주 가까운 친구가 되었다. 우리는 좌석 기차[70]를 타고 시카고로 가기로 했고 그 기차가 탈 만한 것인지 알아보기로 했다.

그 기차는 팰리스 기차[71]보다 훨씬 저렴했다. 엄마는 할인 가격에 표를 사고 우리 화물들과 가방들을 살펴보느라 종일 바빴다. 그래서 오후 4시 셔먼 다비[72] 아저씨와 만나기로 한 시각까지 뛰어다녔다. 셔먼 가족을 만나러 그 집에 가서 로버트 길더슬리브 할아버지,

66 로버트 다비 아저씨, 찰스 보니[73] 아저씨를 만나 재회의 기쁨을 나누었다. 엄마는 어린 아들을 데리고 가지 못한 것이 아쉬웠다. 그 집으로 가는 데 한 시간, 오는 데 또 한 시간이 걸리기 때문에 셔우드를 데리고 갈 시간이 없었다. 그래서 엄마는 아침 9시부터 밤 9시까지 하루 종일 어린 아들을 보지 못했다. 로버트 할아버지가 어린 종손을 보러 엄마와 같이 오셨다. 할아버지는 셔우드가 만난 첫 번째 가족이다. 셔우드에게 금화 20불을 주셨다.

다음 날 아침, 8일 화요일에 우리는 7시 기차를 타고 샌프란시스코를 떠났다. 시카고까지 기차를 갈아타지 않고 가는 직행 열차였다. 우리는 좌석칸에 탔다. 가격은 한 자리당 6불밖에 하지 않았다. 팰리스 기차는 15불이었다. 셔우드에게는 더 많은 자유가 주어졌다. 기저귀를 말리기에도 좋았다. 그리고 6불 정도로 음식과 필요한 접시를 스미스 가게에서 사서 사용할 수 있었다. 여선 삼촌이 하루 세 끼씩 따뜻한 음식을 장만해 주었다. 우리는 구운 감자, 뜨거운 오트밀, 우유, 쌀밥, 구운 사과, 연어, 훈제 소고기, 소다 크래커, 그레이엄 웨이퍼, 생강 쿠키, 마카롱, 복숭아 통조림, 배 통조림, 견과류, 사탕과 과일 그리고 뜨거운 코코아를 먹었다. 팰리스 기차에서는 한 끼당 1불을 지불해야 하지만 우리의 식사비는 평균 10센트밖에 들지 않았다. 우리 외 다른 승객은 두 사람밖에 없었고, 우리는 그 차칸 전체를 거의 독차지했다. 셔우드는 포터에서 또 다른 흑인 친구를 사귀었다. 그는 오마하 출신의 신실한 감리교인인데, 셔우드는 그를 아주 좋아하게 되었다. 집에 가면 셔우드가 분명히 조도 좋아할 거라는 생각이 들었다. 셔우드는 흑인을 좋아하는 성향을 엄마에게 물려받은 것이 확실하다. 셔우드는 흑인들을 전혀 무서워하지 않는 것 같다. 우리는 캘리포니아, 네바다, 유타, 와이오밍 주를 빠르게 지나갔다. 네브라스카, 아이오와, 일리노이 주를 횡단하면 토요일 오전 7시에 시카고에 도착하게 된다.

셔우드는 오늘로 14개월이 되었다. 외투를 입고 26파운드가 나간다(외투는 1½파운드다). 셔우드는 현재 전혀 말을 하지 않는다.
67 "에", "에", "에"로 말하고 싶은 것을 다 표현한다. 뭔가 원하는 것이 있는데 그 소리만으로 통하지 않으면 손가락으로 가리킨다. 그리고 원하지 않을 때는 단호하게 머리를 흔든다. 셔우드는 아직 혼자 걷지 못한다. 그럴 만한 기회가 별로 없었다. 증기선에서는 배가 너무 흔들려서 걸음마를 배우기는커녕 기어 다닐 수도 없었다. 게다가 선실에서는 기온이 종종 82°를 넘는 무더위라서 셔트와 기저귀만 차고 그냥 바닥에 앉아서 노는 게 전부였다. 배 선실에서부터 혼자 바닥에서 일어서기 시작했고, 선 채로 몇 초 동안 우리를 쳐다보며 자랑스러워했다. 그러다 갑자기 배가 흔들리면 넘어졌다. 하지만 곧 다시 일어서곤 했다. 어떤 날 저녁에는 피곤해질 때까지 열 번에서 열두 번 정도 이 동작을 반복했다. 셔우드는 위층 갑판까지 이어지는 계단을 기어서 올라가는 법도 배웠다. 셔우드 뒤에는 여선과 에스더가 지키고 서서 떨어지지 않도록 봐주었다. 셔우드는 배가 아주 출렁일 때도 몇 번씩이나 기어서 올라갔다.

사랑하는 우리 셔우드는 무럭무럭 잘 자라고 있다. 증기선에서는 객실 자기 침상에서 혼자 잘 잤고, 밤에도 우유를 먹기 위해 깨지도 않고 아침까지 잘 잤다. 아침에는 중국인 소년이 신선한 우유와 삶은 달걀을 가져다 주었고, 11시쯤에는 우유 한 통을 마시고는 잠이 들어 한두 시간 잤다. 오후 4시에는 날마다 닭탕 한 그릇을 먹었다.

셔우드는 아직도 매일 관장을 해야 한다. 그리고 집에 가는 내내 한 번밖에 기저귀를 더럽히지 않았다. 기차에서는 에스더 이모와 위칸 침상에서 잤는데, 보통 저녁 8시에 잠들어 다음 날 아침 7시까지 깨지 않고 잤다.

다음 기차는 저녁 8시에
멀리 퍼피랜드를 향해 출발한대요.
삐삐— 집합을 알리는 기적이 울리네요.
"자, 모두 타세요! 침대차에 타세요!"
그런데 "퍼피랜드까지 얼마예요?
너무 비싸지 않았으면 좋겠어요."
아, 요금은— 포옹과 뽀뽀랍니다.
그리고 기관사에게 지불하세요.[74] – 에드가 애보트(Edgar W. Abbott)

68 1895년 2월 10일, 일요일

고아가 주로 말미암아 긍휼을 얻음이니이다(호세아 14:3)

아가야, 어젯밤 네가 잠들었을 때
너의 한숨 소리를 들은 듯해서
너의 작은 아기침대로 살며시 다가가
그 안을 들여다보았단다.
그리고 너의 이마에 뽀뽀를 했단다—
오! 너를 너무나 사랑하기 때문에—

너는 지금 너무 어려서 알지 못하지만
언젠가는 알게 될거야. -유진 필드(Eugene Field)

한나 휘톨 스미스(Hannah Whitall Smith)[75]의 딸이 언젠가 그녀에게 "혹시 제가 저의 어린 루스를 사랑하는 만큼 어머니께서는 저를 사랑하지 않으셨을 수 있을까요?"라는 글을 써보냈다고 한다. 오늘로 셔우드는 15개월이 되었다. 우리 아기는 지금 외할아버지 댁에 있다. 1월 14일 애니 이모의 생일날 이곳에 도착했다. 셔우드는 할아버지 집에 온 후로 $1\frac{1}{2}$파운드가 늘었고, 새 이도 났다. 왼쪽 아랫니다. {머리둘레는 $18\frac{1}{2}$인치, 키는 3인치.}[76] 몸무게는 지금 26파운드가 나간다(옷을 입고). 셔우드를 곡물 바구니에 앉혀서 무게를 쟀는데, 엄마가 애니 이모와 여선과 함께 무게를 재는 동안 착하게도 바구니 안에 잘 앉아 있었다.
셔우드는 할아버지 집에 도착한 첫날부터 걸으려고 노력하기 시작했다. 마침내 흔들리지 않는 굳건한 땅 위에 세운 집에 도착했다는 것을 깨달은 것이다. 첫날 밤 혼자 몇 걸음 걷더니 다음날부터는 조금씩 더 오래 걸었다. 처음에는 신발이 너무 작았기 때문에 조가 좀더 큰 5호 신발을 사다 주었다. 셔우드는 새 신발을 보고는 기분이 좋아져서 얼른 새 신발로 갈아 신고 싶어 했다. 발에 맞는 신발을 신은 후에는 훨씬 잘 걸었으며, 어디든 가고 싶은 데를 혼자서 다녔다. 그리고 지난 2-3일 동안은 기는 것보다 걷는 경우가 더 많았다. 아장아장 걷는 모습이 매우 귀엽다. 보통 두 팔을 흔들면서, 마치 작은 엔진처럼 "히", "훗", "틋" 하면서 다닌다. [일기 원본 69-70쪽 없음]
71 셔우드가 명랑한 얼굴로 자랑스럽게 걸음마를 하는 모습을 엄마가

마음에 담아둘 수 있다면, 이 사진은 추억의 벽에 붙어 있는 사진 중 가장 예쁜 사진이 될 것이다.

오, 작은 발! 오랜 세월을
희망과 두려움을 거쳐 돌아다녀야 하는,
네 짐을 지탱하며 아프고 피 흘려야 하는.
길가의 여인숙 가까이서 나는
고통이 멈추고 안식이 시작되는 여기서
네 갈 길을 생각하면 걱정스럽기만 하다.[77]

외할아버지는 종종 재미삼아 셔우드에게 입을 크게 벌리면 더 잘 걸을 수 있다고 하신다. 그러면 셔우드는 정말로 입을 크게 벌리고 행진을 한다. 하도 많이 벌려서 새로 난 이도 볼 수 있고 목구멍은 물론 마지막으로 먹은 우유까지 보인다. 그런데 아직까지도 우유병을 빨고 있다. 아침에 낮잠을 잘 때마다 우유병을 빨고 밤에 잘 때도 이 애지중지하는 우유병이 있어야 한다. 할아버지 집에서 우유를 바꾸고 음식이 바뀌면 나아질 거라고 생각했던 셔우드의 변비는 오히려 더 심해졌다. 싱싱한 생우유, 부드럽게 삶은 달걀, 애플 소스, 그리고 사과를 통째로 긁어서 먹인 후 글리세린 관장을 해주어도 변을 보지 못했다. 너무 고통스러워서 심하게 울 때면 그 모습을 보는 할머니와 애니 이모까지도 울게 했다. 할머니는 엄마에게 "너는 애기를 위해 무슨 조치를 취해야 할 것 같구나. 안 그러면 죽어버릴 것 같애"라고 말씀하셨다. 그래서 엄마는 크림과 오트밀 죽을 우유에 타서 주고, '무화과 시럽' 한 병을 구해서 매일 밤 셔우드에게 한 숟가락씩 주었다. 이제 셔우드는 관장 없이 매일 아침 변을 보게 되었다. 혀에 있던 설태도 깨끗이 없어졌고, 이제는 날마다 더 건강해지는 것 같다.

72 셔우드는 아직 말을 못 하지만 해주는 말은 잘 알아듣는다. 할머니가 "셔우드, 새 신발 어디 있지?" 하면 얼른 신발을 내민다. "셔우드, 엄마 어디 있지?" 하면 위층을 가리킨다.

지난 달 사랑의 주님께서 셔우드에게 예쁜 여동생을 보내 주셨다. 아기는 1895년 1월 18일 금요일 아침 7시에 이 세상에서 처음으로 눈을 떴다. 아기 이름은 '에디스 마가렛 홀'(Edith Margaret Hall)이다. 몸무게는 7½파운드가 나간다. 셔우드를 데리고 와서 처음으로 아기를 보여 주자 이상하다는 듯이 눈을 커다랗게 뜨고 아기와 엄마를 번갈아 보았다. 그러고는 마치 "고마워요, 엄마, 사랑하는 엄마" 하는 것처럼 자기 볼을 엄마 볼에 부드럽게 대었다. 그런 다음에는 여동생에게 키스를 하고 사랑스럽다는 듯이 아기의 머리카락을 쓰다듬었다. 셔우드는 매일 아기를 보여 달라고 한다. 처음에는 아기가 울 때 따라서 울더니 지금은 누군가가 얼른 아기를 달래 주기를 바란다. 가끔 에스더 이모가 셔우드 팔에 어린 여동생을 안겨 주면 셔우드는 정말 좋아한다.

여선 삼촌, 에스더 이모, 엄마가 아기를 안고 있어도 셔우드는 질투하는 모습을 아직까지 보인 적이 없다.

우리 착한 꼬마 셔우드는 하나님께서 자기에게 주신 보물이 무엇인지 아직 모르고 있다. 하지만 여동생과 지내면서 해가 지날수록 누이가 얼마나 귀한 선물인지 점점 알게 될 것이다.

[뉴욕 리버티에 있는 셔우드 외할아버지 집]

[일기 원본 73–74쪽 없음]

75 1895년 3월 10일

네 고아들을 버려도 내가 그들을 살리리라 네 과부들은
나를 의지할 것이니라(예레미야 49:11)

"오늘은 우리 아가 무엇을 했나요?
빨래와 바느질을 해준 보답으로.
어떻게 우리 아가 빚을 면할 수 있을까요?
안아 주고 보살펴 준 보답으로.
어떻게 엄마는 긴 세월을 기다릴 수 있을까요?
아가 손이 크고 세질 때까지.
누가 이자를 갚을 수 있을까요?
빚더미가 쌓여 간다면."[78]

최근 셔우드는 키는 자라지 않은 것 같지만 몸무게는 2파운드가 늘었고, 첫 번째 어금니가 나왔다. 이제는 혼자 계단을 오르락내리락 할 수 있는데, 이때껏 굴러 떨어진 적이 한 번밖에 없었다. 하루는 여선과 함께 차를 타고 리버티로 나갔는데, 그날은 2월 25일 에스더가 학교에 가기 시작한 날이었다. 여선은 매일 셔우드를 데리고 넓은 곳으로 산책 나가서 말과 소, 어린 송아지들을 보여 준다.
셔우드는 이 산책을 정말 좋아하고 매일 나가자고 조른다. 셔우드는 집안의 귀염둥이가 되어 가고 있다. 할머니 덕분에 셔우드는 무릎에 앉는 것을 좋아하게 되었고, 애니 이모는 가끔 셔우드를 안고 흔들어 준다. 셔우드는 할아버지 무릎에도 종종 올라가 앉는다. 그리고 애니 이모의 강아지 '프리스키'랑 고양이 '마티'와 '뷰티', 할아버지의 커다란 개 '프린스'와 재미있게 논다. 이 녀석들은 어린 셔우드한테 아주 잘해 준다. 하지만 처음에는 셔우드와 노는 것을 싫어했다.

"셔우드와 프리스키"

76 1895년 4월 10일, 수요일

여호와께서…… 고아와 과부를 붙드시고…… (시편 146:9)

"우리의 불완전함에 완전함이 있다."[79]

오늘 셔우드의 몸무게는 30파운드이고 머리 둘레는 19인치이다. 에스더 이모가 매주 학교에서 집으로 올 때마다 말한 것처럼 셔우드가 '점점 작아지는 것' 같다. 사실은 작아지지는 않았지만 키가 크지 않고 옆으로 퍼져서 그렇게 보이는 것이다. 지금 셔우드는 어금니가 네 개 나왔고 송곳니도 나오기 시작했다. 이가 나느라 셔우드는 짜증을 많이 부린다. 아파서 오래 놀지도 못하고 밤에도 울면서 잠을 깬다. 엄마는 이 이가 난 후에는 우리 셔우드가 생살을 뚫는 아픔을 덜 겪었으면 하고 바란다. 지금 셔우드는 잘 자라고 있는 듯하다. 변비 때문에 약을 안 먹은 지도 꽤 오래 되었다. 인산염 소다와 우유만으로 잘 조절되었다. 식탁에서 밥을 잘 안 먹는 편이고,

특히 이가 날 때는 아무것도 먹지 않는다. 그때는 옛 우유병이 가장 친한 친구인데, 때로는 그것을 빠는 것마저도 아파한다. 여선이 너무 바빠서 셔우드를 데리고 나갈 수 없는 날이면 셔우드는 혼자 현관 입구 계단으로 가서 햇빛을 쬐며 이리저리 걷곤 한다. 그런데 하루는 계단에서 떨어지는 바람에 윗입술과 입 언저리가 찢어지고 입 안에서도 피가 많이 났다. 할머니가 셔우드에게 눈, 입, 혀, 이 그리고 귀가 어디 있는지 가르쳐 주셨다. 할머니가 "셔우드, 눈은 어디 있지?" 하시면 셔우드는 작은 검지손가락을 자기 눈 가까이에 댄다. 그리고 손가락이 들어갈까 봐 윙크를 하고 눈을 깜박인다.

77 이번 달에 엄마는 사랑하는 아빠가 남겨주신 돈을 이자가 붙도록 은행에 예치하였다. 엄마는 우리 아들과 딸이 대학에 갈 경비가 필요할 때까지 원금을 건드리지 않으려고 한다. 엄마는 아빠의 지인들에게 편지를 쓰느라 바빴다. 엄마는 오는 11월 24일 전까지 회고록을 완성하려고 한다. 엄마는 또 신문사와 평양 선교부지 구입을 위해 아빠를 지원했던 친구들에게 이제는 그 부지에 기념병원을 건축할 수 있는 자금을 호소하는 편지를 썼다. 어린 셔우드는 이제 거의 모든 말귀를 알아듣는다. 할아버지께 사과를 갖다 드려라, 이걸 주워라, 그건 하지 마라 등 뭐든지 시키는 대로 따른다. 하지만 아직 말은 못한다. "바이 바이" 하면서 헝겊 인형에게 노래를 불러 주고, 에디스가 울면 자기 케이크나 사과를 먹으라고 주거나 아기 젖병을 물린다. 또 아기가 누워 있는 유모차를 흔들어 주면서 "바이, 바이, 바이" 하고 노래를 불러 준다. 어린 동생을 편안하게 해주려고 애쓰는 모습이 정말 사랑스럽고 귀엽다. 할아버지는 어린 손자를 위해 조끼 주머니에 단풍사탕을 조금 넣어

두신다. 셔우드는 그것을 얻으려고 매일 한 번씩 할아버지 무릎 위로 올라가는데, 어떤 때는 달라고 하지 않아도 할아버지가 주시기를 바라면서 한참 동안 무릎 위에 앉아 있기도 한다. 그래도 할아버지가 주지 않으면 주머니를 가리키면서 아기 돼지처럼 "어, 어, 어" 한다. 그러면 단풍사탕을 얻는다. 그러나 셔우드는 아기 돼지와 달리 더 달라고 하지는 않는다. 더 달라고 하는 경우가 거의 없으며, 단 것은 어떤 거라도 조금 먹은 후에는 구슬려도 절대 더 먹지 않는다. 조도 문 뒤편에 있는 우유 저장실 선반에 생강쿠키와 스위트 크래커를 조금씩 두고 있다. 셔우드는 이것도 하나 달라고 날마다 조에게 조른다.

78 1895년 5월 10일, 금요일

서로 기도하라(야고보서 5:16)

"저희 사랑하는 자들을 주님께 데려와
당신 발 앞에 놓습니다.
두렵고 사모하는 희망으로 충만하여
당신의 달콤한 약속을 들으려 합니다.
주님의 은총을 구하는 자에게
그 귀한 믿음을 축복하신다는 약속을.
그리고 주님 날개 그늘 아래서
조용한 쉼터를 찾았습니다."

오늘 꼬마 셔우드 홀이 한 살 반이 되었다. 키는 1인치 자랐지만

몸무게는 반 파운드 줄었다. 셔우드는 밖에 나가는 것을 좋아하고
항상 나가 있으려고 한다. 어느 날 아침 엄마와 여선이 바빠서
셔우드를 그냥 혼자 놀게 놔두었다. 하지만 오래지 않아 양봉장 쪽에서
커다란 울음소리가 들렸다. 조가 먼저 그 소리를 듣고 관절염으로
아픈 연약한 다리를 이끌고 있는 힘을 다해 달려갔다. 그리고 셔우드가
안간힘을 다해 벌들과 싸우고 있는 모습을 발견했다. 벌들은 셔우드의
머리, 얼굴, 손 등에 열두 번도 넘게 침을 쏘았다. 조가 셔우드를
집 안으로 데리고 왔고, 애니 이모와 엄마가 벌침들을 뽑은 다음
할머니가 재빨리 준비해 주신 소다수로 쏘인 곳을 씻겨 주었다.
그러고는 우유를 먹인 뒤 안아서 흔들어 재웠다. 잠에서 깬 후
셔우드는 많이 나아졌고, 쏘인 곳도 그리 부어오르지 않았다.
비록 일주일 동안 쏘인 자리가 표가 나기는 했지만. 하루는 사촌
에바[80]가 셔우드를 위해 새 드레스를 가지고 왔다. 빨간색과 흰색
79 체크무늬 천으로 만든 예쁜 옷인데, 밑 부분에는 사촌 에바가 손수
십자수를 놓았다. 엄마도 할머니의 도움을 받아 새 무명 드레스
두 개를 만들어 주었다. 그리고 셔우드는 6호 신발이 필요하게 되었다.
다른 신발들은 아직 닳지는 않았지만 너무 작아졌다.
할아버지와 셔우드가 함께 사진을 찍었다. 셔우드는 마치 뭘 하러
왔는지 아는 듯이 사진을 잘 찍었다. 모두들 사진이 참 잘 나왔다고
했다. 할아버지도 셔우드도 본 모습에 어울리게 나왔다

아흔 살과 한 살. [외할아버지와 셔우드]

사랑하는 할아버지께서 점점 약해지시는 것 같다. 오래 못 사실 것

같다. 언젠가 할아버지도 사랑하는 아빠가 우리를 떠나셨던 것처럼
그렇게 떠나실 것이다. 어느 늦은 아침녘에 할아버지는 이에 대해
80 엄마에게 말씀하셨다. 떠나실 준비가 되어 있으며 기꺼이 그렇게 하실
거라고 하셨다. 어떤 사람들처럼 무슨 증거를 가지고 있지는 않아도
신약성경에 계신 예수님께서 구원을 위해 오셨다는 말씀 하나하나를
다 믿고 있기 때문에 하나님께서 자신을 구원해 주시리라 믿는다고하
셨다. 이번 여름에 엄마가 캐나다에 가지 않기를 바라시는지
여쭈었더니 할아버지는 갈 준비를 하는 게 좋을 거라고 하셨다.
상태가 좋아질지도 모른다고 하시면서 어떻게 될지 두고보자고 하셨다.

1895년 7월 10일, 수요일

거기서 무슨 일을 당할는지 알지 못하노라(사도행전 20:22)

"다시 한 해를 내디디면서
나는 한 치 앞도 내다볼 수 없다.
하지만 과거는 하나님의 것이고
미래도 그분의 긍휼로 알게 될 것이니
이렇게 모르고 간다,
안다면 못 가는 길을.
하나님과 어둠 속을 걷기 원하네,
밝은 데서 혼자 가기보다.
하나님과 믿음으로 걷기 원하네
보면서 혼자 가기보다."[81]

오늘 아침 셔우드는 20개월이 되었다. 몸무게는 81파운드가 나간다.
여선 삼촌이 일찍 셔우드를 깨워서 씻기고 옷을 입혔다. 그리고 엄마,
누이동생, 박 씨 부부[82]와 함께 뉴욕으로 출발했다. 뉴욕에서 이틀을
지낸 후 노스빌로 가서 프랭크 외삼촌 댁을 방문하고, 일주일이나
열흘 후에는 캐다나에 있는 아빠의 고향 글렌부엘로 갈 것이다.
우리는 오전 11시에 뉴욕에 도착했다. 대도시 뉴욕에 가는 동안
81 셔우드는 착하게 잘 있었다. 엄마 옆에 앉아서 기차 창밖을 보면서
좋은 시간을 보냈다. 말들을 가리키며 "백"(back)이라 부르고, 소를
가리키며 "무"(moo)라고 했다. "새"(bird) 하고 말해 보려고 애도 썼다.
"봐"(see), "이거"(this)라는 말은 잘 한다. 또 '고양이'(kitty)라는
말을 하려고 한다. 이처럼 지난 두 달간 제법 진전이 있었다. 최근
셔우드는 말(horse)을 좋아하게 되었다. 산책을 할 때면 말을 보려고
마구간에 가서 몇 시간씩 있다가 온다. 그리고 말 그림을 발견하면
아주 기뻐한다. 셔우드는 말을 "백"이라고 부른다.
6월 27일은 엄마의 세 번째 결혼기념일이다. 그날 사랑하는
외할아버지께서 우리를 떠나 천국 본향으로 가셨다. 불과 그 전
일요일에 좋아하시는 찬송 〈천국에 내 직분을 분명히 고할 수 있을
때〉[83]를 할머니와 함께 부르셨는데…… 할아버지도 엄마처럼 노래를
잘 못 부르셨지만 종종 이 찬송가와 〈요단강가에 서서〉(On Jordan's
Stormy Banks I Stand), 〈만입이 내게 있으면〉(O for Thousand Tongues to
Sing)을 할아버지만의 독특한 스타일로 주일 저녁마다 부르시곤 했다.
가끔씩 셔우드를 무릎에 앉히고 함께 부르기도 하셨는데, 오래 전
엄마를 무릎에 앉히고 이 찬송가들을 부르시던 기억이 난다.
할아버지는 늘 오래 앓고 싶지 않다고 하셨다. 자기를 돌보느라

사람들을 힘들게 하지 말고 쉽게, 빨리 돌아가기를 원하셨다.
그리고 그 바람대로 가셨다. 돌아가시기 일주일 전에 빙햄턴에 사는
사촌 폴리와 그녀의 남편 호레스 크레리[84]가 할아버지를 방문했는데,
할아버지는 두 사람을 바깥문까지 배웅해 주셨다. 그 후 몇 차례
현관 앞 층계까지 가셨지만 그것이 할아버지의 마지막 외출이 되었다.
82 돌아가시던 주 월요일에는 할머니께 "이번 주를 넘기지 못할 것
같소"라고 하셨다. 우리는 할아버지가 날마다 약해지고 계시다는
것을 알 수 있었다. 할머니가 닭국을 만들어 드리면 맛있게 드셨고,
엄마는 포도 주스를 가져다 드렸다. 매일 우유를 낮에 세 컵, 주무시기
전에 한 컵씩 드셨다. 하지만 배가 안 고프다고 하셨다.
날마다 월터[85] 외삼촌 가족이 할아버지를 뵈러 왔고, 수요일 오전에는
팬트[86] 외삼촌과 엠마[87] 외숙모께서 차를 몰고 오셨다. 목요일에는
해리엇 다비[88] 이모할머니와 리 다비(Lee Darbee) 이모할아버지께서
오셨다. 외할아버지는 잠깐 동안 그들의 방문을 받으셨다. 오후
1시쯤에는 음식을 좀 드시고 주무시기 위해 누우셨다. 오후 4시쯤
깨셔서 월터 외삼촌이 의자로 걸어가시는 것을 도와드렸다. 그리고
외사촌 월터[89]와 애이[90]가 할아버지를 위해 잡은 커다란 강꼬치고기를
가져다 드렸다. 할아버지는 "아주 크네, 군침이 도는데"라고
말씀하셨다. 그날 아침에는 〈크리스천 헤럴드〉에 난 관심 기사를
읽으려고 하셨지만 기운이 없어 못 읽으셨다. 그래서 오후에 엄마가
읽어 드렸더니 내용을 전부 알아들으셨다. 오후에 깨셔서 아무
힘이 없다시며 꿈속에서 풀 깎는 기계를 계속 작동했는데, 그것이
할아버지를 지치게 만들었다고 하셨다. 저녁 무렵 할아버지는
"힘이 있어서 하나님을 찬양할 수 있으면 좋겠다"고 하셨다. 날마다

드시던 음식과 수면제를 드신 후 8시쯤 다시 누우셨고 10시 30분쯤
일어나셨다. 일어나시는 기척을 듣고 할머니께서 가 보셨더니
할아버지는 "잘 잤다"고 하시면서 몸을 일으키시고는 지난 두 달간
자주 하시던 대로 숨쉬기가 수월하게 침대 모서리에 앉으셨다.
"일어나 앉은 김에 먹을 시간이 다 되었으니 음식과 약을 좀 드시는 게
83 좋겠어요"라고 할머니께서 청하자 드리는 대로 모두 잘 받아 드셨다.
할머니께서 "금방 눕지 마세요. 원하신다면 함께 앉아 있을게요"라고
청했지만 할아버지는 눕는 것이 낫겠다시며 침대에 다시 누우셨다.
할머니께서 이불을 덮어드리고 응접실에 있는 긴 의자에 가서
앉으시려는데 바로 그때 코고는 소리 같은 미미한 소리가 들려서
재빨리 할아버지께로 되돌아 가셨다. 하지만 할아버지의 영혼은 이미
떠나셨고 몸은 움직이지 않았다. 할머니는 즉시 엄마를 부르셨다.
엄마는 거기 누워 계시던 할아버지의 모습을 결코 잊지 못할 것이다.
할아버지는 평소 주무시는 것처럼 무릎을 약간 올리고 왼쪽으로 누워
계셨다. 그리고 기도하실 때처럼 한 손을 얼굴에 올려놓고 두
손가락으로 이마를 가리고 계셨다. 마치 어린아이가 자고 있는 것처럼
아주 자연스러웠다. 하지만 그 잠은 누구의 울음으로도 깨울 수 없는
잠이었다. 그리고 할아버지는 노래하시던 그곳에 도착하셨다.

"찬바람 독한 숨이
건강한 그곳에는 미칠 수 없다네.
아픔도 슬픔도, 고통도 죽음도
더 이상 없고 두렵지 않다네."[91]

장례 예배는 일요일 오후에 있었다. 엄마의 어린 아들은 나이가 든 후에야 이 일기와 엄마의 스크랩북에 있는 할아버지의 생애에 관한 글을 읽을 수 있을 것이다.

어린 셔우드는 아빠를 잊었듯이 할아버지도 잊게 될 것이다. 하지만 아빠와 할아버지는 셔우드를 잊지 않으실 것이다. 그리고 그분들은 머지않아 셔우드가 본향으로 올 때까지 셔우드를 돌봐 주시고 기다리실 것이다. 아빠와 할아버지께서 예수님을 따르려고 노력하신 것처럼 엄마의 어린 아들도 기독교인으로 자라 예수님을 따르게
84 해달라고 기도드린다. "사망아 너의 승리가 어디 있느냐 사망아 네가 쏘는 것이 어디 있느냐 사망이 쏘는 것은 죄요 죄의 권능은 율법이라 우리 주 예수 그리스도로 말미암아 우리에게 승리를 주시는 하나님께 감사하노니 그러므로 내 사랑하는 형제들아 견실하며 흔들리지 말고 항상 주의 일에 더욱 힘쓰는 자들이 되라 이는 너희 수고가 주 안에서 헛되지 않은 줄 앎이라"(고린도전서 15:55-58).

어린 셔우드는 할아버지를 그리워했다. 할아버지가 어디 있느냐고 물으면서 침대로 가서 살펴보고는 머리를 흔든다. 그러고는 나와서 그 작은 얼굴에 근심이 가득한 표정을 지으며 텅 빈 할아버지의 의자를 가리킨다. 우리 모두 할아버지를 그리워하지만 할아버지와 36년을 함께 사신 할머니가 특히 외로워하신다. 엄마는 이렇게 금방 할머니를 남겨두고 떠나고 싶지 않았다. 하지만 할머니는 오랫동안 엄마를 기다리고 있는 아빠 쪽 가족들을 방문하는 것이 엄마가 할 일이라고 하셨다. 그래서 그로부터 약 2주 후 우리는 아빠의 본가를 향해 출발했다.

1895년 8월 10일, 토요일, 캐나다 글렌부엘에서

우리가 다 수건을 벗은 얼굴로 거울을 보는 것 같이 주의 영광을 보매 그와 같은 형상으로 변화하여(고린도후서 3:18)

"아이가 태어나면 이내 그 아이가 아버지를 닮았다고 말하지 않는가?
진정 우리가 거듭나면 진실해진 우리를 보고 이내
'저 사람은 하늘에 계신 아버지를 닮았다'고 하지 않겠는가!"[92]

어린 셔우드가 이곳 아빠의 본가에 왔다. 홀 할머니는 셔우드에게
작은 컵을 주셨는데, 이것은 아빠가 다섯 살 때 할머니께서 아빠에게
주신 것이다. 컵에는 "나를 간절히 찾는 자가 나를 만날
것이니라"[93]라고 쓰여 있다. —— 그리고 이곳에는 사랑하는 아빠가
만든 액자, 받침대, 침대들까지 있다. 아빠가 목재창고를 개조해서
85 작업하시던 목공소도 있다. 아빠는 목공 일과 가구 제작을 좋아하셨다.
이곳에는 날마다 아빠를 상기시키는 것이 아주 많다. 아빠의 사랑하는
아버지와 어머니, 형제들, 누이들은 모두 기쁘게 아빠의 아기들과
아이들 엄마를 맞아주셨다. 많은 분이 셔우드가 아빠를 많이
닮았다고 했다. 간혹 어떤 분들은 셔우드가 클리포드[94] 삼촌을
닮았으며 클리포드 삼촌은 형 지미를 닮았다고 했다. 이곳 분들은
사랑하는 아빠를 '지미'라고 부르는데, 모두들 아빠를 많이 좋아하고
사랑했다. 할아버지의 농장이 다른 마을과 꽤 떨어져 있었음에도
여러분이 '지미의 아내와 아기들'을 보러 먼 거리를 찾아오셨다.
100명이 넘는 분들이 첫 2주 동안 다녀가셨다.

{엄마는 아빠가 회심하셨던, 오래된 석조 건물로 지어진 학교에 가 보았다. 아빠는 그 학교에 다니셨다. 아빠의 첫 선생님이셨던 스터전(Sturgeon) 부인도 만났다. 부인은 아빠의 추모사 쓰는 것을 도와주기로 하셨다. 엄마는 아빠가 다닌 에덴스 고등학교(Athens High School)도 보았다.}[95]

셔우드는 지난 한 달간 몸무게가 전혀 늘지 않았다. 하지만 몇 가지 단어가 늘었는데, 실은 단어가 늘었다기보다는 시도만 하던 단어들을 더 분명히 말할 수 있게 되었다는 것이 옳은 표현이다. 이제는 엄마를 따라 '백'(back), '키티'(kitty), '새'(bird), '보츠'(bots), '뚜뚜'(Tute, Tute), '파이'(pie), '엄마'(Mama)라고 발음한다. 그리고 이 단어들을 상황에 맞게 사용한다. 셔우드는 아직도 우유병을 물고 잠을 잔다. 우유병을 위층으로 가지고 가서 착하게 곧 꿈나라로 간다. 그리고 2시간 동안 자고 일어나서 침대에서 내려와 혼자 아래층으로 온다. 화장실에 가고 싶을 때는 말로 알려 주는 편인데, 한국 어린이들처럼 "쉬! 쉬! 쉬!"라고 한다. 포스(Forth) 부인이 셔우드에게 말(horse) 그림이 많이 있는 책 한 권을 주셨다. 그 말들을 에스더 이모가 오려서 여선 삼촌과 손을 맞춰 엄마가 만들어 준 분홍색과 파란색 천으로 된 책에 붙여 주었다. 그러자 셔우드는 정말 좋아했다.
86 그림들을 하나하나 가리키면서 오랫동안 "백"이라고 소리치며 혼자 재밌게 놀곤 한다. 다른 책을 주면 말 그림책을 달라고 애원한다. 다른 책으로는 만족지 않다는 표시를 하면서, 스물네 장 다 말 그림만 있는 '백 책'을 얻을 때까지 계속 "백, 백" 한다.

글렌부엘에 있는 동안 엄마는 아빠 쪽 족보[96]에 대해 알아보았다. 그 결과 홀 가 쪽으로 4세대, 볼턴(Bolton) 가 쪽으로 4세대를 추적할 수 있었다. 엄마는 셔우드의 족보를 잘 기록해서 셔우드의 육아일기에는 홀 가의 계보에 대해 써주고, 에디스 마가렛의 육아일기에는 볼튼 가의 계보에 대해 써주면 좋을 것 같다고 생각했다. 그렇게 해 놓으면 언젠가 아이들은 자신들의 조상에 대해 조금이라도 읽게 될 것이다.

4세대 전 아일랜드 아마 지역에 조지(1세) 홀(George Hall)이라는 사람이
살았다. 그는 마가렛 보이드(Margaret Boyd)와 결혼했고, 그들은
캐디에서 7마일 떨어진 곳에 있는 농장을 임대하여 95년간 그곳에서
행복한 가정을 이루었다. 그들 집에서 가장 가까운 항구는 23마일
떨어진 벨파스트에 있었다. 조지 홀과 그의 아내는 장로교인이었고,
의심할 것도 없이 그 집안은 스코틀랜드계 아일랜드인 자손으로 우리
집안의 훌륭한 인물들, 특히 선교사들을 배출한 집안이다. 그들에게는
제임스(James), 보이드(Boyd)(2세), 사라(Sarah)(2세)라는 세 자녀가 있었다.
조지(1세) 홀은 일찍 사망했고, 그의 죽음 이후 장남 제임스가 농장을
관리했다. 그는 제인 포스터와 결혼했고, 사라(2세)는 로버트 그레이와
결혼한 후 캐나다로 이민을 갔다. 보이드(2세)가 벨파스트로 그들을
배웅 나갔는데 함께 캐나다로 가지 못하는 것을 안타까워했다. 그리고
87 얼마 후 보이드(2세)도 캐나다로 떠났다. 어머니 마가렛 보이드 홀은
스터전 씨와 재혼했고, 그가 죽은 후 로빈슨 씨와 다시 결혼했다.
그리고 로빈슨 씨가 죽은 후 스터전 씨의 아들들을 데리고 캐나다로
왔는데, 그중 한 아들이 우리가 글렌부엘에서 만났던 82세의 로버트
스터전(Robert Sturgeon) 씨다. (마가렛은 말년에 얼굴 상피종을 앓았다. 그리고 그녀의
아들 제임스는 손에 그 병이 있었다. 그러나 이 병으로 두 사람이 사망한 것은 아니다.)

아일랜드의 옛 농장에서 살던 제임스와 그 아내에게는 조지(3세),

사라(3세), 보이드(3세)라는 세 자녀가 있었다. 그들은 대가족이 될 것을 염두에 두고(사실 그들은 12명의 자녀를 두었고 대가족을 이루었다.) 당시 캐나다에 있던 보이드(2세)에게 집으로 오라는 편지를 썼다. 농장에 대한 권리를 매각하고 대가족이 지내기에 더 여유 있는 캐나다로 함께 오기 위해서였다. 보이드(2세)가 왔고, 그들은 임대 권리를 앤더슨 씨에게 팔았다. 보이드(2세)는 엘리자베스 베어드(87세로 아직 살아 계신다)와 결혼했고, 두 형제는 가족들을 데리고 1831년 캐나다로 왔다. 보이드(2세)는 목수였는데 거의 1년간 브로크빌에서 아내와 머물렀다. 제임스는 글렌부엘로 왔고, 그곳에 오두막을 짓고 가족과 함께 살았다. 후에 보이드(2세)와 그의 아내도 글렌부엘로 와서 2년 동안 같은 집에서 함께 살았다. 석공인 제임스는 1842년에 석조 가옥을 짓고 거기서 살았다. 그 집은 잘 수리되어 있으며 최근 홀 가에서 다른 가족으로 넘겨졌다. 이곳에서 그들은 일곱 명의 아들과 세 명의 딸을 각각 남자답고 여자답게 키웠다. 장남 조지(3세) 할아버지는 그 집을 지을 때 돌 나르던 일을 지금도 기억하고 계신다.

88 조지(3세) 할아버지는 1826년 1월 20일 아일랜드의 옛 농장에서 태어나셨고, 1859년 뉴 더블린의 존 볼턴(John Bolton) 씨의 장녀로 1835년 1월 16일 출생한 마가렛 볼턴과 결혼하셨다. 이 젊은 부부는 글렌부엘 농장 가까이에 정착했고, 그 땅은 증조할아버지 제임스로부터 물려받은 것이었다. 그곳에는 통나무집이 있었고, 거기서 그들은 편안하고 아늑하게 지냈다. 그리고 이곳에서 1860년 1월 16일 셔우드의 아빠가 태어났다. 아빠의 이름은 볼턴 외증조할아버지(어머니의 할아버지)의 이름을 따서 윌리엄, 그리고 친할아버지의 이름을 따서 제임스라고 지어졌다. 어린 윌리엄은

한 살이 되기 전에 아버지, 어머니와 함께 키틀리에 사는 수잔 시모어 이모를 방문하러 갔다. 그리고 그곳에서 같은 또래의 사촌 메리 시모어와 톨레도 장로교회의 에반스 목사님으로부터 세례를 받았다. 아빠는 16개월이 됐을 때 걷기 시작했고, 걷기 전에 말을 했다. 아빠는 가끔 통나무 벽에 발라진 석고를 먹곤 했는데 어머니한테 혼나면, "왜요, 엄마. 흙은 맛있어요"라고 대답했다. 또래 남자아이들처럼 아빠도 가끔 말썽을 부렸다. 아버지와 어머니가 멀리 외출하신 어느 날, 아빠와 두 살 어린 여동생 앨리스는 살아 있는 암탉의 털을 전부 뽑아 버렸다. 그리고 한번은 앨리스가 없는 날 누이동생의 고양이를 매달았다. 또 한번은 난로 문을 열고 고양이를 불 속으로 넣으려 했는데 다행히도 그 불쌍한 고양이는 열려 있는 뚜껑으로 도망쳐 목숨을 부지할 수 있었다. 할머니 말씀에 따르면 아빠는 아주 섬세한 아이였고, 그래서 7세가 넘은 봄이 될 때까지 학교에 보내지
89 않았다고 한다. 아빠는 빨리 배웠고, 아홉 살이 되기 전에 2단계 읽기에서 3단계 읽기로 진급했다고 한다. 할머니는 선생님이 서명한 그 진급 카드를 지금도 가지고 계신다.

{할머니께서는 아빠는 늘 믿을 수 있는 아이였다고 하시면서 그래도 한번은 누이동생 앨리스와 말다툼을 하다가 생각이 엉켜버리자 어머니께 달려와 "엄마, 앨리스가 거짓말로 나를 반박하고 있어요"라고 소리친 적이 있다고 한다.}[97]

엄마는 아빠의 회고록이 책으로 쓰여지고 출판되어 셔우드가 앞으로 어린 시절과 소년 시기를 거치면서 참조할 수 있기를 바란다.

하루는 우리 모두가 존 볼턴 외증조할아버지를 뵈러 갔다. 그분은 90세셨다. 1년 전 엉덩이뼈가 탈골되고 다리가 부러지는 바람에

그 후로부터 할아버지는 침대에서 지내고 계신다. 하지만 여전히 건강해 보이신다. 셔우드와 에디스는 할아버지 침대에 앉아서 할아버지가 옆에서 해주시는 말씀을 들었다. 할아버지는 자신의 어머니께서 102세까지 사셨다고 말씀하셨다. 그분은 버몬트에서 오신 네덜란드 후손 마사 엘리엇(Martha Elliott)이며, 1777년 7월 3일에 출생하셔서 1879년 3월 18일에 돌아가셨다. 아빠는 그 할머니를 잘 기억하고 계셨다. 그 할머니가 107세에 돌아가셨다고 하는데, 엄마가 받은 그분의 출생연도가 틀리지 않았다면 그것은 잘못 알려진 것이라고 본다. 증조할아버지의 삼촌 아브람 볼턴은 100세 때에도 나무를 베셨고 103세까지 사셨다고 한다. 볼턴 증조할아버지는 할머니가 자라고 결혼할 때까지 살았던 그 집에서 계속 살고 계신다. 그 집은 석조 건물로, 홀 농장에 있는 집과 흡사하다. 독신이신 헨리 할아버지와 윌리엄 할아버지, 결혼하지 않으신 사라 이모할머니가 증조할아버지와 함께 살고 계신다. 할아버지가 엉덩이를 다치신 후 그 가족 중 가장 어린 윌리엄 할아버지가 지금 간호사 역할을 하신다.

90 그곳을 방문한 날 우리는 벤자민 볼턴의 집에 가서 5대조 할머니 낸시 볼턴{Nancy Higginson Bolton}을 찾아뵈었다. 그분은 정말 아름다운 할머니셨다. 셔우드는 증종조부 보이드 홀의 부인이신 엘리자베스 베어드 홀 할머니도 만났다. 아빠의 1884년도 일기는 이 보이드 할아버지의 죽음에 관한 이야기로 시작된다. 아빠는 이분을 정말 좋아하셨다.

셔우드에게는 삼촌, 고모보다 할아버지의 형제자매가 더 많다. 가까운 곳에 계신 분들은 모두 우리를 방문해 주셨고, 우리도 그분들 대부분을 다시 찾아뵈었다. 캐롤라인 브래들리[98] 이모할머니는 셔우드보다

조금 더 몸집이 큰 어린 딸과 함께 서부에서 오셨다. 상냥한 이분은
홀 할머니의 막내 여동생이다. 다른 여동생 제인 로섬[99] 이모할머니는
그리 멀지 않은 곳에 살고 계시는데 여러 번 우리를 보러 오셨다.
우리도 그 댁에서 하루를 보냈다. 제인 이모할머니는 아빠가 어렸을 때
상당한 기간 동안 할머니와 함께 사셨는데, 그 시절 이모할머니가
아빠와 앨리스 고모를 양쪽에 끼고 찍은 사진을 엄마가 가지고 있다.
그리고 제인 이모할머니는 아빠가 그렇게 좋아하시던 사과 덤플링을
만들어 주신 바로 그분이다. 그 댁을 방문한 날 우리는 저녁으로 사과
덤플링을 먹었다. 그분에게는 세 자녀가 있는데, 장녀 레베카는
브룩빌에서 선생으로 일하고 있고, [비어 있음], 스탠리는 집에 있다.
스탠리는 아빠가 지어준 이름인데 그는 14세 정도 되는 소년이다.
홀 할머니 가족은 성공회에 속해 있다.
7월 31일 수요일 저녁에는 친절한 글렌부엘 주민들께서 그들 모두가
많이 사랑했던 사람의 아내에게 경의를 표하고자 환영회를 열어 주었다.
셔우드는 엄마의 스크랩북에 있는 환영의 글을 읽게 될 것이다.
그 주 일요일 저녁 우리는 한국어 예배를 드렸다. 여선이 한국어
91 성경을 봉독했고, 셔우드는 색동 한복을 입었다. 그리고 [비어 있음]
목사는 모든 사람이 볼 수 있도록 셔우드를 강단에 올려 세웠다.
셔우드는 아주 예뻤고, 모든 사람들에게 볼 수 있는 기회를 주려는
것처럼 천천히 한 바퀴를 돌았다. 엄마는 사람들에게 한국 남자아이의
옷에 대해 조금 설명해 주었다. 그런 다음 평양에서 사역을 시작했을
때의 경험을 들려주었다. 에스더 이모는 〈행복한 나라가 있네〉(There
is a Happy Land)를 한국말로 불렀다. 그리고 자신의 회심에 관한
이야기를 영어로 아주 잘 이야기해 주었다. 모든 사람이 그 예배로 아주

기뻐했다. 그리고 에스더 이모를 위한 비용에 보태라고 12불을 모아 엄마에게 주었다. 비슷한 예배를 린과 에덴스에서도 드렸는데, 총 11불의 모금이 들어왔고 그중 10불은 같은 목적으로 사용될 것이다. 다른 세 군데에서도 방문해 달라는 요청을 받았으나 아쉽게도 사양해야 했다. 엄마가 무척 지쳤을 뿐 아니라 다른 사람들에게도 힘든 일이었기 때문이다. 그리고 초청받은 곳들은 가기 어려운 지역이었다. 우리는 할아버지 집에서 5주 남짓 머물렀다. 그리고 한 주 가량은 브록빌에 있는 앨리스 고모 집에서 보냈다. 방문한 모든 지역에서 우리는 사랑하는 아빠의 친구분들을 만났다. 길로이(Gilroy) 부부는 잠시라도 우리와 만날 수 있어서 무척 반가워했다. 아빠는 이 두 분 생각을 많이 하셨는데, 정말 좋은 분들이었다. 하나님은 캐나다에서 우리에게 따뜻한 친구분들을 많이 주셨다.

뉴욕에서, 1895년 9월 27일. [에스더 부부와 함께 찍은 로제타 가족 사진]

92 1895년 11월 10일, 일요일

네가 사는 날을 따라서 능력이 있으리로다(신명기 33:25)

또 한 해가 저무네!
사랑의 아버지, 다시
일하든지 기다리든지
새해를 당신과 함께하기를!
또 한 해 동안 배우려네.

주님 사랑의 품 안에서
신실하심에 더욱 더 의지하는 법을,
조용히 행복한 안식을 누리는 법을.
또 한 해를 전진하려네.
찬양하는 한 해,
주님의 임재하심을 "살아 있는 동안"
다시 증거하는 한 해를. –하버갈(F. R. Havergal)
{1896년 11월 10일 일기에 기록한 시가 좀더 좋을 것 같다.}[100]

[셔우드 두 돌 때의 머리 타래]

엄마의 어린 아들이 오늘 두 살이 되었다. 첫돌 이후 지난 1년 동안 셔우드는 정말 많은 일을 겪었다. 우리가 겪은 일들을 미리 볼 수 있었다면 그것들을 피하려 했을 것이다.

오, 지혜가 부족한 것이 행복일세, 모르는 것이 복일세.
주님이 오른손으로 날 잡으시고 나를 놓지 않으시네.
그리고 내 영혼을 쉬게 하시네, 사랑하는 주님 품에 안고서.
내 마음이 시험을 꺼리네, 미래를 알려 줄지도 모르는데.
여태껏 난 사랑하는 주님이 허락하신 슬픔만 겪었다네.
그래서 나오는 눈물을 삼키네, "주님이 아신다"라고 속삭이며.
–브레이너드(M. G. Brainard)

93 엄마는 외할머니 집에 돌아온 후로 너무 바빠 셔우드의 육아일기를

쓸 시간이 없었다. 하지만 이제라도 릴리 고모와 존 삼촌이 9월 5일
이른 아침에 캐나다 증기선 '패스포트' 호를 타고 떠나는 우리를
배웅하러 브록빌까지 내려와 주셨다는 것을 말해야겠다. 작별 선물로
홀 할머니는 셔우드에게 예쁜 남색 모자를 보내 주셨고, 앨리스
고모는 새 앞치마를 주셨다.
우리는 정오가 되기 전에 천섬[101]을 지났다. 아주 유쾌한 여행이었고,
온타리오 호수 북쪽 해안에서 토론토로 가는 여행 또한 즐거웠다.
우리는 킹스턴에서 한 시간 반 정도 머물렀는데, 그곳은 아빠가
대학을 다니시던 곳이다. 그곳에서 엄마는 킬본(Kilborn) 박사를 만났다.
그분은 아빠의 절친한 친구 오마 킬본(Omar Kilborn) 박사의 형님이다.
오마 킬본 박사는 중국 서부에서 살다가 지금은 폭동으로 인해 중국
상하이에 계신다. 우리는 6일 오전 토론토에 도착해서 미국 배로
갈아탔고, 그 배는 호수를 건너 루이스턴에 우리를 내려주었다.
세관 관리 때문에 얼마간 지체되었는데, 그 관리는 에스더 이모와
여선 삼촌이 중국인이라며 미국에 올 수 없다고 했다.
우리는 나이아가라 폭포로 가는 기차를 탔다. 폭포에 도착해서 마차를
타고 그 웅장한 풍경을 보러갔다. 셔우드는 폭포를 알아보는 것
같았다. 캐나다 쪽으로 가는 다리를 건널 때 셔우드는 폭포들을
가리켰다. 정오쯤 셔우드와 에디스는 우유를 먹고 마차 안에서 잠이
들었다. 그 사이 엄마, 에스더 이모, 여선 삼촌은 우비를 입고
폭포 아래로 내려갔다.
94 3시 전에 우리는 버펄로로 출발했고, 찰스 외삼촌[102] 댁으로
가기 위해 이어리 철도를 탔다. 우리는 아침 6시부터 오후 6시까지
열두 시간을 여행했다. 배를 세 번 갈아탔고, 기차도 세 번 갈아탔다.

그런데 아이들은 아주 잘 견뎠고, 먼 거리를 움직일 때는 기차보다 배가 수월했다. 찰스 외삼촌과 매기 외숙모, 그리고 외사촌 레나, 찰스 버 노이, 아서, 패니는 반갑게 우리를 맞이해 주었고, 우리는 그곳에서 일주일 동안 즐겁게 지냈다. 그리고 그곳 감리교회에서 캐나다에서 했던 것처럼 한국어로 저녁 예배를 드렸다.

9월 13일 우리는 호넬스빌로 갔다. 사촌 로버트 보니[103]가 마차를 타고 마중나와 주었고, 우리는 그 댁에 가서 유쾌한 시간을 보냈다. 그곳에 있는 동안 셔우드는 우리와 함께 비단 공장과 신발 공장을 둘러보았다. 셔우드는 기계류에 관심을 보였다. 다음 날 우리는 빙햄턴으로 갔다. 사촌 호레스 크레리가 마중나와서 우아한 그의 집으로 우리를 데리고 갔다. 그곳에서 우리는 융숭한 접대를 받았고, 정말 편안히 지냈다. 승마도 했고, 여러 친척들이 우리를 방문해 주셨다. 사촌 윌리엄 셔우드가 우리 셔우드에게 5불짜리 지폐를 주었다. 사촌 폴리 크레리는 캐시미어 양말 네 켤레를 주었고, 엄마에게는 아름다운 검정색 헨리에타 드레스 재료감을 주었다. 그리고 10불을 쥐어 주었다. 이 선물들은 올해 엄마의 생일 선물이 되었다. 9월 19일에는 펜실베니아 주 스크랜턴에 있는 사촌 세스 보니[104]의 집에 머물게 되었다. 엄마는 생일날 지하 300피트 아래에 있는 '1년 내내 검은 다이아몬드를 캐내는' 탄광을 방문하며 축하를 받았다. 그날 밤에는
95 세계에서 가장 큰 주철공장을 둘러보았다.

9월 21일 우리는 노블 부인과 함께 시즈 밀즈에 있게 되었다. 셔우드는 어린 루스 양을 다시 만났다. 루스는 많이 컸고 말도 조금 했다. 루스는 인형을 좋아해서 우리가 그곳에 머무는 동안 우리 애들의 커다란 한국 헝겊 인형을 가지고 놀았다. 셔우드가 루스를 괴롭히곤

했는데, 인형을 볼 때마다 그 인형을 루스에게서 뺏는 시늉을 하며 그 아이를 놀렸다. 그러면 루스는 도와 달라고 울면서 엄마에게로 달려갔다. 24일에는 엄마의 의과대학 친구인 스토켈(Stoeckel) 박사와 그분의 자매인 닥터 버틀러(Butler) 부인을 만나기 위해 윌크스배리로 갔다. 두 분은 엄마가 착한 아기들을 두었다고 생각하셨다. 이곳에서 셔우드는 레이스 공장을 둘러보았다. 25일 밤에는 사촌 마리에트 셔우드가 있는 저지 시로 갔다. 방문 기간 동안 좋은 시간을 보냈다. 우리는 그분들의 친절을 결코 잊지 못할 것이다. 하루는 뉴욕에 계신 아빠의 친구이자 예술가이신 가버(Garber) 씨를 방문해 무료로 아기들 사진을 찍고 왔다. 28일 토요일 밤 우리는 정겨운 농장 집으로 무사히 돌아왔다. 여행 기간 동안 셔우드는 가끔씩 눈을 다치거나 덧니가 나느라 밤에 뒤척인 것을 빼고는 무탈하였다. 캐나다에 있는 동안 몸무게는 늘지 않았고, 키도 그리 자라지 않았다. 셔우드는 활동적이어서 잘 때만 빼고 늘 움직인다. 그리고 매일 두 시간 정도 낮잠을 자는데, 가끔 새로운 곳에 도착하면 곧바로 4시간 정도 잔다. 셔우드는 아직도 젖병을 떼지 못했다.

96 "셔우드와 아기 에디스" [1895년 11월]
1897년 2월 18일 에디스가 엄마의 잉크 병을 가져다가 전부 쏟아 버렸다. 그리고 검지손가락으로 오빠의 사진을 검게 칠해 버렸다. 이것은 아기가 쏟은 네 번째 잉크병으로, 엄마는 에디스를 많이 혼내야 했다.

셔우드의 두 번째 생일에 키는 34인치이고 몸무게는 34파운드이다. 1 인치에 1파운드씩이다. 1년 동안 몸무게는 14파운드가 늘었지만 키는 겨우 3인치 자랐다. 눕혀서 키를 재보았더니 36인치였다.

1년 동안 5인치가 자란 것이다. 머리 둘레는 지금 $19\frac{1}{4}$ 인치로 1인치
커졌다. 그리고 1년 전에는 앞니만 여덟 개였는데 지금은 앞어금니
네 개, 송곳니 네 개, 뒤 어금니 두 개가 순서대로 나왔다. 그래서 지금
셔우드의 치아는 여덟 개에서 열여덟 개가 되었다. 1년 전 셔우드는
손을 짚고 걸었으나 지금은 서서 걷는다. 그때는 첫 신발이 작아지고
97 있었는데 그 동안 다섯 켤레의 신발을 신었다. 처음 두 켤레는
작아졌고, 다음 것은 닳았고, 마지막 두 켤레는 지금도 신고 있다.
신발 사이즈는 6호인데 1년 전에는 4호를 신었다. 그리고 그때는
아무 말도 못했는데 지금은 꽤 많은 단어를 알고 있다.
백(back, 말), 호아-백(whoa-back, 말타기), 키티(kitty), 새(bird), 이거(this),
바이-바이(by-by), 보스(boss), 벌(bee), 물다(bite), 투투(tute-tute),
파이(pie), 마마(mămă), 바우-와우(bow-wow), 거위(goose), 조(Joe), 조의
의자(Joe's chair), 돼지(pig), 케이크(cake), 저녁(supper), 어둡다(dark),
애이(Ai), 조의 부츠(Joe's boots), 마시다(drink)…… 셔우드는 공(ball)을
"보엣"(boet)이라 하고, 여선을 "다"(Dah)라고 부른다. 그리고
마마(mämä)를 캐나다인처럼 "마'마'"(mămă)라고 발음한다. 조(Joe)는
"초"(Cho)와 "듀"(dew)의 중간 소리를 낸다. 또 돼지를 아일랜드인처럼
발음한다. "부어"(Buer)는 경우에 따라 아침, 점심, 저녁 식사를 다
의미한다. 이것은 분명히 엄마가 위층에 있을 때 할머니가 "디-너,"
"서-퍼" 하고 뒤 음절 끄는 소리를 듣고 배웠을 것이다. "다"(Dah)는
엄마가 여선을 부를 때 "여-선-아"라고 하는 데서 비롯된 것 같다.
거위를 발음할 때는 보통 "구" 소리만 낸다. "구스"(goose)에서 "구"
소리만 뽑은 것 같다. 집으로 돌아온 날 "구" 하는 소리를 처음 들었다.
일본 병풍이 우리 방에 쳐져 있는데, 셔우드는 병풍에 그려진 흰

황새들을 가리키면서 "구"라고 불렀다. 그리고 흰 칠면조, 거위, 오리 그림을 보면 같은 소리를 낸다. 엄마는 그 단어를 가르쳐 준 적이 없지만 캐나다에서 누군가가 가르쳐 주었을지도 모르겠다. 그런데 오리는 홀 할아버지 집에만 있었다. 최근에는 어두우면 닥(däk)이라 하고, 무언가를 마시고 싶으면 "다웃"(dout) 하고, 더우면 "학"(hok)이라고 하기 시작했다. 처음에는 더울 때 "불"(fire)이라 했다. 무엇이든 쓰라리거나 아픈 것은 "물었다"(bite)고 한다. 그리고 자기가 아플 때면 "벌이 물었다"(bee bite)고 한다.

98 셔우드는 홀 할아버지 집에서 한 번 더 벌에 쏘였는데, 처음 이곳에서 벌과 놀던 때를 기억하고 있는 것 같다. '물었다'는 셔우드가 아는 유일한 동사로, 문장들은 "바우-와우(bow-wow)가 물었어", "고양이(kitty)가 물었어", "다(Dah)가 물었어" 같은 단순한 문장들이다. 셔우드는 말을 더 하려고 애를 쓰는데, 어느 날 아침에는 엄마가 옷을 입고 있을 때 막 잠에서 깬 셔우드가 "다"(Dah)라고 불렀다.

"다(Dah)는 아침을 먹고 있어요" 했더니 셔우드는 "다"(Dah) 하고는 자기가 먹는 것처럼 입을 벌리고 "부어"(Buer)라고 했는데, 이것은 "여선이 아침을 먹는다"는 뜻이다.

엄마가 뉴욕에 한 주간 가 있었을 때 셔우드는 "마마, 투투, 호아-백"이라고 했다. "엄마가 기차를 타고 갔고, 말이 엄마를 집으로 데려온다"는 뜻이다. 그리고 이제 엄마가 어디 갈 때마다 그렇게 말을 한다. 할머니가 처음으로 그 말을 가르쳐 주신 것 같다. 셔우드는 엄마가 걷는 소리, 그리고 '다'(Dah)가 걷는 소리, 사촌 애이가 걷는 소리를 알고 있다. 그래서 소리를 듣고 누가 오는지 알고 말해 준다. 전에는 자면서 "백"(back)을 불렀는데 이제는 자주 "조"(Joe)를 부른다.

그리고 편지나 신문에 있는 긴 이야기들을 읽는다. 또 식탁에서 숟가락과 포크를 제법 잘 사용한다. 이젠 여러 종류의 음식을 먹는데, 특히 밥을 아주 좋아하며 물을 많이 마신다. 그리고 사과, 배, 고기를 좋아한다. 셔우드는 모든 종류의 고기를 아일랜드식 발음으로 '돼지'(paeg)라고 부른다. 셔우드는 '배'(pear)라고 할 수 있고, 사과와 배를 잘 구분한다. 애이가 이곳에 있는 동안 집토끼를 데리고 왔는데 셔우드가 처음 본 토끼였다. 나중에 셔우드는 장난감 블록에 있는 토끼 그림을 보고 할머니에게 달려가 그림을 보이면서 "애이, 애이"라고 했다. 셔우드는 그림과 사진을 재빠르게 인식한다.

99 할머니께서 셔우드에게 생일 선물로 은화 1불을 주셨다. 그리고 엄마는 버스티드 박사가 첫 크리스마스 선물로 주신 검정털 점핑 강아지를 처음으로 꺼내 주었다. 강아지 목줄에 달린 동그란 벌브를 누르면 강아지는 걷기도 하고 껑충 뛰기도 한다. 셔우드는 이 두 선물을 받고 기뻐했다. 돈을 손에 쥐고 있는 것을 좋아했고, 물론 강아지 장난감도 즐거워했다. 착한 우리 셔우드는 어린 누이동생이 장난감 강아지를 가지고 놀 수 있도록 했다. 요즘 셔우드는 캐나다에서 돌아온 후부터 예전처럼 에디스 마가렛에게 잘 대해 주지 않는데, 키스도 잘 안 해주고 동생을 안아 보게 해달라고 조르지도 않는다. 그리고 걸핏하면 자기가 갖고 싶은 것을 에디스한테서 뺏어간다. 일부러 아기를 때리고, 밀고, 아기 손가락을 밟는 것도 발각되었다. 그래서 엄마는 회초리로 때려 주었다. 그러나 사실 그런 적은 몇 번 밖에 없고, 주로 동생을 재미있게 해주거나 울지 않게 달래려고 모든 것을 기꺼이 양보한다. 셔우드가 결코 양보하지 않는 것이 하나 있는데, 그것은 매일 밤 저녁 먹은 후 "바이, 바이" 하고는 엄마가

앉아서 흔들어 재워 주어야 하는 것이다. 이것만큼은 다른 사람이 못하게 한다. 처음에는 엄마 무릎에 어린 여동생이 앉는 것도 좋아하지 않았는데 지금은 상관하지 않는다. 셔우드는 치통(새 이가 나느라) 혹은 요새 시작된 다리 통증 때문에 밤에 자주 깨곤 한다. 그럴 때면 엄마 침대로 데려가 달라고 조르고 잠이 들 때까지 엄마 침대에 있는다.
100 셔우드는 나름대로 성질이 있는데, 가끔 자기 뜻대로 안 될 때는 바닥에 드러누워 소리를 지른다. 그러나 보통 쉽게 마음을 돌리고 생각을 잘 한다. '회초리'가 무엇을 의미하는지 잘 알고 있어서 그것이 거의 필요가 없다. 옷을 입으려 하지 않을 때나 어린누이동생에게 못되게 굴거나 식탁에서 바른 행동을 하지 않을 때만 가끔씩 사용한다. 셔우드는 지금 속바지를 입는다. 엄마가 이번 겨울을 대비해서 따뜻한 빨간색 플란넬 긴 속바지를 장만해 주었다. 셔우드는 이 옷을 꽤 잘 입고 있다. 물론 가끔씩 잊어버리고 안 입기도 한다. 종합적으로 엄마의 아들은 나이에 비해 아주 착한 꼬마다. 엄마는 셔우드가 나이가 들고 지혜로워질수록 점점 더 좋은 사람으로 자라리라 믿는다. 셔우드는 꽤 잘생겼다. 가버 씨가 찍어 준 최근 사진들은 실물보다 못 나왔다. 그 사진들은 희미하고 끝마무리가 잘 되지 않았다. 할아버지 무릎 위에서 찍은 사진이 더 잘 나왔다.

"셔우드의 손, 2세. 34 파운드, 34인치, [머리 둘레] 19¼ 인치. 키 34인치x2=68인치=다 컸을 때의 키. 5피트 8인치밖에 안 된다!"

101 1896년 1월 10일, 금요일

우리가 다 하나님의 아들을 믿는 것과 아는 일에 하나가 되어 온전한 사람을 이루어 그리스도의 장성한 분량이 충만한 데까지 이르리니

(에베소서 4:13)

"조금씩 조금씩 모든 일이 이루어지듯
믿음의 면류관도 그렇게 얻어지네.
우리 마음의 천국도 그렇게 시작되네,
눈물로써 수고하고 즐겁게 웃으면서.
조금씩 조금씩 돌이킬 수 없는
긴 날과 긴 생이 지나가네. 그러는 중에
새해가 오고 묵은해는 지나가네."[105]

또 한 해가 시작되었다. 오늘로 셔우드는 두 살 2개월이 되었다. 지금 뒤 어금니 한 쌍이 마저 나와서 총 스무 개의 유치가 다 났다. 여선이 새해 선물로 셔우드에게 작은 칫솔을 만들어 주었다. 셔우드는 이 칫솔을 사용해 보고 싶어서 혼자 칫솔질을 하기도 한다. 셔우드는 맨 마지막 젖니 어금니가 나올 때도 아주 힘든 시간을 보냈다. 며칠 밤을 자지 못했고 잘 먹지도 못했다. 몸무게는 지난 생일 이후 1파운드가 빠져서 지금은 33파운드다. 손이 가늘어졌고 키는 1인치가 자라서 지금 서서 재면 35인치가 된다. 셔우드는 키와 몸무게 재는 것을 참 좋아한다. 그래서 재는 데 오랜 시간이 걸려도 얌전히 잘 있고 잘 참는다. 사레스 씨 가게에서 셔우드를 재보니

36파운드였다. 우리 저울로 재는 것이 틀릴지도 모른다. 크리스마스 때 셔우드는 애니 이모랑 엄마와 크리스마스 주일 오전 예배를 드리러 갔다. 셔우드는 아무 짓도 하지 않고 정말 착하게 있었다. 그리고 잠이 들지도 않았다. 셔우드는 음악을 참 좋아한다. 그리고 예배당까지 말 타고 다녀오는 것을 좋아한다. 셔우드는 말을 정말 좋아하는데 할머니의 검은 말 프린스를 '프린스 오스'(Prince orse)라고 부르고 적갈색 말 자네트를 '오스 넷'(orse Net)이라고 부른다.

102 프랭크 외삼촌의 두 아들이 자기들이 쓰던 멋진 장난감을 큰 상자로 하나 가득 셔우드와 에디스의 크리스마스 선물로 보내주었다. 엄마는 그중 몇 개를 월터 외삼촌의 아이들에게 주었고, 몇 개는 나중에 주려고 남겨 놓았다. 크리스마스 아침에 셔우드가 아래층으로 내려오기 전에 여선이 셔우드에게 1불을 주었다. 그리고 식당에는 셔우드의 선물로 양철 말과 수레, 기차 그리고 모슬린 그림책이 있었다. 셔우드는 기뻐하며 검정색 양철 말을 "오스 프린스"라 불렀다. 기차는 투투라 부르고, 시계 그림이 그려져 있는 기관차는 "칵 투투"(cock tute-tute)라 부른다. 그림책은 동물 그림책이었는데, 셔우드는 곰, 사자, 원숭이를 알게 되었고, "bear", "líon", "monk"라고 말한다. 양을 "매에"(mă)라 하고, 얼룩말과 말처럼 보이는 것을 모두 말이라 부른다. 돼지처럼 보이는 동물들은 다 돼지라고 부른다. 셔우드의 단어장이 새로운 말들로 채워지고 있다. 위에 언급한 단어들 외에도 "빛(light), 춥다(cold), 기분(mood), 아기(baby), 소(cow), 하타 두(hȯt'a do), 여보세요(hello), 신발(shoes), 고기(meat), 검정(black), 내 것(mine), 우유(milk), 버터(butter), 예(yes), 아니오(no), 책(book), 포크(fork), 집(house), 너트(nut), 배(boat)" 등을 말할 수 있다. 셔우드는

"검게 어둡다"(black dark)라고 단어를 합치기도 하고, "검고 어두운 게 물었다"(black dark bite)고도 한다. 근래에 들어 셔우드는 어둠을 조금 무서워하게 되었다. 그 원인은 모르겠다. 또 "돼지고기"(pig meat), "소고기"(cow meat), "찬 우유"(cold mėk), "소 우유"(cow mėk), "병 우유"(baudle mėk), "핀스 바우 와우"(Pɍince bow wow, 검정개)라고도 하고, 언젠가 아기 동생이 자기 체크무늬 앞치마를 입자 그것을 가리키면서 "아니, 아니, 내 거"(no, no, mine)라고 했다.

"비-북"(bee–book), "오스-북"(ħorse–book), "투투-북"이라는 말도 한다. 이제 막 자신을 가리켜 "셔루드"(Sherud)라고 부르기 시작했다. 그리고 에디스는 "렐리(Lēllie)" 또는 "아기-렐리"(baby–Lēllie)라고 부른다. 또 "아기의 인형"(baby's doll)이라는 말도 한다. (2단계 단어 30개)

첫눈을 보고 셔우드는 "우유"라고 하면서 바깥으로 나갔다. 그리고
자기한테 날아드는 눈송이를 보고 "벌"이라고 했다. 얼마 후 눈이
103 펑펑 쏟아지자 팔을 뻗고 눈을 향해 달려가서는 "오, 비-북"이라고
소리쳤다. 뭐라고 부르는지 잘 모르는 것은 모두 "카이크"(kike)라고
한다. 셔우드는 그림책과 신문에서 그림을 아주 잘 찾아내는데,
시간이 얼마나 걸리든지 그림을 전부 다 찾아낸다. 그리고 제법 큰
목소리로 "아, 디" "아, 디" 하면서 신문이나 편지에 있는
이야기들을 오랫동안 읽는다.

하루는 월터 외삼촌이 머리 자르는 가위를 가지고 와서 셔우드의 머리를 짧게 깎아주셨다. 셔우드는 최선을 다해 움직이지 않고 얌전히 있었다. 그렇게 짧은 머리를 한 적이 없어서 보기에 좀 어색했다. 머리 모양새가 셔우드를 좀더 아기처럼 보이게 했다. 그러나 머리는 빨리 다시 자라나고 있다.

셔우드는 '나의'(my)와 '너의'(your)를 같은 뜻으로 생각한다. 그래서
가끔 밤에 깨면 "Dah, my" 하는데 이것은 자기 침대로 돌아가는
대신 여선의(your) 침대로 가고 싶다는 뜻이다. 요즘 들어 셔우드는
한동안 낮잠을 자지 않았다. 그래서 보통 저녁을 먹자마자 7시쯤이나
그 전에 "baudle mėk" 혹은 "baudle cow mėk"을 달라고 한다. 그것은
자러 가고 싶다는 뜻이다. 그러고는 우유병을 잡고 금방 잠이 든다.
엄마는 어떻게 우유병을 떼야 할지 잘 모르겠다. 셔우드는 우유병을
잠잘 때 꼭 필요한 것이라고 생각한다. 보통은 잘 때만 우유병을
찾지만 가끔은 낮에도 아기 동생이 먹고 난 우유를 병에 쥐고 마시기도
한다. 봄이 오면 엄마는 한꺼번에 아기들 젖병을 뗄 생각이다.
그러나 젖병을 떼면 지금처럼 쉽게 아기들을 재우지 못할 것이다.
아기들은 지금 흔들어 주지도 않고 무슨 다른 방법을 사용하지
않아도 잘 잔다. 그저 우유병을 주고 눕히기만 하면 잘 자고 밤에
깨어도 우유병을 다시 잡을 때까지 뒤척이다가 우유병을 몇 번 빨고는
잠이 든다. 셔우드는 이제 식탁에서 포크와 숟가락을 정말 잘 사용한다.
104 여러 달 동안 노느라 별로 먹을 생각이 없을 때를 제외하고는 잘
사용하고 있다. 셔우드는 국을 좋아하는데 아직까지는 숟가락으로
먹는 음식을 좋아한다. 빵과 버터도 조금 먹기는 하지만 또래
남자아이들이 먹는 큰 조각은 한 번도 먹은 적이 없다. 케이크와
파이는 제법 먹는 편이고 고기도 조금 먹는데 감자는 잘 안 먹는다.
식탁에서 자주 우유를 달라 하고, 보통 식사와 식사 사이에도 한 번씩
우유를 마신다. 한 컵 가득 마시는데, 이가 스무 개가 났어도 셔우드의

주식은 아직도 우유인 것 같다. 할아버지와 찍은 사진을 보면서 셔우드는 할아버지 조끼 주머니를 가리키고는 입을 오물오물 하며 '먹는' 시늉을 낸다. 할아버지가 사탕을 주셨던 것을 기억하는 것이다. 할아버지 지팡이도 기억하고 있고 지팡이라는 말도 할 수 있다. 셔우드가 좋아하는 〈오닐의 계간지〉(O'Neill's Quarterly)를 살펴보면서 '엄마 것'과 비슷한 칫솔과 빗, 단추걸이, 화장실 물품들을 가려낸다. 그리고 다(Dah)의 것과 닮은 것들도 찾아낸다. 셔우드는 비누 광고와 나란히 있는 책장과 책상을 보면 언제나 엄마 거라고 한다. 자기 뜻을 표현하려고 여전히 몸짓을 많이 사용한다. 꽃그림을 보면 항상 그 그림의 냄새를 맡고, 물을 달라고 할 때는 물 마시는 시늉을 한다. 셔우드는 오늘 두 돌 때 찍은 사진을 보여 달라면서 사진에 있는 모습처럼 손을 펴서 허리에 올리는 시늉을 했다. 그런 다음 엄마에게 일기장에 붙인 자기 머리 타래를 보여 달라는 뜻으로 손가락을 머리 위에 올려놓고 머리카락을 가리켰다. 셔우드는 뜨거운 물주머니를 '엄마의 돼지'라고 부른다. 셔우드와 에디스는 종종 그것을 가지고 잘 노는데, 셔우드는 그 물건을 광고하는 그림을 볼 때마다 그림을 가리키면서 "엄마의 돼지"라고 소리친다.

105 어느 날 셔우드는 작은 인형을 세우려고 안간힘을 쓰고 있었다. 엄마도 그 인형을 세워 보려고 했다. 그러고는 다시 셔우드에게 주면서 "이 인형은 설 수가 없네"라고 했으나 셔우드는 계속해서 세우려고 했다. 그리고 얼마 지나지 않아 엄마는 셔우드의 환호성을 들었다. 가서 보니 아니나 다를까 인형이 서 있는 것이 아닌가. 셔우드는 서 있는 인형을 응시하면서 매우 만족스럽다는 듯이 "셔루드, 셔루드"라고 했다. 엄마는 엄마가 할 수 없다고 생각했던 것을 이뤄낸 엄마의 어린

'셔루드'의 머리를 쓰다듬어 주었다. 셔우드는 두 살 때부터 엄마에게 뽀뽀를 해주었으나 이제는 뽀뽀를 잘 안 해준다. 하지만 해달라고 하면 언제나 지체 없이 뽀뽀를 해준다.
셔우드는 얼마 전부터 식사기도를 할 때면 늘 머리를 숙인다. 그리고 근래에는 스스로 기도를 하려고 한다. 머리를 숙이고 눈을 꼭 감고 무슨 말을 하는 척 중얼거린다. 최근 엄마 방에서 기도할 때 엄마와 함께 셔우드도 무릎을 꿇게 한 적이 있다. 그러자 셔우드는 무릎을 꿇고 조용히 경건하게 있었다. 무엇을 하고 있는지 이해하는 듯했다.

1896년 4월 10일, 금요일

하나님이 주의 종에게 은혜로 주신 자식들이니이다(창세기 33:5)

우리 집의 가장 예쁜 진주는
보시다시피 우리 아이들입니다.
이 두 아이가 얼마나
나에게 귀한지 말로 다 할 수 없어요.

이때껏 찾은 다이아몬드 중
가장 큰 두 개의 다이아몬드랍니다.
세상에서 가장 깊고 찬란한 빛을
발하는 보석이랍니다.

내게 주어진 아이들의 어여쁜 생,

그 값의 작은 한 부분이라도
106 영원토록 내 것이라고는
상상조차 할 수 없습니다.[106] –매티 윌콕스 노블

셔우드는 오늘 두 살 5개월이 되었다. 엄마는 일주일 전에 커틀러 박사의 브룩클린 장로교회에서 젊은 여성 선교 단체를 위한 강연을 하려고 뉴욕 시에 다녀왔다. 그리고 사랑하는 아빠가 우리에게 남겨주신 돈으로 뉴욕 시 북부에 있는 부동산을 5퍼센트의 이자율에 구입했다. 파인 가의 스키드모어(Skidmore) 변호사가 부동산 매매를 친절히 도와주셨다. 스키드모어 변호사는 엄마의 유언장도 써주셨다. 엄마가 사망할 경우 당연히 그 돈은 자식들에게 가게 될 것이다. 그러나 아이들이 아직 어리다면 누군가가 그애들의 보호자가 되도록 명시해야겠다고 생각했다. 그래서 엄마는 프랭크 셔우드 외삼촌과 오마 킬본 박사를 지명했다. 두 분은 엄마처럼 아이들을 위해 애써 주실 것이다. 유산 중 400불은 아빠를 위한 추모 병원 건축을 위해 미리 지정해 두었다. 엄마가 그 병원을 짓지 못하는 경우를 대비한 것이다. 나머지 유산은 셔우드와 에디스가 똑같이 분배하도록 해놓았다. 찰스 외삼촌과 프랭크 외삼촌이 유언 집행자이시다. 셔우드와 에디스는 엄마와 떨어져 있을 때 착하게 잘 있다. 이번에는 셔우드를 데리고 가고 싶었지만 그렇게 할 수 없었다. 셔우드는 빠른 속도로 말을 배우고 있어서 엄마는 지금 그 단어들을 다 따라잡지 못하고 있다. 셔우드가 글을 읽을 때마다 "아-데"(ah-de)라는 소리를 낸 지 한참이 되었다. 그리고 에디스와 편지나 신문, 책을 읽는 척하면서 계속 "아-데, 아-데" 한다. 셔우드는 지금 애니를

"이안"(Ian)이라고 부른다. 이렇게 셔우드는 모든 것을 나름대로 알아서 부른다. 할머니를 "바바"(Baba)라고 하는데, 이것은 스크랜턴 댁 어린 딸들이 자기네 할머니를 부르는 것과 똑같다. 이외에도

107 "크다(big), 너무 크다(too big), 모두 더럽다(all dirty), 쉬, 응가, 눈(snow), 비(rain), 월크(wolgk, 물), 진크 월크(gink wolgk, 물을 마시다), 넘어지다(fall down), 하늘(sky), 어렵다(hard), 먹는 걸 보다(see eat), 들이키다(drink it up), 감자(potatoes), 슬리퍼(slippers), 약(medicine), 담요가 모두 없어지다(blanket all gone), 아래층(downstairs), 위층(upstairs), 침대(bed), 자다(sleep), 행복한 날(happy day), 가버리다(go away), 아기 손을 회초리로 때리다(whip baby hands), 이버티(리버티)로 가다(go to Ibety[Liberty]), 엄마가 위층에서 글을 쓴다(Mamma witen upstairs), 팔꿈치(elbow), 밖으로 나가다(go outdoors), 집 안에서(in the house), 아기가 운다(baby cry), 칠면조(gobble turkey), 병아리(chickie), 송아지(calf), 사슴(deer)"이라는 말을 한다.

1896년 7월 10일, 금요일

가난한 자를 보살피는 자에게 복이 있음이여 재앙의 날에 여호와께서 그를 건지시리로다(시편41:1)

의무를 다하는 자가 가장 즐거운 인생을 산다네.
크건 작건 우리의 선행은 끊어지지 않는 실로 촘촘히 짜여 있네.
그 사랑이 우리를 고귀하게 하네.
세상은 나팔을 불지 않고 종을 치지 않아도

생명책에 적힌 빛나는 공적이 말하리라.

생의 임무를 마친 후 그대의 사랑이 복을 노래하겠네.
한숨 짓는 그대의 입술에 닿는 아이의 키스가 그대를 기쁘게 하겠네.
그대가 섬긴 가난한 자가 그대를 부자로 만들고
그대가 도운 병자가 그대를 강하게 하겠네.
그대가 모든 것 다해 바친 섬김으로 말미암아 그대는 섬김을
받으리로다.[107] –브라우닝 부인

엄마는 오늘 사랑하는 셔우드에게서 멀리 떠나 있다. 엄마는 이번 여름에 크리스천 헤럴드 프레시 에어 어린이 캠프에서 주치의로 일하고 있다. 그래서 나이액에 있는 론 산(Mt. Lawn)에서 지내면서 아픈 아이들을 돌보고 있다. 캠프 수장인 클롭시(Klopsch) 박사는 엄마가 자녀들을 데려오는 것이 부적합하다고 생각하셨다.
108 대신 엄마에게 2-3주마다 한 번씩 자녀들과 주말을 함께 지낼 수 있는 특혜를 주셨다. 이 긴 시간 동안 사랑하는 아이들과 떨어져 지내는 것이 정말 힘든 일이겠지만 이번 여름에는 이렇게 하는 것이 가장 좋은 선택이라고 엄마는 생각했다. 그리고 이번 가을에는 I.M.M.S.[108] 일을 하면서 121 E. 45번가에서 다시 아이들과 생활할 수 있게 될 것이다. 엄마는 아이들이 모두 건강하고 외갓집에서 여선 삼촌과 다른 분들의 보살핌을 잘 받을 것을 알고 있다. 그리고 외갓집에 있는 것이 나이액에 있는 것보다 아이들을 위해 더 나을 것 같다. 어젯밤 론 산에 있는 어린이 30여 명이 구토하면서 아팠다. 엄마는 그 아이들을 모두 방문하느라 많은 시간을 보냈고 새벽 2시까지 잠을 못 잤다. 대부분의

간병인들은 전혀 도움이 안 되었으므로 엄마와 수간호사는 아이들을 씻기는 일까지 모든 일을 둘이서 다 해야 했다. 엄마는 오늘 아주 피곤하다. 그리고 너무 오래 서 있으면 가끔 그렇듯이 왼쪽 아킬레스건의 힘이 빠졌다.

아기들을 보러 엄마는 집에 벌써 한 번 다녀왔다. 6월 22일부터 뉴욕에서 일을 시작했고, 매일 꽤 많은 어린이들을 진찰하고 있다. 한 주에 95명을 본 적도 있다. 이렇듯 이 어린이 캠프는 빨리 채워진다. 아이들은 열흘간 머무르기 때문에 월요일, 화요일, 수요일에는 검진할 어린이들이 없다. 그래서 뜻밖에도 엄마는 집에 갈 수 있었다.

차스 그레고리(Chas Gregory)와 함께 말을 타고 일단 그의 집으로 간 다음 할머니 집까지 걸어갔다. 집 문이 모두 잠겨 있었기 때문에 엄마는 부엌을 통해 집 안으로 들어갔다. 그리고 셔우드가 할머니 침대에서 낮잠을 자고 있는 것을 확인한 다음 위층으로 올라가서 아기가 침대에서 깊이 잠들어 있는 것을 보았다. 할머니도 주무시고 계셨다. 에디스가 먼저 잠에서 깨어났다. 두 아이는 엄마를 보고 정말 기뻐했다.

109 셔우드는 계속 살이 빠지고 있다. 겨우 32파운드 나간다. 일 때문에 집을 떠나기 전에 엄마는 셔우드를 데리고 화이트 호수와 베델에 잠깐 다녀왔다. 나흘간 다녀오면서 엄마는 이 변화가 셔우드에게 좋은 영향을 주기를 바랬다. 그러나 셔우드는 집을 떠나 있는 동안 너무 안 먹었고 우유도 거의 손을 대지 않았다. 집에 돌아오자 입맛이 조금 나아진 듯했지만 엄마는 예전에 시도했던 대구간유 초코액을 계속 섭취하는 것이 최선이라는 생각이 들었다. 그것을 먹어 주는 셔우드는 정말 착한 아이다. 엄마가 두 아기들에게 이유식을 시작한 5월 1일

이후에도 셔우드가 'baudle mėk'를 못 잊고 있을 수 있다. 처음에는 우유병에 우유를 넣어주지 않고 밤에 우유를 마신 후에 그냥 빈병을 주었다. 하지만 셔우드는 그러기 전부터 체중이 빠지기 시작했다. 빈 우유병에 신경을 쓰는 것 같지도 않았다. 우유병에 우유를 넣어 달라고 한 적도 한두 번뿐이었다. 베델에 갔을 때는 아예 우유병을 두고 갔다. 처음 이틀 동안은 우유병을 찾지도 않고 잠들었는데, 둘째 날 아침에 깼을 때는 우유병을 달라고 했다.

하지만 그 후로는 다시 우유병을 찾지 않았다. 셔우드에게서 우유병을 떼는 것은 엄마가 걱정했던 것만큼 그리 힘들지 않았다. 셔우드의 젖병을 떼면서 에디스에게도 더 이상 우유병을 주지 말라고 여선에게 당부했다. 셔우드가 여행에서 돌아온 후 더 이상 집에는 우유병이 없었다. 2년 만에 처음 있는 일이었다. 더 이상 우유병을 씻지 않아도 되니 조금 어색하다. 그러나 아주 좋다. 그리고 더운 날씨가 다시 시작되고 있으므로 지금이 젖병을 떼기에 제일 좋은 시기라고 생각한다.

110 엄마가 집에 있을 때면 셔우드는 늘 엄마 침대에서 엄마 옆에 가까이 누워서 자고 싶어 한다. 잠이 들면 여선이 셔우드를 안아서 아기침대에 눕힌다. 그러면 보통 밤새 깨지 않고 잘 잔다. 간혹 잠을 깨서 '쉬'가 마렵다고도 한다. 셔우드는 이제 오줌 싸는 일이 거의 없고 기저귀도 잘 버리지 않는다. 이번 가을이면 셔우드가 바지를 입어도 괜찮을 거라고 엄마는 생각한다. 우리 셔우드는 이토록 착한 아이다.

엄마가 멀리 갈 때면 셔우드는 "셔우드 안 울어요. 언젠가 셔우드도 투투 타고 갈 거예요"라고 한다. 셔우드는 이제 엄마가 기록할 수

없을 정도로 말을 잘 한다. 그리고 벌써 이야기 읽어주는 것을 좋아
하기 시작했다. 하루는《빨간 망토 소녀》를 읽어 주었더니 점점 그
이야기에 빠져들기 시작했고, "나쁜 늑대—할머니 물어—불쌍한
할머니"라고 했다. 그림에도 대단한 흥미가 있다. 그림 안에 있는
모든 것을 눈여겨보는데, 꽃, 나비, 새, 접시, '불쌍한 마의 코트'(poor
mah's coat), 까마귀, '할머니의 지팡이' 등 그림 속에 있는 모든 것들을
눈여겨본다.
프랭크 외삼촌, 킷 외숙모, 그리고 사촌 벨트[109]와 클레어[110]가 이번
여름에 할머니 집에서 3주간을 지내기 위해 오기로 되어 있다.
사실 7일날 출발한다고 했으니 이미 할머니 집에 와 있을 것이다.
프랭크 외삼촌 가족은 코호 시에 살고 있는데, 삼촌의 두 아들은 무척
시골에 오고 싶어 했었다. 모두들 정말 좋은 시간을 보내고 있으리라
믿는다. 그 다음에는 릴리 고모와 사촌 레베카가 캐나다에서 우리를
방문하기 위해 올 것이고, 고모가 도착하면 엄마는 다시 산에서
내려갈 것이다. 바로 1년 전 이날 우리는 프랭크 외삼촌과 캐나다에
계시는 분들을 방문하기 위해 출발했다. 그때에 비해 셔우드의
몸무게가 1파운드 밖에 늘지 않았다는 것이 좀 이상하다! 요즘
111 셔우드의 몸무게가 잘 늘지 않아서 엄마는 걱정스럽다. 정신적으로
성장하고 있어서 그럴지도 모르겠다. 엄마는 셔우드가 전반적인
변화를 경험하고 다른 장소에서 지내 보는 것이 유익할 거라고
생각한다. 그래서 조만간 엄마는 클룹시 박사를 만나서 아이들을
어린이집(C.H.C.H.)[111]에 데려오는 것을 허락해 줄 수 있는지 이야기해
보려고 한다. 그분은 우선 간병인들을 모두 살펴본 후 이 기관과
연관된 아이들을 데려오는 것에 대해 다르게 생각해 보는 것이

옳은지 두고 보자고 했다. 하지만 엄마의 다음 돌아올 때까지 셔우드의 상태가 호전되지 않으면 클롭시 박사는 엄마의 아기들이 캠프에 오는 것을 허락지 않을 것이다. 엄마가 다른 사람들의 자녀들을 위해서는 이렇게 많은 일을 하지만 정작 자신의 아이들은 이곳에 데려오지 못할 정도로 잘 돌보지 못한다는 사실이 안타깝기만 하다. 다(Dah)가 같이 오면 아이들을 돌보는 데 엄마가 많은 시간을 쓰지 않아도 될 것이다. 그리고 엄마는 기꺼이 아이들의 숙박비를 지불할 것이다. 그러나 클롭시 씨는 이러한 나의 사정을 사람들이 이해하지 못할 것이고, 또 어린이집이 아이들을 키울 능력이 있는 집안의 자녀들을 보살핀다고 여길 거라며 걱정하는 것 같다. 그래서 결국 다음에 엄마가 아이들을 데려오기로 한다면 차라리 캠프 길 건너편에 있는 이웃에 숙박비를 내고 아이들을 데려다 놓는 것이 더 현명한 방법인 듯하다.

112 1896년 11월 10일, 화요일

하나님이여 주는 나의 하나님이시라 내가 간절히 주를 찾되(시편 63:1)

{작년 생일에 인용한 하버갈의 시를 보라. 그리고 이 시를 그곳에 사용하라.}[112]

나뭇잎이 바래고 떨어진다. 바람이 거칠고 사납다.
새들은 지저귀기를 그쳤다. 그러나 너에게 해줄 말이 있단다, 아가.
하루하루가 끝날 때마다 어둠과 차가움이 더해 가더라도
눈부시게 빨간 장미의 뿌리는 눈 속에서도 살아 있단다.

그리고 겨울이 지나면 가지에는 새순이 돋고
메추라기는 클로버로 돌아오며 제비는 처마로 돌아올 것이다.
울새는 가슴에 밝은 새 조끼를 입고
길가의 예쁜 꽃은 태양과 이슬로 빛날 것이다.
오늘은 나뭇잎이 휭휭 날리고 시내는 말라 물소리 안 들려도
그러나 네게 해 줄 말이 있단다, 아가야. 봄은 분명히 올 거라고.
거칠고 추운 날이 있겠고 혹독한 비바람도 휘몰아칠 거야.
그래, 여기 있는 우리에게 좋은 일들만 오는 것은 아니란다, 아가야.
그러니까 행복했던 기쁨이 어여쁜 여름의 빛살을 잃을 때
장미의 뿌리가 어떻게 눈 속에서 살아남았는지 생각해 보렴.
―《반스 읽기 교본 3》 중 〈11월〉[113]이라는 시에서.

셔우드의 세 돌 잔치도 두 돌 때와 마찬가지로 외할머니 집에서 보냈다. 하지만 이번에는 엄마와 누이동생이 뉴욕에 있어서 혼자 생일을 맞이해야 했다. 엄마는 9월 28일부터 일을 하기 위해 아이들을 데리고 121 E. 45번가에서 살았다. 그러나 10월 28일 로체스터에서 열린 여성해외선교회 집행위원회 총회에 참석하러 가는 길에 리버티에 들러 셔우드를 사랑하는 할머니 곁에 남겨 두었다. 셔우드가 그곳에서 지내는 동안 엄마는 우리 아들이 아주 잘 지내고 있다는 보고서를 받았다. 할머니는 셔우드가 더할 나위 없이 얌전하게 지내고 있으며, 할머니와 잠을 자고 모두에게 동무가 되어 준다고 하셨다. 할머니께서는 추수감사절 바로 전에 셔우드를 뉴욕에 있는 엄마와 동생한테 데려다 줄 계획을 세우셨다. 엄마는 셔우드의 생일 선물로 《엄마를 돕는 사람들》(Mama's Helpers)이라는 작은 이야기책을

두고 왔다. 그리고 애니 이모는 혼(Horn) 씨 이발소에서 셔우드의
머리를 잘라 주었다. 할머니는 새 신발 한 켤레를 주셨고, 조는 장갑
113 한 쌍을 사주었다. 셔우드의 생일날은 맑았으며, 셔우드는 바깥에서
놀면서 재미있게 지냈다고 할머니께서 편지에 쓰셨다. 여기 어린
셔우드가 처음으로 엄마에게 보낸 편지를 붙여 놓는다. 엄마는
2년 전 이때 셔우드가 사랑스런 작은 손으로 평양에 계시던 아빠에게
비슷한 손편지를 썼던 것을 기억하고 있다.

[셔우드가 엄마에게 보낸 편지]
"사랑하는 어머니, 당신의 사랑하는 아들, 셔우드."
"이것은 셔우드가 동생과 엄마에게 보내는 것이야"[편지에 할머니가 쓴 내용]

[3세 때 머리 타래]

"3세 때 셔우드의 손. [체중] 34 파운드, [키] 37¼인치, [머리 둘레] 19¾인치"

셔우드는 지난 한 해 동안 신체적으로는 그리 많이 자라지 않았으나 정신적으로 더 성장했다. 몸무게는 같지만(34파운드) 머리 둘레는 19¾ 인치로 ½ 인치가 늘었고, 키는 37¼ 인치로 3¼ 인치 자랐다. 그래서 작년보다 훨씬 더 호리호리해졌다. 손을 그린 그림을 비교해 보아도 알 수 있을 정도다. 엄마는 셔우드가 1년 전보다 체중이 늘지 않았다는 생각에 걱정스러워하지만 그래도 셔우드는 건강한 것 같고 외모도 잘생겼다. 그리고 바지를 입기 시작한 뒤로 오히려 통통해 보이고 살도 쪄 보인다. 처음 보는 사람들은 항상 셔우드를 "튼튼하고 건강해 보이는 남자아이"라고 한다. 셔우드는 9월 이후부터 바지를 입고 있어서 비록 오늘로 세 살밖에 안 된 '아직까지는 아기'이지만

'꼬마 사나이'처럼 보인다.

114 이렇게 어린 나이에 셔우드는 벌써 사고가 종교적으로 기울어진 것 같다. 기특하게도 1년 동안 교회에서 행동이 반듯했고 교회에 가는 것을 좋아한다. 그리고 얼마 전부터 "이제 저는 잠자리에 듭니다"라고 기도한다. 그리고 할머니 집에서 자러 갈 때도 그렇게 기도하는 것을 거의 잊은 적이 없으며, 상기시켜 주지 않아도 항상 스스로 기도에 대해 생각하고 있다고 할머니께서 말씀하셨다. 그리고 한번은 혼자서 기도를 처음부터 끝까지 다 했다고 한다. 하지만 보통 한두 구절을 반복해 주면 따라하는 것을 좋아한다. 셔우드는 여러 번 "하나님은 어디에 계셔요?"라고 물었다. 한번은 "하늘나라에 계시지"라는 대답을 듣고 1분 정도 생각하더니 다시 물었다. "하나님은 죽었어요?" 아빠가 죽었고 하늘나라에 갔다고 들었던 내용과 연관시킨 것이 분명했다. 하지만 오래 전에 이렇게 생각하는 것을 잊어버렸고 이제는 이 주제에 대해 생각할 때면 "하나님은 죽지 않았어요, 하나님은 내 마음 속에 계셔요. 그리고 하나님은 아빠가 계신 곳에 계셔요"라고 말한다. 셔우드는 죽고 싶다고는 하지 않지만 자주 하늘나라에 가고 싶다고 한다. "언젠가 나는 하늘나라에 갈 거예요"라고 하거나 "다음 주에 나는 하늘나라에 가고, 언젠가 돌아올 거예요"라고 한다. 한번은 할머니께 "나는 하늘나라에 가고 싶어요"라고 하고는 갑자기 "하지만 떨어질지도 몰라요"라고 덧붙였다.

2월 10일 셔우드의 키는 38¼ 인치였다.

115 1897년 5월 10일

주께서 이르시되 그 날 후로는 그들과 맺을 언약이 이것이라 하시고 내 법을 그들의 마음에 두고 그들의 생각에 기록하리라(히브리서 10:16)

"아이와 같은 마음으로 주님을 배우고
주님께 저의 미래를 맡깁니다.
아직 걷지 않은 인생 길 그 발자국마다
주님의 사랑이 인도하실 것입니다."[114]

3년 6개월 때 셔우드 가족.

6개월 이상 셔우드의 육아 일기를 쓸 시간이 없었다. 지금 셔우드는
세 살 반이 되었다. 위 사진은 최근에 찍은 사진인데 셔우드가 아주 잘
나왔다. 지난 번 생일 이후 셔우드의 겉모습은 그리 많이 변하지 않았다.
116 키는 3인치 정도 자랐지만, 몸무게는 반 파운드만 늘었다. 지금 키는
3피트 4인치이고, 머리 둘레는 20인치, 몸무게는 34½파운드다.

이 갈색 양복 바지와 코트와 조끼는 작년 크리스마스 때 엄마가 사준 것이다. 엄마랑 할머니와 함께 코호에 사는 프랭크 외삼촌 가족을 방문하러 가기 전에 산 옷이다. 우리는 그곳에서 한 주 정도 지냈는데, 셔우드도 아주 즐거운 시간을 보냈다. 사촌 벨트와 클레어가 셔우드에게 아주 잘해 주었다. 셔우드는 종종 프랭크 외삼촌 집에 다시 가자고 한다.

지난 6개월 동안 셔우드는 조금밖에 변하지 않았지만 일기장을 들추어

2년 전 이맘 때 할아버지 무릎에서 찍은 사진과 이번에 찍은 사진을
비교해 보면 무척 흥미롭다. 이 사진을 찍기 전에는 셔우드가 그
사진에 있는 모습과 비슷한 것 같았는데, 이제는 누가 봐도 셔우드가
얼마나 성숙해졌는지 금방 알 수 있다. 다른 사진은 귀여운 아기
얼굴이지만 이 사진은 의젓한 어린 소년 같다. 각 사진은 그 나름대로
사랑에 빠진 엄마의 눈에 완벽해 보인다.
셔우드와 에디스는 오랫동안 잘 놀다가도 간혹 틀어져서 말다툼을
하고 싸우기까지 한다. 보통 셔우드가 먼저 울면서 엄마한테 달려와
자기보다 격렬한 어린 누이동생으로부터 구해 달라고 한다.
그러면서도 셔우드는 동생을 사랑한다. 어느 날 밤에는 셔우드와
에디스가 아기 침대에서 같이 잠이 들었는데, 무슨 이유로 엄마가
에디스를 엄마 침대로 데리고 갔다. 셔우드는 밤중에 깨어서 여동생이
없어졌다는 생각에 울기 시작했다. 엄마가 무슨 일이냐고 묻자
117 "아기를 찾을 수 없어요, 흑흑" 하며 울었다. 종종 동생을 아프게
하거나 동생에게 짓궂은 짓을 했을 때는 재빨리 "그러려고 한 것이
아니라…, 잊어버렸어요"라고 하거나 "이제 다시는 안 할게요"라고
한다. 언젠가 셔우드가 길에서 어떤 고약한 아이를 본 일에 관해
말한 적이 있다. 어떻게 해서 그 아이가 나쁘게 되었냐고 물었더니
"그 아이는 회초리로 때려 줄 엄마가 없어서요!"라고 했다.
셔우드는 요즘 기도를 잘 하지 않는다. 기도하는 것을 자주 잊어버린다.
가끔 상기시켜 주면 너무 피곤하다거나 곧 하겠다고 한다. 6주 동안
우리와 함께 계시던 할머니가 집으로 돌아가신 지 얼마 되지 않은
어느 날, 할머니가 외로울 거라는 생각이 들었던지 할머니를 위해
기도했다. "바바가 울지 않게 해주세요"라고. 하루는 놀다가 갑자기

"이제 기도할 거야" 하고는 자기 작은 의자 앞에 무릎을 꿇더니 "예수님, 구세주"라고 했다. 그다음은 무슨 말을 해야 할지 생각이 안 나는 듯 잠시 멈추더니 "다 했다" 하고는 다시 가서 놀기 시작했다. 셔우드는 기도에 대해 아주 엄숙하고도 심각하다. 그래서 장난으로 기도한 것 같지는 않았다. 그리고 지금까지 그 기도를 반복한 적도 없다. 어느 날 저녁 창문을 통해 어두워져 가는 밖을 내다보면서 "나는 하나님께서 어둠이 오게 한다고 생각해요"라고 했다. 한번은 "왜 하나님은 비가 오게 하나요?"라고 묻기도 했다. "나무, 풀, 꽃에 마실 물을 주시고, 목욕할 수 있게 해주시려고"라고 대답해 주자 아주 만족해했다.

2월과 3월, 두 달 동안 셔우드는 집에서 두 블럭 정도 떨어진 곳에 있는 유치원에 다녔다. 처음에는 거기 가는 것을 아주 좋아해서 집에 오려고 하지 않을 정도였다. 셔우드는 9시 30분부터 정오까지 아침 시간에만 갔고, 오후에는 낮잠을 잤다. 셔우드는 "학교에 간다"면서 그곳에 가는 것을 아주 중요하게 여겼다. 셔우드는 블럭과 구멍에 작은 말뚝을 집어넣으면서 놀았다. 그리고 한 주에 두 번씩 구멍 뚫린 작은 카드에 바느질을 했는데, 셔우드는 이 작업을 아주 좋아했다.
118 빨대와 색종이로 목걸이도 두 개 만들었다. 셔우드는 노먼(Norman) 선생을 좋아했고 그녀도 셔우드를 착한 아이라고 불렀다. 그러나 노먼 선생은 주로 유치부를 마치고 초등학교 입학 준비를 하는 아이들을 돌보느라 셔우드에게 동시, 노래, 게임 등을 가르쳐 줄 시간이 없었다. 셔우드는 작은 의자에 그냥 조용히 앉아서 수업을 방해하지 않고 있다가 집으로 왔다. 엄마는 셔우드가 더 이상 배우는 게 없어서 좀 실망스러웠고, 유치원을 그만 두어야겠다는 생각을

하고 있었다. 그런데 갑자기 셔우드가 스스로 그만 다니고 싶다고 했다. 엄마는 다시 가라고 달랠 수가 없었다. 전에 물어볼 때는 늘 "쿨(Kool, 학교)에 가는 것이 좋아요"라고 했는데…….

셔우드가 유치원에서 꿰맨 카드.

지금까지는 아무도 셔우드의 말씨를 교정해 주려 하지 않았었다. 셔우드는 "나를 클리포드를 보러 가도 돼요?"(Can me go up see Clifford?)라고 하거나 "나를 잘라도 돼요? 나를 종이를 전부 집어도 돼요?"(Can me cut; – me pick papers all up?)라고 묻는다. 셔우드는 '풀다'(untie)가 무엇을 의미하는지 알고 있다. 그러나 무엇을 묶어 달라고 할 때 "이것을 풀어 주세요"(untie it up)라고 말한다. '예'라고 대답해야 할 때 'yes'나 '에스'(ess)라는 단어를 사용하기 시작한 지도 얼마 되지 않았다. 셔우드는 항상 묻는 질문에 완전한 문장으로 대답했는데, 이는 분명한 답을 주고 싶어 했기 때문이다.

119 5월 20일이면 엄마가 의료 선교부 학생들을 위해 디커니스 홈에서 하던 일이 끝난다. 그러면 엄마는 셔우드를 데리고 필라델피아로 가서 20일과 21일에 열리는 의대 동창회에 참석할 예정이다. 셔우드는 엄마의 '쿨'(Kool, 학교)과 엄마의 선생님들을 만나는 것에 아주 큰 기대를 걸고 있다. 그런 다음에는 에스더 이모한테 "굿 바이" 인사를 하러 볼티모어로 갈 것이다. 에스더 이모는 그곳에 있는 의과대학에서 첫 해를 성공적으로 마쳤다. 에스더 이모를 만난 뒤에는 사랑하는 할머니와 에디스가 있는 리버티로 돌아가서 한국으로 출발할 때까지 그곳에서 여름을 보낼 것이다.

엄마는 다시 한국에 가서 사역을 맡기로 했다. 그것은 엄마가 한국에서
돌아올 때 바라던 것이다. 만약 여성해외선교회에서 엄마를 보내는
것이 적합하다고 생각하면 말이다. 현재 여성해외선교회에서는 엄마를
한국에 다시 보내기를 원하고, 한국 선교부에서도 엄마가 돌아오기를
몹시 바라고 있다. 엄마는 이것이 하나님께서 바라시는 일이라
생각한다. 엄마는 많은 기도를 했다. 하나님의 뜻이 아니라면 한국으로
가는 길을 막아 주시고 이곳에서 할 일을 열어 달라고.
그런데 한국의 사역은 여성해외선교회와 한국 양쪽에서 활짝 열려
있고, 이곳에서의 사역은 막히고 있다. 겨울 내내 엄마가 한 일은 아주
힘든 일이고, 다우콧(G. D. Dowkoutt)[115] 박사로 인해 매우 불편했다.
다우콧 박사는 엄마에게 그 일을 맡겨 놓고는 나중에는 자신이 그
자리를 원했다. 운영위원회에서는 엄마가 있어 주기를 주장하면서도
다우콧 박사와 그분 가족이 국제의료선교회 사택에 머무르도록
허용했으며, 다우콧 박사는 사사건건 엄마를 힘들게 했다. 그곳에서는
개선의 여지가 없었고, 엄마는 여성 관리인들이 엄마의 지위를 맡을
120 적당한 인물을 찾을 때까지만 그 사역을 감당하기로 했다.
보스워스(J. B. Bosworth) 부인이 지난 6주간 동안 엄마의 사역을
도와주었고 그분이 내년도에 엄마의 지위를 맡도록 임명되었다.
엄마는 벌써 할머니 집에서 지낼 때 꼭 필요하지 않은 물건들,
즉 셔우드의 흔들말과 흔들의자, 높은 의자, 그림책 몇 개 등을 싸서
한국에 가져갈 커다란 상자에 넣었다. 셔우드는 종종 한국에 가는
것에 대해 이야기한다. 그리고 가끔 "하나님, 한국 사람들을 축복해
주세요"라고 기도한다.

❧ [헤고(Hego) 호 항로 지도. 나가사키와 부산을 오간 헤고 호는 니폰 유센 카이샤 라인(Nippon Yusen Kaisha line<N.y.k. line>)에 의해 운항되었다.]

121 1897년 11월 10일 수요일, 한국, 제물포

비록 아이라도 자기의 동작으로 자기 품행이 청결한 여부와
정직한 여부를 나타내느니라(잠언 20:11)

"하나님의 크신 계획 중에 있는 작은 생명,
나이가 늘수록 얼마나 헛되어 보이는지.
되는대로 하고 할 수 있는 만큼만 하렴,
무한한 전체의 움직임을 변화시킬 수 있도록!
끝없이 펼쳐진 그물에 한 땀이 되어,
바다의 밀물과 썰물에 한 방울 물이 되어.
이 한 땀이 없으면 무늬에 구멍이 생긴다네.
엉킨 실들이 지나간 곳에 흠이 진다네.
참 목적에서 실패한 인생은
하나님이 의도하신 완전한 계획을 그르친다네."[116]

오늘은 셔우드의 네 번째 생일이다. 태어난 날에 태어난 곳인 한국에 도착한다면 아주 기막힌 우연의 일치가 아닐 수 없을 것이다. 그런데 그렇게 되었다. 우리는 오전 9시에 헤고 호를 타고 한국에 도착했고, 10시쯤 거룻배에서 내려 육지를 밟았다. 4년 전 오늘 셔우드가 처음으로 모습을 드러냈던 바로 그 고향에 온 것이다.

하지만 이번에는 셔우드를 맞아 줄 사랑하는 아빠가 계시지 않았다. 존스 목사가 미국 세인트 폴에서부터 우리와 함께 여행한 부인과 어린 딸을 마중 나오셨다. 그리고 폴웰(M. W. Follwell)[117] 부인이 평양에서 내려와 여동생 릴리안 해리스(Lillian Harris)[118] 박사를 맞아 주셨다. 또 페인(J. O. Paine)[119] 양과 프레이(L. E. Frey)[120] 양이 서울에서부터 피어스(N. Pierce)[121] 양을 마중 나왔다. 해리스 박사와 피어스 양은 세인트 폴에서부터 우리와 동행했는데, 두 분 모두 여성해외선교회 선교사로서 서울에서의 사역을 돕기 위해 왔다.
122 제물포에 사는 존스 가족을 제외한 우리 모두는 11일 밤 서울로 가는 강 증기선의 운항을 기다리기 위해 스튜어드 호텔로 갔다.

지난 일기를 쓴 이후 6개월간 너무도 많은 일들이 있었기 때문에 간략하게 정리해야겠다. 그러나 덜 중요한 것들이 언급되는 반면 반드시 기록해야 할 것들이 빠지게 될 것이 분명하다. 자주 기록할 시간이 없는 것이 유감이지만 엄마는 1년에 두 번 정도밖에 일기를 쓸 수가 없다.

우리는 남쪽 지역을 여행하고 6월 1일쯤 할머니 집으로 돌아왔다. 즐겁게 보낼 수 있었던 시간들이지만 엄마는 한국으로 돌아갈 준비를 해야 했기 때문에 많은 시간을 즐겁게 보낼 수는 없었다.

여러 가지 일들 외에 아빠의 책 문제도 있었다. 안타깝게도 엄마는 엄마가 맡았던 다른 일들 때문에 1년 동안 아빠의 책에 전혀 손 대지 못하고 있었다. 엄마는 그 일을 반드시 끝내서 한국으로 가기 전에 출판을 해야겠다고 마음먹었다. 그래서 6주 동안 꾸준히 원고 작업을 했고, 7월 15일에 출판 일정을 논의하기 위해 뉴욕으로 갔다.

엄마는 거의 한 달 동안 그곳에 머물면서 교정 작업을 시작했고, 의료 수련 사역도 좀 하고, 한국에 갈 준비를 하기 위해 쇼핑도 많이 했다.
엄마가 없는 동안 할머니와 '다'(여선)가 셔우드와 에디스를 돌봐
주었다. 비록 '다'가 예전만큼 큰 도움이 되지 못해서 사랑하는
할머니를 걱정시켰지만 말이다. 그는 엄마가 미국에 데려올 때 한
약속과 달리 우리와 한국으로 돌아가지 않기로 했다. 그래서 엄마는
여선에게 가능한 한 빨리 일할 곳을 구하라고 했다. 엄마는 이제
여선이 필요치 않았지만, 한국으로 돌아가는 길에 행여 그가 도움이
123 될 수 있을까 하여 그냥 그를 데리고 있었을 뿐이다. 여선이 달리
결정하리라는 것을 알았더라면, 엄마는 뉴욕에서 그를 데려오지
않았을 것이고, 5월에 그곳에서 여선에게 구해 주었던 일을 계속 하게
했을 것이다. 여선은 엄마에게 다시 도시에서 할 일을 구해 달라고
했다. 하지만 여선은 자신이 할 수 있는 유일한 일인 요리나 빨래,
다림질은 하지 않겠다며 단호히 거절했다. 그래서 엄마는 그에게 어떤
일도 구해줄 수 없었다. 여름 내내 엄마는 여선을 거두느라 일주일에
4불을 지불했으나 그 비용만큼 그는 도움이 되지 못했고 근심을
끼쳤으며 걱정거리가 되었다. 하지만 얼마 후 여선은 이를 뉘우치고
더 잘하기 시작했으며, 엄마가 찾아주는 일이면 어떤 일이든 기꺼이
하겠다고 했다. 그래서 엄마는 샌드포드(A. B. Sandford) 목사 댁에 좋은
일자리를 구해 주었다.

에디스는 5월 한 달 동안 할머니와 지내면서 '바바'(Baba) 대신 '할머니'(Gamma)라고 말하는 것을 배웠다. 하지만 셔우드는 집으로 돌아온 후에도 여전히 바바라고만 불렀다. 할머니께서 '할머니'라고 말하게 하려고 여러 번 시도해 보았지만 셔우드는 그렇게 못하는 듯했다. 할머니는 셔우드의 말꼬리를 잡으려고도 해 보셨다. 셔우드가

"나는 그 말을 못해요" 하면 얼른 받아서 "무슨 말을 못한다고?"라고 물으셨다. 그러나 셔우드는 "나는 'you'라고 못해요"라고 대답했다. 그런데 6월 말 어느 날 밤에 셔우드는 갑자기 자신이 그 말을 빠르게 반복하므로 할 수 있다는 것을 발견했다. 간-마(Gan-ma) 감-마(Gam-ma) 감마(Gamma)! 그리고 그날 이후로는 할머니를 그렇게 불렀다. 엄마가 기도할 때 가끔 셔우드는 엄마에게 큰 소리로 기도해 달라고 한다. 한번은 엄마가 기도를 끝내자 "조와 콜버트[122]를 위한 기도를 안 했어요"라고 했다. 아무도 셔우드에게 그런 말을 해준 적이 없지만, 셔우드는 콜버트 이모부가 우리와 같이 교회에 가지 않는다는 사실을 알아챘다. 그리고 왜 가지 않느냐고 물었고 자기가 가자고 할 거라고 했다. 엄마는 셔우드가 그렇게 할까봐 걱정이 되었다.

124 콜버트 이모부는 가톨릭 신자였고, 누군가가 셔우드에게 그렇게 하라고 시켰을지 모른다고 오해할 수 있었다. 그러나 셔우드는 이모부에게 교회에 가자고 하지 않았다. 언젠가 셔우드는 '하나님의 정원'을 보고 싶다고 했다. 엄마는 그 아이가 어디서 그런 표현을 들었는지 잘 모르겠다. 셔우드는 절대로 엄마 외에는 다른 사람에게 무엇을 요구하지 않는다. 한번은 머리를 자를 때가 되었는데, 엄마는 월터 외삼촌에게 이발 가위를 가져와 달라는 부탁을 계속 잊고 있었다. 어느 날 할머니와 월터 외삼촌이 식탁에 계셨는데 셔우드가 엄마에게 말했다. "할머니한테 월터 외삼촌더러 가위를 가져오라고 말해 달라는 부탁을 잊지 마세요." 그것은 참으로 간접적인 부탁 방법이었다. 9월 6일에 우리는 정든 고향집, 보금자리를 떠나 서부로 얼굴을 돌려 극동으로 향했다. 사랑하는 분들께 '안녕'을 고하기란 정말 힘든 일이었다. 감리교회에서는 우리를 위해 멋진 환송회를 마련해

주었고(셔우드와 에디스는 한복을 입었다), 한국에 건립될 아빠의 기념병원 [비어 있음] 을 위해 모금해 주었다. 사촌 폴리 크레리도 50불을 보내 주었다. 엄마는 어느 날 조와 그가 기독교인인 것과 기독교인임을 드러내는 것에 대해 꽤 길게 이야기를 나누었다. 전에 한국으로 갈 때에도 엄마는 조와 이런 대화를 했는데, 그때 조는 자신이 교회 명부에 이름이 올라 있는 기독교인과 다를 바 없이 착하게 살고 있다고 주장했다. 그런데 이번에는 더 감동받았고, 교회에 가서 견습자 명단에 자기 이름을 올리겠다고 약속까지 할 뻔했다. 조는 늘 자신의 선한 습관에 대해 말한다. 그래서 엄마는 조에게 구세주의 공로를 구하지 않고 자신의 힘만으로 선하다고 생각하는 것이 아닐까 염려한다고 했다. 그러자 조는 아니라면서, 자신은 주님이 도우셨음을 알고 있고, 기도를 믿으며, 천국에 가기를 바란다고 했다. 나중에 할머니의 편지에서 조가 엄마에게 자신은 30년이 넘도록 '이제 잠 자려고 눕습니다'라는 기도와 '주기도문'을 기도해 왔다고 전해 달라고 했다. 사랑하는 올드 블랙 조, 그 이야기는 정말 애처로웠고, 엄마는 울 수 밖에 없었다.

125 월터 외삼촌이 할머니의 농장을 빌려서 올겨울을 그곳에서 지낼 것이다. 그래서 사랑하는 할머니는 그들과 지내실 수 있게 되었고 잘 보살핌을 받으실 것이다. 사랑하는 할머니, 만약 한국까지 가는 힘든 여정을 견뎌 내시리라는 확신이 있었다면 우리는 정말로 할머니를 모시고 오고 싶었고, 할머니도 그러고 싶어 하셨다. 할머니는 우리의 이별이 덜 힘들도록 록랜드까지 우리와 함께 오셨다.

그렇게 하면 할머니께서 우리를 조금이라도 덜 그리워하게 해드릴 수 있을 것 같았다. 우리 할머니는 참으로 용감하시다. 우리가 떠나는 것을 막으려 하신 적이 없다. 조가 우리에게 우리를 보내기가 지난번보다 더 힘들고 우리가 가는 것이 옳지 않아 보인다고 했을 때도, 할머니는 괜찮다고 하셨다. 그러시면서 지난번보다 보내기 쉬운 것은 지금은 엄마가 무엇을 해야 할지 알고 있을 뿐더러 아기들의 위로를 받을 것이며, 또한 한번 갔다가 무사히 돌아온 적이 있으므로 다시 만날 수 있다는 희망 속에 살 수 있기 때문이라고 하셨다. 자신의 유익을 구하지 않는 어머니의 마음으로 할머니는 오로지 엄마만 생각하셨고 자신은 전혀 생각하지 않으셨다.

[4세 때 머리 타래]

"셔우드의 4세 때 손. 4세. 키는 40인치, 머리 둘레는 20인치."

126 그렇게 우리는 떠났고, 우티카까지 왔다. 그곳에서 우리는 다음 날까지 교통편을 기다리면서 첫 밤을 보내야 할 상황이었는데 다행히도 존스 목사 본가에서 즐거운 시간을 보낼 수 있었다. 셔우드는 존스 할아버지와 잘 놀았고, 할아버지는 셔우드가 착한 아이라고 하시면서 이른 아침에 셔우드를 데리고 산책도 하셨다. 그다음 우리는 존 루사(D.B. St. John Roosa)[123] 선생의 누이이신 [비어 있음] 부인을 방문했다. 존 루사 선생은 엄마가 맨해튼 안이과병원에서 수련의 과정을 거칠 때 엄마를 가르쳐주신 분이다. 다음 날 저녁 우리는 엄마의 의과대학 동창 메리 브라이언(M. Bryan)[124] 박사가 사는 뉴욕 주 오그덴스버그에 도착했다. 또 그다음 날에는 선교사 회의가 있었다. 셔우드와 에디스는 한복을 입고 참석했고, 엄마는 한국에서 했던 사역에 대해 잠깐 동안 가벼운

연설을 했다. 셔우드와 에디스는 이곳에서 좋은 시간을 보냈다. 브라이언 박사 자매와 그분의 조카딸은 아이들에게 친절히 대해 주었고, 내 집처럼 편안하게 지낼 수 있도록 배려해 주었다. 브라이언 박사는 아이들 옷 갈아입히는 것과 돌보는 것을 도와주면서 엄마의 짐을 들어주었다. 한국에 가는 길에 이렇게 많은 도움을 받아 본 적이 없다. 마지막 날 아침에는 브라이언 박사가 아이들이 한복을 입고 있는 모습을 찍어주었다. 그리고 나중에 현상된 사진들을 보내주었는데, 이 사진들을 보면 당시 아이들이 어떤 모습이었는지 알 수 있다. 그녀는 더 잘 나온 사진들이 있으면 나중에 보내 주겠다고 했다.

[네 살 적 한복 입은 셔우드]

네 살 적 셔우드 [누이동생 에디스와 함께 한복을 입고 있다.]

127 우리는 오그덴스버그에서 세인트 로렌스를 거쳐 아일랜드 벨에 있는 브록빌까지 갔다. 셔우드가 아주 좋아했다. 윌 그레이[125] 고모부가 부두까지 나와서 우리를 맞아 주었다. 우리는 곧 앨리스 고모 댁에 도착했다. 셔우드보다 약간 나이가 많은 사촌 해리는 우리를 기다리면서 안전 그네를 타다가 잠들었는데 곧 깨어났다. 2년 전에 왔을 때는 셔우드가 더 컸는데 지금은 해리가 더 크다. 아이들은 재미있게 잘 놀다가 좀 다투기도 했다. 그래도 착한 사촌 해리는 셔우드와 에디스가 자기 장난감을 가지고 놀 수 있게 해주었다. 사촌 모드와 앨런은 너무 많이 자라서 다음에 만날 때면 어른이 되어 있을 것 같다.

우리는 캐나다에서 18일 동안 있었다. 대부분의 시간을 홀 할아버지 집에서 지냈다. 앨리스 고모와 사촌 해리가 우리와 함께 할아버지 집으로 와서 일주일 동안 함께 지내다 갔다. 우리는 제인 로섬 이모할머니 댁에도 다녀왔는데, 좋은 시간을 가졌다. 제인 이모할머니와와 사촌 엘피는 셔우드와 에디스 돌보는 것을 많이 도와주셨다. 셔우드는 제인 이모할머니의 오리들을 좇아다니는 것을 아주 좋아했는데, 하루는 오리를 따라 연못까지 들어가 버렸다. 발이 다 젖고, 앞치마에는 흙이 묻고, 멋진 새 밀짚모자에서는 물이 뚝뚝 떨어졌다. 아이들은 제인 이모할머니와 같이 가서 모이를 주는 것도 재미있어했다.

엄마 생일에는 우리 모두 아빠의 절친한 친구였던 길로이 부부 댁에서 지냈다. 그리고 보이드 홀[126] 작은할아버지 댁도 방문해서 즐거운 시간을 보냈다. 투리세(Tourisse) 댁과 퍼시벌(Percival) 댁에서는 어린 여우를 보았다. 이 두 가정 모두 우리 아이들에게 많은 관심을 보여 주셨다. 투리세 댁에서는 처음으로 메이플 시럽을 먹었는데 아이들이 참 좋아했다.

하루는 볼턴 증조할아버지 댁을 방문해서 즐거운 시간을 보냈다. 부러진 엉덩이뼈 때문에 아직 침대에 누워 계시지만 쾌활하셨고 만족해 하셨다. 92세의 할아버지는 셔우드에게 아빠에 대해 이야기해 주셨고, 아들 윌리엄 할아버지와 함께 노래도 불러주셨다.

128 브록빌로 떠나기 전날 길로이 부인께서 엄마와 셔우드를 내시(Nash) 부인 댁에 데려다 주셨다. 내시 부인은 우리가 방문해 주기를 몹시 바라셨고, 우리는 좋은 시간을 가졌다. 셔우드는 내시 할아버지와 함께 안전 그네를 타고 놀았다. 내시 부부는 오래되고 큰 석조 주택에서

살고 계셨는데, 집이 멋지고 널찍했으며 편리하게 수리되어 있었다. 아빠를 무척 아끼셨던 내시 부인은 우리에게 아빠에 관한 많은 이야기를 들려주셨다. 언젠가 캠프 모임에 갔는데 부인은 고질병이던 두통이 너무 심해서 밤 기도회 중에 자리를 떠야만 했다고 한다. 다음 날 아침 머리가 쪼개지듯 아플 때 아빠가 텐트 안을 들여다보면서 "내시 부인, 머리가 좀 어떠세요?" 하고 묻더란다. "내가 두통이 있다는 걸 어떻게 알았니?" 부인이 의아해 하자 아빠는 윈터(Winter) 씨가 "다른 이유로는 기도회를 떠날 누이가 아니"라고 해서 알게 되었다고 하더란다. "그래, 정말 많이 아팠어." 부인이 고백하자 아빠는 자신의 텐트로 돌아가 부인을 위해 기도드렸다고 한다. 마침 그때 어느 남자아이가 신선한 송어 몇 마리를 아빠에게 가지고 왔는데, 아빠는 그 송어를 가지고 다시 내시 부인에게 와서 텐트 안으로 고개를 들이밀고 또 한 번 괜찮은지 물어보더라는 것이었다.
그래서 아빠가 방문해 준 뒤 곧 두통이 말끔히 사라졌으며, 그녀의 여동생에게도 그렇게 전했노라고 했더니 아빠는 "주님을 찬양합니다" 하고서는 생선이 부인께 좋을 것 같다며 그 신선한 물고기들을 부인에게 주었다고 한다. 그 생선들은 아빠가 선물 받은 것이며, 부인께 드리려고 일부러 산 것이 아니라고 안심시키면서 말이다. 부인은 물고기를 손질해서 아빠를 초대할 테니 같이 먹자고 했고, 아빠는 그렇게 했다고 한다. 아빠는 자주 부인을 보러 그 댁에 들렀으며, 부인은 아빠를 자식처럼 생각했다고 한다.
9월 27일, 우리는 캐나다태평양철도(C.P.R.)를 타고 브록빌을 떠났다. 새벽 2시에 칼턴 교차로에서 선로가 바뀌었고, 그후 세인트 폴까지 갔다. 세인트 폴에는 29일 아침 8시 45분에 도착했다. 그곳에서

129 우리는 마가렛 제인[127]의 삼촌 집에 가서 존스 부인, 마가렛 제인과 함께 즐거운 시간을 가졌다. 저녁에 우리는 사우스 다코타 주 빅터에 있는 데이빗 파월[128] 이모부 댁으로 출발해서 9월 30일 오전 11시에 그곳에 도착했다. 그런데 밤에 셔우드가 아팠다. 구토했고 열이 났다. 그리고 레처까지 가는 내내 잠만 잤다. 데이비드 이모부가 레처까지 마중 나오셨고, 우리는 그 집까지 초원을 가로지르며 10마일을 갔다. 엄마는 셔우드를 곧바로 침대에 눕히고는 피직약을 먹였다. 셔우드가 할머니 집을 떠난 후 처음으로 먹은 약이다. 목이 좀 아프다고 했지만 엄마에게 스프레이 약이 없어서 셔우드는 목 헹구기를 배웠고 곧잘 따라했다. 아침이 되자 셔우드는 많이 나아졌다. 그리고 하루가 더 지나자 본래의 셔우드로 돌아왔다. 포도 씨를 너무 많이 먹은 게 문제였던 것 같다. 셔우드는 지친 듯했고 버터 밀크를 마시고 싶어 했다. 그래서 파월 이모가 셔우드를 위해 우유를 저어서 버터 밀크를 만들어 주셨다. 아, 셔우드가 얼마나 좋아하던지!
큰 잔에 가득 채워진 우유를 단번에 마셔 버렸다!

셔우드는 다코타에서 아주 좋은 시간을 가졌다. 사촌 제이슨[129]은 자신이 어렸을 때부터 가지고 있던 그림책들과 장난감, 엄마가 만들어 준 스크랩 그림책, 청년이 된 지금까지 간직하고 있는 북 마크를 다 보여 주었다. 제이슨은 지금 24세다. 엄마가 만들어 준 그림책은 20년이나 되었지만 완벽한 상태로 보관되어 있었다. 종이에 무명천을 덧대 만들었고 가장자리에는 분홍색 테두리를 했으며, 파란색과 검정색 책장이 번갈아 끼워져 있었다. 검정색 겉표지는 분홍색 리본으로 묶여 있었다. 엄마는 셔우드가 이것을 보고 배우고, 또 자기 물건들을 잘 간수하기를 바란다. 셔우드가 그런 편이기는 한데

동생에게 부수는 것을 배워 파괴적이 되기 전까지는 더 얌전하게 놀았었다. 에디스도 자라면서 이제는 갈수록 얌전해지고 있다. 파월 이모가 당신을 기억하라고 셔우드에게 멋진 그림 접시를 주셨다. 에디스에게는 사촌 비라[130]가 똑같은 접시를 주었다.

130 《닥터 윌리엄 제임스 홀 목사의 생애》[책 표지와 목차]
"캐나다와 미국의 젊은이들에게 애정을 담아 헌정함.
그들에게 용기를 주기 위해 홀 박사는 자기 인생의 이야기가 기록될 수 있기를 기대했다."
"친구로서 남겨줄 수 있는 가장 풍성한 유산은 끝나지 않은 사역이다."

브록빌을 떠나기 전에 엄마가 여름 내내 작업한 아빠의 생애에 대한 책 완성본을 처음 받았는데,그 사실을 기록하는 것을 잊어버렸다. 캐나다로 떠날 때까지 엄마는 수정본의 마지막 장을 다 읽지 못했다. 이렇게 빨리 책이 나올 수 있게 출판사가 일을 잘한 것이다. 엄마는 우선 500권을 인쇄했다. 엄마에게 청구된 비용은 [비어 있음] 였는데 엄마가 들인 시간을 제외한 금액이다. 기회가 있었다면 바꾸고 싶은 부분이 몇 군데 있지만 서둘러 만든 책이라는 것을 고려해 볼 때 상당히 괜찮게 만든 책이라고 생각한다. 당연히 엄마는 다른 사람들이 이 책을 어떻게 생각할지 무척 궁금하다. 이 책이 많은 사람들에게 자극이 되기를 바란다. 그리고 엄마의 어린 아들도 이 책을 읽을 수 있을 만큼 자랐을 때 자극을 받을 수 있기를 바라며 기도한다. 캐나다에서는 스탠리 로섭 이모할아버지, 클리포드 삼촌, 길로이 씨가 이 책의 대리인 역할을 해주실 것이다. 엄마는 판매하는 책 한 권당 25센트를 수고비로 받도록 할 것이다. 리버티에서는 사랑하는 올드 블랙 조가 책을 판매할 것인데, 조는 판매가격인 1.50불에서

15센트만 받기로 했다. 25부는 무료로 나누어 주어야 했지만 나머지를
131 모두 팔면 엄마는 [비어 있음] 을 청산할 수 있다. 책을 판매해 얻은 수입의 첫 100불은 아빠의 기념병원을 위해 사용할 것이다.

10월 6일, 우리는 세인트 폴에서 존스 부인과 그레첸(Gretchen), 그리고 새로 한국으로 임명된 릴리언 해리스 박사와 피어스 양을 만나서 좌석 기차를 타고 밴쿠버까지 함께 여행했다. 객차 안에는 다른 승객이 네 명밖에 없었다. 여섯 살쯤 되어 보이는 어린 소녀가 한 명 있었는데 그 아이는 우리 아이들과 잘 놀았다. 엄마의 아기들과 존스 부인의 아기는 잘 놀지 않는데, 이번에는 엄마의 아기들이 그레첸 못지않게 잘못을 저질렀다. 지난 겨울 뉴욕에 있던 우리를 방문한 이후 그레첸은 많이 나아졌지만 셔우드와 에디스는 오히려 퇴행했다. 밴쿠버에 도착하기 바로 전날 엄마는 그 여섯 살짜리 아이가 백일해에 걸렸다는 사실을 알게 되었다. 그 아이의 부모들이 이야기해 주었더라면 어린 아이들과 같이 놀지 않게 하였을 것이다. 겨울이 다가오고 있는 이 시기에 백일해에 걸리면 좋지 않기 때문이다.

"로키산맥 기슭과 셀커크산에서 채취한 나뭇잎들"

셔우드는 이 기차 노선을 아주 좋아했는데, 특히 로키산맥에 이르자 매우 즐거워했다. 오랫동안 조용히 앉아 창밖으로 보이는 웅장한 경치를 구경하더니 그 다음에는 인디언들 찾는 것을 좋아했다. 그러다가 야생 거위를 파는 인디언들을 몇 명 보았다. 날씨가 추운 탓에 인디언들이 기차 역에 많이 나와 있지 않았다.

132 [밴쿠버에서 일본까지 타고] 온 엠프레스 오브 인디아 호.

[인디아 호에 함께 승선한 동료 선교사들]
중간 열 왼쪽에 셔우드가 있다. 사진에는 머독 매켄지(Murdock Mackenzie) 목사, 그로스벡(Grosbeck) 목사 부부, 밴다이크(Vandyke) 목사 부부, 케언즈(Cairns) 목사 부부, 닥터 스키너(Sknner) 목사, 그리피스(Griffith) 목사, 벨(Bell) 목사, 존스(Jones) 부인, 해리스(Harris) 박사, 피어스(Pierce) 양."

일요일은 밴쿠버의 커머셜 호텔에서 지냈다. 에디스는 아파서 케이블카를 못 탔지만 셔우드는 혼자서도 아주 재미있는 시간을 보냈다. 10월 11일 우리는 엠프레스 오브 인디아 호를 타고 항해를 시작했다. 배에는 16명의 선교사들이 있었고, 3개월 된 아기와셔우드, 에디스 그리고 그레첸이 있었다. 이외에도 어린이들이 10명 더 있었고, 100명 정도 되는 어른 승객들이 1등실에 있었다. 첫날 오후와 저녁에는 안개가 끼었지만 항해는 순조로웠고 모두 잘 지냈다. 아이들에게는 엄마가 아침과 점심을 먹기 한 시간 전에 그리고 저녁을 먹기 두 시간 전에 식당에서 식사가 제공되었다. 그래서 엄마는 저녁 식사를 알리는 첫 신호가 울리면 셔우드와 에디스를 침대에 눕혔다.
아이들은 대체로 엄마가 자기 전에 잠들었지만, 셔우드는 착하게 잘 있으면 맛있는 것을 가져다 달라는 조건을 걸었다. 그래서 엄마는 너트와 건포도 등을 작은 박엽지에 싸가지고 와서 거실에 있는 셔우드의 침상 옆 접의자 위에 올려놓는다. 셔우드는 잠에서 깨면 그것을 집어서 아주 맛있게 먹는다. 때로 엄마는 무화과를 가져오기도 하는데, 동생은 좋아하지만 셔우드는 별로 좋아하지 않는다.
항해 둘째 날 아침에 일어나려 했으나 배멀미가 나서 하루 종일 침대에 누워 있었다. 셔우드와 에디스는 엄마만큼 토하지는 않았으나

24시간 동안 아무것도 먹지 못했다. 다음 날 아침에 셔우드는 밥을 먹고 얼마 동안 멀미를 했지만 토하지는 않았다. 그리고 정오쯤에는 흔들리는 배 안에서도 잘 걸어다닐 수 있게 되었고, 나머지 항해 동안 건강하고 행복하게 지냈다. {멀미를 하면서 셔우드는 "마치 배가 언덕을 올라가는 것 같다"고 했다.}[131] 항해를 마칠 때까지 셔우드는
133 입맛이 좋은 편이었고 정말 잘 먹었다. 그래서 캐나다를 떠날 때 34파운드였던 몸무게가 —다시 재보지는 못했지만—분명히 늘었을 거라고 확신한다. 배에는 7-8세 정도 되는 어린 남자아이가 있었는데, 셔우드는 그 아이와 말을 가지고 아주 잘 놀았다. 그 아이는 요코하마에서 내렸고, 셔우드는 나가사키로 가는 내내 그 아이를 그리워했다.

나가사키 청동 말 사원(Temple of the Bronze Horse)에서 [채취한] 녹나무 잎(Camphor-wood).

셔우드는 매일 밤 하나님께 배가 물에 가라앉지 않게 해달라고 기도했다. 사실 셔우드는 지난 겨울 뉴욕에서 요셉(Yoseph) 박사가 배를 타고 떠나시는 것을 본 후로 거의 매일 밤 이렇게 기도드려 왔다. 10월 28일 우리는 나가사키에 도착했고, 정들었던 엠프레스 호를 떠나게 되었다. 몇 번씩이나 그 배로 돌아가자고 할 정도로 셔우드는 그 배에서 정말 즐겁게 지냈다. 셔우드는 갑판 위에서 열린 달리기에 참가한 기념품으로 "H.R.S. 엠프레스 오브 인디아"(H.R.S. Empress of India)라고 금색실로 새겨진 모자 밴드를 얻었다. 그 밴드를 사촌 벨트가 셔우드에게 준 해군 모자 주위에 둘러 주었더니 아주 좋아했다. 우리는 한국으로 가는 일본 증기선 히고 호를 기다리며

나가사키에서 열흘 동안 머물렀다. 셔우드는 처음 사나흘은 아주 건강한 것 같았는데 11월 4일에는 백일해와 비슷한 증상을 나타냈다. 기차에서 만났던 어린 소녀로부터 감염된 것으로 보인다. 6일에는 셔우드가 많이 나았고, 그날 저녁 우리는 히고 호를 타고 떠났다.

셔우드의 백일해(Pertussis)?
10월 6-9일-세인트 폴과 밴쿠버에서 노출됨.
11월 4일-이틀간 몸이 안 좋더니 점심 시간에 기침을 하고 토함. 밤에 뒤척이고 열이 남.
11월 5일-아침 체온 99.8°, 심박수 150, 호흡수 36. 오후 체온 100.4°, 심박수 130, 호흡수 28.
6일-아침 체온 98.4°, 심박수 112, 호흡수 32. 오후 5시, 히고 마루를 타고 항해.
열은 더 이상 없고, 기침 약간. 몇 번 심하게 기침을 했지만 백일해의 특징적인 기침소리(후프, whoop)는 없음.
8-11일-콧물이 심하게 남.
7-9일-배멀미,
9일-점심을 토한 후부터 10일 아침까지 더 이상 아무것도 먹지 않음. 아프고 나서 처음 2-3일은 변비였지만 그 뒤로는 정상.
치료-열이 날 때 아코나이트(Aconite), 카스토리아(Castoria) 두 번. 나중에 적은 양의 드로세라(Drosera)를 하루 서너번 씩.
11월 12일-병이 시작된 지 1주일. 호흡수는 정상 20, 약간 거침. 더 이상 구토나 변비가 없음. 후핑 기침은 아직 없고 심한 기침도 하지 않는다. 드로세라를 하루 1-2드램 복용하고 로툰다(Rotunda) 6미님을 2온즈 물에 타서 하루 네 번씩 복용.
11월 20일-그냥 감기를 앓았는지도 모르겠다. 셔우드, 에디스, 그레첸 모두 후핑 기침을 하지 않았다. 하지만 셔우드와 에디스는 같은 증세로 아팠고, 이어서 에디스는 카타르성 폐렴(catarrhal pneumonia)을 앓았다.

다음 날에는 배멀미를 했다. 11월 8일 월요일을 부산에서 지내며 로스 박사와 점심 식사를 했다. 우리 모두 타고 온 일본 증기선 음식을 별로 좋아하지 않았기 때문에 정말 맛있게 점심을 먹었다. 일본인들은 중국인들만큼 요리를 하지 못하는 것 같다. 선장, 승무원, 선원들이 모두 일본인이었고, 그들은 우리에게 친절하려고 애썼다. 어린이들

세 명 다 배의 일등석을 탔다. 우리는 월요일 저녁에 다시 출발했다.
화요일 정오까지는 순항했으나 그 후로 갑자기 파도가 너무
134 거칠어졌다. 파도가 일렁이면서 셔우드와 엄마는 점심을 토해냈다.
동생은 잠들어 있어서 점심을 먹으러 가지 않았는데, 잠에서
깨어나자마자 엄마에게 달라고 졸랐던 사과를 토해냈다. 우리는 모두
옷 입은 채로 누워 버렸다. 너무 지쳐서 밤새도록 겉옷까지 모두
입은 채로 있었다. 아침에 항구 가까이 왔다는 소식에 기분이 한결
나아졌다. 씻고 정돈을 좀 한 다음 간단하게 아침 식사를 했다.
9시쯤 증기선이 외항에 정박했고, 우리는 돛단배를 타고 오랫동안
노를 저어 해안가로 왔다. 그리고 이미 적은 것과 같이 11월 10일
오전 10시에 육지에 도착했다.

땅에 닿았을 때 엄마는 셔우드에게 네 번 뽀뽀를 해주었다. 그리고 처음으로 셔우드가 몇 살인지 가르쳐 주었다. 셔우드는 자기 나이가 "네 살"이라고 맞게 말 할 수 있지만 자주 잊어버린다. 그래서 "몰라요" 하거나 가끔은 "다섯 살"이라고 하는데, 그 숫자는 종종 팝콘 장수가 "팝콘이 5 센트"라고 외치는 소리를 흉내 내면서 알게 된 것이다.

엄마는 셔우드에게 대나무로 만든 작은 안락의자와 집짓기 블록 상자도 주었다. 그 블록으로 셔우드는 벌써 예쁜 구조물을 만들 수 있다. 셔우드는 이 두 선물에 흡족해했다.

어느 날 엄마가 담배 연기에 대해 불평했을 때 셔우드가 물었다.

"엄마, 왜 하나님은 남자들이 담배를 못 피우게 하지 않으세요?"

엄마는 이렇게 대답해 주었다. "그렇게 해달라고 구하면 하나님이 들어주시는데, 남자들은 그렇게 구하지 않는단다."

셔우드는 외할머니께 여러 번 답장을 썼고, 다(Dah)에게도 한 번 썼다.
셔우드는 그들을 기억하고 있으며, 애니 이모, 콜버트, 조를 위해
항상 기도하고 가끔씩 다른 친구들을 위해서도 기도한다.
엄마는 우리 어린 아들이 선한 사람으로 자라기를 바라며 지금도
그런 사람이기를 진심으로 기도하고 바란다. "어린 아이일지라도
그의 행실로 알게 된다"고 성경은 말씀하고 있기 때문이다. 그래서
135 셔우드가 주위의 이교도 어린이들에게 빛을 전하는 작은 선교사가
되기를 바란다. 셔우드는 지금 엄마 옆에서 글을 쓰고 있다. 무엇을
쓰고 있느냐고 물었더니 '예수님 군사 종교'에 대해 쓰고 있다고 했다.
그리고 이렇게 덧붙였다. "여기에 '세상에 충만한 예수님'이라고
썼어요." 엄마는 셔우드가 이미 선교 설교[132]를 쓰기 시작했다고
생각한다. 엄마는 셔우드가 전에는 이런 표현을 하는 것을 들어본
적이 없다. 그리고 이때까지 '종교'라는 말을 한 적도 없는 것 같다.

[132] 1897.11.14. 일요일-셔우드의 첫 설교.

하지만 왠지 이 단어가 셔우드의 머릿속에 자리 잡고 있었음이 분명하다. 일본에서 가져온 인력거를 타고 호텔에서 존스 부인 댁까지 가면서셔우드는 거리에서 풍기는 냄새에 대해 이렇게 말했다. "사람들이 여기서 돼지를 키우는 것 같아요. 그 냄새와 비슷해요." 셔우드는 여러 번 바지 속에서 무는 '모기'에 대해 말했다. 아직 한국의 벼룩에 대해 모르기 때문에 이것을 모기라고 생각하는 것이다. 벼룩들은 처음 엄마가 이곳에 왔을 때 엄마를 좋아했던 만큼 셔우드도 좋아하는 것 같다. 셔우드는 온 몸이 물렸는데 동생은 전혀 물리지

않았다.

일본 배에서 멀미가 너무 심했어서 셔우드는 태평양을 지나는 증기선에서 한 배멀미는 잊은 듯하다. 미국으로 돌아가는 것에 대해 말할 때면 "멀미를 안 했던 좋은 배를 타고 가고 싶어요"라고 한다.

136 1898년 3월 10일, 목요일, 한국 서울

네 하나님 여호와께서 이 사십 년 동안에 네게 광야 길을
걷게 하신 것을 기억하라(신명기 8:2)

"때때로 내가 걷고 있는 길 위로
구름이 어둡게 내려앉네.
하지만 어둠을 지나도, 밤을 지나도
내 마음은 두려움을 모른다네.
가까이 내 옆에서 걷고 계신 친구가 계시므로,
'끝까지 함께하리라' 나직이 속삭여 주는 친구가."[133]

셔우드가 한국에서 지낸 지 4개월이 되었다. 대부분의 시간을 서울에서 보냈다. 셔우드는 잔디가 돋고 꽃이 피고, 우리에게 돈이 장만되면 평양에 가자고 한다. 엄마도 2개월 안에 그렇게 되기를 바란다. 동대문에 있는 새 집과 이곳에 있는 새 건물이 아직 완공되지 않았기 때문에 여성해외선교회의 모든 사역자들이 지금 이 옛날 장소에서 함께 지내고 있다. 커틀러 박사와 루이스 양은 병원에서 지내고 있고, 페인 양과 프레이 양은 이전의 양육원에서 지낸다.

로스와일러(L. C. Rothweiler)[134] 양은 원래 있던 자기 방에 남아 있고, 해리스 박사와 피어스 양은 스크랜턴 부인이 지내던 방에서 묵고 있다. 엄마와 우리 아기들은 옛날 한문 교실에서 지내고 있다. 엄마가 이곳에서 사용했던 사랑채는 부엌과 식당이 되었다. 그러나 2-3개월 안에는 모두가 흩어지게 될 것이 분명하다. 페인 양(아마 커틀러 박사도)은 미국으로 귀국할 것이고, 로스와일러 양과 해리스 박사는 동대문으로 가게 될 것이다. 그리고 엄마와 아기들은 평양으로 가기를 원한다. 어쨌든 지금은 모두 하루 세 번씩 식당에서 한 식구로 만나고 있다. 비용은 분담하고 있다. 엄마는 두 사람 몫을 내고 있다. 연료비는 엄마 방 하나에만 60엔이 넘게 든다. 이때까지 연료비 외의 지출도 많았다. 12월부터 5월까지 한 달에 일인당 평균 53불 23센트가 들었다. 엄마가 한 사람 몫이고, 에디스와 셔우드가 한 사람 몫이다(한 달에 112불 52센트).

2월에 접어들 때까지 셔우드와 에디스는 서울에서 잘 지냈다. 바로
137 그전에 보모가 두 아이를 데리고 어느 현지인 집(요셉 아버지 집)에
다녀왔는데, 자신의 이마 머리를 고르게 뽑기 위해서였다. 그곳에서 아이들이 홍역에 노출되었다. 셔우드는 한국을 떠나기 직전에 이미 홍역을 앓았기 때문에 다시 홍역에 걸리지 않을 거라고 생각했다. 그래서 밖에도 자주 나가게 했고, 에디스만큼 주의를 주지 않았다. 그러나 에디스와 같이 셔우드도 홍역에 걸려 버렸다. 처음에는 에디스만큼 아파 보이지 않았는데 나중에는 에디스보다 더 힘들어했다. 에디스는 곧 나았지만 셔우드의 병세는 두 주간이나 더 계속되더니 2월 19일에는 아주 심각해져서 엄마뿐 아니라 커틀러 박사와 해리스 박사도 아주 위험한 상태라고 생각하게 되었다.

겨드랑이 체온이 105½°였고, 거의 24시간 동안 고열이 계속되었다. 우리는 이것을 셔우드가 폐렴이나 복막염 또는 다른 어떤 아주 심각한 병에 걸릴 징조로 여겼다. 그러나 다행스럽게도 그런 일은 일어나지 않았고, 아직까지 우리는 그 병의 원인을 모른다. 엄마는 너무너무 걱정되어서 간절히 기도드렸다. 하나님의 뜻이라면 우리 아들을 엄마에게 남겨 달라고. 다른 분들도 합심해서 간절히 기도해 주셨다. 펜윅(M. C. Fenwick)[135] 목사는 그 다음 날 교회에서 대중기도를 해주셨다. 그리고 다행스럽고 감사하게도 하나님께서는 다시 한 번 셔우드를 엄마에게 남겨 주셨다. 체온이 몇 시간 동안 일정한 속도로 8°가 내려갔다. 그리고 며칠간은 정상 이하의 체온 상태를 유지했다. 그리고 그 후로 아주 많이 나아졌다. 아직까지 숨이 좀 가쁘기는 하지만……. 우리 아들도 아빠처럼 엄마에게, 또 셔우드를 아는 모든 사람들에게 큰 위로와 도움을 주는 사람이 되기를 소망하며 기도한다. 하나님께서는 지금까지 두 번이나 셔우드를 엄마에게 돌려주셨다. 사지(死地)에서 건져 주셨고 엄마의 기대 이상으로 자비를 베풀어 주셨다. 참으로 긍휼하시고 좋으신 분, 정말 좋으신 하나님이시다.

홍역(Rubeola)에 이은 병(?)

2월 5일–오후 6시, 체온 103.8°. 오후 5:30, 산토닌(Santonin) ½그래인, 칼로멜(Calomel) ½그래인, 무화과 시럽(Syrup of Figs) 2드램.
오후 6:30, 백부자(Aconite), 겔세미움(Gelsemium), 장뇌(Camphor)와 브리오니아(Bryonia) 각각 ⅙미님.
저녁 9:30 체온 99.8°, 심박수 145. 땀을 흘리다.
2월 6일–오전7 시, 체온 102.4°, 심박수 138. 산토닌과 칼로멜 각각 ½그래인.
오전 8:00, 변을 잘 보다.
오전10:30, 체온 100.4°, 심박수 120.

오전11:00, 두 시간 잠을 잠.
오후 1:30, 체온 99.8°, 심박수 128. 갈색 설사, 담즙과 점액, 회충은 없음.
2월 7일-오전 7시, 체온 100.4°. 메스껍다고 함. 어제 오후 4시에 너트를 좀 주었다.
무화과 시럽을 다시 먹이다.
오후 3시, 담즙이 섞인 대변을 보다.
저녁 8시, 체온 99.8°, 심박수 96.
2월 8일-오늘은 괜찮은 것 같다. 오후에 추위를 좀 탔고 기침을 함.
2월 9일-콧물을 흘리고 기침을 좀 함. 방향 암모니아정(Spts. Ammonia Arom.)을 복용하다.
오후 1시, 피곤해하고 잠을 잠. 호흡수 36, 심박수 130.
저녁 8시, 자면서 땀을 흘리다. 호흡수 36, 심박수 130.
2월 10일-홍역이 발발하다. 1월 28일에 노출. 그러나 예전에 홍역을 치렀음. 체온 100.5°.
2월 11일-계속 홍역 발발 중. 저녁 8시, 체온 98.5°, 심박수 96, 호흡수 24.
2월 12일-발진이 사그라지고 있다. 상태 양호.
2월 13일—발진이 다 없어졌다. 저녁 7시에 난로 앞에서 스폰지 목욕을 하고 옷을 갈아입었다.
2월 14일—다 나은 것 같다. 오후에 밖에 너무 오래 있어서 지치다. 잠을 잘 못 이루고 몹시 피곤하다고 불평함.
2월 15일—옷을 안 입으려 하고 왼쪽 귀와 배가 좀 아프다고 함. 변을 잘 보았으나
무화과 시럽을 정오에 한 번 더 주었다.
정오, 체온 102°, 심박수 160. 키니네 1그래인과 열감기 정제를 1알 주었다.
저녁 7시, 체온 102.2°, 심박수 168.
2월 16일—아침 7시, 체온 101.8°.
아침 8시, 스위트 오일과 열감기 정제 1알을 먹였다. 소량의 굳은 변을 보다.
오전 11시, 스위트 오일과 물을 주입. 후에 소량의 변을 보다.
정오, 체온 102.4°, 심박수 172, 호흡수 34.
오후 1시, 키니네 1그래인.
오후 4시, 열감기 정제.
오후 5시, 체온 101.2°. 주입했던 오일과 물만 배설하다.
저녁 7시, 상태가 나아졌고 고기 수프와 무우를 좀 먹다. 키니네 1그래인도 복용.
저녁 8시, 오일, 무화과 시럽, 방향 암모니아정.
밤 9시, 자면서 땀을 좀 흘림. 심박수 104.
2월 17일-상태가 좋고 변을 잘 보다. 아침을 잘 먹다.
아침 8:30, 체온 99.6°, 심박수 124. 키니네 1 그래인. 방향 암모니아정 3미님을 복용.
오전 10시, 옷을 입고, 점심도 잘 먹다. 낮잠.
오후 3:30-4:30, 바깥에서 놀고 저녁을 잘 먹다.
저녁 8시, 취침. 심박수 112.
2월 18일—오늘은 괜찮은 것 같다. 오전에 1시간 반 동안 바깥에서 놀았다. 점심을 조금만

먹고, 낮잠을 ½시간 잤다. 오후 3-4시에는 인력거를 타고 외출. 병원에 잠깐 내려갔다 돌아와서 저녁을 조금 먹었다. 몹시 피곤하고 잠이 와서 목욕을 못 하겠다고 해서 그냥 재움.
저녁 9시, 체온 105.2°, 심박수 130, 호흡수 38. 소변을 보다. 키니네 1그래인과 열감기 정제.
2월 19일—아침 7시, 체온 103.5°, 심박수 150, 호흡수 40. 산토닌 ½그래인, 칼로멜 ½그래인, 스위트 오일 1½ 드램을 먼저 주고 나머지 반 알을 주었다.
아침 8:30, 잠을 자다. 코코아 몇 숟가락만 먹음. 심박수160, 호흡수 44. 아침에 말할 때 얼굴 근육이 신경성 경련을 일으키는 것을 목격했다. 그러나 성격이 밝고 기가 죽지 않음.
오전 10시, 체온 105.4°. 코코아를 조금 달라고 했다. 찬 스폰지로 닦아 주고 키니네 1그래인을 주었다. 찬물을 조금 마시다. 경련을 더 하고 몹시 피곤해 보인다.
오전 11시, 배 위에 겨자를 조금 얹어 주었다. 잠을 자고 싶다고 함. 찬물 백을 머리에 얹고 잠이 들었다.
오전 11:30, 깨워서 겨자를 치웠다. 피부가 바알갛게 되었고 배가 나아졌다고 했다. 가슴, 목, 입술을 스위트 오일에 섞은 테레빈유로 문질러 주었다. 아질산 에테르(Spts. Aetheris Nitrosi) 물약을 2드램 주었으나 반 정도, 아마 3방울밖에 먹지 않았다. 복용량은 5미님(방울)에서 2드램. 코코아를 달라고 했으나 한 모금밖에 마시지 않았다.
정오, 체온 T 105°, 심박수 165, 호흡수 40. 잠. 자면서 가끔씩 경련을 일으킴. 무릎을 세우고 있음. 아질산 에테르 5미님을 복용. 아무것도 안 먹으려고 함.
오후 1:30, 계속 잠만 잠. 한참 설득해서 약을 먹이고 물을 조금 마시게 했다. 그리고 어젯밤 9시 이후 처음 소변을 보았다. 커틀러 박사에게 아무 데도 아프지 않다고 했다. 그러고는 "아야, 귀가 아파요" 했다. 머리에 찬물 백을 계속 얹고 있다. 솜에 테레빈유를 뿌려서 배에 얹어 주었다. 눈이 뜨겁다고 해서 한참 동안 스폰지를 대어 주었다.
오후 4시, 디지탈리스 추출물 ⅕미님, 아질산 에테르. 오렌지 2개에서 짜낸 즙을 마셨다. 소변을 보다. 체온 104.7°, 심박수 135. 미지근한 물로 관장을 해주었다. 장이 잘 움직여 주었다.
오후 6시, 체온 102.5°, 심박수 126, 호흡수 30. 땀을 줄줄 흘림. 따뜻한 알코올로 닦아주었다. 디지탈리스 추출물 ⅙미님. 우유 1온스에 멜린즈 식품(Mellin's Food)과 위스키를 조금 섞어서 먹였다.
저녁 7시, 잠. 오렌지물도 안 마시려고 함.
저녁 8:30, 체온100°. 키니네 2그래인을 직장으로 투여했다. 철분 1드램, 우유와 멜린즈 식품 ½온스.
밤 10시, 소변을 보다. 변이 마렵다고 했으나 보지 못했다. 우유와 멜린즈 식품 2드램.
밤 11시, 체온 98.8°, 심박수 116, 호흡수 26. 철분 1드램.
자정, 체온 99.4°. 두세 번 "아야, 배가 아파요" 했다. 하지만 이번에는 방광에 손을 얹고 아프다고 했다. 테레빈유를 솜에 묻혀 배 위에 얹어 주었다.
새벽 3:30, 체온 97.8°, 심박수 104. 철분 ½드램을 우유 ½온스에 타서 주었다. 오렌지물을 조금 마셨다. 뜨거운 다리미와 물병으로 침대를 따뜻하게 해주었다. 키니네 3그래인을 직장으로 투여했다.

아침 7시, 체온 98.6°. 키니네 1그래인을 입으로 주고 빽빽한 연유 1온스를 멜린즈 식품과 함께 준 뒤 물을 먹였다.

2월 20일—아침 8시, 소변을 보다. 요비중(Specific gravity) 1015. 소변에 알부민 없음.

오전 9 시, 체온 98°, 심박수 116. 우유 2온스와 오렌지 1개를 먹었다.

오전 11시, 소변을 보고, 3시간 동안(오전 7시-10시) 코코아 3온스를 마셨다.

오전 11:30, 키니네 ½ 그래인, 오렌지물.

정오, 체온 99.7°, 심박수 112, 호흡수 20. 기분이 좋음. 아직 잠이 안 온다고 한다.

처음으로 먹을 것을 달라고 했다. 연유와 멜린즈 식품을 조금 먹었다.

오후 1시, 레몬 젤라틴을 무우와 먹었다. 잠을 조금 잤고, 땀을 흘렸다.

오후 4:30, 체온 98°, 심박수 92. 키니네 1그래인, 오렌지물. 소고기 물 5온스를 마셨다.

오후 5:30, 우유 4온스를 마시고 소변을 보았다.

오후 6:30, 밀크 토스트를 조금 먹었다.

저녁 8시, 체온 97.5°(입), 심박수 88. 소변을 보고 잘 준비를 했다.

저녁 9 시, 반 시간 정도 조용히 자고 있다. 땀을 흘렸다.

2월 21일—새벽 3시, 체온 97.2°, 심박수 78.

아침 7시, 체온 97.4°. 소변을 보다. 키니네 1그래인. 오렌지물. 아침으로 오트밀과 우유, 코코아를 먹었다.

오전 10시, 소변을 보고 대변을 보려고 애를 썼으나 보지 못했다. 우유를 조금 마시고 케이크를 한 조각 먹었다.

오후 1시, 체온 97.4°, 심박수 85. 토스트와 우유, 레몬 젤라틴을 점심으로 먹었다.

키니네 1그래인. 변을 잘 보았다. 보리알과 깍지가 섞여 있고 소변 주위로 거품이 일었다.

오후 1:15, 잠, 축축함.

오후 3시, 초콜릿 푸딩.

오후 6시, 닭과 수프와 커스터드.

밤 10시, 체온 97°, 심박수 70. 종일 침대에 있었다. 침대에서 1시간 정도 앉아 있었다.

옷을 입고 밖에 나가고 싶어 했다.

2월 22일—새벽 4시, 체온 97.2°, 심박수 72. 따뜻한 우유와 멜린즈 식품을 주었다.

오전 10시, 체온 97.4°, 심박수 92(앉아 있은 지 1 시간 후). 시리얼린(cerealine)과 우유, 토스트, 코코아를 아침으로 먹었다.

정오, 밀크 토스트, 올리브 푸딩, 케이크 한 조각.

오후 1시, 체온 97.4°, 심박수 70. 난로 앞에서 스폰지 목욕을 한 후 옷을 갈아입고 10분 만에 잠이 들었다. 요비중 1022, 알부민 없음.

오후 4시, 남은 토스트로 요기를 했다.

저녁 8시, 체온 97.4°, 심박수 72. 기침을 약간 했다. 무화과 시럽.

2월 23일—오전 8시, 일어나 옷을 입었다. 키니네 1그래인. 어제부터 질산 ½미님을 하루 세 번씩 복용. 변을 잘 보고 혀가 조금 깨끗해졌다. 또 한 번 작은 변.

오후 1시, 체온 97.8, 심박수 92. 아침나절에 잘 놀고 점심도 잘 먹었다.
저녁 7:30, 체온 98°, 심박수 72. 1½시간 동안 낮잠을 잤다. 저녁을 잘 먹었다.
2월 24일—아침 7시, 체온 98°. 처음으로 아침을 먹으러 갔다.
저녁 8시, 체온 98.8°, 심박수 92. 잠깐 낮잠을 잔 것 외에는 종일 일어나 있었고 밥도 잘 먹었다. 키니네와 질산을 계속 복용 중.
3월 1일—혀가 깨끗해졌다. 질산과 키니네를 중단. 간유를 주기 시작했다.
3월 15일—심히 앓고 난 후 2주 동안 입맛이 좋다가 지금 다시 나빠졌다.

[로즈 E. 무어 부인이 보낸 편지][136]
친애하는 홀 부인,
무어 씨와 저는 조만간 부인을 통해서 부인의 선교부에 헌금을 하려고 합니다. 부인은 자신을 위해서는 아무것도 가지려 하지 않는 분임을 잘 알기 때문이지요. 하지만 이 작은 선물은 받아 주시겠는지요? 제가 해산할 때 베풀어 주신 부인의 크나큰 친절에 대한 저의 사랑과 감사의 징표입니다. 부인이 얼마나 잘 해주셨는지를 생각할 때마다 저는 평생 부인께 보답할 수 없으리라는 생각이 듭니다.
이 작은 외투와 모자는 지금 홀(Hall) 아기에게는 너무 클 것입니다만 날씨가 좋아져서 그 애가 외출을 많이 하게 될 때면 잘 맞으리라 생각합니다. 그리고 어린 아기들은 빨리 자라기에 금방 옷이 작아지기도 하고요. 사랑스러운 아기가 오늘은 더 나아졌기를 바랍니다. 하나님께서 속히 셔우드의 건강을 온전히 회복시켜 주시고, 아기와 어머니에게 풍성한 은혜를 베풀어 주시기를 바랍니다.
사랑하는
로즈 E. 무어

[M. F. 스크랜턴의 편지(1897.2.20)]
친애하는 홀 부인,
오늘 오후에 펜윅 씨가 돌아오셔서 셔우드가 몹시 아프다는 소식을 전해 주셨습니다. 그분이 생각하는 것만큼 상태가 나쁘지 않기를 바라고 있습니다. 부인은 그렇게 심각하다고 생각하지 않으시지요, 그렇지요? 오늘 저녁에는 셔우드의 상태가 어떤지 정말로 알고 싶습니다. 저희에게 좋은 소식이 들려올 수 있기를 바랍니다.
염려와 사랑을 보내며,
M. F. S.

[윌리엄 B. 스크랜턴 박사의 편지(1897. 2. 21)]
친애하는 홀 부인,
오늘 셔우드는 어떤가요? 오늘은 셔우드가 많이 나아서 부인의 걱정이 사라지기를 바랍니다. 오늘 제가 해 드릴 수 있는 것이 있는지요?

마음을 다하여, 진심으로,
W. B. 스크랜턴

138 아이들 보모가 일을 참 잘한다. 그녀는 부지런하며, 세례 받은 기독교인이다. 하지만 아이들과 놀아주고 아이들을 재미있게 해주는 능력은 거의 없다. 아이들이 해야 하는 일을 안 하려고 할 때 조금이라도 할 수 있도록 달래지를 못한다. 그리고 가끔씩 상황을 더 악화시키기까지 한다. 하지만 다른 일은 참 잘해서 더 이상 잘할 수는 없겠지 하면서 엄마는 그녀와 헤어지는 것을 꺼리고 있다. 여러 여선교사들과 함께 지내는 이런 집에서 어린 두 아이를 데리고 사는 것은 어려운 일이다. 모두가 엄마는 아니지만 각자 나름대로 아이들이 어떻게 행동해야 하는지 잘 안다고 생각하고 있다. 그러나 지금까지 심각한 문제가 일어난 적은 없다. 단지 엄마는 대부분의 여성들이 엄마가 아이들을 따끔하게 제대로 훈계하지 않는다고 생각한다는 것을 느낄 뿐이다. 엄마도 아이들이 좀더 반듯하기를 바라지만, 그 애들은 아직 자기 평판에 상관하지 않는, 그저 어린 아이들일 뿐이다. 아이들은 주로 식당에서 숙녀들과 만나서 식사를 하지만 따로 작은 상 앞에 둘이 앉아서 먹는다. 그리고 여덟 분의 숙녀들에게 식사가 제공될 때까지 조용히 앉아서 음식을 기다려야 하기 때문에 부산스러워지기 쉽다. 가끔 낮은 의자에 앉아 있으므로 쉽게 빠져 나가기도 한다. 아이들은 자기들끼리 있기 때문에 식탁 예절은 나아지지 못하고 오히려 퇴보하고 있다. 엄마는 아이들이 어린이용 높은 의자에 앉아서 우리와 함께 식사를 한다면 나아질 거라고 생각하지만 식탁이 그만큼 커 보이지 않는다. 작은 집이라도

우리 집에서 우리끼리 지낼 수 있으면 좋겠다. 숙녀들은 아이들에게 거의 관심을 기울이지 않는다. 그래도 로스와일러 양이 가장 많은 관심을 주는 편이다. 우리 아이들은 누구에게 귀여움을 받는 것을 상관치 않는 아이들이라서 그런지도 모른다. 그러나 지금까지 우리는 다 함께 행복하게 잘 지내고 있고, 우리의 유대관계가 어색해진 것 같지는 않다.

139 셔우드는 한국말을 빨리 습득하지 못하고 있다. 젊은 보모가 오히려 우리 아이들이 그녀의 한국말을 배우는 것보다 아이들이 하는 영어를 더 빨리 배우고 있다. 아이들은 보모 외에 다른 한국인들은 별로 만나지 않는다. 나는 아이들이 루이스 양의 두 한국인 "zúls"[셔우드의 아기 말투로 girls]들과 같이 놀 수 있기를 바랐는데 루이스 양은 그녀의 아이들이 우리 아기들과 놀기에는 너무 착하다고 생각하는 것 같다. 그래서 우리 아이들은 주로 아펜젤러 목사의 자녀들과 논다.

셔우드와 메리는 친한 친구로 많은 시간을 같이 보내며 잘 노는데, 나이가 더 많은 메리가 지시하는 편이고 셔우드는 순순히 따르는 편이다. 하루는 메리가 셔우드에게 어느 의자에 앉으라고 했는데, 셔우드가 이의를 제기했다. 그러자 메리는 집에 가겠다면서 나가는 척했다. 셔우드는 울음을 터뜨렸고 메리는 다시 와서 셔우드에게 자기 말대로 하겠느냐고 물었다. 그러자 셔우드는 눈물을 글썽거리며, 메리가 상냥한 미소를 지으며 지시하는 그 의자에 앉았다.

한국어에 대해 말하자면, 두 아이는 이미 한국식 감탄사인 "아이고"라는 말을 사용한다. 그리고 신발을 "비신"이라고 부른다. 그리고 "감사합니다"를 한국말로 하고, "어셔어셔," "조심ᄒᆞ오"[137]라는 말도 할 줄 안다. 셔우드는 다른 말들도 좀 할 수 있었는데, 엄마는 지금 그 말들이 생각나지 않는다. 하지만 앞서 말했듯이 셔우드는 미국 아이들하고만 놀았기 때문에 아직까지 한국말을 많이 익히지 못했다.
영어에서는 더 이상 엄마가 셔우드의 어휘를 추적할 수 없을 정도다. 아기 때 쓰던 말과 발음이 점점 줄어들고 있어서 엄마가 섭섭할 지경이다. 커틀러 박사가 어른처럼 의젓하게 말하는 법을 셔우드에게 가르치려고 할 때면 엄마는 제발 그만두라고 부탁하고 싶은 심정이다. 지금까지 엄마가 아이들의 말투를 고쳐 주지 않았음에도 아이들 스스로가 서로에게 '아기 말투'를 쓰지 않았으므로 이제는 그 말투를 잊어버린 것 같다. 때때로 자연스레 하는 아기 말투는 엄마에게 너무 사랑스럽게 들리고, 엄마는 그 소리들이 듣고 싶다. 로스와일러 양은 셔우드에게 "얼마큼 엄마를 사랑하니?" 묻고는, 셔우드가 "Berry lots"라고 대답하는 것을 듣기 좋아한다. 셔우드는 뒤집어진 것(inside out)을 "바깥쪽이 나왔다"(outside up)고 하고, 매듭(knots)을 "두드린다"(knocks)고 한다. 또 "잠근다"(lock)를 "두드린다"(knock)고 한다. {"사자가 갇혔다"를 "사자가 맞았다"(The 'Ion is knocked)고 하고, "매듭짓다"를 "매듭을 두드린다"(tie in a knock)고 한다. 먹다(eat)의 과거형 먹었다(ate)를 "ute"라 하고, 보다(see)의 과거형 보았다(saw)를 "sawed"라고 한다. 옷을 입다(dress)와 옷을 벗다(undress)를 모두 "푼다"(untie it up)고 표현한다.}[138]

140 크리스마스 날 밤에는 "만약 키스마스 날이 내일 다시 오지 않는다면 나는 쭉을 거야"(I'll Kie, if Kismas day don't come again tomorrow)라고 했다. 새해 들어 셔우드는 적절한 때와 장소에서 "실례합니다"라는 말을 하기 시작했다. 셔우드는 잘 기억하고, 엄마가 무엇을 잊어버릴 때

상기시켜 주기도 한다.

셔우드는 상상력과 사고력을 조금씩 사용하기 시작했다. 얼마 전에는 에디스에게 주려고 산 멋진 유리 호루라기에 대해 말하면서 에디스가 그것을 아주 조심스럽게 다뤄야 한다고 했다. 그리고 나중에는 호루라기를 사지는 않았고 다만 그것을 살까 생각("sunk")만 했다고 말했다. 하루는 "사자들이 하나님을 물 수 있어요?"라고 묻더니 좀더 생각해 보는 듯했다. 그러고는 스스로 그 질문에 대답했다.

"하나님은 피가 없죠?" 그러더니 한 단계 더 추론을 늘려서 "만약 나에게 피가 없다면 사자들이 나를 물지 않겠지요?"라고 했다. 또 하루는 우리 학교 여학생들에게는 엄마가 없느냐고 물었다. 대부분의 여학생들은 하나님을 모르는 이교도 어머니를 모시고 있다고 대답해 주었더니, "왜 그 사람들은 하나님을 모를까요? 하나님이 그들을 만들지 않았나요?" 하고 물었다.

언젠가 약간 허기를 느꼈는지 셔우드는 검지와 중지를 가깝게 세워 V자 모양을 만들면서, "엄마, 시계를 보세요. 점심 시간이에요"라고 했다. 시계를 쳐다보니 아니나 다를까 시계 바늘은 11시 5분을 가리키고 있었다. 셔우드는 우리가 점심을 먹으러 갈 때 항상 시계 바늘이 대략 그 위치에 있던 것을 예의 주시하였음이 분명했다. 그것은 네 살짜리 어린 아이로서는 대단한 관찰력이었다고 엄마는 생각한다.

셔우드는 뉴욕에서 1년 전에 크리스마스 선물로 받은 흔들목마를 여전히 좋아한다. 종종 먼지를 털어 주고, 갈기와 꼬리에 빗질을 해준다. 가끔씩 목마에게 기도하라고 지시도 하고, 목마가 착한 말이 되게 해달라고 기도한다. 셔우드는 하나님께서 착한 사람을 기뻐하신다고 생각한다. 그리고 자신이 착한 아이일 때는, "지금

하나님이 행복하시겠지요?"라고 한다. 한번은 착한 일을 해서
하나님을 기쁘시게 할 거라더니 엄마한테 달려와서 "하나님이
141 하! 하! 하! 웃으시는 소리를 들었어요" 하면서 행복하게 하하하 웃는
소리를 냈다. 예수님이 마음속에 거하시기를 청하면 그 속에 있는 나쁜
것들을 모두 좇아내 주신다는 말을 듣고 즉시 이렇게 기도하기도 했다.
"예수님, 여기 제 마음 속에 오셔요." 그리고 며칠 동안 예수님이
자기 마음에 오셨다고 느끼고 있었으며, 정말로 더 착해졌다.
외할머니의 팔이 부러졌다는 소식을 들은 후에는 매일 밤 이렇게
기도했다. "할머니 팔이 잘 낫게 도와주세요. 뼈가 다시 자라게
해주세요." 그리고 자주 "병원에 있는 사람들이 모두 잘 낫고 하나님과
예수님에 대해 들을 수 있게 도와주세요"라고 기도한다. 하루는
사슬에 묶여 있는 죄수들을 보고 그 사람들에 대한 이야기를 듣고 난
뒤 이런 제안을 했다. "누군가 감옥에 있는 죄수들에게 설교하러
가야 해요." 셔우드는 자신이 한 질문에 곧잘 스스로 대답한다.
하루는 "하나님은 엄마들을 어떻게 만드셨어요? 사람들이 석탄 뭉치를
만드는 것처럼 이렇게 (손으로 무언가 빚는 시늉을 내면서) 하시나요?" 하고
물었다. 그러고는 작은 흔들의자에 앉아서 곰곰이 생각해 본 후 이런
대답을 했다. "하나님께서 어린 아기들을 만드셔요. 그리고 같은
방법으로 엄마들도 만드셔요."

사랑하는 할머니가 셔우드에게 보낸 편지를 여기 옮겨 놓는다.
"사랑하는 셔우드야, 네가 보낸 친절한 편지를 받고 정말 기뻤단다.
네가 착한 아이가 되려고 노력하며 네 엄마 생각을 해준다니 기쁘구나.
할머니는 네가 착한 사람이 되어 엄마를 힘들게 하지 않기를 바란단다.

네가 할머니를 생각해 주고 할머니 사진에 뽀뽀해 준다니 정말 기쁘구나. 할머니도 네 사진 보는 것을 좋아한단다. 한복을 입고 있는 네 사진이 정말 잘 나왔더구나. 할머니는 네 생각을 아주 많이 한단다. 네가 아플 때 건강하게 해달라고 하나님께 기도드리고, 네 엄마가 귀국할 때 너도 살아남아서 미국으로 돌아오기를 기도한단다.
또 편지를 써서 보내 주렴. 할머니.
1898년 4월 17일"

셔우드의 친구, 해리스 박사로부터 온 편지

한국, 평양
1898년 4월 1일

마스터[139] 셔우드 홀
한국, 서울

친애하는 셔우드 군,
셔우드가 보내준 친절한 편지가 지난 화요일 오후에 도착했어. 말할 필요도 없이 선생님은 셔우드의 호의에 정말 기뻤어. 자, 이번에는 셔우드가 아기 플로렌스(Florence)[140]를 보고 기뻐할 것 같아. 이 여자아기는 정말 착하고 가끔씩 아주 사랑스러운 미소를 짓지. 셔우드가 평양에 와 만나게 되면 정말 좋아할 거야. 바람이 연기를 방으로 역류시켜 숨 쉬기가 곤란한 이곳에서 아기로 존재한다는 것이 어떻다는 것을 셔우드는 이미 잘 알고 있어서 다행이야. 선생님은 물론이고 이 아기도 셔우드가 건강히 잘 있다가 평양에 와서 아기랑 루스와 메이(May) 노블과 함께 놀 수 있기를 바라고 있어. 선생님이 루스와 메이에게 셔우드가 보내준 편지를 읽어 주었어. 모두 셔우드로부터 소식을 듣게 되어 아주 기뻐했지. 루스와 메이도 셔우드와 에디스에게 많은 사랑을 보낸대.
그리고 셔우드가 빨리 와서 함께 놀 수 있기를 바라고 있어. 오늘 아침에는 해가 밝게 떠서 플로렌스는 어린 존 베어드를 보러 갈 거야. 그리고 존과 같이 점심을 먹을 거래.
그래서 선생님은 서둘러 아기를 준비시켜야 해. 아기가 셔우드와 에디스에게 사랑스러운 미소를 보내네. 이 짧은 편지를 통해 전할 수 있는 모든 사랑을 우리 셔우드와 에디스에게 보내면서 다시 한 번 친절한 편지를 선생님에게 써 주어서 고마워.
선생님도 곧 서울 우리 집으로 내려갈 거라고 엄마께 전해줘.

엄마와 에디스에게도 많은 사랑을 보내며, 우리 셔우드에게 가장 큰 사랑을 보낸다.
사랑으로, 릴리안 해리스.

142 1898년 11월 10일 화요일, 평양에서.

모든 것이 하나님께로서 났으며(고린도후서 5:18)

"이 태양 밝은 땅 어딘가에
더 부드럽고 사랑스런 것이 있을지 모르나,
나는 주님께서 축복으로 주신
꼭 쥔 두 손으로 인해 감사를 드린다네.

그날 내 손 안에 살며시
부드러운 작은 손이 들어왔다네,
내 여정에서 나를 강하게 해주는
사랑스런 그 어루만짐이 필요하던 때에.

신비롭고 감미롭게 작은 손이 말하는 듯했네,
"사랑해요, 이해해요."
그리고 내 두려움을 잔잔케 했다네,
심장의 뜨거운 눈물이 그 작은 손에 떨어질 때."[141]

[손 그림]
"5세. [몸무게] 41파운드, [키] 42½인치, 머리 20¼인치."

[5세 때 머리 타래]

다시 셔우드의 생일이 다가오고 있다. 올해로 5세가 된다. 키는 작년보다 2½인치 컸지만, 머리 둘레는 겨우 ¼인치 늘었다. 몸무게는 41파운드이다.

143 엄마가 일기를 쓴 지 9개월이 지났다. 그 9개월간 정말 바쁘게 지냈다. 하지만 바빴다는 것이 그중에서 가장 쉬운 일이었다. 그 기간 중 초기에 또 다른 엄청난 슬픔이 우리에게 다가왔다. 크나큰 첫 번째 슬픔 가운데 있던 우리에게 하나님께서 보내 주신 '작은 위로자' 에디스, 그 은총의 아이가 우리 품을 떠났다. 평양에 있는 우리 새 집에 안주하기도 전에 벌어진 일이다. 하나님께서 에디스를 데려가셨다는 소식을 처음 들었을 때 셔우드는 "아빠가 에디스를 간절히 원했기 때문"이라고 했다. 셔우드는 누이동생을 그리워하고 있다. 그 아이가 있었으면 하고 간절히 바라고 있다. 가끔씩 셔우드는 얼마나 기다려야 예수님이 오시고, 에디스가 다시 살아날 것인지 묻곤 한다. 셔우드는 여러 번 이런 말을 했다. "오, 에디스가 여기 있다면 나는 에디스를 정말 많이 사랑해 줄 거예요. 그리고 정말 잘해 주고 다시는 안 싸울 거예요."

에디스가 마지막으로 예쁜 흰옷을 입고 있던 날 셔우드는 엄마와 함께 동생을 보러 갔다. 셔우드는 그 모습이 단지 에디스의 몸일 뿐이며 영혼은 떠나갔다는 사실을 깨달은 것 같았다. 셔우드는 하얀 클로버 꽃을 따서 동생 손에 쥐어 주었다. 에디스를 만지는 것을 조금 무서워하는 듯했지만 곧 동생의 이마에 뽀뽀를 해주었다. 그리고 아름다운 예배가 끝난 뒤 예쁘고 하얀 관에 있는 에디스를 보며 마지막 인사를 할 때 한 번 더 뽀뽀해 주었다. 당시에는 이에 대해 아무 말도 안 했지만, 나중에 아주 차가운 것을 묘사할 때면 여러 번 이렇게 말했다. “그것은 에디스의 이마처럼 차갑고……
차가웠어요.”
동생의 사랑스러운 몸이 아빠가 있는 한강가 언덕에 안장될 때
셔우드는 그 광경을 보지 않았지만 이에 대해 이해하고 있다.
셔우드는 묻었다는 것을 “심었다”고 하면서 그것을 죽음에서 다시
살아나는 것과 결부시켰다. 그리고 예수님을 모르는 한국인들도
죽은 사람들을 ‘심는다’는 것을 알고 놀라워했다. 9개월이란 시간은
셔우드의 성장을 자세히 기억하기에는 너무 긴 시간이다. 특히 엄마가
144 여러 가지 다른 일을 하느라 정말 여념이 없어서 어린 아들을 잘
관찰하지 못했기에 더욱 그러하다. 하지만 엄마는 잠깐이나마 시간을
만들어서 셔우드와 같이 보내고 있는데, 그것은 바로 식사시간이다.
점심을 먹은 후에는 늘 셔우드가 낮잠을 자기 전에 옆에 앉아서 책을
읽어 준다. 그리고 셔우드가 자는 동안 엄마는 진료소의 환자들을
돌본다. 셔우드는 엄마가 일을 다 마치기 전에 깨기도 하는데,
어떤 때는 진료소로 와서 치료하는 것을 구경하기도 한다. 그리고
나가서 놀라고 하면 아주 착하게 바로 나간다. 엄마가 산책하거나
왕진 갈 때면 셔우드도 늘 같이 간다. 우리 집에 인력거가 있어서
몇 번은 인력거를 타고 다녀오면서 좋은 시간을 보내기도 했다.
셔우드는 낮잠을 자기 때문에 밤에는 늦게 잠자리에 든다. 그래서
저녁 때 엄마와 함께 좋은 시간을 보낸다.
셔우드는 새 기도를 배웠다. 이 기도는 예전에 하던 “이제 잠자려고
눕습니다”처럼 시작을 해주지 않아도 혼자서 잘 한다. 때때로
옛날 기도를 하기도 하지만 새로 배운 이 기도를 사랑스럽고
경건하게 드린다.

"선한 목자 되신 예수님, 들어주세요.
오늘밤 예수님의 어린 양을 축복해 주세요.
어둠을 뚫고 저에게 가까이 오셔서
아침햇살이 비칠 때까지 자는 것을 지켜 주세요."

어린이의 저녁 기도[142]

"선한 목자 되신 예수님, 들어주세요.
오늘 밤 예수님의 어린 양을 축복해 주세요.
어둠을 뚫고 저에게 가까이 오셔서
아침 햇살이 비칠 때까지 자는 것을 지켜 주세요."

종일토록 예수님의 손이 저를 인도하셨어요.
그 보살핌에 예수님께 감사드려요.
저를 입혀 주시고 먹여 주시고 따뜻하게 해주셨어요.
저의 저녁 기도에 귀 기울여 주세요.

저의 죄를 다 용서해 주시고
제가 사랑하는 친구들을 축복해 주세요.
제가 죽으면 하늘에 데려가 주시고
거기서 예수님과 행복하게 살게 해주세요.

셔우드는 요즘 예전에 하던 것처럼 즉흥적인 기도를 잘 덧붙이지도 않고, 매일 밤 에디스와 함께 친구들의 명단을 훑으면서 하나님께 드리던 축복기도도 잘 안 한다. 한번은 평소 하던 대로 "하나님, 동생을 축복해 주세요"라고 했다. 그러고는 혼잣말로 "오, 에디스를 위해서는 더 이상 기도할 필요가 없지"라고 했다. 그 후로는 그 기도를 하지 않았다. 누군가가 아프거나 배를 타고 떠나게 되면 셔우드는 그들을 기억하여 기도해 준다. 셔우드는 또 좋은 아침 기도를 배웠는데, 처음 한동안은 시작을 해주지 않아도 혼자서 즉흥적으로 하더니 이제는 그 기도를 자주 하지 않고, 하더라도 "이제 눕습니다"같이 시작을 해주기를 기다린다. 이 기도는 이렇다.

"저는 지금 잠에서 깨어나 일어났어요. 주님께서 저의 삶을 지켜 주시고, 아침부터 저녁까지 제가 하는 모든 일을 옳은 길로 인도해 주시기를 기도합니다."

145 셔우드는 엄마와 번갈아 가며 식사 기도를 하는데, 항상 다음과 같이 기도한다.

"위대하신 하나님, 좋으신 하나님, 이 음식을 주시니 감사합니다. 모든 사람들을 먹여 주시고 우리에게 일용할 양식을 주옵소서." 아니면 "우리에게 매일 일용할 양식을 주세요"라고 짤막하게 기도한다.

초여름에 셔우드는 사물의 성장을 관찰하는 데 큰 흥미를 갖게 되었다. 특히 심는 것을 목격했던 식물에 관심이 많았다. 하루는 비가 알맞게 온 후 바람이 조금 불면서 해가 다시 나왔다. 엄마는 우리 셔우드가 현관 앞 계단에서 이렇게 말하는 소리를 들었다.

"잔디들이 머리를 흔들면서 '하나님, 비를 내려 주셔서 감사해요' 하네요. 그리고 꽃들과 옥수수도 머리를 흔들면서 '하나님, 우리를 깨어나게 해주셔서 감사해요' 하네요." 어느 날은 이렇게 물었다. "하나님이 꽃들과 하늘에 페인트를 칠하셨어요?" 또 한번은 "나는 하나님의 생각을 생각하고 있어요"라고 했는데, 사실 우리 셔우드는 자주 그러는 것 같다. 아, 셔우드가 늘 그랬으면 좋겠다.

[외할머니의 편지 1]
사랑하는 내 손자 아가,
엄마랑 잘 지내고 있니? 잘 지내고 있기를 바란다. 다음에는 네 고양이에 대한 소식도 알려주렴. 조가 보내준 씨앗이 싹 텄니? 네 몸무게와 엄마의 몸무게가 얼마인지는 말하지 않았더구나. 알려주면 좋겠다. 셔우드는 착한 아이지? 할머니.

[외할머니의 편지 2]
사랑하는 내 아가,
할머니는 널 많이 많이 사랑한단다. 네가 할머니와 이곳에 있는 네 친구들을 잊지 않기를 바란다. 너의 어린 사촌들은 모두 잘 지내고 있단다. 그리고 우리한테는 착한 고양이 네 마리가 있단다. 너와 루스가 한 마리씩 가져가고, 우리가 흰 고양이와 검은 고양이를 가지고 있으면 좋겠구나.
여기 할머니가 함께 보내는 신문기사들을 네 엄마와 노블 부인이 읽었으면 해. 그 후에는 네 엄마가 간직했으면 좋겠다. 이 기사들은 메리앤(Maryann) 이모가 받은 신문에서 할머니가 찾은 것이란다. 오렌지 카운티 신문에 난 두 기사인데 네 엄마가 읽고 간직하기를 바란다. 우리는 네가 착한 아이기를 바라고 있어. 너와 네 엄마의 체중이 얼마나 되는지 알고 싶구나. 다음 번 편지에서 알려주렴. 생활용품은 충분히 있니? 집에 돌아올 때까지 쓸 수 있겠니? 안녕, 하나님께서 우리를 도와주시고 지켜주시기를. 할머니.

셔우드는 5주가 넘게 자기 생일을 기대하면서 날짜를 세고 또 세었다. 처음에는 몇 일요일 남았다고 세더니 나중에는 몇 날이 남았다고 세었다. 셔우드는 이제 시간에 대한 개념이 생기기 시작한 것이다. 며칠 전 어느 환자분이 셔우드가 고양이를 가지고 싶어 한다는 말을 듣고 고양이를 한 마리 가져왔다. 검정과 흰색이 섞인 예쁜 새끼고양이인데 아주 착하고 얌전하다. 셔우드는 이 고양이를 처음에는 '스크랜턴 박사'라고 부르고 싶어 하더니 나중에는 '벙커 씨'라고 부르고 싶어 했다. 하지만 훌륭한 신사들을 그런 식으로 불려서는 안 된다고 일러 주었다. 그래서 마침내 셔우드가 고른 '실버 문'(Silver-moon)이라는 이름으로 부르기로 했다. 셔우드는 오랫동안 고양이 혹은 쓰다듬어 줄 수 있는 '살아 있는 무엇'을 갖고

싶어 했기 때문에 그것을 얻고자 자주 기도했다. 그랬기에 '실버 문'은
자기 생일 선물로 하나님이 주신 것이라고 했다. 외할머니는
반짝반짝 빛나는 은화 1불을 주셨고, 수잔은 분홍색 한국 비단에
셔우드가 오래 살기를 바라는 한문 글귀를 초록색으로 수놓아 만든
146 넥타이를 주었다. 루스는 작은 찻주전자를 주었고, 루스의 메이(May)
이모는 종이 인형을 보내 주셨다. 엄마는 노아의 방주와 한국에서
행복을 나타내는 색깔로 만든 옷 한 벌을 주었다. 바지는 선홍색 비단
플러시 천으로 만들었고, 같은 천으로 블라우스의 테두리를 둘렀다.
블라우스는 셔우드의 돌복을 짓고 남은 천으로 만들었다. 선홍색
플러시 천으로 에디스의 겨울 드레스를 만들려고 했는데 결국은
그 천으로 만든 옷을 셔우드가 입게 되었다. 남자아이에게는 너무
밝아 보이는 것 같지만 나쁘지 않다. 한국인들이 많이 칭찬해 주었다.

[외할머니의 편지 3]

셔우드에게
네가 보내 준 편지와 씨앗을 받고 정말 기뻤단다. 그곳 사람들은 그 씨앗을 먹는 거니? 아니면 그걸로 무엇을 하지? 너는 고양이나 강아지 또는 토끼를 길러 본 적이 있는지, 주로 무얼 가지고 노는지 궁금하구나. 생일날 좋은 시간이었기를 바란다. 다음 번 편지에서 말해 주렴. 엄마가 걱정하지 않게 착하고 진실한 사람이 되려고 노력해 다오. 할머니도 그런 착한 손자를 원한단다. 다음 편지에는 네 동무들에 대해서 말해 주렴. 어떤 아이들이니? 할머니.

[외할머니의 편지 4]

셔우드, 내 사랑하는 손자 아가,
어떻게 지내고 있니? 할머니는 네가 착하고 엄마를 기쁘게 해주려고 노력하는 아이기를 바란다. 새 집은 마음에 드니? 한국말은 좀 배웠니? 할머니 생각에는 네가 요즘 엄마랑 같이 자는 것 같은데, 그렇니? 동생이 없어서 여전히 외로운 거니? 네가 떠난 지 1년이 되었구나. 할머니는 네가 다시 올 때까지 나머지 3년 동안도 하나님께서 우리를 안전하게 지켜 주시기를 바란단다. 그리고 선교사님들 모두를 축복해 주시기를 기도한단다. 사람들을 복되게 하기 위해 그분들이 바치는 사랑의 노고를 기억해 주시기를 바란다. 어린 랄프 레슬리(Ralph Leslie)와

넬리 에디스(Nelly Edith)는 둘 다 착하단다. 그곳에 사과, 배, 포도는 있는지 궁금하구나. 종종 편지해 주렴. 할머니를 대신해서 엄마에게 뽀뽀해 주고, 엄마는 할머니를 대신해서 네게 뽀뽀해 주기를 바란다. 할머니.

셔우드의 생일을 축하해 주려고 오후에 몇 분의 손님이 오셨다. 피쉬(A. Fish) 박사[143]와 베스트(M. Best) 양[144]은 한국인 결혼식에 참석하느라 오지 못했지만 평양에 계시는 나머지 숙녀들과 아이들이 참석했다. 웹(Webb) 부인,[145] 리(Lee) 부인[146]과 마일로(Milo)와 아기, 폴웰(Follwell) 부인과 아기는 아직 중국에서 돌아오지 않았다. 그래서 노블 부인과 루스, 베어드(Baird) 부인,[147] 존과 윌리엄, 웰즈(Wells) 부인[148](스콧은 오지 않았다), 그리고 셔우드가 '새 색시'라고 부르는 헌트(Hunt) 부인[149]이 오셨다. 우리는 팝콘, 뉴욕에서 온 사탕(1년 전 제니 인트만이 준 것이지만 신선하고 맛있었다), 리본 케이크, 생강 케이크, 치즈,코코아 그리고 너트를 넣고 크림을 바른 생일 케이크를 먹었다. 케이크 위에는 초 다섯 개를 꽂았고, 음식이 나왔을 때 셔우드가 불을 붙였다.

손님들이 돌아가신 후에는 수잔, 요리사와 그의 아내, 보이, 문지기 그리고 보모를 불러서 같은 음식으로 대접했다. 모두 행복한 하루를 보냈다. 엄마는 보통 수요일에는 근무를 쉬는데, 이번 주에는 우리 셔우드의 생일을 즐겁게 마련해 주기 위해 목요일을 비우려고 수요일 날 환자들을 보았다.

엄마는 올해 셔우드의 새 사진 두 장을 갖게 되었다. 하나는 6월에 있었던 루스의 생일 파티에서 찍은 것이다. 여기 붙여두면 좋을 것 같다. 웹 할머니가 리 아기와 폴웰 아기를 무릎 위에 앉혀 놓고 계시고, 할머니 한 쪽에는 마일로 리, 다른 쪽에는 루스 노블이 서 있다.

그리고 존 베어드가 루스 옆에 서 있다. 셔우드는 스콧 웰즈와 함께
147 멍석 위에 앉아 있다. 그리고 8월에 우리를 떠나 하늘나라로 간 아기
메이 노블이 있다. 모두 아주 잘 나왔다. 웰즈 박사가 찍으셨다.

"루스의 생일 파티에서"
[뒷줄 : 마일로 리, 웹 할머니와 무릎 위에 리 아기와 폴웰 아기, 루스 노블, 존 베어드.
앞줄 : 스콧 웰즈, 셔우드 홀, 메이 노블]

또 다른 사진은 폴웰 박사가 9월 어느 날 우리 새 집에서 찍어 주신 것이다. 흔들목마 위에 앉아 있는 셔우드와 앞 마당에 서 있는 엄마 사진인데, 실제로 보이는 것보다는 집에서 많이 떨어져 있었다.
앞 계단에 앉아 있는 보모와 침모가 잘 보인다. 나팔꽃이 절정이어서 현관 앞 계단에 그늘이 드리워졌다.

[폴웰 선교사가 찍어 준 로제타의 평양 집]

"웹 할머니와 평양 어린이들" [Children's Missionary Friend에 실린 로제타 홀의 글]

"한국-이 사진은 아픈 어린 아기들을 위해 작년에 건립된 에디스 마가렛 기념 병동이다."

148 엄마 생각에 우리 셔우드는 관찰력이 뛰어난 듯하다. 엄마보다 정확하게 사물을 관찰하는데, 그럴 수 있는 이유 중 하나는 시력이 엄마보다 좋기 때문이다. 셔우드는 웹 할머니 얼굴에 주름살이 있다는 사실을 알아채고는 (주름살이 별로 없으신데도) 할머니들은 모두 외할머니와 웹 할머니처럼 얼굴에 '베인 자국'이 있는지 물어보았다. 우리가 처음 평양에 도착해서 노블 목사 댁에서 지낼 때 우리 방에는 여러 색깔로 물들인 양탄자가 바닥에 깔려 있었고, 외할머니 집에 있던

것과 흡사한 병풍이 쳐져 있었다. 침대도 침대틀 없이 스프링 위에 그냥 이불을 깔게 되어 있었는데, 외할머니 집에 있을 때 우리가 사용하던 식이었다. 낮에는 침대를 세워서 벽에 기대어 놓고 그 앞에 병풍을 쳐 놓았었다. 엄마는 그 유사성을 느끼지 못했지만 셔우드는 즉시 그것을 알아채고는 할머니 집에 있던 우리 방과 비슷하다고 했다. 그리고 커틀러 박사가 우리를 방문했을 때 빨간색과 흰색 줄무늬가 있는 블라우스를 입고 왔는데, 그 옷은 애니 이모가 에디스에게 준 인형옷과 비슷했다. 셔우드는 한눈에 그것을 알아보고 에디스의 인형옷과 비슷하다고 했다. 엄마 책상 옆에 걸려 있는 〈영감〉(inspiration)이라는 제목의 그림에는 작은 천사들이 배를 타고 내려오면서 저녁노을 속에 앉아 있는 한 여인에게 장미꽃을 던져 주는 장면이 있다. 셔우드는 그 그림을 유심히 살펴본 후 이렇게 물었다. "에디스도 저 천사들처럼 옷을 입지 않고 있어요?" 그러고는 자주 하던 대로 스스로 대답했다. "내 생각에는 한국 교회에 있는 그림 속 예수님처럼 부드러운 하얀 드레스를 입고 있을 것 같아요." 셔우드는 예수님이 구름 두루마리를 입고 하늘로 승천하는 그림을 보고 마음에 새겨 놓았던 것이 분명하다. 셔우드는 이제 어떤 말들이 생각을 표현하기에 적합한지 제법 개념이 잡힌 듯하다. 닭다리를 '드럼스틱'이라고 부르는 것을 좋아하지 않는다. 한번은 엄마가 벽(wall)을 울타리(fence)라고 했더니, "엄마, 벽을 울타리라고 불러서는 안돼요. 벽은 돌로 만들어졌으니까 이건 벽이에요. 울타리는 철조망으로
149 만들어진 거예요"라고 했다. 어디서 그렇게 많이 배웠는지 엄마는 도무지 모르겠다. 하루는 스키너(Skinner)[150] 박사에 대해 말하면서, "저는 그 이름이 싫어요, 듣기에 좋지 않아요"라고 했다.

버츠(H. A. Buttz)[151] 박사의 이름도 셔우드가 좋아하지 않는 이름이다. 외할머니의 이름 '셔우드'는 좋은 이름이라고 생각한다. 그리고 악마(devil)를 사탄(satan)이라고 부르는 것을 좋아하지 않는다. "내 생각에 사탄은 예쁜 이름인 것 같아요. 그렇게 생각해요"라고 한다. 때때로 셔우드는 벌 받는 것을 아주 분하게 여기고 오랫동안 감정이 상해 있다. 그리고 모진 생각을 마음에 품기도 한다. 언젠가는 이런 말을 했다. "내가 죽었으면 좋겠어요. 엄마도 나처럼 큰소리로 울게 만들고 싶어요." 셔우드는 실수나 잘못된 행동에 대해 온갖 변명을 만들어 내는 데 탁월하다. 엄마는 셔우드가 어디서 '나는 천성적으로'라는 표현을 배웠는지 모르겠는데 아무튼 셔우드는 이 말을 자주 한다. 가끔씩 엄마는 셔우드가 잘못 그 자체보다도 잘못된 행동이 들킨 것에 더 마음 상해할까 봐 걱정된다.

셔우드는 '마음을 바꾸다'(change my mind)를 '마음을 묶다'(chain up my mind)라고 하는데 아직까지 엄마는 고쳐 주지 못하고 있다. 사실 엄마에게는 그 소리가 너무 진귀하게 들린다. 어느 날 아침에 셔우드가 한국 교회에 안 갈 생각이라고 했다. 그래서 "알았어"라고 했는데 잠시 후 셔우드는 "내 마음을 묶기로 했어요. 거기 가면 벙커 부인을 만날 수 있을지도 몰라요"라고 했다. 셔우드는 벙커 씨 부부를 아주 좋아한다. 그분들은 여름 동안 평양에서 한참을 지냈는데, 셔우드를 많이 귀여워해 주시고 셔우드가 금광[152]에 대해 묻는 많은 질문에 친절하게 대답해 주셨다. 벙커 씨 부부는 금광에서 사역하고 계신다.[153] 셔우드는 얼마 전에 벙커 부인으로부터 친절한 편지를 받았다. 부인은 금광에 대해 더 설명해 주셨다. 셔우드는 정말로 금광에 가보고 싶어 한다.

[벙커 부인이 셔우드 홀에게 보낸 편지]

지티발비(Chitte Balbe)[154]
1898년 11월 5일

사랑하는 셔우드야, 나는 네 생각을 자주 하고 있고, 지금 너에게 이곳에 대해 그리고 이곳 제련소에서 금광석으로부터 금을 쇄광해 내는 과정에 대해 적어 보낼 거란다. 먼저 너와 네 엄마가 잘 지내고 있기를 바라고, 루스가 너랑 좋은 친구이기를 바란다. 루스와 루스의 부모님께도 안부 전해 주렴.
이 작은 마을은 산 아래에 자리 잡고 있는데, 주위는 온통 산과 산으로 첩첩이 둘러싸여 있단다. 그래서 눈에 보이는 것은 산들뿐이고 그 사이사이로는 계곡이 있으며 물이 흐르고 있단다. 이 산이 바로 금산(gold hill)이고, 산 밑에는 제련소가 있단다. 별로 높지도 길지도 않으며 그렇게 넓지도 않지만 이 산에는 아주 질 좋은 금이 매장되어 있단다. 이 제련소에는 1000파운드 무게의 도광분쇄기(쇄광기, 도광기)가 20개나 있단다. 나는 쇄광기가 무엇인지 그것을 직접 볼 때까지 몰랐단다. 자, 이제 최선을 다해 쇄광기가 무엇인지 말해 줄게.
쇄광기는 큰 신발을 신은 기다란 쇠막대란다. 이렇게 생겼지. →[그림]
이 거대한 쇄광기는 오르락내리락 기계로 작동되는데, 내려오면서 금광석을 깨어서 잘게 부순단다. 쇄광기가 쿵쿵 방아를 찧는 동안 호스를 통해 물이 그 안에 계속 흐르면서 먼지들을 씻어 내고, 금은 수은판에 모아진단다. 그렇게 수은판 위에 단단한 아말감(금과 수은의 합금) 상태로 두었다가 벗겨서는 곱게 갈아 뚜껑과 파이프가 달린 커다란 접시에 넣고 벌겋게 달아오를 때까지 열을 가한단다. 그러면 수은은 증기로 변해 파이프를 통해 나가서 찬 물에 닿아 응축되어 채집된 후 다시 금을 모을 때 사용된단다.
쇄광기가 작동하는 동안에는 당연히 금을 긁어낼 수 없기 때문에 2주에 한 번씩 기계를 멈추고 합금을 긁어낸단다. 이걸 '청소'(clean up)라고 부르더구나. 나도 청소하는 걸 한번 도운 적이 있는데 내가 긁어낸 것만 나에게 주었어도 나는 엄청난 부자가 되었을 거야. 근데 하나도 안 주더구나! 정말 아쉬운 일이지, 그치?
각 쇄광기 앞에는 쇄광기 안에 남아 있지 않고 체에 걸러져서 씻겨 내려온 금을 모으는 길고 커다란 판이 놓여 있단다. 이 판은 매일 청소한단다. 쇄광기는 번갈아 가면서 방아질을 하는데 먼저 1 번이 쿵 찍고 나면 다음은 4번이, 그러고는 2번, 5번, 3번 이런 식으로 계속 쿵쿵쿵 찧는단다. 이렇게 쇄광기들은 자기들끼리만 말을 한단다. 밤낮으로 자지도 않고 말이야.
금에서 수은이 모두 빠진 후 증류기를 식히면 드디어 순금이 모습을 드러낸단다. 그리고 다시 한 번 벌겋게 달궈진 뒤에는 벽돌 같은 모양으로 찍혀서 팔리게 된단다. 금 한 덩이는 50파운드까지 나가기도 해. 금이 물처럼 흘러나오는 모습은 참 예쁘단다.
순 노랑물이 말이야. [그림]
셔우드야, 부디 건강하고 많이 먹고 잘 자라서 엄마를 도울 수 있는 사람이 되기를 바란다!

네가 지금 너의 엄마에게 위안이라는 걸 나는 알아. 엄마에게 내 사랑을 전해 주렴. 그리고 내가 종종 너와 네 엄마를 생각하고 있으며 우리가 만나게 되기를 바란다고 얘기해 줘. 배달부가 떠나기 전에 노블 부인에게도 편지를 써야 하기 때문에 이제 그만 마칠게.
많은 사랑을 보내며, 애니 E. 벙커.

셔우드는 종종 천국에 대해 말하고 질문한다. 그리고 천국에서는 아프지도 않고 울지도 않을 거라는 사실을 좋아하지만, "난 어른이 될 때까지는, 지쳐버리기 전에는 하늘나라에 가고 싶지 않아요"라고 한다. 수잔이 자기가 덮을 누비이불을 꿰매고 있는데, 셔우드도 바느질을 하고 싶어 했다. 그리고 루스의 인형한테 줄 이불을 만들기 시작해서 세 조각을 꿰맸는데, 아직 끝내지 못했다. 엄마는 다섯 살이 될 무렵 처음으로 바느질을 시작했고 다섯 살이 지난 여름부터 학교에 다녔다.
150 그래서 셔우드에게도 다섯 살이 지나면 공부를 시작해야 한다고 일러두었다. 셔우드는 "헨디(Hendy)[155]와 아이다 아펜젤러가 수업을 받는다"는 것을 알고 있기 때문에 이 말이 무슨 뜻인지 알았고, 공부를 시작하기를 기대하고 있었다. 엄마는 지금 셔우드의 생일이 3주쯤 지난 뒤 이 일기를 쓰고 있으므로 셔우드가 수업을 받는 것에 여전히 흥미가 있으며 행여 공부하기 싫어할까 노심초사하지 않아도 되겠다는 말을 덧붙이고 싶다. 낮에는 엄마가 셔우드를 규칙적으로 가르칠 시간이 없고 저녁 식사를 마친 후에야 시간이 나는데, 그 시간대는 어린애가 수업을 받기에 최상은 아니다. 하지만 셔우드는 하룻밤도 거르지 않고 공부를 하자고 한다. 일요일조차도 쉬지 않으려고 한다. 셔우드는 늘 엄마 책상에서 엄마 무릎에 앉아 반 시간 동안 열심히 공부하는데, 때로는 졸리기 전까지 한 시간 동안 공부하기도 한다. 엄마는 셔우드에게 영어보다 한글을 먼저 배우게

했다. 한글이 더 간단하고 쓰기 쉽기 때문이다. 엄마는 적어도 한글이 셔우드가 눈으로 익히고 말로 배우기에 훨씬 쉬울 거라 생각했고, 한글을 먼저 배워 두면 나중에 영어도 훨씬 빨리 배울 거라는 생각이 들었다. 물론 영어를 배우는 것에 비해 한글을 재미있게 가르쳐 주지는 못하지만 지금까지는 아주 잘 익히고 있다.

[셔우드의 한글 공부]
"셔우드가 처음 시도해 본 한글 쓰기"
"어마니"-"처음으로 셔우드가 어머니라고 적은 글"
98-99년 가을 "어마니".

셔우드는 이 한글 음절과 단어들은 어디서든 즉시 알아차린다: 아, 가(go), 오(come), 고, 코(nose), 이(this), 다(all), 보(see), 소(cow), 어, 라.[156]
그리고 셔우드는 이 글들을 열심히 받아쓰기 연습을 한다. 비록 다른 공부를 하는 것보다 더 빨리 지쳐버리기는 하지만…….
셔우드는 새 단어 찾아내는 것을 그 무엇보다도 좋아한다. 그리고 새 단어를 배우면 그걸 찾으려고 책장을 수없이 뒤진다. 그때마다 엄마보다 더 빨리 그 단어들을 발견하고 찾아낸다. 아침 기도회와 예배 시간에는 한글 성경과 찬송가를 넘기면서 자기가 아는 모든 글자들을 찾아낸다. 이렇게 계속 나아간다면 머지않아 셔우드는 우리와 함께 아침 성경공부 구절들도 읽을 수 있게 될 것이다.
151 영어처럼 잘 이해할 수는 없을지라도 음성학적으로 한글이 더 정확하기 때문에 영어보다 발음을 쉽게 배울 수 있다고 엄마는 생각한다. 셔우드는 누군가가 이야기를 읽어주는 것을 아주 좋아한다. 엄마는 셔우드가 낮잠을 자려고 누우면 매일 한두 개씩 이야기를

읽어 준다. 그러다 낮잠에서 깨면 더 이상 읽어 달라고 조르는 법이 없다. 밤이 길어진 겨울인데도 조르지 않는다. 일요일에는 긴 성경 이야기를 기대하는데, 몰튼(Morton) 부인의 '예수님 이야기'를 읽어 주면 3장까지 주의 깊게 듣는다. 자주 성경을 그대로 읽어 주기도 하는데, 셔우드가 한국 교회에 걸려 있는 그림을 보고 흥미를 갖게 된 주제나 우연히 듣게 된 이야기에 대한 구절을 찾아서 읽어준다. 셔우드는 자주 스데반 집사가 돌에 맞은 이야기, 세례 요한 이야기, 창조 이야기, 홍수 이야기 등을 들려 달라고 한다.

최근 있었던 일요일 성경 공부는 하나님이 기도에 응답하심을 믿는 것에 관한 주제였다. 셔우드는 공부 시간에는 별 관심을 보이는 것 같지 않았는데, 나중에 알고 보니 그 주제가 가슴 속에 각인되었던지 그날 밤 평양의 강 근처 마을에서 큰 불이 났을 때 그 불을 보더니 동정심으로 가득 차서 집을 잃게 된 불쌍한 사람들을 위해 기도하자고 했다. 그 불은 셔우드가 처음 목격한 큰 불이었고 한국에는 소방차나 미국에 있는 불 끄는 수단이 하나도 없다는 이야기를 들었기 때문에 "하나님께 불을 꺼 달라고 같이 기도해요" 하더니 그렇게 기도드렸다. 눈을 뜨기 전 마지막 부분에서는 "믿습니다"라고 덧붙였다. 기도드린 후 다시 밖을 내다보더니 불길이 많이 작아졌다고 했다. 엄마가 보기에도 불길이 줄어든 것 같았다.

셔우드는 메리 아펜젤러를 많이 그리워하고 있다. 지난 몇 달 동안 메리 이야기를 하지 않고 넘어간 날이 거의 없었다. 그런데 셔우드는 지금 루스 노블과 친해지고 있다. 루스가 한 달간 서울에 가고 없는 동안에는 존 베어드가 참 좋은 아이라고 생각했다. 셔우드는 친구들과 놀기를 좋아한다. 혼자 노는 것에는 만족하지 못한다. 다만 지금은 고양이가 있어서 루스를 오라고 하거나 루스네 가겠다고 조르지 않고도 하루를 잘 보내기도 한다.

{아펜젤러 부인이 보낸 편지에서 메리가 얼마나 셔우드를 보고 싶어 하는지, 그리고 방바닥에 드러누워 셔우드를 찾아 달라고 소리치며 울었다고 적은 내용을 보고 무척 좋아했다. 그리고 그 부분을 여러 번 다시 읽어 달라고 했다.}[157.]

[아펜젤러 부인의 편지]

"부인이 보내주신 편지를 정말 즐겁게 읽었습니다. 부인께서 새 사역을 잘 하고 계신다니 저희도 기쁩니다. 저희 모두는 사랑하는 어린 셔우드가 보고 싶습니다.
저희 아이들은 셔우드와 셔우드의 여동생을 따뜻하게 기억하고 있습니다. 지난 겨울에 아이들은 참 좋은 시간을 함께 가졌었지요. 부탁하신 부인의 저장고에 있던 물건들을 마펫 형제 편에 보내드렸는데, 아직 못 받으셨으리라 생각됩니다. 하나님께서 부인을 축복하시기를 기원합니다. 수잔에게도 안부 전해 주세요. 수잔이 이곳 사역을 도울 수 없게 되어 아쉽답니다. 셔우드에게 사랑을 보내며,
진심으로, H. G. 아펜젤러 가족."

152 1899년 5월 10일, 수요일

그러므로 무엇이든지 남에게 대접을 받고자 하는 대로
너희도 남을 대접하라(마태복음 7:12)

"행복은 거래할 수 없는 것이다.
물고기를 잡듯이 그물에 담는 것도 아니다.
우리 인생에서 때론 놓치는 것이
가지는 것보다 도움이 될 수 있다.
선은 추구함에 있지 않고

크고 작음을 상관치 않는다.
그냥 행하고 행하며
우리가 받고자 하는 대로 행하는 것일 뿐이다."
-앨리스 케리(Alice Cary)

[짐 실은 망아지에 타고 있는 셔우드]

시간은 정말 빠르게 지나간다. 엄마는 너무 바빠서 셔우드에게 온 변화들 중 몇 가지밖에 적지 못하겠다.
지난 12월에 엄마는 셔우드를 루스 노블의 집에 맡겨두고 한 주간 짧은 시골 여행을 다녀왔다. 엄마가 진짜로 갔다는 사실을 알게 되고 밤에 엄마와 함께 잠을 잘 수 없다는 것을 알았을 때 셔우드는 정말로 기꺼워하지 않았다. 하지만 셔우드는 아주 잘 적응했고 착하게 지냈다. 그리고 엄마가 집으로 돌아오자 뛸 듯이 기뻐했다. 다음에는 반드시 자기를 데리고 가야 한다고 했다. 그래서 올 3월에 다녀온 여행에는 셔우드도 같이 갔다. 우리는 김창식이 살고 있는 마을 근처까지 배를 타고 간 뒤 내륙으로 들어갔다. 셔우드는 짐 실은 망아지를 타고 갔는데, 이 여행을 아주 즐거워했다. 우리가 배에서 내려 첫 밤을 보낸 곳에서는 두 마리의 '씨암탉'이 우리와 같은 방에 있었다. 이 동네에서 셔우드는 올해 새로 나온 할미꽃을 꺾었다.

[셔우드의 청원서]
사랑하는 엄마.
엄마가 빨리 왔으면 좋겠어요. 나는 노블 부인이 주무시러 갈 때까지 안 잘래요. 다음번에 멀리 갈 때는 가기 전에 말해 주세요. 엄마가 간 곳에 대한 이야기를 정말 듣고 싶어요.

[셔우드의 청원서 뒷면]

"오와리 마루(Owari Maru), 제물포에 4월 3일, 4월 22일, 5월 3일, 6월 24일, 7월 15일 입항."
"남포에서 김 씨 댁-
가마꾼 500. 평양에서 1300을 줌.
말 타고 김 씨 댁으로: 150+20. 평양에서 1300을 줌. 오늘 밤에 200-300을 줄 것."
닥터 홀 부인.

삼화에서 셔우드는 김 씨의 아이들과 같이 놀았다. 남포에 머물 때는
153 길에 풀어놓은 흑돼지 새끼들과 놀면서 할미꽃을 따기도 했다. 우리는
남포에서 부활절을 보냈고 기쁜 예배를 드렸다. 이날 남포에서는
처음으로 '헌금'이 거두어졌고 셔우드가 자기 모자에 헌금을 받았다.
평양 돈 131냥이 헌금되었는데, 한 냥은 어림잡아 반 센트 정도이다.
김창식은 아빠가 평양에서 모았던 첫 번째 헌금에 대해 사람들에게
이야기해 주면서 그때 헌금이 지금 남포에서 모은 금액보다 적었지만
당시 자체 교회를 지을 수 있게 만들었다면서 이 돈이 남포에 교회를
지을 수 있는 씨앗 돈이 되기를 바란다고 했다.

"할미꽃"

외할머니가 보낸 짧은 편지

셔우드에게.
할머니는 우리 셔우드가 노블 부인 댁에서 지내면서 엄마가 여행을 잘 떠나도록 해준 것이 대견하구나. 엄마는 며칠간 떠나 있었니? 할머니는 너에게 줄 누비이불을 만들기 시작했단다. 잘만 하면 네가 집에 돌아왔을 때까지 바느질을 마쳐서 사용할 수 있을 것 같다. 항상 착한 아이가 되거라. 그리고 엄마를 위해 심부름도 하고 가사 일을 돕기 바란다. 알아서 네가 할 수 있는 만큼 최선을 다하기 바란다. 할머니

1899년 봄 셔우드의 매듭 작품.

우리는 육로를 통해 사흘 만에 집으로 돌아왔다. 하룻밤은 삼화에서, 그리고 하룻밤은 강서에서 보내면서 각각 흥미로운 모임들을 가졌다. 우리는 총 여섯 마을을 방문했고, 450리(약 150마일)[158]를 여행했다. 우리는 열한 가정에서 가르쳤고, 하루 두세 번 정도 여성 모임을 가졌으며 때로는 네 번 모임을 갖기도 했다. 어디서나 셔우드가 제일 큰 구경거리였다. 사람들이 처음으로 보는 외국 남자아이였기 때문이다. 셔우드는 방해가 되지 않고 오히려 도움이 되었다. 내가 결혼했고 아들이 있다는 사실은 외국인의 관습을 몰라서 우리 미혼 선교사들을 잘 이해하지 못하는 이곳 사람들과 친숙해지는 데 도움이 되었다.

이른 봄 동안 셔우드는 천 조각을 좀더 꿰맸고, 이 카드도 바느질을 해서 만들었다. 나중에는 많은 공을 들여 엄마를 위해 같은 스타일로 커다란 편지함을 만들어 주었다. 한 번 바느질을 할 때마다 두 시간씩 꾸준히 작업에 매달렸다.

154 평양에 도착한 지 1년이 되는 5월 1일, 우리는 서울에서 열리는 정기 총회에 참석하기 위해 노블 씨, 폴웰 박사 부부 그리고 플로렌스와 함께 길을 떠났다. 남포까지 사흘간 배를 타고 가서 다시 그곳 여관에서 닷새 동안 더 머물렀다. 마침내 제물포로 가는 증기선에 올랐고, 제물포에서는 존스 목사 댁에서 이틀을 보낸 후 서울로 갔다. 셔우드는 친구들과 다시 만나 같이 놀 수 있게 되어 아주 기뻐했다. 이제는 메리 아펜젤러가 무섭지 않다고 하면서, 그렇게 된 이유가 메리의 곱슬머리가 얼굴을 약간 가리고 있기 때문이라고 했다. 그런데 맨 처음 그레첸을 만났을 때는 아주 수줍어하면서, "그레첸의 얼굴이 훤히 다 보여서" 그렇다고 했다. 그레첸은 머리를

뒤로 넘겨 빗어서 단단히 땋고 있었다.

서울에 있는 동안 셔우드는 운행이 시작된 전차도 몇 번 타 보았다. 그러나 폭동이 일어나는 바람에 전차 운행이 중단되었다. 평양에서 내려오기 전에 엄마는 셔우드의 충치 몇 개를 때우려고 했다. 아래 앞어금니와 위 중간 송곳니에 충치 자국이 생겼다. 셔우드가 잘 참아 주었지만 엄마는 충치를 잘 치료할 수 없었고 충치에 박았던 봉도 금방 빠져 버렸다. 어느 날 남포에서 딱딱한 빵을 씹다가 첫 이를 잃었다. 오른쪽 아래 중간 송곳니이다. 그리고 한 달 후에는 왼쪽에 있는 짝지 송곳니를 엄마가 빼주었다. 서울에 머무는 동안 치과에 가서 충치에 좀더 좋은 봉을 박았다. 이것은 영구치가 나올 때까지 유지될 것이다.

어느 날 별로 몸이 좋지 않던 셔우드가 이런 말을 했다. "제 이마를 조인트('joint')가 돌로 쾅 때린 것 같아요." 셔우드는 giant를 'joint'라고 한다. 엄마는 한 번도 셔우드의 그 말투를 고쳐준 적이 없다. '조금씩'(little by little)이라는 말도 늘 'by little by little'이라고 한다.
155 "여름은 어떻게 오나요? 해가 뜨는 것처럼 'by little by little' 오나요?"
이렇게 묻기도 하고 또 "나는 'by little by little' 자라나요?"라고 묻기도 한다.

의료 사역에 너무 바빠서 엄마는 우리 셔우드가 무슨 말을 하고 어떻게 변하는지 제대로 다 적을 시간이 없다. 언젠가는 엄마도 리빙스톤처럼 이런 말을 적을 것 같다. "나는 종종 선교사라는 내 직업에 대해 생각에 잠겨본다. +++ 비록 미비한 점들이 많았을지언정 후회로 인한 아픔은 조금도 없다. ++ 그러나 이교도들을 가르치는 데 힘을 다 쏟아 부으면서 시간의 일부를 쪼개 자녀들과 놀아주는 것은 내 임무가 아니라고 느낀 것이 후회스러울 뿐이다. 보통 하루의 힘든 정신적, 육체적 노동에 지쳐서 저녁에는 아이들과 놀아줄 기운이 남아 있지 않았다. 아이들이 어릴 때 내 품 안에 있는데도 놀아 주지 못했고, 아이들은 빨리 자라서 떠나 버렸다. ++++ 더 이상 내가 놀아 줄 상대가 없다는 것을 깨우쳐 주었다."

셔우드가 채집한 '흰 민들레꽃'.

156 1899년 11월 10일, 금요일

나의 날은 베틀의 북보다 빠르니(욥기 7:6)

"아이는 저녁마다 내 무릎에 앉아 있었지.
'3에 3'(Three and Three)[159]을 더한 나이의 그 소년이란다.
햇볕에 그을린 얼굴에 맑고 파란 눈은
나를 쳐다보며 행복하게 웃었지.
황혼이 질 때 나는 아이를 꼭 끌어안고
'내 사랑하는 어린 아들아' 부르고는 물어보았지,
'엄마는 한동안 궁금했단다.
그 조그맣던 아기는 어디로 가버렸을까?'

나에게 긴 하얀 옷을 입은 아기가 있었지,
지금 너처럼 안아서 흔들어 주던 아기가.
머리는 노랑비단처럼 부드럽고

두 눈은 수정같이 파랬단다.
작은 손은 분홍빛으로 물들인 꽃 같았는데,
보아라, 네 손은 이렇게 힘센 갈색손이잖아.
아기가 살며시 나갔나 봐, 잃어버린 것 같아, 어쩌지?
보세요, 우리 아기가 어디로 갔는지 아시나요?

내 목소리는 그때의 달콤하고도 성스럽던
생각이 떠오를 때마다 목 멘단다.
엄마가 된 첫 기쁨이 내것이던 때가 언제였나요?
내 얼굴에 후회의 그늘이 있었나요?
튼튼한 두 팔로 내 목을 꼭 감싸면서
'3에 3'을 더한 나이의 소년이 말하네요.
'그 아기는요—아기는 소년나라로 갔대요.
모르셨나요? 그 아기가 바로 저예요!'[160]

'시간의 할아버지'(Old Father Time)[161]는 11월 10일을 돌려서 다시 금요일이 되게 했고,[162] 나의 어린 아들은 여섯 살이 되었다. 셔우드는 신발을 신고 키가 3피트 9인치로, 2$\frac{3}{4}$인치가 늘었다. 몸무게는 46$\frac{1}{2}$파운드 나간다.

157 우리는 오후에 간단한 차 모임을 가지며 축하했는데, 어른과 아이들을 모두 초대했다. 생일 케이크는 크림을 바른 호두 케이크였고, 그 위에 꽂힌 여섯 개의 초에 셔우드가 불을 붙인 다음 잠시 후 불어서 껐다. 생일 케이크 외에도 다른 케이크와 크래커, 사탕, 팝콘을 먹었다. 셔우드가 정말 좋아했던 작은 불꽃놀이도 있었다.

엄마는 올해도 의료 사역을 계속하면서 에디스 마가렛 어린이 병동을 세우느라 몹시 바빴다. 그래서 우리 셔우드가 무슨 말을 하고 무엇을 하는지 많은 관심을 쏟을 수 없었다. 흥미롭고 재미있는 모습과 일상이 있어도 엄마는 달리 생각할 일이 너무 많아서 그때가 지나면 곧 잊어버리게 된다.

한두 사례를 들자면, 셔우드는 폴웰 부인이 그 댁 젖소에게서 우유를 짠다는 사실을 알고 있었다. 그래서 지난 여름에 노블 가족이 소를 가지고 있다는 말을 듣게 되었을 때 셔우드는 "누가 소의 젖을 짜나요? 노블 목사님이 하시나요, 노블 부인이 하시나요?"라고 물었다. 친절하게도 스왈른(W. L. Swallen)[163] 부인이 그녀의 자녀들을 가르치는 일요일에 셔우드도 올 수 있게 허락해 주셨다. 그래서 셔우드는 성경 구절을 많이 배웠다. 지난 7월에는 요한복음 3장 16절을 배운 후 '멸망'과 '영생'에 대해 설명해 달라고 했다. 그러고는 자기가 천국에 못 가게 될까 봐 두렵다고 했다. "음, 성경은 '그를 믿는 자마다' 천국에 들어갈 거라고 했고, 너는 예수님을 믿고 있잖아, 그렇지?" 그렇게 엄마가 말했더니 "네, 믿고 있어요. 하지만 늘 마음에 두고 있지는 않아요"라고 대답했다. 셔우드는 믿음과 사역이 함께 가야 함을 느끼고 있는 것이 분명하다.

몇 달 전 셔우드가 성경 구절을 암송하는 것을 듣고 엄마는 그 나이(5세) 때 성경 구절을 전혀 몰랐다고 말해 주었다. 그러자 셔우드는 "나는 커서 좋은 'humjun'(남편, husband)이 될 거라는 생각이 들어요"라고 했다. 엄마가 웃자 셔우드는 "그 단어는 잘 발음이 안 돼요. 남자아이가 어릴 때 humjun이라는 말을 못하면 커서도 그 말을 못하나요?"라고 물었다. 셔우드는 종종 커서 '엄마의 humjun'이 될 거라고 생각하는 듯이 말한다. 다른 사람의 남편이 된다는 것은 전혀 생각도 안 하는 것 같다.

158 셔우드의 생일이 지나고 그다음 주에 우리는 다시 시골 여행을 떠났다. 이번에는 모두가 짐 싣는 망아지를 타고 북쪽으로 300리, 즉 100마일을 갔다. 해가 짧아서 나흘이 걸렸는데, 가끔은 어두워진 후에도 이동했다. 밤에 머문 여관들은 좋지는 않았지만 돌아오는 길에 갑작스레 머물게 된 여관보다는 나았다. 우리는 최종 목적지인 운산에 도착하게 되어 기뻤다. 벙커 씨의 지원으로 오 씨가 이곳 운산에서 선교 사역을 할 수 있게 되었고, 엄마는 오 씨의 아내 수잔나와 딸 루시도 운산에서 함께 사역하도록 설득했다.

오 씨 가족은 경치 좋은 곳에 위치한 제법 좋은 집에 살고 있었다. 함께 온 우리 집 보이가 방을 치우고 가져 온 간이침대를 놓아 주어서 우리는 편안히 지낼 수 있었다. 보이가 식사를 준비해 주었고, 우리는 열흘 동안 즐겁고 유익한 시간을 보냈다. 셔우드와 루시는 좋은 친구가 되었다. 루시 외에도 어린 여자아이들 여섯 명을 매일 오게 해서 주간학교를 시작했다. 이후로 주간학교는 평균 출석률이 양호한, 열 명의 학생이 모이는 학교로 성장했다.

우리는 많은 가정으로부터 심방을 와달라는 초대도 받았는데, 각 가정에서 교리 문답과 복음서를 팔았다. 여성들을 위한 저녁 모임에서는 많은 사람이 우리가 알려주는 복음에 흥미를 갖게 되었다. 마지막 일요일에 여러 명이 기독교인이 되기로 결심하고 자신들의 이름을 제출했다. 그리고 주물들(fetishes)을 버리고, 술을 만들지도 않고 팔지도 않기로 서약했다.

운산은 금광에서 가까운 곳이어서 여러 계층의 사람들이 함께 살고 있으므로 대다수 가정이 술주정뱅이들의 요구를 들어주는 데 빠져있었다. 이곳은 사역하기에 실망스러운 장소이고, 지금까지 복음에 거의 관심을 가지지 않았다. 그러나 오 씨 부부는 우리의 방문으로 용기를 얻었고, 이제 그리 힘들지 않으리라 생각한다.

6("3+3")세 때의 셔우드. [짐 실은 망아지를 타고 운산 금광으로 가고 있다.]

금광에서 보내는 동안 셔우드뿐만 아니라 수잔과 금용이도 아주 즐겁고 재미있어 했다. 벙커 부인이 셔우드에게 보낸 편지에서 이미 설명했기 때문에 엄마는 그에 대해서는 생략하려고 한다.
159 광산에 있는 미국인들은 우리를 보고 매우 기뻐했다. 감독관이신 테일러(G. A. Taylor)[164] 씨는 이렇게 말씀하셨다. "부인과 어린 아들의 방문을 받은 경축일이었습니다." 도시락을 싸갔지만 그분들이 주는 점심을 대접받았다. 그분들과 식탁에 빙 둘러 앉아서 점심을 먹는 것이 좋을 듯했다. 그분들은 우리가 떠나기 전에 셔우드의 주머니에 너트와 사탕을 채워 주셨다. 엄마가 이를 뽑아 준 적이 있는 어느 광부는 셔우드에게 은화 한 전을 또 쥐어 주었다. 불쌍한 사람들……, 어머니, 아내, 누이들로부터 멀리 떨어져 지내는 그들을 보고 엄마는 측은한 마음이 들었다. 이곳에 있던 벙커 부인마저 떠났기 때문에 이제는 외국인 여성이 한 명도 없다. 셔우드는 금광 방문을 정말 즐거워했고 다시 가고 싶어 한다. 여행 동안 아주 얌전했고, 때로는 말에서 내리지도 않고 거의 한 나절을 갔다. 어떤 때는 엄마가 탄 말의 고삐를 잡고 마부 흉내를 내면서 걷기도 했다. 셔우드는 마부가 되고 싶지만 자전거를 구해서 탈 것 같다고 했다. 여행 내내 셔우드는 아주 잘

지냈고, 엄마는 셔우드를 데리고 오기를 잘했다고 생각했다. 셔우드는 광산에 있을 때 한국인들 사이에서 짧은 설교를 하기도 했다. 사람들에게 술을 마시지 말고 담배도 피우지 말라고 했고, 예수님을 사랑하고 천국에 가라고 했다.

[셔우드가 쓴 한글]
'어마니 사랑하오', '사랑' '사람' '아기'.

'예수 인도하소셔 어둡고 길 모리니 나를 도아주쇼셔.'

여행에서 돌아온 후부터는 지난 겨울에 중단되었던 한국어 공부를 조금이나마 다시 시켜 보려고 했다. 셔우드는 배운 것을 모두 기억했다. 겨울 동안 한 주에 세 번 이상은 공부를 못 했고, 겨우 30분씩밖에 수업을 받지 못했지만 셔우드는 많은 단어를 읽을 수 있고 꽤 어려운 문장도 읽을 수 있다. 석판 위에다 글씨도 꽤 잘 쓰는데, 가장 잘 쓴 것을 보관해 놓지 못했다. 여기에 그 글씨를 옮긴다. "예수 인도ᄒᆞ쇼셔, 어둡고 길 모로니 나를 도아주쇼셔"[165]라고 적었다. 셔우드는 이 찬송가를 거의 다 읽을 수 있다.

160 앨리스 피쉬 박사 결혼식에서, 1899.

[머리 타래]

[6세 손그림] "6세. 키 45 인치, 46½ 파운드."

161 1900년 5월 10일, 화요일, 중국 즈푸(Chefoo, China)

여호와를 경외하는 도는 정결하여 영원까지 이르고 여호와의 법도 진실하여 다 의로우니 금 곧 많은 순금보다 더 사모할 것이며 꿀과 송이꿀보다 더 달도다(시편 19:9-10)

"우리는 온전해지려고 이곳에 있습니다.
오직 그리스도만이 우리의 필요를 아십니다.
귀한 보석이 가장 갈기가 힘들듯이
우리는 하나님이 손수 지으신 보배입니다!

[스왈른 자녀들이 보낸 생일 파티 초대장]
"내일, 1900년 2월 22일 3시 티파티에 셔우드를 초대합니다."
올리베트, 윌버, 거트루드.

엄마와 셔우드는 5월 1일 이곳 즈푸에 도착했다. 텐진으로 휴가를 갈 계획이었으나 제물포에서 배를 타기 직전에 벤(R. R. Benn)[166] 박사로부터 이번에는 그곳으로 오지 않는 것이 좋겠다는 전갈을 받았다. 그곳에 악성 성홍열 전염병이 돌고 있기 때문이다. 그래서 대신 상하이로 가기로 했다. 즈푸에서는 상하이로 가는 첫배를 탈 때까지만 머물 생각이었다. 즈푸는 엄마와 아빠가 신혼여행을 왔던 곳이기 때문에 이곳에 오래 있으면 엄마의 외로움이 더 커질까 두려웠기 때문에, 엄마는 아주 많이 우울한 상태였다. 그러나 즈푸는 정말 아름다운 곳이다. 프라이스 부인은 우리를 아주 편안히 대해 주셨고, 셔우드는 바다, 조개껍데기, 모래, 불가사리를 보고 더할 나위 없이 행복해했다. 이런 셔우드를 그렇게 빨리 이곳에서 떠나게 한다는 것은 잔인한 것 같았다. 그래서 엄마는 이곳에서 열흘 정도 머물기로 했다. 우리는 내일 겐카이 호를 타고 떠날 것이다. 8년 전 엄마와 아빠가 이곳에 올 때 타고 온 바로 그 배다. 셔우드는 이곳이 천국 같다고 생각한다. 그리고 이것이 엄마가 늘 생각하던 완벽한 꿈이라고 여긴다. 지금 이 집에는 하숙인이 거의 없어서 셔우드는 8시에 우리와 함께 저녁을 먹고 난 후 거실—셔우드는 이 방을 '놀이방'이라고 부른다—로 가서 9시 30분까지 있는다. 셔우드는 오후에 긴 낮잠을 자기 때문에 이렇게 늦게까지 버틸 수 있다.

162 셔우드는 이 집에 계시는 프라이스 씨 부부, 왓츠 존스(Watts Jones) 부인과 그녀의 여동생 배즐리(Badgely) 양에게 세련되지 못한 매너로 많은 즐거움을 선사하고 있다. 셔우드가 숙녀 손님 두 분의 이름을 익히는 데 오랜 시간이 걸렸고, 그분들을 지목할 때 그냥 "그분"이라고 했다. 하지만 이제는 그분들의 이름을 부른다. 늘 'Mr.'와 'Mrs.' 호칭 사용법을 어려워했는데, 프라이스 씨를 "남자 프라이스 부인"이라고 부르곤 한다.

셔우드는 하루 종일 모래사장에서 길과 벽을 만들거나 돈놀이를 하기 위해 작은 돌들을 모으면서 놀고, 때론 양계장에 가서 놀기도 한다. 그리고 C.I.M.[167] 어린이들과 두 번 소풍을 다녀왔다. 셔우드는 저녁을 먹은 뒤 거실에서 숙녀 분들과 함께 있는 것을 좋아한다. 그리고 배즐리 양과 "어떤 빨간 물건을 보고 있을까요?"(I see something red)라는 놀이를 하거나 좋아하는 색깔놀이를 한다. 이곳에 아이들 세 명이 온 적이 있는데, 셔우드는 그 애들과 골무 감추기 놀이를 하고 놀았다. 마지막 며칠 저녁에는 숙녀분들이 돌아가면서 이야기를 해주셨다.

셔우드에게도 이야기를 한번 해달라고 부탁을 하셨는데, 셔우드는 큰 용기를 내서 시도해 보았지만 이야기들은 짤막하고 두런두런 더 만들어내지 않으면 별 내용이 없었다. 셔우드가 좋아하는 이야기는 어린 여자아이가 엄마를 위해 달걀을 구하러 갔다가 닭장에 가서 방울뱀 두 마리를 본 이야기이다. 그다음에는 보통 계속해서 엄마가 어렸을 때 작은 회색 뱀을 가지고 놀았던 이야기를 한다.
즈푸에 온 후 셔우드는 외할머니와 루스에게 멋진 편지를 썼다.
오늘은 중국인이 셔우드가 신을 예쁜 갈색 가죽 신발을 완성해 주었다. 오늘 밤 마지막 만찬 때 검정 벨벳 바지와 크림색 캐시미어블라우스를 입고 이 신발을 신고 나타날 것이다. 이 바지와 블라우스를 만든 천은 에디스가 캐나다에서 받은 것이다. 그러나 이때껏 그냥 두었다가 이제야 비로소 오빠의 옷감으로 사용되었다. 오늘 밤이 이곳에서의 마지막 저녁이 될 것이다.

셔우드 홀에게, 루스로부터.
"셔우드야, 네가 집으로 오고 있다니 기쁘다."

163 1900년 11월 10일, 토요일

내 아들아 나의 법을 잊어버리지 말고 네 마음으로 나의 명령을 지키라 그리하면 그것이 네가 장수하여 많은 해를 누리게 하며 평강을 더하게 하리라 인자와 진리가 네게서 떠나지 말게 하고 그것을 네 목에 매며 네 마음판에 새기라 그리하면 네가 하나님과 사람 앞에서 은총과 귀중히 여김을 받으리라 너는 마음을 다하여 여호와를 신뢰하고 네 명철을 의지하지 말라 너는 범사에 그를 인정하라

그리하면 네 길을 지도하시리라(잠언 3:1-6)

아이는 즐겁게 놀러 갔대요.
그런데 하루 종일 생각이
은실처럼 구불구불 돌았대요.
행복한 금발 머리속에서—
"엄마가 그랬어요, '아이야 최선을 다하렴.
너는 하나님의 위대하신 계획의 일부란다.'"

아이는 반짝반짝 빛나는 별과
비를 담은 구름밖에 몰랐대요.
어떻게, 왜, 무엇을 위해 이상한 것들이 있는지 몰랐대요—
학교에서 어린애일 뿐이지만
이렇게 생각했대요. "이건 하나님의 위대하신 계획의 일부야.
나도 최선을 다해야 해." - 마가렛 샌스터(Margaret Sanster)

[셔우드의 7세 머리 타래]

[셔우드가 엄마에게 보낸 추수감사절 카드]
"추수감사절-엄마에게"

지난 두 달 동안 셔우드는 일곱 살 생일을 몹시 기대하고 있었다. 셔우드는 평양에 있는 외국인 어린이 중에서 제일 나이가 많다. 셔우드와 엄마는 작은 파티를 구상했는데, '달걀 찾기' 놀이를 어린 아이들이 좋아할 거라고 생각했다. 그래서 6주간에 걸쳐 사용될 달걀들의 속을 말려 놓았다가 어제는 포도 젤리로 채워 넣었다.
달걀들을 주홍색과 초록색으로 칠했고, 몇 개는 하얀색으로 그냥
두었다. 금용이는 멋진 호두 케이크도 만들었다. 크림을 입히고
색색의 캐러워이 사탕을 그 위에 뿌린 다음 양초 일곱 개를 꽂았다.
그리고 너트 사탕과 땅콩을 준비했고, 마실 코코아도 준비했다.
지난 2-3일 동안 셔우드는 학교에서 '바쁜 시간' 중에도 다양한 색깔의
봉투를 열두 개 만들었다. 그리고 엄마는 달걀 그림 밑에 초대 문구를
164 써 넣었다. "11월 10일 2시에 오셔서 제가 달걀 찾는 것을 도와주세요."
그리고 모든 카드에 셔우드가 서명했다. 열 명의 어린이를 초대했는데,
어린 아기들을 제외하면 모두 초대한 것이다. 그리고 웹 할머니와
오길비(L. Ogilvy)[168] 선생을 초대했다. 노블 부인과 폴웰 부인도 그날
오후에 오시라고 했다. 모두 초대에 응했고 아주 즐거운 시간이 되리라
기대했는데 정오부터 비가 내리기 시작했다. 웹 할머니께서만 길을
나서도 괜찮겠다며 마일로를 가마에 태우고 오셨다. 잠시 후 노블
부인과 루스 그리고 앨든(Alden)이 왔는데, 그것이 모인 전부였다.
우리는 3시까지 다른 사람들을 기다렸다가 달걀 찾기를 시작했다.
모두 다섯 개씩 찾았고, 앨든만 세 개를 찾았다. 나머지는 엄마가
찾아서 생일케이크 등과 함께 오지 못한 사람들에게 보냈다. 그리고
모두가 달걀 찾은 상을 받았는데, 소리 내는 거북이, 악어, 앵무새 등
이었다. 실수로 달걀이 깨지자 그 안에 젤리가 들었다는 것을 알게
되었고, 모두들 깜짝 놀라며 즐거워했다. 몇 개 안 되는 빈 달걀들도
서로에게 던지면서 '달걀 포격' 놀이에 사용했다. 불꽃놀이도 하려
했지만 비가 와서 못했다. 모두들 좋은 시간이었다면서, 함께 즐거운
시간을 나누지 못한 사람들을 아쉬워했다.

셔우드의 생일 아침 식사로 수란(poached egg)을 올린 뜨거운 국수
한 사발을 수잔이 보내주었는데, 셔우드는 아주 좋아했고 엄마한테도
나눠주었다. 수잔은 또 예쁜 유리그릇에 사탕을 담아서 주었다.
에스더 의사와 그녀의 여동생 김 베시(Bessie Kim)는 하얀 비단 목도리를
주었고, 루스와 앨든은 배드민턴채를 선물로 가지고 왔다.
셔우드도 장난감 하나를 상품으로 받았는데, 엄마는 손에 가지고 있던
열두 개 중 마지막으로 남은 상품도 주었다. 초대한 열 명의
어린이들에게 하나씩 보내고 남은 것이었다. 오늘 아침 10시에는
엄마가 준비한 선물을 주었는데, 멋진 상자에 담긴 그림물감이었다.
아이들이 떠난 후 셔우드는 아빠의 모자 안에서 광을 낸 나무달걀을
발견했다. 이것은 열리는 달걀인데, 그 안에는 골무와 검정색과 하얀색
면실이 감긴 작은 실패들이 있었다. 셔우드는 이 두 가지 선물을
165 아주 좋아했다. 웹 할머니가 보내주신 예쁜 제비꽃도 있고, 외할머니가
보내주신 은화도 있다. 사랑하는 외할머니를 이제 다시는 이 세상에서
볼 수 없게 되었다. 우리가 중국에 가 있을 때 셔우드가 그곳에서
할머니께 편지를 쓰고 있던 바로 그날 5월 5일 하나님께서 본향으로
데리고 가셨다. 다시 행복한 집에서 함께 모여 살 수 있기를 소망했기에
할머니의 소천은 커다란 슬픔이 되었다. 할머니의 부고 소식을 받은
그날 밤 셔우드는 온 마음을 다해 엄마를 위로해 주었다.
"울지 마세요. 엄마, 울지 마세요, 엄마가 우니까 나도 울게 되잖아요."
셔우드는 이 말을 하고 또 했다. 그리고 아주 서럽게 한참을 울었다.
셔우드는 할머니의 죽음이 우리 두 사람에게 무엇을 의미하는지
알고 있는 듯했다.

"하나씩 하나씩 의자가 비어 가네,
한때 사랑하던 이가 앉았던 의자가.
하나씩 하나씩 의자가 채워지네,
천국 아버지의 집에는.

우리가 잠드는 것은 영원한 잠이 아니라네,
외롭고 조용한 무덤에서의 잠은—
가져가시는 주님을 찬양하세.
주시는 주님을 찬양하세.

[셔우드가 그린 크리스마스 카드]
"메리 크리스마스"

[셔우드의 글쓰기 수업과 그림 수업]

셔우드는 종종 학교에서 배운 것들에 대해 언급하는데, 그러면서 엄마를 놀라게 한다. 어느 날 아침에는 옷을 입으면서 '콘글로미스'(Conglomis)[169]에 대해 이야기했다. 엄마가 설명해 달라고 하자 그 아이는 "왜 콘글로미스, 그 사람이 미국을 발견했잖아요. 맞죠?"라고 했다.

166 크리스마스 날, 평양에 있는 모든 선교사들과 아이들은 노블 목사 댁으로 초대되었다. 저녁을 먹은 후 평양에서는 처음으로 크리스마스 트리가 세워졌다. 학교 어린이들이 나무를 장식하기 위해 종이 화환과 제등을 많이 만들었다. 그리고 어린이들을 위한 멋진 선물들이 많이 있었다. 셔우드는 커다란 호랑이를 선물 받고 아주 기뻐했다.

그 호랑이는 나무 밑에서 계속 움직이는 것처럼 보였다. '산타 클로스'가 선물을 나누어 주었고, 모든 프로그램이 대성공이었다.

엄마를 놀래 주기 위해 학교에서 '바쁜 시간' 중에 만든 1900년 크리스마스 카드. [셔우드는 열두 달짜리 달력을 리본으로 묶어 만들었다.]

오길비 양은 어린이들이 노래 부르는 재롱잔치를 준비했고, 셔우드는 〈나의 늙은 암말〉(That Old Mare of Mine)이라는 시도 낭송했다.

나의 늙은 암말[170]

나를 바꿔치고 싶나요, 그런가요 아저씨? 아, 정말 모르겠어요.
왜 당신이 나의 수키(Sukey)를 즉각 천 불에 사지 못했는지 말예요.
나의 늙은 암말.
예, 그녀의 가죽은 텁수룩하고요. 정말 볼품도 없어요.
예 어르신, 관절염이 맞아요. 그리고 그녀는 고약한 무릎도 가졌어요.
하지만 그런 말씀은 제게 아무 소용이 없어요. 제겐 그녀 밖에 없답니다.
나의 늙은 암말.

당연히 저는 알죠. 수키가 못마땅하고 참 성가실 수 있다는 것을요.
하지만 당신은 여자의 천성이 그런 것을 감안해 주셔야 해요.
나의 늙은 암말.
당신이 왼쪽으로 그녀를 당기면 아마도 오른쪽으로 가려고 할거예요.
대포가 날아와도 무서워하지 않지만 별거 아닌 종이 한 장에도,
아니 무슨 허연 것만 보여도 놀라서 껑충 뛴답니다.
나의 늙은 암말.

그러나 내 눈이 어두워져서 못 보게 되면 나는 그녀의 시력을 믿을 거예요.
그녀는 나를 안전하게 인도해 줄 거고, 칠흑 같은 밤에도 기민할 거예요.
나의 늙은 암말.
내가 때리면 그녀는 그저 꼬리를 한 번 흔들고 다시 걸어갑니다.
또 때리면 머리를 흔들고요. 싫으면 멈칫 합니다.
하지만 감각이 무딘 건 아니죠. 모든 걸 다하지만 말만 안 하죠.

나의 늙은 암말.

대체로 그녀는 숙녀랍니다. 자신의 연인이 볼 수 있다는 걸 알면 말이죠.
그리고 당신이나 나보다 훨씬 더 진취적이랍니다.
나의 늙은 암말.
그녀의 동작이 좀 느리고 시작이 힘들지만
우리는 같이 늙어 가는 걸요. 그리고 그녀는 내게 너무 소중해요.
아저씨, 나는 그녀가 헤어지고 싶어한다고 생각하지 않아요.
나의 늙은 암말.
사과주가 내 머리를 어지럽게 했던 때를 기억해요.
수키가 여기 없었더라면 나는 죽었을 거예요.
나의 늙은 암말.
그녀가 길 한 가운데서 나를 붙잡고 집으로 데리고 왔죠.
그리고 다시는 헤매거나 떠돌아다니지 못하게 했죠.
거품 이는 사과주를 보게되면 바로 그녀 같은 말에게 묶어둬야 해요.
나의 늙은 암말.

당신의 천국에 대해서 말해도 되고, 당신의 지옥에 대해서 말해도 돼요.
거기에는 사람도 있도 말도 있고 소도 있고, 그리고 거기엔 그녀도 있어요—
나의 늙은 암말.
그녀는 이 동네를 휩쓴 가장 놀라운 화제거리였습니다.
비록 그녀의 머리에 맞는 금관은 없었지만
나의 수키를 피터가 절대로 거절할 수는 없어요.
나의 늙은 암말.

167 희망찬 1901년이 시작되었다. 셔우드는 평양에 있는 우리 작은 학교에서 공부를 잘 하고 있고, 에스더는 의사가 되어 엄마를 도우러 귀국했다. 어린이 병동도 완공되어 잘 사용되고 있고, 여성 병원을 위한 기초가 놓이고 그 건물을 위한 목재도 준비되었으며, 새 주간학교(Day School)로 쓸 건물과 사택이 마련되고 이를 위한 재료들도 미국에 주문해 놓았기 때문에 엄마는 마음이 좋지 않을 이유가, 올 한 해를 기쁘게 보내지 않을 이유가 하나도 없는 것처럼

보이는데, 그런데도 엄마는 그렇지 못했다. 오랫동안 너무 무리한 것이다. 지난 봄 중국 휴가 이후 괜찮아진 줄 알고 엄마의 한계를 넘어서고 있다는 것을 깨닫지 못했다. 엄마는 건물 계획과 건축 등으로 점점 더 바빠졌고, 진료소와 병원을 운영하며 시골 여행, 전도부인 돌보는 일, 맹아학교에 관한 모든 일을 주관하면서 에스더와 수잔 그리고 셔우드에 대한 염려 등 이 모든 것들로 인해 신경 쇠약에 걸려 버렸다. 그래서 엄마는 3월에 오길비 선생님께 셔우드를 맡기고 우리 집을 돌보면서 셔우드와 등하교해 달라고 부탁하고 건강을 회복하기 위해 제물포와 서울로 내려갔다. 엄마의 상태가 호전되기 시작해서 셔우드에게 돌아올 계획이었는데 서울에서 열린 정기 총회 마지막 날 엄마는 큰 충격을 받았다. 선교부에서는 엄마가 변화된 환경에서 장시간 휴식을 취하지 않고는 사역하기에 부적합하다고 결론을 내렸고, 엄마가 원하는 바가 아니었으나 미국에 가서 휴식을 취하라는 결정이 내려졌다. 그래서 셔우드를 평양에서 불러오게 되었고, 박 에스더 박사와 그녀의 가족이 셔우드를 데리고 서울로 내려왔다. 에스더는 서울에 있는 옛 병원[171]에 임명되었다. 언스버거(M. F. Ernsberger)[172] 박사는 볼드윈 진료소로 갔고, 해리스 박사는 엄마가 평양에서 하던 일을 맡게 되었다.

셔우드가 그린 새해 카드.

[셔우드의 편지 1]
1901년 4월 8일
사랑하는 엄마,
글쓰기 시간에 엄마를 많이 많이 사랑한다고 쓰고 싶었어요. 저는 잘 있어요. 좋은 시간을 보내고 있어요. 엄마를 보게 되면 정말 좋을 거예요. 조금만 더 있으면 엄마가 올 거예요. 엄마를 사랑해요. 그리고 요즘은 착한 아이예요.

엄마의 어린 아들,
셔우드.

[셔우드의 편지 2](날짜 미상)
사랑하는 엄마,
엄마를 사랑해요. 노블 부인과 루스는 오늘 스콧 집에 가셨어요. 그리고 루스는 학교에 왔어요. 우리는 쉬는 시간에 재밌게 놀았어요. 마일로가 못 찾게 숨었어요. 재미있었어요. 수잔이 금광에 갔다가 금광석을 가져다 주었어요. 오길비 선생님이 벽시계를 고쳐 주셔서 지금은 제 시간에 종을 쳐요.
오늘 아침에 엄마가 보내신 두 번째 편지가 도착했어요. 오길비 선생님이 편지를 읽어 주신다며 저를 깨워서 일어났어요. 선생님이 편지를 읽어 주신 다음 아침을 먹으러 갔어요. 금용이가 아픈 발을 끌면서 집에 왔어요. 그래서 오길비 선생님이 목요일까지 오지 말라고 했어요. 긴 편지를 쓰고 싶지만 저는 그렇게 할 수 없어요. 시간이 너무 많이 걸려서 저는 이 편지를 보내고, 또 편지를 쓸 거예요. 오길비 선생님이 그러시는데 편지를 길게 쓰려다 못 부치는 것보다 짧은 편지를 쓰는 것이 낫다고 하셨어요.
사랑하는 엄마, 더 쓰고 싶지만 그렇게 할 수 없어요. 사랑하는 엄마, 편지를 지금 끝내야 되서 미안하지만 그렇게 해야 해요. 엄마가 제 소식을 듣고 싶어 하시니까요.
저는 쓰는 게 너무 느려요.
많은 사랑을 보내며, 셔우드로부터.

[셔우드의 편지 뒷면에 쓴 오길비 선생의 추신]
추신: 박사님이 이 편지를 읽을 수 있으실지 모르겠습니다. 셔우드는 글을 쓰면서 너무 피곤해졌어요. 그래서 이 편지를 끝낼 수 없을 줄 알았는데, 이렇게 셔우드는 편지를 다 작성하고 다시 베껴 썼답니다. 루이스 오길비.

6월 7일, 엄마와 셔우드는 우리 선교부의 루이스 양과 장로교 선교부의 스트롱 양과 다시 고향으로 향하게 되었다. 우리를 맞아 줄 할머니가 안 계시기 때문에 진짜 고향으로 가는 기분은 아니지만 어쨌든 미국으로 가는 것이었다. 우리는 호놀룰루에서 [비어 있음] 해변까지 마차를 타고 가서 즐거운 하루를 보냈다. 세인트 존의 빵(St. John's-bread)[173] 등을 꺾기도 했다. 7월 4일에는 넓은 태평양에서 아주 즐거운 프로그램이 있었다.[174] 셔우드에게 기억될 사건은 정오에 황동 대포를

170 발사한 일이다. [일기 원본 168-169쪽 없음] 대포가 터지면서 셔우드는 서너 군데 상처를 입었는데 그중 두 군데에서 피가 났다. 셔우드는 엄청 놀랐지만 많이 다치지는 않았다. 그러나 일등석에 탔던 한 중국인은 심한 부상을 입었다. 애국심을 고취하는 노래들과 연설들 외에 여러 경주들이 있었다. 실과 바늘 경주, 자루 경주, 감자 경주, 장애물 넘기가 있었다. 셔우드와 여섯 살짜리 여자아이가 달리기를 했는데, 셔우드가 부상을 입는 바람에 그 여자아이가 이겼다. 이 아이는 선장의 딸이고, 그 가족은 마닐라에서 돌아오는 중이었다. 사람들은 여자아이에게 네 살 어린 것을 감안해서 그만큼 앞선 거리에서 시작할 수 있게 해주었다. 선장의 딸은 체구도 나이도 셔우드와 비슷했지만 어쨌든 셔우드는 일곱 살이었기 때문에 사람들은 그 아이가 셔우드보다 먼저 출발할 수 있게 해주었고, 덕분에 그 아이는 쉽게 이길 수 있었다.
저녁 때 샘 아저씨와 콜럼비아 부인이 멋진 선물들을 나누어 주었다. 경주에서 이긴 소녀에게 아름다운 장식품을 주었고, 경주에서 진 셔우드에게도 배 깃발 모양의 작은 은으로 만든 핀을 주었다. 셔우드는 이 핀을 대단히 소중하게 생각한다. 저녁에는 멋진 지팡이 도보(cane walk)[175]가 있었다. 춤도 추었지만 이 니폰 호에는 필리핀에서 돌아오는 흥겨운 사람들이 많이 타고 있어서 거의 매일 밤마다 춤을 춘다.

[셔우드의 니폰 호 티켓과 승객 명단]
1901년 6월 22일 요코하마 출발, 7월 7일 샌프란시스코 도착.

1901년 니폰 호 7월 4일 저녁 식사.

7월 7일, 우리는 무사히 샌프란시스코에 도착했다. 그리고 바로
옥시덴탈 호텔로 가서 며칠간 묵었다. 로버트 길더슬리브 할아버지와
외사촌 로버트 다비가 우리를 보러 오셨다. 프랭크 외삼촌한테서
연락이 왔는데, 엡워스 동맹 회의(Epworth League Convention)[176]에
참석하기 위해 샌프란시스코에 오는 중이라고 하셨다. 그래서 우리는
그 회의 기간 동안 계속 샌프란시스코에 머물러 있기로 했고,
기어리 가에 괜찮은 숙소를 구했다. 그리고 몇몇 모임에 참석했다.
외사촌 로버트가 우리를 즐겁게 해주었는데, 엄마가 별로 외출하고
싶지 않을 때 셔우드를 공원이나 다른 곳에 데려가 주었다. 하루는
길더슬리브 할아버지가 셔우드와 루이스 양, 엄마를 데리고 물개를
볼 수 있는 데로 가주셨다. 그곳에서 점심을 먹고 골든 게이트
공원으로 가서 캥거루와 들소를 보았다. 외사촌 로버트가 셔우드와
171 엄마를 알라메다에 사는 길더슬리브 할아버지 집에 데려다 주어서
그 댁에서 하루를 지내기도 했다. 길더슬리브 할아버지는 셔우드에게
할아버지가 겪은 전쟁 이야기를 해주셨다.
할아버지는 남북전쟁(War of the Rebellion)에 참여했었다. [비어 있음]
이분이 바로 전에 우리가 샌프란시스코에 왔을 때 셔우드에게 금화
20불을 주신 그 할아버지다. 우리는 샌프란시스코에서 2주를
지냈는데, 신문에서 뉴욕과 동부가 놀랄 정도로 덥다는 소식을 듣기는
했지만 샌프란시스코 날씨는 기분 좋게 선선했고, 우리는 동부의
무더운 날씨를 피할 수 있었다. 프랭크 외삼촌이 샌프란시스코에
도착하셔서 엄마에게 뉴욕 캐스틸에 있는 찰리 외삼촌 집에 가서
외삼촌이 서부 여행을 마칠 때까지 셔우드와 있으라고 조언해 주셨다.
그리고 여행을 마치는 대로 셔우드를 프랭크 외삼촌 집으로 데리고

갈 것이고, 엄마는 찰리 외삼촌이 계시는 캐스틸이나 클리프턴 스프링스에 있는 요양원에 들어가 있으면 된다고 하셨다.
그래서 우리는 동부로 가는 기차를 탔고, 외사촌 로버트가 배웅해 주었다. 샌프란시스코에서 버펄로까지는 우리 둘이서만 객차를 타고 갔다. 스트롱 양은 세인트 헬레나 요양원에 들어갔고, 루이스 양은 북부선을 타고 세인트 폴까지 갔다.

범 미국 박람회(Pan-American Exposition) 중 타조 농장 방문, 뉴욕 버펄로.

"줄리아, 셔우드(7세 9개월), 패니. 캐스틸에서 버니가 찍어 줌."

버펄로에서 우리는 범 미국 박람회를 관람했다. 셔우드는 미드웨이에 있는 타조 농장을 혼자 보러 갔다. 정류장으로 돌아오는 전차가 너무 자주 서는 바람에 우리는 늦게 되었고, 서두르느라고 셔우드는 채선이가 준 초록색 지팡이를 전차에 두고 내려 버렸다. 셔우드는 그 지팡이를 한국에서 떠날 때부터 여태껏 내내 가지고 왔다. 우리는 이어리 철도를 타고 캐스틸까지 갔고, 밤 10시쯤 그곳에 도착했다. 찰리 외삼촌이 말과 마차를 끌고 정류장에 나와 계셨다. 그리고 곧 매기 외숙모가 따뜻하게 맞아주셨다. 사촌 버니와 아서, 패니 그리고 줄리아를 만났다. 셔우드는 이곳에서 아주 즐겁게 지냈다. 사촌들도 셔우드가 온 것을 좋아했고, 프랭크 외삼촌이 셔우드를 너무 일찍 데리러 오셨다고 생각했다. 셔우드가 프랭크 외삼촌과 함께 떠날 때가 되자 아서는 엄마와 떨어지기 싫어서 우는 셔우드의 모습을 보고 싶지 않다며 달아나 숨어 버렸다. 그런데 돌아와서 매기 외숙모께 셔우드가 떠난 것에 대해서 물어보고는 셔우드가 전혀 울지 않았다는 데 무척 놀라워했다.

172 엄마는 1900년 11월 10일 기록을 마친 뒤로 1902년 11월 10일까지 일기장에 손도 대지 않았다. 그리고 이제 이 일기장도 별로 남지 않았기 때문에 엄마는 셔우드가 생일, 크리스마스 등을 어떻게 보냈는지 보여 주는 편지들을 좀 삽입하고, 너무 많이 기록하지 않는 게 좋을 거라고 생각한다. 셔우드와 엄마는 8개월 동안 떨어져 지냈다. 10월에 단 한 번 프랭크 외삼촌 집에 들렀을 뿐이다. 그것도 뉴욕 지부 정기 총회를 마치고 요양원으로 돌아가는 길에 겨울 옷가지를 챙겨 가려고 열흘 정도만 방문했던 것이다.

173 [엄마가 셔우드에게 보낸 편지]

요양원, 캐스틸, 뉴욕
1901년 8월 19일

나의 사랑하는 셔우드,
엄마가 잘 지내고 있다는 것을 알려주고 싶어 편지를 쓴다. 상태가 많이 좋아졌는지는 잘 모르겠지만 더 나빠지지는 않았단다.
프랭크 외삼촌이 편지와 우편물을 통해 우리 셔우드가 정말로 착하게 지내고 있다는 말씀을 해주셔서 엄마는 정말로 감사하다. 엄마는 네가 계속 그렇게 지내기를 바란다. 나쁜 버릇들과 싸우면서 하나님께 도와달라고 청하는 것을 잊지 말거라.
셔우드야, 너보다 나이 많은 사촌들과 잘 지내기를 바란다. 너는 사촌들로부터 항상 좋은 대접을 받으려고 하면 안 돼. 네가 어리다고 잘해 주기만 바라면 너는 이기적인 아이가 되어 버릴 거야.
프랭크 외삼촌께 트렁크를 열 필요가 없다고 말씀드려 주렴. 방해가 안 되는 곳에 그냥 놔두시라고 해. 입을 만한 옛날 옷들이 좀 있니?
루이스 간호사한테서 편지가 왔단다. 세인트 폴에 있는 오빠네 집에서 아주 행복하게 지내고 계신대.
엄마가 지내는 방에는 헬렌 팍스(Helen Fox)라는 아주 예쁜 어린 여자애가 있단다. 헬렌은 겨우 두 돌이 지났지만 아주 영리하고 말을 잘 한단다.
방금 헬렌이 "a, b, c, d, e, s를 쓸 줄 안다"고 하는구나.

학교가 다음 월요일에 시작하는지 아니면 그다음 주에 시작하는지, 미국 학교를 네가 좋아할지 궁금하구나. 한국과는 매우 다를 거야. 사랑하는 오길비 선생님이 너를 그리워하실 거야. 너도 선생님이 보고 싶을 테고. 벌써 오길비 선생님으로부터 편지를 받았을 것 같구나. 아직은 캐나다에서 어떤 편지도 오지 않았지만 틀림없이 그곳으로 간 편지가 있을 것 같다.

지나가다 어떤 집 현관에 네것과 똑같이 생긴 흔들목마가 있는 걸 보았단다.

엄마는 저녁 식사 후 거의 매일 저녁 찰리 외삼촌 집에 간단다. 어제는 거기서 점심을 먹었고, 찰리 외삼촌이 말을 태워 주셨단다. 그 말에는 아직 재갈을 물리지 않았는데, 엄마 생각에는 말이 아직 전염병에서 다 낫지 않았기 때문인 것 같아.

애니 이모로부터 편지를 받았지만 아직 답장을 쓰지 못했단다. 친절하게도 너를 돌봐주겠다고 하셨단다. 하지만 그곳에서는 네가 학교에 잘 다닐 수 없을 것 같아. 조(Joe)는 하루 속히 우리가 집에 올 날을 고대하고 있다는구나. 오, 엄마도 정말 그렇게 하고 싶단다.

하지만 지금은 결코 집에 돌아갈 수 없을 것만 같다. 편지지가 가득 차서 이제 그만 써야겠구나.

너와 너를 친절히 돌봐주시는 분들께 많은 사랑을 보내며,

너의 사랑하는 엄마.

174 1901년 셔우드의 생일과 크리스마스

십일 월[177]

나뭇잎이 바래고 떨어진다.
바람이 거칠고 사납다.
새들은 지저귀기를 그쳤다.
그러나 너에게 해줄 말이 있단다, 아가.

하루하루가 끝날 때마다 어둠과 차가움이 더해 가더라도
눈부시게 빨간 장미의 뿌리는 눈 속에서도 살아 있단다.

그리고 겨울이 지나면 가지에는 새순이 돋고
메추라기는 클로버로 돌아오며 제비는 처마로 돌아올 것이다.

울새는 가슴에 밝은 색 조끼를 입고
길가의 예쁜 꽃은 태양과 이슬로 빛날 것이다.

오늘은 나뭇잎이 휭휭 날리고 시내는 말라 물소리 안 들려도
그러나 네게 해줄 말이 있단다, 아가. 봄은 분명히 올 거라고.

거칠고 추운 날이 있겠고 혹독한 비바람도 휘몰아칠 거야.
그래, 이곳에 있는 우리에게 좋은 일들만 오는 것은 아니란다, 아가.

그러니까 행복했던 기쁨이 어여쁜 여름의 빛살을 잃을 때
장미 뿌리가 어떻게 눈 속에서 살아남았는지 생각해 보렴.
-《반스 읽기 교본 3》(Barne's Third Reader)[178]에서

⚘ 선물들:[179]
여선으로부터 1.00[$],
프랭크 외삼촌 아이들로부터 장난감.
클래이턴(Clayton) 부인이 은수저, 여선이 칫솔,
사진 12장.

⚘ **[요양원에 있던 엄마와 프랭크 외삼촌 댁에 있는 셔우드의 상봉에 관한 메모]**
존스타운(Johnstown)에서 즐거운 시간을 가졌다. 셔우드는 크고 통통해졌다.
내가 자연스러워 보이기는 한데 뭔가 조금 달라졌다고 했다—"나이가 조금 들어 보이는 것 같아요." 셔우드는 초급 한글 공부 책을 절반 정도 복습했는데, 서너 단어만 잊어버렸고 꽤 잘 하였다. 그러고는 피곤해져서 새로 배우는 단어의 뜻을 기억하지 못했고, 방금 잘 읽었던 말도 잊어버리곤 했다. 그래서 책을 치우게 했다.
기차역으로 나를 마중 나온 셔우드가 먼저 나를 발견했다. 셔우드를 만나서 정말 기뻤다.

175 엄마와 떨어져 있던 8개월 동안 셔우드가 쓴 유일한 편지

⚘. 존스타운, 뉴욕
1902년 3월 7일

사랑하는 엄마,
엄마에게 편지를 쓸 시간이 되었다는 생각이 들었어요. 젠(Jen) 외숙모와 벨(Belle), 아모스(Amos) 아저씨가 지난 주에 오셨고, 글로브스빌에서도 네 분이 오셨어요. 벨과 저는 아주 즐거운 시간을 보냈어요. 저희는 말놀이를 했구요, 블럭을 가지고도 재밌게 놀았어요. 더 이상 생각이 안 나서 이만 마쳐야겠어요. 셔우드.

[엄마의 편지-찰스 외삼촌 댁에서 셔우드에게 보낸 편지]

캐스틸, 뉴욕
1902년 4월 5일

사랑하는 나의 셔우드야.
우리 편지가 서로 엇갈린 것 같구나. 편지가 늦어서 미안해. 하지만 지난 며칠간 캐스틸에서 해야 할 일들이 무척 많았단다.
오늘 엄마는 로저 부인의 오두막에서 찰리 외삼촌 집으로 이사했단다. 좀더 일찍 옮기려 했는데 2-3일 동안 엄마 몸이 짐을 쌀 수 있을 만큼 좋지 않았어. 그리고 찰리 삼촌 가족도 방을 고치고 넓히느라 바쁘신 것 같아서 엄마는 서두르지 않았단다. 짐을 싸느라 피곤했지만 작년 가을만큼 힘들지는 않았단다. 너에게 썼듯이 엄마는 그린 박사님과 짧은 인터뷰를 했는데, 우리 둘 다 피곤했기 때문에 엄마의 기대만큼 만족스럽지는 않았어. 그래서 떠나기 전에 그분을 다시 한 번 만났으면 해. 그분께서 정기적으로 '가정 방문'을 해주셨으면 한단다. 헤어지기 전에 그렇게 권장하셨기도 하고.
엄마는 프랭크 외삼촌이 만우절에 보내주신 친절한 편지를 받고 기뻤단다—그 편지는 절대로 만우절 장난 편지가 아니야. 벨트가 너에게 그럴싸한 장난을 친 것 같구나. 엄마에게는 아무도 만우절 거짓말을 하지 않았고, 엄마도 다른 사람에게 그러지 않았어. 요양원에서 몇몇 분들은 만우절 바보가 되기도 했지만 말야.
프랭크 외삼촌이 화요일 날 존스타운을 떠나신다니 아무리 엄마가 원해도 그 전에는 외삼촌 집에 갈 수 없을 것 같구나. 목요일쯤에나 갈 수 있을 것 같다. 혹시 다른 날이 너나 키트 외숙모에게 더 좋다면 알려 주렴. 그린 박사님은 너무 바쁘셔서 엄마가 서둘러 떠난다면 아마 다시 만날 수 없을 거야. 이번 주에 엄마가 너와 있어 주었더라면 참 좋았을 텐데. 외삼촌 댁 아이들이 메이필드에 가 있는 동안 네가 그 애들을 그리워했으리라는 생각이 든다.
프랭크 외삼촌께 아직도 팬턴 외삼촌한테 편지를 못 썼다고 전해 주렴. 외삼촌 편지를 받고 곧 바로 편지를 쓰려 했는데 그러지 못했단다. 이곳을 떠나기 전에는 꼭 편지를 써 보내도록 할게. 농장 소식은 더 이상 듣지 못했지만, 사실 엄마는 아직도 애니 이모에게 답장을 안 보냈단다. 다음 주에 애니 이모에게 먼저 편지를 써야 할 것 같다.
지난번 편지에 네가 그렇게 훌륭한 선교 사역을 하고 있어서 정말 기쁘다는 말을 잊었단다. 네가 엄마를 능가할 것 같다는 생각이 드는구나.
엄마가 너의 글을 보고 실망했다고 했을 때 너와 프랭크 삼촌도 매기 외숙모와 같은 기분이었겠지? 외숙모는 엄마가 너에게 너무 많은 것을 기대한다고 생각하신대. 하지만 작년 이맘때 네가 엄마에게 써 준 편지를 동봉해 줄 테니 보거라. 분명히 그 편지는 지난번 글보다 낫기에 엄마는 실망할 이유가 있다고 생각한다. 다시 보내는 네 편지와 작은 포지(Posey)를 잘 간직해 주렴. 엄마는 그것을 아주 소중히 생각한단다. 그 글은 네 나이에 정말 잘 쓴

글이다. 엄마는 네가 곧 더 잘 쓸 수 있기를 바라고 있단다. 지금 더 노력하고 있다니 기쁘구나. 이제 잘 시간이야. 내가 가기 전에 너나 키트 외숙모께 한 번 더 편지 쓰려고 노력할게. 그리고 언제 가게 될는지도 알려 줄게.
사랑하는 너의 어머니.

[프랭크 셔우드 외삼촌 편지에서 발췌한 내용과 동봉된 신문 기사]
추신: 셔우드는 작은 선교 사역을 하고 있단다. 우리 교회의 베시 호스 부인이 YWCA에서 선교회를 인도하게 되었는데 마침 한국에 대해 이야기를 나누려고 한다면서 네 올케 키트에게 한 가지 부탁을 했단다. 셔우드에게 한국 물건들을 가지고 와서 설명을 좀 해달라고 말이야. 키트는 가져갈 수 있는 물건들을 골랐고, 셔우드도 기꺼이 가겠다고 했단다. 모두들 좋은 시간을 보냈고 셔우드를 만나게 되어 기뻤단다. 그 자리에 세인트 폴 루터 교회에서 온 부인들이 몇 분 있었는데, 오는 수요일에 한국 물건들을 가지고 자기네 교회에도 와 달라고 했단다. 그래서 셔우드는 그 교회에도 갈 거야.

존스타운 Y.W.C.A.
4시 예배
지난 일요일 오후에 있었던 선교회는 특별히 흥미로웠다. 최근 의료 선교사인 어머니와 함께 한국에서 고국으로 온 셔우드 홀 군이 와서 한국인에 관한 흥미로운 이야기를 해주었고, 한국인이 입는 복장과 사진들을 보여주었다. 예배 시간에 한국인에 대한 기사와 그들의 관습에 대한 몇 가지 기록들을 읽어주었다.

[사촌 패니가 셔우드에게 보낸 편지]

캐스틸, 뉴욕
1902년 4월 5일

사랑하는 셔우드,
요즘 잘 지내고 있지? 오늘은 내 생일이고 좋은 날씨란다. 나는 새 드레스, 둥근 빗, 황금닭이 달린 펜대, 초코렛, 오렌지, 생일 케이크, 반짇고리, 대추를 받았어.
네 어머니는 이제 계속 우리 집에서 지내고 계신단다. 너를 자주 볼 수 있었으면 좋겠다.
나는 6학년이고 켈로그 선생님 반에 있어. 학교에서 너와 같은 책으로 공부하고 있고 5단계를 읽고 있단다. 금요일 날 네 어머니 요양원에서 판매할 태극기를 색칠해서 55센트를 벌었어. 그럼, 이만 줄일게. 곧 답장해 줘.
너의 사랑하는 사촌,
패니.

176 셔우드가 "여왕의 영어"(Queen's English)를 사용한 예문[180]

'그 책은 아주 ínerstraíng(interesting, 재미있다)', 'Emínately(evidently, 분명히)' 그것은 그들이 처음으로 본 사진기였다.' '나를 unrupt(distrupt, 방해하지) 마세요.' 바툼(Batúm)에서 어느 비오는 밤에 비가 쏟아진다(pouring)는 표현을 '일어났을 때 비가 주전자로 퍼붓는다(pitchering)'는 새로운 방식으로 말했다. '매를 좀 맞아야 한다'를 '육체적인 처벌(cortical punishment)을 좀 받아야 한다'고 하기도 했다. 하루는 커틀러 박사가 읽어준 이야기에 대해 이렇게 말했다.

"사람들이 어린 여자애를 box-chatter(chatterbox, 수다쟁이)이라고 불렀어요. 커틀러 박사님은 말을 많이 하는 아이를 box-chatter라고 부른다고 하셨어요." 'Emínately', 셔우드는 좀 비틀리게 말을 하고 있다. 셔우드는 글렌 로겐 호에서 전에 들어본 적이 없는 용어들을 많이 접하게 되었다. 엄마에게 와서 '무례하다'(rude)가 무슨 뜻이냐고 묻기도 하고 '건방지다'(cheek)가 '속이다'(cheat)와 같은 뜻인지, 토미 엄마가 'I'll tan you'(때려 줄 거야)라고 하는 말이 무슨 뜻인지도 물었다.

지난 가을 뉴욕 전차에서 셔우드는 반대편에 앉아 있는 아가씨를 보고 "엄마, 저분이 예쁘다고 생각하지 않아요? 얼굴이 예쁜 게 아니라 피부가 예뻐요"라고 했다. 엄마와 이 말을 엿들은 주위 사람들은 포복절도하며 웃었다.

177 1902년 8월 14일-셔우드와 엄마는 브루클린으로 가는 이른 아침 기차를 타고 리버티를 떠났다. 어제 저녁 조와 애니 이모 가족에게

'안녕'을 할 때는 그리 힘들지 않았다. 이제는 5년간의 사역을 못 마치고 한국에서 돌아오는 일이 없을 것 같기 때문이다. 하지만 평양에 있는 선교사들이 셔우드와 엄마의 행동에 이상한 오해를 하고 있었기에 우리가 한국에 가야 하는지 의문스러웠고, 우리는 다시 미국으로 영원히 돌아올 것 같기도 했다. 한국에 가는 것이 옳다고 생각되었고, 관계자들이 우리가 같이 가는 것을 제안한다면 짐을 싸서 갈 준비가 되어 있기는 했지만. 셔우드는 오늘 아침 알바니에서 산 멋진 파란색 모직 모자를 기차 창밖으로 잃어버렸다. 그래서 기분이 몹시 상했다. 기차역에서 트렁크를 열고 셔우드가 별로 좋아하지 않는 파란 오리 모자를 꺼내는데 10센트가 들었다. 베일즈(Veils) 부인 댁에서 점심을 먹었고, 셔우드는 엠마 외숙모가 주신 상자에 담아 간 토끼를 돌보았다. 그리고 브루클린으로 가서 엄마의 옛 동창 템퍼런스 그레이(Temperance Gray) 부인의 따뜻한 마중을 받았다. 부인은 셔우드가 한국으로 가는 데 비용으로 쓰라고 40불을 주었고, 우리 평양맹아학교에도 첫 해에 50불을 주었다. 이곳에서 열흘간 머무는 동안 셔우드는 프로스펙트(Prospect), 브롱크스(Bronx), 센트럴 공원을 방문했고, 에덴 박물관[181]에서도 즐거운 오후와 저녁 시간을 보냈다. 그곳에서 셔우드는 자신의 왕[182] 에드워드 7세의 대관식을 보았다. 정말 멋있었다.

[넬리와 조지 매케이지(George McKage), 애니 이모의 자녀들]

8월 15일 – 한국에서 [비어 있음]라고 쓰인 해외 전보가 왔다. 그럼에도 불구하고 이곳에 있는 우리 선교사 동료 모두는 우리가 한국으로 가야 한다고 생각하고 있다. 커틀러 박사와 만나서 이 문제에 대해 이야기를 나누고 나서 그분도 우리가 함께 돌아가야 할 거라고 생각하는 듯해서 엄마는 그렇게 하는 것이 옳은 일이라고 결정했고,
178 커틀러 박사에게 브루클린으로 와서 아침에 우리와 아틀란틱 하이랜드(Atlantic Highlands)로 가서 이 문제에 관해 스키드모어(H. B. Skidmore)[183] 부인과 한 번 더 이야기해 보자고 청했다. 그리고 그분이 여전히 승인한다면, 우리는 알바니로 가는 밤배를 타고 프랭크 삼촌 집에 가서 작별 인사를 드린 후 캐나다로 가겠다고 했다. 그날 아침(8월 22일) 우리 모두가 스키드모어 부인 댁에 갈 준비가 되어 있을 때 셔우드와 엄마는 스키드모어 부인으로부터 9월 3일 커틀러 박사와 함께 한국으로 돌아갈 것을 공식적으로 명하는 편지를 받았다. 그래서 그 시간 이후 문제가 해결되었다고 생각했다. 하지만 아틀란틱 하이랜드로 갈 준비가 다 되어 있었고, 엄마는 이 여행이 커틀러 박사에게 유쾌한 시간이 되리라 생각했기에 우리는 길을 떠났다. 셔우드는 토끼를 데리고 갔다. 증기선에서 셔우드는 [비어 있음] 부인과 좋은 친구가 되었고, 몇몇 다른 숙녀분들과도 친구가 되었다. 여행은 즐거웠으며, 우리는 스키드모어 부인의 축복을 받고 기쁘게 그 댁을 나섰다. 허드슨 강을 거슬러 가면서 탐조등과 여러 가지를 구경하며 여행을 즐겼다.

[아틀란틱 하이랜드에 있는 스키드모어 부인 댁에서. 셔우드는 토끼를 안고 있다.]

캐나다에 있는 앨리스 그레이 고모 댁에서. [앞줄 왼쪽이 셔우드]

1902년 8월 23일 - 토요일 아침 일찍 프랭크 삼촌이 배로 와주셨고,

우리는 즐거운 시간을 가졌다. 월요일에 캐나다를 향해 떠나서 8월 25일 브록빌에 닿았고 8월 27일 글렌부엘에 도착했다. 우리는 일주일 동안 홀 할아버지 집, 제인 이모할머니 집, 앨리스 고모 집, 사촌 레베카네서 즐거운 시간을 가졌다. 많은 친구들이 우리를 보러 와주었다.

1902년 9월 1일 – 노동절. 갔던 길로 다시 미국으로 돌아왔다. 무슨 연유인지 모르나 우리 짐이 아직 도착하지 않았는데 우리는 다음 날 아침까지 그 사실을 몰랐다. 사람들은 다음 날 아침에 짐이 올 거라고 했지만 짐은 오지 않았다. 알바니에서 출발하는 '애디론댁' 일반열차를 기다리는 동안 셔우드는 엄마가 자기를 두고 떠난 줄 알고 무척 겁이 났다. 그리고 오랫동안 이 일을 서운해 했다.

1902년 9월 2일 – 10시에 뉴욕에 도착했다. 짐을 못 찾아 왔기에 종일 짐이 어디 있는지 알아보느라 꽤 많은 돈을 썼다. 엄마의 벨트 가방을 가지고 다니던 셔우드는 기어이 그 안에 있던 엄마의 지갑, 금시계, 우표 등을 가방과 함께 몽땅 잃어버렸다. 우리는 가방을 찾으려고 경찰서를 두 군데 들렀고, 다음 날 아침에 탈 증기선을 예약하는 등 동분서주하느라 새벽 2시까지 깨어 있었다. 잃어버린 가방과 짐은 결국 못 찾았다. "셔우드는 대서양을 건너는 동안 《엉클 톰스 캐빈》을 아주 재미있게 읽었다. 앞의 사진에서 셔우드 옆에 앉은 아멜리아 가렛도 항해 마지막 저녁 때 그 책을 마쳤다."

런던으로 가는 세인트 폴 호 티켓
1 – 표지
2 – 아메리칸 라인: 뉴욕–사우스햄프턴–(런던–파리)

3-승선자 명단. 마가렛 에드먼즈 양과 메리 커틀러 박사도 2등객실 승객 명단에 있다.
4-셔우드와 로제타가 앞줄 왼쪽에서 세 번째와 네 번째에 서 있다.
5-2등객실에 토끼와 함께 있는 로제타와 셔우드.
6-셔우드가 앞에 앉아 있고, 로제타는 그 뒤에 서 있다.

[손그림]
"9세, 키 52¼인치(4피트 4¼인치), 몸무게 67파운드, 머리 둘레 [비어 있음]."

[머리 타래]

179 1902년 9월 3일 - 세인트 폴 호를 타고 9월 10일 도착 예정으로 런던으로 항해를 시작했다. '토끼'도 데리고 갔다. 에드먼즈 양은 캐나다에서 태어났고, 훈련받은 간호사로서 앤 아버(Ann Arbor)에서 왔으며, 이번에 우리와 함께 가게 되었다. 커틀러 박사는 9월 12일 출항하는 N.Y.K. 라인을 예약한 줄로 생각하고 있었는데 알고 보니 예약되어 있지 않았고, 글렌 라인(Glen Line) 이라는 화물선 말고는 11월 7일 전에는 아무 배도 예약할 수 없었다. 시베리안 기차를 고려해 보았으나 결국 모두 글렌 로간 호를 예약하는 게 낫겠다는 데 동의했다. 그 배는 양철 화물을 싣고 10월 16일 스완지(Swansea)를 출발해서 러시아령 아르메니아(Russian Armenia)의 바툼으로 갔다가 거기서 러시아산 석유를 싣고 일본으로 가는 배였다.
셔우드의 모국 수도 방문에 대한 글은 작은 기행문 '에드워드 7세 국왕의 대관식 때 다녀 온 세계 중심 도시'를 보기 바란다.

1902년 11월 10일, 월요일 [내용 없음]

180 셔우드에게 든 비용(Sherwood's Expenses)

첫 번째 해[1893-1894]

첫 번째 아기 옷	20.00
홀릭스 푸드	15.00
크림와 오트밀	3.00
연유	13.00
펩신(과 그에 든 우표 값)과 다른 약들	2.00
기저귀로 쓰인 수건(1개)	1.00
아놀드 사의 뜨개 기저귀 18개	3.00
안에 차는 뜨개 기저귀 12개	1.00
기저귀로 쓴 한국 천(1개)	0.50
아놀드 사의 뜨개 밴드 3개〔1.20〕, 뜨개 속바지 2개〔1.80〕	3.00
양말 뜨개실	2.00
작은 사진 36개	6.00
첫 번째 짧은 옷들, 바느질	0.80
켤레 사이즈 3과 4의 신발(2켤레)	0.75
켤레 긴 양말(3켤레)	0.75
안전핀과 멜빵	0.75
젖병과 젖꼭지	0.50
한국에서 고용한 일손	24.00
합계	98.80

선물들

존슨 부인으로부터 코바늘로 뜬 모자 하나
스크랜턴 부인으로부터 아기 양말 3켤레
한국인 친구들로부터 한국식 아기 양말 6켤레
무어 부인으로부터 모자와 긴 외투
전킨 부인으로부터 코바늘로 뜬 파우더 꽂이(powder socket)
레이놀즈 부인으로부터 하얀 긴 드레스 하나
조가 보낸 크리스마스 선물 $1.00
노블 부인이 주신 크리스마스 선물 아기 담요
루이스 부인과 커틀러 박사로부터 아기 코끼리와 강아지
크리스마스 트리에서 얻은 실로 뜬 공
버스티드 박사로부터 (작동하는) 검은 강아지

181 두 번째 해[1894-1895]

생일 기념 드레스	2.00
일본산 유모차	6.00
연유	5.00
홀릭스 푸드	5.00
무화과 시럽과 인산염소다	3.50
드레스(3), 앞치마(4), 허리띠(2), 모자(1), 스카프(1)(시카고에서)	10.00
신발(사이즈 5) 1켤레	0.50
긴 양말 4켤레	1.00
셔츠(3벌), 회색 모직실(샌프란시스코에서)	0.75
Bird's eye 기저귀(2개)	1.75
뜨개 기저귀 12개	3.00
갈색 신발(사이즈 $5\frac{1}{2}$)(1켤레)	0.50
묵직한 신발(사이즈 6)(2켤레)	2.00
깅엄 드레스, 앞치마, 바느질	3.00
면 셔츠(리버티에서)(2벌)	0.60
모슬린 잠옷(4벌)	1.00
생일 사진(한국에서) 12장	2.50
할아버지와 찍은 사진 12장	4.00
아기 침대(3.25) 방에 놓는 의자(1.25)	4.50
젖병와 젖꼭지	0.50
은으로 만든 컵과 냅킨 링	1.00
미국에서 고용한 일손	96.00
합계	154.10

선물들

생일 선물
할머니로부터 1.00
노블 부인으로부터 밝은 파란색 플렌널 드레스
스크랜턴 부인으로부터 코바늘로 뜬 모자와 벙어리장갑
여선과 에스더로부터 모피로 가장자리가 둘러진 토시
메리로부터 비단 토시
앨리스로부터 한국식 어린이 양말
실비아로부터 한글을 수놓은 흰색 비단 손수건

전킨 부인으로부터 흰색 색슨산 벙어리장갑
헐버트 부인으로부터 코바늘로 뜬 밤에 신는 양말 2켤레
루이스 양으로부터 잠옷 1개, 잠옷 윗도리 2개
헨리 아펜젤러로부터 두꺼운 외투(앨런 가의 아들이 입었던 것)
엠마 외숙모로부터 깅엄 드레스 하나(사촌 에바가 수놓아 줌)
젠킨스 부인으로부터 앙고라 털로 가장가리를 댄 어린이용 외투 하나.
샌프란시스코의 로버트 아저씨로부터 금화 $20.00
웹스터 박사로부터 5.00
빙햄턴의 사촌 윌리암 셔우드로부터 5.00
홀 할머니로부터 파란색 펠트로 만든 응달 나리(Turk's cap)
가버 씨로부터 사진 12장
폴리 크레리로부터 캐시미어 긴 양말 3켤레

182 **세 번째 해**[1895-1896]

빨간 모직 속바지(3벌)	1.80	
검정 모직 기저귀용 긴 바지(1벌)	1.00	
고무신 사이즈 $6\frac{1}{2}$(1켤레)	0.40	
갈색 색슨 지방 벙어리장갑(1켤레)	0.35	
무화과 시럽(1개)	0.40	
기저귀 사이즈 3〔모슬린〕 29센트씩(3개)	0.87	
입으로 부는 장난감 올갠	0.17	
긴 양말 멜빵	0.20	
무화과 시럽 큰병(1개)	0.75	
속바지(2벌)	0.50	
페리스 셔츠(Ferris waists) 35센트씩(2벌)		0.70
속바지(2벌)	0.50	
첫 번째 정장〔바지 사이즈 4, 허리 사이즈 3세용〕		1.98
바지(5세용)(2벌)	1.40	
셔츠(1벌)	0.50	
신발과 넥타이(각 1벌씩)	1.50	
무화과 시럽(1개)	0.75	
대구 오일을 섞은 초콜릿 에멀션(2개)	1.50	
일손 $100〔절반만 지불〕, 7~9월 생활비 $6.00		106.00
합계	122.62	

선물들

생일 선물
할머니로부터 은화 1불
여선으로부터 $1.00
여선으로부터 칫솔

크리스마스 선물
벨트와 클레어로부터 장난감과 책들
클레이턴 부인으로부터 "5포인트"은수저
조로부터 칼과 포크
벨트로부터 외투와 모자

183 네 번째 해-3세 생일부터 4세 생일까지 [1896-1897]

선물들

생일 선물
할머니로부터 새 신발 1켤레
애니 이모로부터 이발비
조로부터 벙어리장갑
엄마로부터 책

크리스마스 선물
보트너(Botner) 양으로부터 장난감 시계와 줄
엄마로부터 흔들목마
제니 인트맨과 다른 분들로부터 사탕과 너트
조로부터 유리컵 1개, 가죽 지갑, 색칠공부 책
할머니로부터 손수건들
제인 이모할머니로부터 빅토리아 주빌리(Victoria Jubilee) 손수건
홀 할머니로부터 $1.00
외할머니로부터 $1.00
아넷트 파월로부터 도자기 접시 1개
엄마로부터 일본 장난감들

갈색 정장, 5세용(1벌) 1.98

흔들목마(1개)	2.98	
파란색 겉옷	2.98	
너만(Nauman) 부인 학교 2월 학비	2.00	
너만 부인 학교 3월 학비	2.00	
깅엄 앞치마(2벌)	0.70	
파란색 세일러 옷(1벌)	1.00	
노란색 블라우스(1벌)	0.69	
셔츠(2벌)	0.58	
벌워스(Burworth) 부인 지원금	4.00	
모자(오닐에서)(1벌)	0.75	
싼 모자(3벌)	0.75	
신발(9사이즈 $8\frac{1}{2}$, 뉴욕에서)(1켤레)	1.50	
두꺼운 신발(리버티에서)(1켤레)	1.00	
약	0.50	
좋은 밀집 모자(블루밍데일에서)(1벌)	1.50	
얇은 파란색과 검정색 모직으로 만든 세일러 복(1벌)		1.98
두꺼운 모직 세일러 바지(1벌)	0.50	
갈색 모직 바지(1벌) 0.50, 뜨개 속바지(2벌) 0.50		1.00
파란색 옥양목 셔츠(1벌)	0.45	
무화과 시럽〔0.40〕, 초콜릿 에멀션〔0.70〕	1.15	
여행 경비, 음식, 과일 등등(미국에서)	1.50	
옥시덴탈 호텔	0.70	
세인트 폴에서 밴쿠버까지 식비	0.52	
팁	1.75	
일본에서 장난감	0.73	
S. S. 티켓(밴쿠버에서 나가사키까지)	80.75	
일본에서 인력거	0.50	
9일 동안의 일본 체재비	2.50	
제물포까지 증기선 티켓	7.00	
합계	124.94	

184 1897년 11월 10일부터 1898년 11월 10일까지

스튜어드 호텔 숙박비	금화 8.00
화물, 세금, 여행 용돈	5.00
대나무 의자(1개)	5.00

러시아인 가게에서 신발(사이즈 10)(1켤레)〔1.50〕		
일주일 만에 수선비〔0.15〕	1.65	
사이즈 10(러시아인 가게에서)(1켤레)	1.90	
신발 사이즈 10(뉴욕에서)(1켤레)	1.50	
모직 긴 양말(2켤레), 뉴욕에서〔1.00〕, 고무줄〔0.20〕		1.20
무화과 시럽과 약	0.75	
인력거꾼	0.25	
1/18 잡화점, 땔감 등등	13.15	
1/18 시카고 주문	7.65	
1/18 샌프란시스코 주문	3.03	
1/18 영국 주문	3.10	
1/18 12월 생활비	4.33	

5번째 생일부터 평양으로 간 이후 기록하지 않음.

프랭크 외삼촌 집에 있는 동안

신발 수선	1.15
기침약	0.25
모자	0.35
정장	3.50
고무신 ?	0.15
셔츠	0.25
덧신	1.00
셔츠와 속바지	0.50
쓰기 연습책	0.10
신발	0.95
바지	0.39
멜빵	0.15
고무신	0.15
합계	7.84

185 ⚚ R. T. 스틸스(R. T. Stiles) 교수.
셔우드의 평양 선생님 중 한 분.
1918년, 로스앤젤레스, 76세.
1163 E. 12번가.

‘첫 사춘기’ 때의 셔우드. 1906년 9월 10일.
12세 생일 때 셔우드의 머리 타래

[뒤표지]

[뒤표지 덧싸개]
셔우드 홀의 육아일기
1893년 11월 10일 한국 서울 출생부터 혼자 글을 쓸 수 있게 된
1902년 11월 10일 까지. 그리고 1906년 사춘기의 첫 모습.
뉴욕 주 리버티의 스콧(Scott) 목사의 요청으로
셔우드 홀 박사가 런드(Lund) 양을 통하여 보냈고,
런드 양는미국의 피난선인 ‘마리포사’(Mariposa) 호를 타고
태평양을 건너와 캘리포니아 주 로스 앤젤레스에서
우편으로 부쳤으며, 1940년 12월 7일 뉴욕 시에 도착했다.

주

1. 음력으로 10월, 양력 날짜로 10일을 뜻하는 듯하다. 1893년 11월 10일은 음력으로 10월 3일이다.
2. 로즈벨트 렌슬러 셔우드(Rosevelt Rensler Sherwood).
3. 루이스(Ella A. Lewis 1893–1927) 선교사는 간호사로, 뉴욕 디커니스 홈에서 로제타와 함께 일했다. 1891년 북감리교 선교사로 한국에 와서 1927년까지 36년 동안 한국에서 사역한 후 양화진외국인선교사묘원에 묻혔다.
4. 그레이트하우스 부인은 당시 한국 정부의 법률 고문 클래런스 그레이트하우스(Clarence R. Greathouse, 1846–1899)의 어머니다. 그레이트하우스 장군은 한국에 도착하기 전 1886년부터 1890년까지 일본 요코하마에서 미국 영사로 재직했다.
5. 메리 M. 커틀러 박사는 1892년 한국에 도착했고, 감리교 선교부에서 여성 의료 사역을 했다.
6. 헬렌 헌트 잭슨(Helen Hunt Jackson)의 시.
7. 4드램(dram)은 약 7그램(1dram=1.7718452gram). 약용식 도량형 환산법으로 무게를 드램으로 나타낼 때는 'ʒ' 표시를 하고 뒤에 로마 숫자를 달았다.
8. 10미님(minis)은 약 10방울. ♏은 미님의 약자. 1미님=0.01616115199밀리리터.
9. 홀릭스 식품은 제임스 홀릭(James Horlick)과 윌리암 홀릭(William Horlick)이 설립한 홀릭스 회사에서 만든 맥아유(malted milk)다.
10. 북장로교 선교회 호레스 알렌(Horace Allen) 박사.
11. 장로교 선교회 로즈 무어(Rose E. Moore) 부인. 사무엘 무어(Samuel F. Moore) 목사가 그녀의 남편이다. 로제타는 셔우드 출산이 임박한 상황에도 무어 부인의 출산을 도와주었고, 무어 부인은 이에 감사 편지를 로제타에게 보냈다. 무어 부인은 편지에서 셔우드 선물과 선교 후원금을 보내겠다고 했다. 무어 부인의 편지는 1898년 3월 10일 일기가 쓰여 있는 곳에 첨부되어 있다.
12. 남장로교 선교회 윌리엄 레이놀즈(William D. Reynolds) 선교사의 부인.
13. 북감리교 선교회 윌리엄 노블(William A. Noble) 목사 부부는 1892년 서울에 도착했고, 1934년까지 평양에서 전도 사역을 했다.
14. 존 버스티드(John B. Busteed) 박사는 1893년 한국에 도착했고, 서울에 있는 시병원에서 의료 사역을 했다. 홀 가족과 노블 가족은 버스티드 박사가 한국에 오는 비용을 지원하기 위해 집을 함께 사용했다. 버스티드 박사는 병환으로 1897년 뉴욕으로 돌아갔고, 1901년 사망했다.
15. 14쪽과 17쪽은 로제타가 한국 선교사로 떠나기 전에 일하던 곳에서 돌본 환자들에 관한 기록이다. 1889년 11월에서 12월까지의 기록으로, 14쪽은 매기 오닐(Maggie O'Neil) 부인과 제임스 로빈슨(James Robinson) 아기의 병상 일기이고, 17쪽은 어느 부인의 해산에 대한 설명이다. 15쪽과 16쪽은 일기 원본에 없다.
16. 외할머니 피비 길더슬리브(Phoebe Gildersleeve).

17. 셔우드가 태어난 지 4개월이 되는 생일. 로제타는 매달 10일을 기념하여 육아일기를 적었다.
18. 셔우드가 'out'이라고 한 말에서 따온 표현.
19. 이사벨라 루시 버드(Isabella Lucy Bird, 1831-1904, 비숍은 결혼 후의 성)는 19세기 영국의 탐험가 이자 작가, 사진가, 동식물 연구가다. 그녀는 한국을 탐험하기 위해 1894년부터 1895년까지 머물며 명성황후를 알현했을 뿐 아니라 청일전쟁과 동학혁명, 고종이 중국과의 조공 관계를 포기하는 것 등을 목격했다. 그녀는 명성 황후 시해와 그 후에 일어난 일에 대한 보고서도 썼다.
20. '조'의 이름은 조시아 윌슨(Josiah Wilson)이다. 그는 미국 남북전쟁이 일어나기 전 남쪽에서 탈출한 흑인 노예였는데, 로제타 가족 농장에서 일하면서 가족 내에서 많은 역할을 했다. 1894년 당시 조시아는 69세였다.
21. 마가렛 버 노이(Margaret Ver Noy), 로제타의 이복 오빠인 찰스 허드 셔우드(Charles Hurd Sherwood)의 부인. 그들은 뉴욕 주 캐스틸(Castile, New York)에서 살았다.
22. 프랭크 로즈벨트(Frank Rosevelt Sherwood, 1858-1938) 목사, 로제타의 이복 오빠. 그는 캐서린 앤 맥킨리(Catherine Anne Mackinlay, 애칭 Aunt Kit)와 결혼했다.
23. 모드 그레이(Maud Gray), 윌리엄 제임스 홀의 여동생 앨리스 홀 그레이(Alice Hall Gray)의 딸.
24. 마가렛 벵겔(Margaret Bengel) 양은 교육 사업을 위해 1890년 로제타와 함께 한국에 왔다. 그녀는 조지 히버 존스(George Heber Jones) 목사와 1893년 결혼했고, 존스 부부는 제물포로 발령이 났다.
25. 박여선은 윌리엄 홀의 마부였으며 에스더(김점동)와 결혼했다. 그의 이름은 '박유산'으로 많이 알려져 있으나 이 책에서는 '박여선'으로 번역했다. 이에 대해서는 《로제타 홀 일기 4》 119쪽 각주 101 참조.
26. 김창식(1857-1939) 목사는 올링거(Ohlinger) 선교사의 요리사였는데, 기독교인이 된 후 한국에서 처음으로 안수를 받은 목회자(ordained preacher)가 되었다.
27. 북장로교 선교부의 사무엘 마펫(Samuel Moffett) 목사.
28. 한석진(1868-1939) 목사는 사무엘 마펫 선교사의 조력자였다. 그는 1907년 평양 신학교를 처음으로 졸업한 일곱 명 중 한 사람이다.
29. 오석형은 윌리암 제임스 홀 박사와 그의 조력자 김창식이 1893년 평양 감리교 선교부를 개설했을 때 첫 번째로 복음을 받아들인 사람이다. 그의 딸 오봉래는 시각장애인이었는데, 로제타는 그녀를 위해 1894년 한국에서 점자를 개발했다. 그리고 이는 우리나라에서 시각장애인을 위한 특수교육의 시발점이 되었다.
30. 로제타가 나중에 덧붙인 내용이다.
31. 로제타가 나중에 덧붙인 내용이다.
32. 동학농민혁명(1894년).
33. 동학농민혁명 때 조선에 들어온 일본군은 조선 조정의 철수 요구를 거부하고 1894년 7월 23일 경복궁을 점령했으며, 고종의 아버지 흥선대원군을 불러들여 김홍집 친일내각을 구성했다.
34. 1894년 7월 25일 충청도 아산만 해전(풍도 해전)과 7월 28일 천안 부근 육상전투(성환 전투)에서 모두 일본이 청나라를 이겼다. 이에 8월 1일 청나라가 일본에 선전포고를 함으로써 청일전쟁이 시작되었다.
35. 장로교 선교부 C. C. 빈튼 (C. C. Vinton) 박사.
36. 앨리스 머지(Alice Muzzy)의 시.
37. 앤 벨 셔우드(Anne Bell Sherwood, 1867년 출생), 로제타의 여동생. 그녀는 콜버트 맥케이지(Colbert Mckage)와 결혼했다.

38. 김 마리아(Mary Kim), 결혼 후의 이름은 신 마리아(Mary Shin).
39. 로제타는 '염금영이'라는 소년의 이름을 한글로 기록했다.
40. 로제타는 첫돌을 맞는 아들을 위해 시를 썼다.
41. 아들의 첫돌을 축하하는 로제타의 시.
42. 로제타는 실비아가 손수건에 수놓은 글자를 한글로 옮겨 적었다.
43. 새 보모로 온 박에스더의 언니 김마리아(Mary Kim)인 듯하다. 같은 이름을 사용한 사람들 중에는 '메리 스파크스 휠러'(Mary Sparks Wheeler)라는 세례명을 가진 봉선이와 황메리가 있다.
44. 로제타는 프록터의 〈첫 슬픔〉(A First Sorrow)이라는 시 중 'long'이라는 단어를 'sweet'로 바꾸었다.
45. 로제타는 1894년 셔우드의 여객선 티켓을 여기에 붙여놓았다. 티켓에는 요코하마를 출발하여 호놀룰루를 경유하여 샌프란시스코에 이르는 항로와 승객 명단(명단에 '홀 부인과 어린이'라고 쓰여 있다), 로제타가 기록한 항해일지가 기록되어 있다. 이 배에 박여선과 에스더 부부도 동했는데, 에스더와 여선은 서로 다른 객실에 머물렀던 것 같다.
46. 루이스 보이드 테이트(Lewis Boyd Tate, 1862–1929) 목사는 1892년 남장로교 선교사로 내한하여 매티 잉골드(Mattie Ingold) 박사와 1905년에 결혼했고, 전주와 청주에서 1923년 은퇴할 때까지 사역했다. 그의 누이 마르다 사무엘 테이트(Martha Samuel Tate, 1864–1940)도 50여 년 동안 한국에서 선교사로 일했다.
47. 벼룩이나 이, 빈대 등에 의해 감염되는 풍토병으로 회귀열병(relapsing fever). 로제타는 이 병의 이름을 한글로 '임병'이라고 적었다.
48. 로제타가 나중에 덧붙인 내용이다.
49. 양화진외국인묘지를 가리킨다. 당시 이곳에는 1890년 안장된 헤론 선교사와 3명의 선교사 자녀가 묻혀 있었다.
50. 장로교 선교부 올리버 R. 에비슨(Oliver R. Avison) 박사.
51. 로제타가 일기 가장자리에 덧붙인 내용이다.
52. 존 볼턴(John Bolton)은 윌리엄 제임스 홀 박사의 외할아버지다.
53. 릴리 홀(Lillie Hall)은 윌리엄 제임스 홀의 여동생이다.
54. 장로교 선교부 그래함 리(Graham Lee) 목사.
55. 1893년 8월 26일 일기는 1894년 12월 10일 일기 가장자리 여백 부분에 기록되어 있다. 로제타는 일기와 윌리엄 홀이 지은 시를 함께 적었다.
56. 빈튼 선교사는 1894년 가을에 첫 아들을 잃고 양화진에 묻었는데 이 일을 말하는 것이다.
57. 로제타는 일기 옆 여백에 피더스톤(W. R. Featherstone, 1846–1875)의 시(〈My Jesus I Love Thee〉) 3연을 덧붙였다. "I will love Thee in life, I will love Thee in death, And praise Thee as long as Thou lendest me breath; And say when the death dew lies cold on my brow, If ever I loved Thee, my Jesus, 'tis now."
58. 로제타는 윌리엄 홀이 순직한 날의 일기 옆 여백에 패니 포레스터(Fanny Forrester)의 시 〈사랑하는 어머니〉(Sweet Mother)를 적었다. 패니 포레스터는 에밀리 C. 저드슨의 필명이다. 그녀는 침례교 버마 선교사였던 애도니럼 저드슨(Adoniram Judson)과 결혼하여 딸과 아들을 낳았다. 하지만 결혼한 지 4년도 채 안 되어 그녀를 선교지에 남겨 두고 남편이 죽었다. 이 시는 남편과 사별한 후 그녀가 쓴 것이다.
59. 로제타는 크로스비의 찬송시 원문을 일기에 첨부해 놓았다.

60. 프란시스 리들리 하버갈(Frances Ridley Havergal)의 〈나의 생명 드리니〉(Take My Life and Let It Be).
61. 툴리어스 클린턴 오케인(Tullius C. O'Kane, 1830–1912) 목사가 작시, 작곡한 찬송 〈Sweeping through gates〉. 〈어린양의 피로 씻김 받았네〉(Washed in the Blood of the Lamb)라고도 알려져 있다.
62. M. E. 그레이트하우스 부인이 쓴 추도 편지.
63. 조지 히버 존스(George Herber Jones) 목사가 쓴 추도 편지.
64. 부자(aconite, 附子)는 해열제, 진통제로 사용되었다.
65. 존 W. 채드윅(John W. Chadwick)이 작시한 찬송 〈It Singeth Low in Every Heart〉의 2절과 3절.
66. 필립 제임스 베일리(Philip James Bailey)의 글.
67. 이사야 27:8.
68. 엘리자베스 배럿 브라우닝(Elizabeth Barrett Browning)의 시.
69. 로버트 길더슬리브(Robert Gildersleeve), 로제타의 외삼촌.
70. Tourist Car. 좌석이 침대로 바뀌는 침대차.
71. 풀먼 팰리스 기차(The pullman Palace Car)는 좌석 기차보다 더 고급스런 기차로 잠자는 좌석, 일등석 식당칸, 리클라이너 의자, 화장실, 이발소, 도서관 등 편의 시설이 있었다.
72. 셔먼 다비(Sherman Darbee), 로제타의 외사촌, 로제타의 이모 헤리엇 길더슬리브 다비(Harriet Gildersleeve Darbee)의 아들.
73. 찰스 보니(Charles Bonney), 로제타의 외사촌, 로제타의 이모 엘리자베스 길더슬리브 보니(Elizabeth Gildersleeve Bonney)의 아들.
74. 이 시의 제목은 〈양귀비 마을행 기차〉(Poppy–Land Express)다.
75. 한나 휘톨 스미스(1832–1911)는 미국에서 19세기 대각성 운동이 일어났을 당시의 전도자이자 개혁자, 그리고 중요한 대중 설교가 겸 저술가였다. 그녀는 영국과 아일랜드에서 일어난 경건주의 운동 당시의 저술가이기도 했고, 여성 참정권 운동과 절제 운동에서 활발하게 활동했다.
76. 로제타가 일기 가장자리에 덧붙인 내용.
77. 헨리 W. 롱펠로우(Henry W. Longfellow)의 시.
78. 케이트 우드랜드(Kate Woodland)의 시 〈빚 갚기〉(Paying Her Way)에서.
79. 엘리자베스 배럿 브라우닝(Elizabeth Barrett Browning): "하나님의 위대하심이 우리의 불완전함에 넘치며 우리의 불안정에 안정을 주신다"(God's greatness flows around our incompleteness; Round our restlessness, his rest).
80. 에바 벨 셔우드(Eva Bell Sherwood), 로제타의 오빠 월터 셔우드(Walter Sherwood)의 딸.
81. 메리 가디너 브레이너드(Mary Gardiner Brainard)의 시 〈모르고〉(Not Knowing)에서.
82. 박여선–에스더 부부.
83. 아이작 왓츠 작시 〈When I can read my title clear to mansions in the skies〉
84. 폴리 버 크레리(Polly Burr Crary, 1833–1899)는 로제타의 고모 폴리 셔우드 버(Polly Sherwood Burr)의 딸이다. 그녀는 가죽 가공업계에서 저명한 사업가였던 호레스 H. 크레리와 결혼했다.
85. 월터 힐 셔우드(Walter Hill Sherwood, 1859–1943), 로제타의 오빠.
86. 윌리엄 팬턴 셔우드(Willian Fanton Sherwood), 로제타의 오빠. 그는 의사였다.
87. 엠마 티스(Emma C. Tice), 로제타의 오빠 윌리엄 팬턴 셔우드 박사의 부인.

88. 해리엇 길더슬리브(Harriet Gildersleeve), 로제타의 이모. 그녀는 리 다비(Lee Darbee)와 결혼했다.
89. 월터 셔우드 주니어(Walter Sherwood Jr.), 로제타의 오빠 월터 힐 셔우드의 아들.
90. 애이 M. 셔우드(Ai M. Sherwood), 로제타의 오빠 월터 셔우드의 맏아들.
91. 찬송가 〈요단강가에 서서〉(On Jordan's stormy Banks I stand). 사무엘 스테넷(Samuel Stennet) 작사.
92. 《The Heathen Woman's Friend》. Woman's Foreign Missionary Society, Methodist Episcopal Church, vol. 27.
93. 잠언 8:17.
94. 클리포드 홀(Clifford Hall), 윌리엄 제임스 홀 박사의 막내 남동생.
95. 로제타 홀이 일기 가장자리에 덧붙인 내용이다.
96. 로제타가 기록한 셔우드 홀의 아버지 윌리엄 제임스 홀 족보에는 같은 이름이 여러 번 나온다. 독자들의 이해를 돕기 위해 동명이인의 이름 뒤에 1세, 2세, 3세를 붙여 구별했다. 즉, 윌리엄 제임스 홀을 기준으로 1세는 증조부 세대, 2세는 조부 세대, 3세는 아버지 세대를 뜻하는 것이다. 따라서 이 족보상 '조지 2세 홀'은 셔우드홀의 할아버지, '제임스 홀'은 증조할아버지, '조지 1세 홀'은 고조할아버지다.
97. 로제타가 일기 가장자리에 덧붙인 내용이다.
98. 캐롤라인 볼턴 브래들리(Caroline Bolton Bradley), 윌리엄 제임스 홀 박사의 이모.
99. 제인 볼턴 로섬(Jane Bolton Rowsom), 윌리엄 제임스 홀 박사의 이모.
100. 로제타가 일기 가장자리에 덧붙인 내용이다. (Better for Nov. 10. '96 and use that here).
101. 캐나다 온타리오 주와 미국 뉴욕 주 사이를 흐르는 세인트로렌스 강에 있는 1500여 개 섬들. 대부분 캐나다령이며, 여름철 휴양지로 유명하다. 홀가의 휴양지도 이곳에 있다.
102. 찰스 허드 셔우드(Charles Hurd Sherwood), 로제타의 오빠. 그는 마가렛(매기) 버 노이(Margaret Ver Noy)와 결혼했고 변호사였다.
103. 로버트 보니(Robert Bonney)는 로제타의 이모 엘리자베스 길더슬리브 보니(Elizabeth Gildersleeve Bonney)의 아들이다.
104. 세스 보니(Seth Bonney)는 로버트 보니와 형제간이다.
105. 루엘라 클라크(Luella Clark)가 쓴 시 〈조금씩 조금씩〉(Little by little).
106. 감리교 선교부의 노블 부인이 지은 시.
107. 엘리자베스 바렛 브라우닝(Elizabeth Barrett Browing)의 시 〈즐거운 인생〉(The Sweetest Lives).
108. 국제의료선교회(International Medical Missionary Society).
109. 로즈벨트 렌슬러 셔우드(Rosevelt Rensler Sherwood, 1885-1919)는 프랭크 셔우드 목사 부부의 장남이다.
110. 클래런스 맥킨레이 셔우드(Clarencee MacKinlay Sherwood, 1888-1923)는 프랭크 셔우드 목사 부부의 막내 아들이다.
111. Christian Herald Children's Home.
112. 로제타가 덧붙인 내용이다. 즉, 로제타는 지난 생일(1895.11.10)에 기록한 하버갈의 시와 이번에 수록한 시의 위치를 바꾸기를 바라고 있다.
113. Alice Carey(1820-1871)의 시 〈11월〉(november).
114. Charlotte Elliot(1789-1871)의 시.

115. Dr. George D. Dowkoutt.

116. 수잔 쿨리지의 시 〈한 땀〉(Single Stitch)에서.

117. 메리 W. 해리스(Mary W. Harris)는 1893년 교육 사역을 위해 한국에 왔고, 1897년 의학 박사인 E. 더글라스 폴웰(E. Douglas Follwell) 목사와 결혼했다. 그 후 1920년까지 평양에서 봉사했다.

118. 릴리안 해리스(Lillian N. Harris, 1863–1902) 박사는 E. 더글라스 폴웰 부인의 여동생으로, 1897년에서 1902년까지 감리교 의료 선교사로 사역했다. 한국에서 봉사하던 중 발진티푸스로 사망했다.

119. 조세핀 페인(Josephine O. Paine, 1869–1909)은 교육 사역을 위해 1892년에 내한했고, 1909년 험난했던 순회 전도 여행 사역 중 브라이트 병(Bright disease, 신장병)이 악화되어 사망했다. 《Woman's Missionary Friend》, January 1910, p.11.

120. 룰루 E. 프레이(Lulu E. Frey, 1868–1921)는 교육 사역을 위해 1893년에 내한했고, 1920년 사망할 때까지 이화학당 교장으로 봉사했다.

121. 넬리 피어스(Nellie Pierce)는 교육 사역을 위해 1897년에 내한했다. 1904년 성서협회(Bible Society) 휴 밀러(Hugh Miller) 목사와 결혼했다.

122. 콜버트 맥케이지(Colbert Mckage), 로제타의 여동생 애니의 남편.

123. 다니엘 베넷 세인트 존 루사(Daniel Bennet St. John Roosa, 1838–1908) 박사는 유명한 안이과 전문의였으며, 뉴욕 의과대학(New York Post-Graduate Medical School)을 설립하였고 동대학 학장을 역임했다.

124. 메리 브라이언 박사(Dr. Mary Bryan)는 1890년 로제타가 뉴욕 디커니스 홈에서 하던 일을 인수받았고, 후에 인도에서 의료 선교사로 봉사했다.

125. 윌리엄 그레이(William Gray)는 윌리엄 제임스 홀 박사의 누이 앨리스의 남편이다.

126. 보이드 홀(Boyd Hall), 홀 할아버지(Grandpa Hall)의 남동생.

127. 마가렛 제인은 그레첸(Gretchen)이란 애칭으로 불리며, 조지 히버 존스 목사와 마가렛 벵겔 존스 부인의 딸이다.

128. 데이빗 M. 파월(David M. Powell) 목사는 로제타의 언니 아다 엘비라 셔우드(Ada Elvira Sherwood)와 결혼했다. 아다가 죽은 후에는 로제타의 또 다른 언니 애덜린 아넷 셔우드(Adaline Annette Sherwood)와 결혼했다.

129. 제이슨 굴드 파월(Jason Gould Powell), 데이빗 M. 파월 목사와 애덜린 아넷 셔우드의 아들.

130. 비라 파월(Vira Powell), 제이슨 굴드 파월의 누이.

131. 로제타는 셔우드의 이 말을 일기 여백에 덧붙였다.

132. 로제타는 셔우드가 그린 낙서 위에 '셔우드의 첫 설교'(Sermon)라고 덧붙였다. 로제타는 셔우드가 자신의 생각을 표현한 그림을 '설교'라고 생각한 것 같다.

133. 작자 미상.

134. 루이스 C. 로스와일러(Louise C. Rothweiler, 1853–1921)는 1887년 W.F.M.S.에 의해 한국으로 임명되었는데, 독일 감리교회에서 파견한 최초의 선교사였다. 그녀는 1899년까지 교육 사역을 했다.

135. 말콤 C. 펜윅(Malcolm C. Fenwick, 1863–1935) 목사는 1889년 내한한 침례교 첫 선교사다.

136. 무어 부인의 이 편지는 로제타가 셔우드를 낳기 전에 자신의 출산을 도와준 것에 대한 감사의 편지로, 태어날 아기인 셔우드에게 옷을 선물로 주고, 로제타가 속한 선교회에 헌금을 하겠다는 내용이다. 편지 내용으로 보아 1893년 크리스마스 일기에 첨부되어야 할 것으로 보이지만 1898년 3월 10일 일기에 첨부되어 있었다.

137. 로제타는 '비신', '어셔어셔'와 '조심ᄒᆞ오'를 한글로 적었다.

138. 이 부분은 로제타가 일기 가장자리에 덧붙인 내용이다.

139. 마스터(Master)는 어른에게 "Mister"라고 하듯 어린이에게 하는 존칭이다.

140. 릴리언 해리스 박사는 언니 메리 해리스 폴웰의 해산을 위해 평양에 갔고, 플로렌스는 갓 태어난 조카딸이다.

141. 프랭크 L. 스탠턴(Frank L. Stanton)의 시 〈작은 손〉(A Little Hand).

142. 로제타는 이 시의 1연은 일기에 직접 옮겨 적고 시 원문을 일기장에 첨부했다.

143. 장로교 선교부 엘리스 피쉬(Alice Fish) 박사는 1897년 한국에 왔고, 1899년 사무엘 오스틴 마펫 목사와 결혼했다. 1912년 딸 마가렛을 사산한 후 며칠 뒤 이질로 사망했다.

144. 장로교 선교부 마가렛 베스트(Margaret Best, 1867–1942) 양은 1897년 교육 사역을 위해 한국에 왔고, 1937년까지 사역했다.

145. 웹 부인은 그래함 리(Graham Lee) 부인의 어머니다.

146. 장로교 선교부 블랑세 웹 리(Blanche Webb Lee) 부인은 1892년 남편 그래함 리 목사와 함께 한국에 도착했다.

147. 애니 로리 아담스 베어드(Annie Laurie Adams Baird) 부인은 1890년 남편 윌리암 베어드 박사와 함께 장로교 선교부에 의해 한국 선교사로 임명되었다. 그녀의 남동생 제임스 에드워드 아담스(James Edward Adams) 목사 또한 1894년 아내 넬리 딕 아담스(Nellie Dick Adams)와 함께 한국으로 왔다.

148. 장로교 선교부의 제임스 헌터 웰즈(James Hunter Wells) 박사 부부는 1895년 내한해서 1915년까지 사역했다.

149. 벌사 핀리 헌트(Bertha Finley Hunt) 부인은 윌리엄 B. 헌트(William B. Hunt) 목사와 약혼한 상태에서 1898년에 내한했다.

150. 엠퍼레스 오브 인디아 호에 타고 있던 스키너 박사.

151. 헨리 앤슨 버츠(Henry Anson Buttz, 1835–1920) 박사는 후에 드류 대학교(Drew University)가 된 드류 신학교(Drew Theological Seminary)의 4대 총장이 되었다.

152. 운산금광. 평안북도 운산군에 있던 운산금광은 동양광업개발주식회사(Oriental Consolidated Mining Company)에 의해 운영되었다. 촉대, 국산동, 매봉, 삼봉, 대바위, 다리골 등 북면 일대에는 금이 아주 풍부했는데, 특히 다리골과 대바위에 매장량이 많았다.

153. 당시 벙커 부부는 광부들을 대상으로 전도 사역과 의료 사역을 하고 있었다.

154. 이답리(泥踏里). 영어로는 "Chittabalbie"라고 적기도 했다. E. W. Mills, "Gold Mining in Korea," The Transactions of the Royal Asiatic Society Korea Banch, vol.7, May 1916, p.23, 26. 셔우드 홀 박사는 자서전 《닥터홀의 조선회상》(With Stethoscope in Asia: Korea)에 'Cheraepalpe'라고 기록했다. MCL Associates, 1978, p.189.

155. 헨리를 셔우드가 아기말로 부르는 발음. 헨리 아펜젤러는 헨리 G. 아펜젤러 목사의 아들이다.

156. 로제타는 '아, 가, 오, 고, 코, 이, 다, 보, 소, 어, 라' 등의 글자를 한글로 적었다.

157. 로제타가 일기 가장자리에 덧붙인 내용이다.

158. 로제타는 일기에 '450li or about 150miles'라고 썼다. 450리는 약 180킬로미터, 150마일은 약 240킬로미터이므로, 거리 환산에 약간의 착오가 있었던 것 같다. 로제타는 1899년 11월 10일 일기에도 300리를 100마일로 기록했다.

159. “Three and three”는 셔우드가 여섯 살임을 의미한다. 원본 시에 ‘Two and two’로 적혀있는 것을 로제타는 셔우드의 나이에 맞게 고쳐 적었다.

160. Ida Reed Smith. 〈대답〉(The Answer) 혹은 〈소년나라로 간 아기〉(The baby Went Boyland)라는 제목의 시.

161. ‘시간의 할아버지’는 ‘Father Time’이라고도 불리는 시간을 의인화한 가상의 존재로, 큰 낫과 모래시계를 든 노인의 모습이다.

162. 셔우드가 태어나던 1893년 11월 10일도 금요일이었다.

163. 북장로교 선교부의 윌리엄 L. 스왈른(William L. Swallen) 목사 부부는 1892년 내한하여 1939년까지 봉사했다.

164. 조지 테일러(George A. Taylor 1829-1908)는 동양광업개발주식회사(Oriental Consolidated Mining Company)의 운산금광 기술책임자로 1897년 내한하여 1908년 사망했다. 서울 양화진외국인선교사묘원에 아들과 함께 묻혀 있다.

165. 로제타는 아들 셔우드가 쓴 한글을 그대로 옮겨 적었으며, 여백에는 셔우드가 쓴 한글을 스크랩해 두었다.

166. 레이첼 R. 벤(Rachel R. Benn) 박사는 1890년부터 톈진에서 의료 사역을 했다. 로제타와 벤 박사는 1890년 처음 선교사로 파송되었을 때 시카고에서 요코하마까지 함께 여행했다.

167. 중국 내륙 선교부(China Inland Mission).

168. 루이스 오길비(Louis Ogilvy) 양은 1903년 찰스 모리스(Charles Morris) 목사와 결혼하고, 1915년까지 평양에서 봉사한 후 1927년 모리스 목사가 사망할 때까지 원주에서 봉사했다.

169. 아메리카 대륙을 발견한 탐험가 콜럼부스(C. Columbus)를 말하는 것이다.

170. 폴 던바(Paul Laurence Denbar, 1892-1906)의 시. 던바는 오하이오 주 데이턴에서 출생한 흑인 시인이자 소설가로 흑인 사투리로 시와 단편을 써서 명성을 얻었다. 로제타는 이 시의 1연은 손으로 옮겨 적었고, 나머지는 잡지를 오려서 일기에 첨부했다. 던바가 지은 이 시는 모두 6연으로 되어 있으나 로제타가 오려 붙인 잡지에는 마지막 6연이 없고 4연과 5연의 순서도 바뀌어 실렸다. 옮긴이는 던바의 시 전문을 번역해 수록했다.(이 시는 일기 원본 164쪽에 첨부되어 있으나 일기 내용의 흐름에 따라 166쪽 부분에 수록했다.)

171. 보구여관(保救女館, Caring for and Saving Woman’s Hospital).

172. 엠마 F. 언스버거(Emma F. Ernsberger, 1864-1934) 박사는 1899년 의료 선교사로 한국에 도착한 후 1920년까지 봉사했다.

173. 콩과의 지중해의 상록수(Ceratonia siliqua)로 캐럽(carob) 나무라고도 알려져 있다. 껌(gum)을 만들어 내는 달콤한 식용 과육과 씨를 함유하고 있는 이 식물의 꼬투리는 식품회사에서 고정제(stabilizer)로 사용되었다.

174. 배에서 7월 4일 미국 독립 기념일 행사가 진행되었다.

175. 미국에서 여러 사람들이 지팡이를 짚고 줄지어 걸어가는 것은 주권과 독립의 상징이다.

176. 1889년 미국 클리블랜드에서 시작된 미국 감리교의 청년신앙운동 단체. 신앙과 사회봉사 실천을 목표로 시작되었고 해외 선교에도 적극적으로 참여했다.

177. 앨리스 케리(Alice Carey)의 시 〈November〉.

178. 반스 뉴 내셔날 리더스(Barnes’s New National Readers)는 교과서 시리즈로 1권부터 6권까지 있었다.

179. 이 선물 목록은 1895년 크리스마스와 1896년 새해 선물인 것 같다. 1896년 1월 10일 일기 참조. 여선은 1900년 4월 28일에 볼티모어에서 폐결핵으로 사망했다.

180. 이 기록은 1902년 늦여름 미국에서 한국으로 돌아갈 때 기록한 것이다. 로제타와 셔우드는 뉴욕에서 런던으로 갔고, 그다음 글렌 로겐(Glen Logan) 호을 타고 코베로 갔다. 그 배는 흑해(Black Sea)를 거쳐 항해했다.

181. 맨해튼에 있는 에덴 뮤제(Eden Musée)는 1884년에 문을 열었는데, 그곳에는 밀랍 작품들이 많이 소장되어 있고, 음악회와 마술 랜턴 쇼, 인형극 등 특별한 오락 공연들이 바뀌가면서 진행되는 놀이 센터였다. 또한 유명한 그림들이 소장되어 있었고, 초기 활동사진(motion pictures)의 전시장이 되기도 했다.

182. 셔우드는 아버지의 국적인 캐나다인으로 등록되어 있었고, 캐다다는 영국령에 속해 있었기 때문에 영국 왕은 곧 "셔우드의 왕"이었던 것이다.

183. H. B. 스키드모어(H. B. Skidmore) 부인은 여성해외선교회의 통신 담당 비서였다.

해설

100년이 지난 오늘도 뜨겁기만 한 사랑

이용민(한국기독교역사학회 총무이사)

1.

아빠인 윌리엄 제임스 홀과 엄마인 로제타 셔우드 홀에게는 두 명의 자녀가 있었다. 큰아이는 윌리엄 제임스 홀이 평양 지역 담당 개척 선교사로 선발되면서 많은 세월을 떨어져 지내야 했던 아들 셔우드 홀이고, 작은아이는 윌리엄 제임스 홀이 마지막 숨을 내쉴 때 엄마 뱃속에서 자라고 있던 딸 에디스 마가렛 홀이다. 로제타 홀은 각각 이 두 아이에 대한 육아일기를 기록하여 후손에게 남겼는데, 이 일기는 바로 첫째 셔우드 홀에 대한 육아일기다.

《로제타 홀 일기 5》는 셔우드 홀이 태어난 1893년 11월 10일 토요일 오전 10시를 기해 시작되며, 실질적으로는 1900년 11월 10일 토요일자로 끝나지만, 그 이후에 해당하는 내용으로, 셔우드 홀이 엄마 로제타 홀에게 쓴 편지 등으로 꾸며진 일기가 9세 생일을 맞은 1902년 11월 10일 월요일자로 셔우드의 왼손 그림 바탕에 키, 몸무게, 머리둘레 등을 적고, 머리타래를 붙인 채 기록되어 있다. 그리고 맨 뒤에는 셔우드에게 들어간 비용이 첫해부터 시작해서 세세하게 내역별로 기록되어 있다.

그런데 이 육아일기를 둘러싼 별도의 겉 포장지에는 이 일기의 여행 경로가 기록되어 있다. 즉, 이 일기는 뉴욕 리버티의 얼 스콧 목사의 요청으로 셔우드 홀 박사가 런드 양에게 보냈고, 런드 양은 이 일기장을 들고 미국의 피난선 '마리포사' 호를 타고 태평양을 건너 캘리포니아의 로스앤젤레스에서 우편으로 부쳤으며, 1940년 12월 7일 뉴욕에 도착했다고 적혀 있다. 이로 미루어 아마도 육아일기는 엄마인 로제타 홀이 아니라 셔우드 홀이 보관하고 있었으나 자신이 한국을 떠날 때 미국으로 가져갈 수 없는 상황이었으며, 결국 다른 누군가를 통해 뉴욕까지 가져올 수밖에 없었던 급박한 장면을 연상하게 된다. 이 육아일기가 안전하게 전달된 과정에 대한 구체적인 정황은 확실하게 알기 어려운 형편이지만, 별도의 에피소드가 있을 것으로 여겨진다.

참고로 지금까지 발간된 〈로제타 홀 일기〉의 날짜들을 살펴보면, 이 육아일기의 시기적 위치가 가늠될 수 있으리라 생각한다. 《로제타 홀 일기 1》은 1890년 8월 21일에서 같은 해 9월 23일까지, 《로제타 홀 일기 2》는 1890년 9월 24일에서 1891년 5월 17일까지, 《로제타 홀 일기 3》은 1891년 5월 15일에서 같은 해 12월 31일까지, 그리고 《로제타 홀 일기 4》는 1892년 3월 8일에서 1894년 10월 1일까지 기록되어 있다. 《로제타 홀 일기 5》는 《로제타 홀 일기 4》와 1년 정도가 겹친다고 할 수 있는데, 《로제타 홀 일기 4》에 자세히 나와 있지 않은 여러 가지 중요한 내용들을 확인할 수 있는 것도 바로 이 육아일기다.

2.

윌리엄 제임스 홀과 로제타 셔우드 홀의 첫 아기 셔우드 홀에 대한 육아일기는 〈로제타 홀 일기〉의 부록이나 속편으로서의 의미가 아닌 전혀 새로운 차원의 중요한 작업이라고 평가해야 마땅하다. 지금까지 한국에 왔던 선교사가 선교사로서 자신의 선교활동에 관한 내용을 일기로 기록한 문헌은 알렌의 일기와 아펜젤러의 일기, 베른하이젤의 일기 등 드물게나마 찾아볼 수 있지만, 이 일기와 같이 자신의 자녀 한 사람의 성장과정을 육아일기로 남긴 사례는 로제타 홀의 경우가 유일하다고 여겨진다. 따라서 특별히 선교사의 자녀 양육에 관한 자료라는 측면에서도 이 육아일기의 중요성은 대단히 크다고 할 수 있다.

또한 이 육아일기에는 《로제타 홀 일기 4》에 나오지 않는 중요한 내용들, 예를 들어 윌리엄 제임스 홀의 죽음과 그의 장례 일정, 로제타 홀이 미국으로 돌아갔다가 다시 한국으로 오게 되는 과정에서 미국 내 여러 선교부와의 관계에 대한 이야기, 제임스 홀의 전기를 쓰게 되는 과정에 관한 내용, 로제타 홀이 서울과 평양에서 다시 선교사로 활약하는 모습들에 관한 내용 등이 자세하게 기록되어 있는데, 이에 관련된 내용은 다른 자료에서는 쉽게 찾아볼 수 없는 것들이다.

특히 이 육아일기는 기존 일기와는 다르게 일기를 작성하는 주체가 한 개인으로서의 '나'가 아니라 '엄마'로 되어 있다. 이는 로제타 홀이 육아일기를 기록하면서 철저하게 엄마와 자녀의 관계에서 아이 눈높이에 시점을 맞추고 있으며, 이는 장차 이 일기의 실제적 주인공인 셔우드 홀에게 읽히기 위함이었음을 확인할 수 있다. 여기에는 셔우드 홀이 태어나서 만 아홉 살이 될 때까지 셔우드 홀에 관한 극히 일상적인 내용들이 아주 특별하게 서술되어 있다. 즉 육아에 관한 모든 내용이 상세하게 기록되어 있는 것이다.

이 육아일기의 또 다른 특징 하나는 아이가 태어난 1893년 11월 10일을 기점으로 매달 10일로 날짜를 맞춰 한 달 전체에 해당하는 내용들을 압축적으로 정리해 놓았다는 점이다. 따라서 이 육아일기는 일기에 나타나는 특정 시점을 기준으로 맥락을 구분하는 것이 아니라 육아일기의 내용을 토대로

《로제타 홀 일기 4》를 대조하며 읽어 가면서 육아일기의 전체적인 시기 구분을 따로 설정해야 할 필요가 있다. 물론 특정한 날을 기념으로 찍은 사진이나 그림, 별도의 기록 같은 것들이 육아일기에 첨부되어 있어서 로제타 홀이 아들 셔우드 홀에 대해 특별히 강조하는 부분들이 부각되어 있다.

이런 점을 감안하면, 이 육아일기는 크게 세 부분으로 구분할 수 있다. 첫째 부분은 1893년 11월 10일 셔우드 홀의 탄생에서 시작하여 아빠인 윌리엄 제임스 홀이 순직한 후 양화진에 묻히기까지에 해당한다. 둘째 부분은 1894년 12월 14일《로제타 홀 일기 1》에 나왔던, 미국에서 한국으로 오기까지의 여정을 역순으로 하여 박에스더 부부를 대동하고 미국으로 돌아가서 지냈던 시기이다. 셋째 부분은 1897년 11월 10일 셔우드 홀의 네 번째 생일날 다시 한국에 도착하여 이전의 선교사역을 계속 이어가는 모습을 담아내고 있다.

이렇게 구분할 수 있는 각각의 시기를 통해 로제타 홀은 엄마와 자녀의 관계로서 셔우드 홀과 함께했던 일상들을 상세하게 기록하고 있다. 그런데 여기에는 기쁘고 행복한 순간들보다는 슬픔과 안타까움으로 마음을 태웠던 순간들이 훨씬 많이 등장하는데, 바로 이점이 더욱 주목해서 살펴보아야 할 대목이다. 엄마와 아들의 관계가 아빠를 넘어 주변의 많은 사람들과의 관계를 통해 더욱 풍성하게 전개되는 동시에 신앙적인 측면에서 하나님 아버지가 그들의 관계에 개입하는 모습으로 그려지고 있기 때문이다.

3.

이제 이렇게 구분한 각각의 부분에 대해 중요한 맥락을 짚어가는 것으로 독자들의 이해를 돕고자 한다. 극히 개별적인라고 할 수 있는 엄마와 자녀의 관계에서 작성된 육아일기에 특별한 한국 교회사적 의미를 밝히려는 시도 자체가 별로 소용이 없어 보이기 때문이다. 우선 첫 번째 부분은 앞서 언급한 대로 셔우드 홀의 탄생에서 시작한다. 즉《로제타 홀 일기 5》는 셔우드 홀이 태어난 1893년 11월 10일 금요일 오전 10시부터 시작하는 것이다. '그의 평생을 여호와께 드리나이다'라는 사무엘상 2장 28절 말씀과 함께 갓 태어난 부드러운 분홍빛 아기에게 "우리 아가"라고 첫 인사를 하는 장면이다.

이 장면에 앞서 로제타 홀은 일기장 앞면을 할애하여 남편 윌리엄 제임스 홀의 사진과 나란히 자신의 사진을 넣어둘 예정인바, 대신 어여쁘게 핀 큼지막한 장미꽃 한 송이 그림을 붙이고 그 아래 자신의 이름을 적어두었다. 그 밑으로는 꽃으로 장식된 "In God We Trust"라는 엠블럼 그림을 넣었다. 그 뒤로는 셔우드 홀이 입은 옷을 만든 옷감 조각 30여 종을 붙여 놓았다. 그리고 여백을 활용하여 '어머니로서 할 수 있는 가장 달콤한 일은 아기의 앙증맞은 옷을 만드는 것이다'라고 썼다. 그 뒷장에 나오는 셔우드가 자신이 태어난 집 앞에서 1899년 여름에 찍은 사진도 인상적이다.

로제타는 자신의 아이와 처음 만났을 때의 인상과 느낌을 감격적으로 기록했다. 건강하고 예쁘고 귀여운 아이였다. 그런데 셔우드는 생후 4일째부터 황달을 앓았고, 변비가 심했다. 한 달째 되는 날인 12월 1일 아빠가 평양으로 떠나고 난 후에는 거의 한달 내내 급성 위염에 시달렸다. 생후 6주가 지날 무렵에는 주변에서 아이가 이 세상에 오래 있지 않을 거라는 말이 들리기 시작했다. 그러나 셔우드는 아빠가 돌아오고 난 후 좋아지기 시작했다. 로제타 홀은 '아빠가 함께 계시다는 것, 그 자체가 엄마는 물론 아기에게도 큰 도움이 된다는 사실이 증명되었다'고 기록하는 것으로, 처음으로 닥친 셔우드의 위기를 넘길 수 있었다.

셔우드가 5개월이 되었을 때, 엄마는 셔우드를 안고 사진을 찍었다. 그동안 셔우드는 주변에 반응을 보이며 잘 웃는 아이로 자라고 있었다. 그리고 셔우드는 서울을 떠나 평양으로 가서 지내게 되었는데, 이빨도 나기 시작했고 가끔 기자묘에 가서 놀기도 했다. 평양에서는 처음인 외국인 아기를 보려고 수많은 사람들이 와서 관심을 보였다. 그러다가 소위 1894년 5월 10일

'평양 기독교인 박해사건'을 겪고 난 후, 그 여파로 6월 6일에는 평양에서 철수하여 다시 서울로 와야 했다. 서울에서도 셔우드는 온순하고 명랑하며 잘 웃는 아이로 자라고 있었다.

청일전쟁이 발발한 후 10월 1일, 아빠는 또다시 평양으로 떠났다. 그래서 셔우드는 11월 10일 첫 돌을 아빠 없이 보내야 했다. 그녀는 '오늘 우리는 얼마나 아빠를 그리워했는지 모른다'라고 썼다. 그처럼 커다랗던 그리움이었기에 충격은 더욱 컸을 것이 틀림없겠다. 발진티푸스에 걸려 이미 많이 쇠약해진 아빠가 서울에 도착했을 때는 너무 늦어 서울의 모든 의료역량이 총동원되었지만 별다른 차도 없이 정신력으로만 버텨내는 상태가 지속되었다.

> 그리고 11월 24일 토요일 해질 무렵 아빠는 마지막 숨을 쉬셨다. 아빠의 두 손은 엄마의 두 손을 잡고 있었고, 아빠의 눈은 엄마의 눈을 바라보고 있었다. 엄마는 부드럽게 사랑스러운 두 눈을 감겨 드렸다. 그러고 나서 아빠의 눈이 엄마의 눈을 다시는 볼 수 없을 거라는 생각에 아빠의 눈을 한 번 더 뜨게 했다. 마지막으로 오랫동안 볼 수 있도록. 아빠의 눈은 여전히 밝고 맑아서 아빠의 사랑스런 영혼이 그 몸을 떠난 것처럼 보이지 않았다. 엄마는 마지막으로 아빠의 눈을 감겨드리고 그 방을 떠났다. 그리고 사랑하는 어린 아들을 안고 와서 하나님께 아들을 위해 자신이 더 용감하고 강해질 수 있게 도와달라고 기도했다. 그리고 아직 복중에 있는 어린 아기를 위해 기도했다. -1894년 12월 10일, 월요일 일기에서

그날 일기는 '불쌍한 우리 셔우드! 지난 달 너는 세상에서 가장 소중한 것을 잃었단다. 너는 어려서 지금은 그 상실에 대해 아무것도 모르겠지만 시간

이 지나면 느끼게 될 거야. 비록 내가 너로 인해 아픈 것만큼은 아니겠지만 말이다'라고 미국으로 돌아가면서 쓴 글로 시작되었다. 여기에는 윌리엄 제임스 홀이 병에 걸리고 나서의 구체적인 경위와 장례 일정에 관한 세부 사항들이 담겨 있다. 그리고 셔우드와 엄마, 박에스더 부부가 함께 미국으로 떠나는 모습이 있다. 잠시 휴식을 취한 후 2년쯤 뒤에 다시 평양에 와서 아빠가 못다 이룬 사역을 계속하고자 하는 다짐과 함께였다. 따라서 독자들은 여기서 멈추면 안 된다. 남편에 대한 로제타 홀의 마음은 두 번째, 세 번째 부분으로 계속 이어지기 때문이다.

4.

두 번째 부분은 4주에 걸쳐 태평양을 횡단하는 증기선과 대륙을 횡단하는 열차를 타고 미국의 고향집으로 향하는 여정으로 시작한다. 셔우드는 힘든 여정을 잘 이겨내고 무사히 외할아버지 집에 도착했다. 며칠 후 그곳에서 여동생인 에디스 마가렛 홀이 태어났다. 셔우드는 혼자서도 잘 걷게 되었다. 셔우드가 20개월 되는 날인 7월 10일 아빠의 고향 글렌부엘로 가는 새로운 여정을 시작하게 되는데, 엄마가 자녀들을 데리고 아빠의 고향에 가서 아빠의 흔적들을 더듬어보려 했기 때문이다. 그리고 이것은 다음 사역을 위한 일종의 첫 번째 과정이 되었다. 여기서 확보한 자료들을 바탕으로 엄마는 아빠 《윌리엄 제임스 박사 회고록》(The Life of Rev. William James Hall, M. D.)을 작성할 수 있었기 때문이다.

하지만 그녀의 공식적인 업무는 이듬해 여름부터 시작되었다. 크리스천 헤럴드 어린이 캠프에서 주치의로 일하면서 사역을 시작하여, 국제의료선교회에서도 일을 맡게 된 것이다. 또한 미국 감리회 여성해외선교회 임원으로 활동했다. 그리고 다시 한국에 가서 일할 수 있는 방법을 모색했다. 당시 그녀의 상황이 일기에 다음과 같이 기록되어 있다.

엄마는 다시 한국에 가서 사역을 맡기로 했다. 그것은 엄마가 한국에서 돌아올 때 바라던 것이었다. 여성해외선교회에서 엄마를 보내는 것이 적합하다고 생각하면 말이다. 현재 여성해외선교회에서는 엄마를 한국에 다시 보내기를 원하고, 한국 선교부에서도 엄마가 돌아오기를 몹시 바라고 있다. 엄마는 이것이 하나님께서 바라시는 일이라 생각한다. 엄마는 많은 기도를 했다. 하나님의 뜻이 아니라면 한국으로 가는 길을 막아주시고 이곳에서 할 일을 열어달라고. 그런데 한국의 사역은 여성해외선교회와 한국 양쪽에서 활짝 열려있고 이곳에서의 사역은 막히고 있다. -1897년 5월 10일 일기에서

이처럼 육아일기의 둘째 부분에서는 아버지 집에서 휴식을 취하며 둘째 딸을 낳고 아이들을 키우며 천천히 사역을 시작하여 마침내 다시 한국으로 돌아갈 방편을 마련하는 전반적인 과정이 전개된다. 로제타는 한국으로 돌아가기 위해 짐을 꾸리기 시작했다. 남편을 기념하는 병원을 짓고자 하는 마음도 잊지 않고 있었다. 그렇게 1897년 9월 6일, 그녀 일행은 정든 고향집 보금자리를 떠나 한국으로의 여정을 시작했다.

셔우드 홀 육아일기의 마지막인 셋째 부분은 로제타 홀이 셔우드와 에디스를 데리고 한국으로 돌아오는 장면에서 시작된다. 셔우드가 태어난 한국에 셔우드의 네 번째 생일인 1897년 11월 10일, 제물포 도착을 기념하게 되었던 우연의 일치를 남다르게 여기면서 한국 땅을 다시 밟았다. 서울에서 수개월 지내는 동안 로제타 홀과 셔우드는 평양으로 가고 싶어 했다. 그동안 2월에서 3월 사이의 40일 정도를 셔우드는 홍역 등으로 많은 고생을 했다. 그리고 엄마와 셔우드에게는 또 다른 큰 아픔의 시간이 다가왔다.

그토록 원했던 평양에 가서 새 집으로 들어가기도 전에 일어난, 갑작스러

우면서도 크나큰 아픔이었다. 여동생 에디스가 1898년 5월 23일 가족의 품을 떠난 것이다. 셔우드는 아빠가 에디스를 간절히 원했기 때문이라고 생각했다. 3월 10일자 일기 뒤에 나오는 11월 10일자 일기, 그 사이 9개월 동안의 일들은 로제타 홀에게 일기를 쓸 수 있는 시간적인 여유를 줄 수 없을 만큼 급박하게 흘러가고 있었던 정황을 암묵적으로 보여 주는 것이라 할 수 있다. 그녀는 평양에 남편을 기념하는 기홀병원과 딸을 위한 에디스 마가렛 기념병동을 설립했으며, 매일 환자들을 돌보는 의료선교사로서의 사역에 전념하면서도 셔우드와 밥을 같이 먹거나 함께 산책을 하기 위해 노력했다.

1899년 봄부터 셔우드는 엄마를 따라 평양을 중심으로 하는 전도구역 여러 곳을 방문하는 선교여행에 동참했다. 5월 1일에는 서울에서 열리는 정기총회에 참석하여 오랜만에 그리운 친구들을 만나 신나게 놀기도 했다. 정신없이 바쁜 사역 가운데서도 로제타 홀은 셔우드에게 소홀히 하지 않도록 신경을 쓴 것 같다. 선교사로서 후회로 인한 아픔은 없지만, 복음을 전하는 데 온 힘을 쏟아 부으면서 시간의 일부를 쪼개 자녀들과 놀아 주는 것은 자신의 임무가 아니라고 느꼈던 것이 후회스러울 뿐이라는 심정을 간접적으로 표현하기도 했다.

셔우드가 여섯 살이 되고 난 다음 해 5월, 엄마와 셔우드는 즈푸에 도착했다. 당시 엄마는 조금 우울한 상태였고, 신혼여행을 왔던 곳이기에 외로움이 더 커질까 두려웠지만 셔우드는 그곳을 천국처럼 여기며 즐거워했다. 일곱 살이 되었을 때 셔우드는 학교에 다니면서 더욱 의젓해졌다. 평양에서 로제타 홀의 사역은 1901년이 시작되면서 그동안 무리했던 것이 현상으로 나타나게 되었다. 겉으로는 평양병원은 물론 어린이병동도 잘 운영되고 있으며, 새롭게 만들 학교를 위한 재료들도 미국에서 도착할 예정이었다. 그러나 한국 선교부에서는 그녀의 상태를 진단한 결과 미국으로 돌아가서 휴식을 취하도록 했던 것이다. 이에 따라 로제타 홀은 셔우드와 함께 안식년을 삼아 미국으로 가서 지내게 되었는데, 그 때의 일들을 추가적으로 기록하는 것으로 1900년 11월 10일자로 끝이 나는 셔우드 육아일기를 마무리하고 있다. 나머지 부분인 1902년 11월 10일 셔우드의 아홉 번째 생일 때까지는, 그녀가 셔우드와 주고받은 편지와 사진 등과 셔우드에 대해 측정한 신체 기록 등으로 채웠다.

5.

이상에서 살펴본 내용은 로제타 홀 육아일기의 본질에 해당한다고 할 수 없다. 정작 로제타 홀이 셔우드에 대해 기록한 육아일기에는 주변의 정황과는 크게 관련이 없는 셔우드 홀 자체에 대한 그녀의 관심이 집중되고 있기 때문이다. 앞서 구분한 각각의 세 부분에서 공통적으로 나타나는 것도 마찬가지로 로제타 홀의 아들 셔우드 홀 자체에 대한 관심과 그에 대한 기록이 이 육아일기의 본질임을 보여 준다고 할 수 있다.

우선 처음부터 일관되게, 그녀는 셔우드 홀에 대한 어떤 변화에 주목하고 있다. 이를테면 신체의 변화 과정에 대한 철저한 기록이 그것이다. 그녀는 매달 셔우드 홀의 신체 사이즈를 측정하여 키와 몸무게, 머리둘레 등을 기록으로 남겼다. 그리고 최소한 일 년에 한 번 이상 손바닥을 그대로 따라 그린 셔우드의 손그림을 그렸고, 언제 처음 이빨이 나오기 시작했는지, 어떻게 빠졌는지, 충치를 치료했던 내용들까지 빠짐없이 기록했다. 또한 셔우드가 사용했던 말들의 단어를 하나하나 기록하여 그것이 어디에서 비롯된 것인지까지 생각하며 사용하는 단어 숫자를 기록했고, 이는 영어를 배우는 과정뿐 아니라 한국어를 익히는 과정에서도 적용되었다.

특히 셔우드 홀의 행동을 일일이 관찰하여 그것이 변화되어 가는 과정을 지속적으로 살피고 있으면서, 셔우드가 새롭게 관심을 갖게 되는 영역에 이르기까지 주의 깊게 체크했다. 아픈 상황에서는 병에 걸리게 된 순간부터 회복되기까지 하루하루 진단 내용과 처방 및 그에 따른 결과를 기록으로 남겼다. 로제타 홀에게는 셔우드 홀의 매일 매 순간이 소중했던 것이다. 이와 같이 로제타 홀 육아일기에는 자녀에 대해 다시 생각해 보아야 할 내용들이 교훈처럼 담겨 있다.

해설을 쓰는 본인 역시 두 아이를 키우면서 그 옛날 선교사들은 어떻게 자녀를 키웠을까 오래 전부터 궁금해하고 있었다. 내한 선교사 자료 그 어디에서도 육아에 관한 세세한 기록을 찾아볼 수 없었기 때문이다. 그런데 특별히 내한 선교사 가운데 남편과 딸을 이 땅에 묻는 아픔을 간직하고 있으면서도 한국 여성의학 분야에서 탁월한 업적을 남긴 로제타 홀의 육아일기를 살펴보게 되면서 궁금증이 해소되었을 뿐만 아니라 육아에 있어서 스스로를 되돌아보게 되었다. 그리고 따로 새 노트 한 권을 꺼내 들었다. 아이들에 관한 일기를 쓰기 위해서다. 비록 출생 후부터의 기록은 아니지만 10대를 살아가기 시작하는 아이들의 소년기를 쓰고자 하는 것이다. 로제타 홀 육아일기를 계기로 우리 자녀들에 대해 새롭게 접근할 수 있는 방법을 찾게 되었다. 그리고 무엇보다 아빠가 곁에 있는 것 자체가 엄마는 물론 아이들에게 큰 도움이 된다는 사실을 새삼 깨닫게 되었다. 로제타 홀 육아일기를 통해 앞으로 한국 교회사에서 선교사들의 구체적인 생활사가 폭넓게 밝혀지기를 진심으로 바란다.

옮긴이

김현수 *Hyunsue Kim*

경북 문경에서 태어나 열세 살 때 미국으로 이주했다. 애리조나 의과대학을 졸업했으며, 미국 하버-UCLA 메디컬센터에서 내과 전공의, 하버-UCLA 메디컬센터와 에머리 의과대학에서 혈액학·종양학 전임의와 인디애나 주 그레이터 라파예트 종양학 연구소 주치의를 역임했다. 현재 콜로라도 스프링스 로키마운틴 암센터에서 일하고 있다.
의료선교사의 소망을 가지고 기회가 주어질 때마다 전 세계를 찾아 의료봉사 활동을 펼치고 있으며, 평양에 의과대학을 세우는 일에 동참하고 있다. 미국 생활 중 알게 된 선교사 후손들과 교류하면서 그들이 보관하고 있는 선교 자료들이 유실되는 현실을 개선하기 위해 2010년 에스더재단을 설립했다.

문선희 *Sunhee Song Moon*

연세대학교에서 역사학과 신학을 공부했으며, 연세대 대학원에서 교회사를 전공하여 신학석사(Th. M.) 및 신학박사(Ph. D.) 학위를 받았다. 신학석사 과정을 마친 후 미국 캘리포니아산호세로 이주하였고, 2000년부터 한인 2세를 비롯해 미국에서 생활하는 이민자들을 위해 설립된 코너스톤교회(Conerstone Church of Silicon Valley)에서 교육봉사자로 섬기는 한편 번역가로 활동하고 있다. 2010년부터 에스더재단 이사로 참여하여 한국 교회 초창기에 파송된 미국 출신 선교사들의 기록을 우리글로 옮기는 일에 헌신하고 있다. 옮긴 책으로《로마서 주석》(공역, 로고스 출판사),《켈트 성인들 이야기》(공역, 기독교문서선교회),《헤럴드 램의 칭기스칸》(코리아닷컴) 등이 있다.

해설

이용민 *Yongmin Lee*

연세대학교 대학원에서 한국교회사 연구로 신학박사 학위를 받았다. 내한 선교사들의 한국에서의 활동과 본국 교단 선교부와의 관계에 대해 관심을 두고 연구하고 있다. 현재 한국기독교역사학회 총무이사 및 아시아기독교사학회 총무이사로 섬기고 있다.

에스더재단 Esther Foundation

교육과 자선을 목적으로 미 연방 세법에 의해 비영리 법인단체로 승인받아 2010년 4월 설립되었다. 한국 최초의 여의사 박 에스더를 기리는 마음에서 '에스더재단'이라고 이름 지었다. 에스더재단은 초창기 내한 선교사들이 남긴 선교 자료들을 발굴하여 책으로 발간, 번역, 출판, 배포하는 일을 중점적으로 추진하고 있다. 이와 함께 치유를 통해 복음을 전하는 선교 사업도 세계 곳곳에서 펼치고 있다.

–

양화진문화원 Yanghwajin Institute

양화진외국인선교사묘원에 안장된 선교사 및 한국 기독교 역사에 대한 자료 수집과 연구를 수행 · 지원하고, 교회와 사회를 잇는 소통의 도구가 되기 위해 한국기독교선교100주년기념교회에 의해 2005년 설립되었다. 전택부 유품 기증을 계기로 양화진문화원 내에 양화진기록관Yanghwajin Archives을 설립 · 운영하고 있으며, 초기 선교사들의 기록물도 보존 관리하고 있다.

로제타 홀 일기 5

Diary of Rosetta S. Hall V

2017. 5. 22. 초판 1쇄 인쇄
2017. 5. 30. 초판 1쇄 발행

지은이 로제타 홀
옮긴이 김현수·문선희
엮은이 양화진문화원
펴낸이 정애주
국효숙 김기민 김의연 김준표 김진원 박세정
송승호 오민택 오형탁 윤진숙 이한별 임승철
임진아 정성혜 차길환 최선경 한미영 허은

펴낸곳 주식회사 홍성사
등록번호 제1-499호 1977. 8. 1.
주소 (04084) 서울시 마포구 양화진4길 3
전화 02) 333-5161
팩스 02) 333-5165
홈페이지 www.hsbooks.com
이메일 hsbooks@hsbooks.com
페이스북 facebook.com/hongsungsa
양화진책방 02) 333-5163

ISBN 978-89-365-1232-3 (93230)
ISBN 978-89-365-0543-1 (세트)

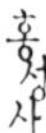